ENCYCLOPEDIA OF RAWHIDE AND LEATHER BRAIDING

Bruce Grant showing a braided quirt (in right hand) and twist-braid reata, braided rawhide reins, braided rawhide headstall, and braided chin strap (in left hand) at the Miracle of Books Fair in Chicago. The articles in the author's left hand are held together by braided rawhide hobbles. Photo: *Chicago Tribune.*

ENCYCLOPEDIA OF RAWHIDE AND LEATHER BRAIDING

VISUAL & PERFORMING ARTS
CHICAGO PUBLIC LIBRARY

BRUCE GRANT

CORNELL MARITIME PRESS
Centreville, Maryland

Library of Congress Cataloging-in-Publication Data

Grant, Bruce, 1893–
    Encyclopedia of rawhide and leather braiding.

    Incorporates material from the author's Leather braiding, and How to make Cowboy horse gear.
    Bibliography: p.
    1. Leather work.   2. Braid.   I. Title.
TS1040.G75   745.53′1   72-10407
ISBN 0-87033-161-2
ISBN 13: 978-0-87033-161-9

Manufactured in the United States of America
First edition, 1972; ninth printing, 2006

This book is affectionately dedicated to the memory of the late
Felix M. Cornell, counselor and friend

A Partial List of Other Books by Bruce Grant

THE ADVENTURES OF ROBIN HOOD
AMERICAN INDIANS: YESTERDAY AND TODAY
BOY SCOUT ENCYCLOPEDIA
MY COWBOY BOOK
COWBOY ENCYCLOPEDIA
CYCLONE
DAVY CROCKETT, AMERICAN HERO
EAGLE OF THE SEA
FAMOUS AMERICAN TRAILS
FIGHT FOR A CITY
FIRE FIGHTERS
HOW TO MAKE COWBOY HORSE GEAR
MY INDIAN BOOK
ISAAC HULL, CAPTAIN OF *OLD IRONSIDES*
KNOW YOUR CAR AND HOW TO DRIVE
LEATHER BRAIDING
LEOPARD HORSE CANYON: THE STORY OF THE LOST APPALOOSAS
LONGHORN: A STORY OF THE CHISHOLM TRAIL
NORTHWEST CAMPAIGN: THE GEORGE ROGERS CLARK EXPEDITION
PANCHO: A DOG OF THE PLAINS
PONY EXPRESS
RIDE, GAUCHO
SIX GUN: A STORY OF THE TEXAS RANGERS
THE STAR-SPANGLED ROOSTER
THOMAS TRUXTUN, CAPTAIN OF *THE CONSTELLATION*
TONG WAR! A HISTORY OF THE CHINESE TONGS IN AMERICA
   (With Eng Ying Gong)
A TRIP IN SPACE
WARPATH: A STORY OF THE PLAINS INDIANS
ZACHARY, THE GOVERNOR'S PIG

CONTENTS

Slit Braids

Flat Braids

Flat Braids (cont.)

Round Braids

Round Braids (cont.)

Crocodile Ridge Braids

Crocodile Ridge Braids (cont.)

Square, Rectangular, Spiral, Twist Spiral, Oval and Triangular Braids

Buttons

Buttons (cont.)

Edge-Braiding

Buckle and Ring Coverings

Other Braided Coverings

Handle Coverings

Hobbles

Turk's-heads

Turk's-heads (cont.)

Braided Knots

Braided Knots (cont.)

Lazy-Man Button and Pampas Button Knots

The Braiding Detective

Braided Appliqués

FOREWORD

This book comes as the result of almost a lifetime of work. It comes, too, as the inevitable consequence of two prior books, as well as numerous magazine articles on braiding, and from the encouragement of friends and fellow craftsmen in this country and many parts of the world.

Since the two books, *Leather Braiding* and *How to Make Cowboy Horse Gear*, became widely circulated among rawhide and leather braiders, I have exchanged letters and information with braiding enthusiasts and professionals in many sections of the globe. I also have made two trips to the Argentine, where I had worked years ago as a newspaper man; six or more to Mexico; and traveled about America's West.

I first became interested in braiding as a youngster in Texas. Years later, when I returned a trifle shaken from France where I was a war correspondent in World War II, I took up the craft with renewed interest and as a form of therapy. It was then that I realized there was hardly anything written in English on the subject—no definitive book, certainly—and so I wrote my first article, "The Vanishing Craft of Braiding," for the *Western Horseman* magazine. The response to this, as I explain later, was most encouraging.

The late Felix M. Cornell, of the Cornell Maritime Press, became interested, and the two above-mentioned books resulted. These are now incorporated in this volume, with a wealth of new material I have collected since their publication.

There are so many people I want to thank for their help and encouragement, that it would take many pages to list them all. Many will be given due credit in various sections of this book. However, I wish to thank especially:

A.G. Belcher, editor, *The Craftsman*, Fort Worth, Texas; Romeo Del Castillo, late secretary of the National Association of Charros, Mexico City; Hilario Faudone, Argentina; Luis Alberto Flores, author of *El Guasquero (The Rawhide Worker)*, and writer of gaucho braiding for *El Caballo* magazine, Buenos Aires; Martín Gómez, Argentina; Richard Grimler, Guatemala; Alfredo Guraya, Argentina; C.W. Halliday, West Australia; Roy Harmon, Las Cruces, New Mexico; John Walter Maguire, Argentina; David Morgan, Austral Enterprises, Seattle, Washington; James Morrison, New Zealand; Francis Ian Maclean, Queensland, Australia; Justo P. Saënz (h), writer and horse breeder, Argentina; Henry Schipman, Jr., writer and artist, Las Cruces, New Mexico; Dick Spencer III, publisher, Chuck King, editor, and Barbara Emerson, editorial secretary of the *Western Horseman*, Colorado Springs, Colorado; and R.M. Williams, author of *The Bushman's Handcrafts*, Australia.

I wish to express my appreciation to Larry Spinelli for permission to use his excellent drawings from my book, *Leather Braiding*.

There are many others I would like to thank again, especially Douglas Lamoureaux, Edward Larocque Tinker, L.H. Rutter, Karl Vogel, M.D., and Burt Rogers. These last named have passed over the Great Divide but in the text of this book, their names are used in the present tense—as I like to think of them in that way.

And most certainly I wish to thank my wife, Catharine Bauer Grant, for her tolerance and understanding under such trying circumstances as having for years our entire house in Winnetka, Illinois, converted into a rawhide and leather workshop.

THE ROMANCE OF LEATHER BRAIDING

When man first realized what a useful and serviceable thing his own skin was he got busy trying to figure out how he could turn to practical account the skins and hides of other animals. This was the genesis of leather and the beginning of civilization.

With the skins and pelts prehistoric man tanned or cured he was able to clothe himself and thus hunt and forage during the winter months and travel and search for game in colder climates. He could make more comfortable homes in which to live, put together better tools with which to work, manufacture boats in which to cross streams, and assemble more efficient weapons for waging war.

Leather was an important factor during the remote Stone Age and while there is slight chance of archeologists ever discovering any of the actual leather apparel and craftsmanship of primitive man, the uses of leather have been revealed from sculptures and drawings found on walls of prehistoric caves. This crude art dates back from 20,000 years B.C. and indicates that man and his mate dressed in hides and skins.

However, pieces of leather articles, including light caps, aprons and undressed goat skins have been found in Egyptian tombs of 2500 B.C.

Man's weapons metamorphosed from stone to bronze and from bronze to steel. Other things changed in his life and his ways of living, but not leather. He tanned the hides in much the same fashion as before and he utilized the leather in a similar way. Even in this day of the Atomic Age the preparation of leather has changed but little.

What is more interesting from our viewpoint is that man's ingenuity was challenged to find means of joining pieces of leather, fastening leather to other materials and shaping leather in forms to suit his needs. He used leather thongs for a wide variety of purposes. He sewed his garments together with them, he secured his war-heads to his weapons with them, he made ropes, handles and buttons, and he used leather thongs for hinges and leather for buckles and brads in place of the various metal fastenings common today.

Thus is leather associated with man in his transition from the brute into the thinking and reasoning individual, from the ignorant into the cultured, and from the cultured into the artistic. He used leather more and more and at one period the things he made represented the highest state of artistic development and his leather handcraft was a most beautiful and attractive art.

The actual tanning of leather has been traced to the Bronze Age, which is roughly estimated from 2500 to 800 B.C. Prior to that it is believed that primitive man preserved his hides in a more or less pliable and imputrescible condition by treating the pelts with the grease and brains of the animal itself, much after the fashion in which American Indians make their buckskin. Or, as the Eskimos do today, early man might have used urine in tanning his leather.

It is certain that a chrome, formaldehyde or alum tannage was unknown.

However, during the Bronze Age the fleshy sides of the hides were rubbed with salt and alum, stored in cool placefor a few days and then stretched and pulled. The fatty sides were scraped and limestone sand rubbed in. The skins were stretched and dried.

This method came down to the Romans who perfected it in producing their fine leather known as *aluta*. This soft leather was said to have even been used by the Roman ladies for fashioning their "beauty spots."

The Greeks, also, were adept in the tanning and utilization of leather. The first Greek leather worker is cited as Tychios of Boetia, a native of Hyle. He is credited by Homer with having made the shield of Ajax, and Pliny termed him the inventor of tanning.

In those days leather and skins were used for beds, blankets, rugs, curtains, coverings for chairs and couches, and for shoes as well as for many other purposes. A deerskin bed was believed to protect the sleeper against snakes and priests slept on special skins when they wished to invoke oracles in their dreams.

The Bible contains frequent mention of leather. In Genesis 3:21 we find: "Unto Adam also and to his wife did the Lord God make coats of skins, and clothed them." It also tells that Moses dyed rams' skins.

In Butler's *Lives of the Saints* he writes of St. Crispin and St. Crispinian working with their hands at night making shoes. St. Crispin today is the patron saint of the shoemakers, and this honorable trade can boast such American examples as Noah Worcester, D.D., known as the Apostle of Peace; Roger Sherman, the patriot; Henry Wilson, the Natik Cobbler, and John Greenleaf Whittier, the Quaker Poet.

Hans Sachs, the shoemaker poet of Nuremberg, known as the Nightingale of the Reformation, in 1568 wrote a verse in which he told how he prepared his own leather:

> "I dry the skins out in the air
> Removing first each clinging hair.
> Then in the Escher stream I dash them
> And thoroughly from dirt I wash them.
>
> Cow-skin and calf in tan I keep,
> Long months in bark-soaked water steep
> Then with a brush of hair I scrape them
> And on the selling counter drape them."

There are many wise and pithy sayings having to do with leather. One proverb has it, "Men cut large thongs from other men's leather." Unemotional men are said to have "thick hides," or they are "thick-skinned," while those with stubborn ideas are "hide-bound." We still use such expressions as "I'll tan your hide," "He's a skinflint," and "Give him a leather medal."

Carlyle in his *Sartor Resartus* comes to the conclusion that the old-world grazier became sick of lugging his slow ox about the country till he got it bartered for corn or oil, and would take a piece of leather and thereon stamp or scratch the mere figure of an ox, or *pecus*. He would put this in his pocket and call it *pecunia*, or money. Here is the derivation of our word *pecuniary*, and even today in modern slang we speak of a dollar bill as a "skin." We "skin" a man in a trade and when we do him out of something illegally it is by use of the "skin-game."

Ancient history is replete with references to leather and leather work. Unbelievable as it might seem there were even leather cannon! These guns, in calibers from 1-pounders to 4-pounders, consisting of a copper tube covered with several layers of mastic and wrapped with rope or twine on top of which was put a coat of plaster, were finally covered with leather. They were used as early as 1349 by the Venetians.

There were, of course, leather cups, leather bottles, leather chests and many other utility articles of leather. There is a complete literature on leather bookbinding and ancient leathercraft. Leather was in wide use—and even today there is hardly a person who does not have some form of leather about him—shoes, hatbands, pocketbooks, billfolds and such.

The most important of the historical notices on leather—from our viewpoint—has to do with the ancient Phoenicians. These people invaded North Africa probably in or around the year 1600 B.C. and transmitted their leathercraft to the Moors.

The Moors at the beginning of the Eighth Century crossed the Straits of Gibraltar and penetrated Spain. Here they inaugurated a brilliant civilization. In Cordova, the capital, the leather industry gave origin to several trades, one of which was harness-making. What leathers are more famous than Cordovan, Spanish and Morocco!

The *guadamacileros* of Spain could not be surpassed for their wonder creations of figured leather, for unlike the heavily lacquered and painted leathers of today these Spanish artists always subordinated their decorations to the leather itself. The leather never lost character. This art originated in the city of Ghadames in the Sahara, where the ghadamesian leather came from.

From the Ninth to the 18th centuries Europe had been reconquered and the Arabs expelled. But they left behind them not only their leather art, which included elaborate braiding and thong work, but their techniques for executing these things.

So in 1520 when Hernando Cortes introduced the first horses into America, he brought, too, men well versed in the understanding and teaching of leatherwork and the art of braiding.

It is not difficult from that point to trace the introduction of fancy braidwork into the United States. The Mexican *vaqueros* who rode the dusty trails of the plains and brought up their cattle from below the Rio Grande and those of the pre-gold rush cattle drives of California during the last century were expert *trenzadores*, or braiders. They were masters of leather braiding and leather decoration. Some were *charros* to whom the horse and his decoration or equipage was the primary object of life.

These Mexicans inspired our own cowboys to take pride in their gear and in those times a braided bridle with fancy woven knots scattered along the reins was a beautiful thing to behold—not to speak of the hatbands, belts, pistol holsters, saddles, quirts and other gear and appurtenances.

The Spanish craft of leather braiding and decoration spread, too. It would be interesting to an anthropologist or archeologist to trace, for example, the Spanish woven knot, built upon the sailor's well-known Turk's-head knot. I have seen woven finger rings of split bamboo made by the Igorotes of the Philippines which are exactly like those knots on Spanish and Arabian whip and knife handles.

The Argentine *gaucho* makes the same type of woven knot as does the native Indian of Mexico. The entire course of Spanish civilization could well be traced through this intricate and decorative knot.

The term "lost art" might be applied to leather braiding. However, it is a loose and generic term used in connection with most handcraft today. The greater part of our handcraft should be designated as a developed art. We continually see where improvements have been made in ancient workmanship by the use of modern scientific methods and by machine operation and cultivated design.

Just as the development of the bow and arrow in archery makes these modern implements far superior to those of the ancients, especially the savages, so are textile weaving and many other arts and crafts as far advanced.

It might be better to say that leather braiding is an almost forgotten and highly neglected art. It is not necessary now to join things with leather thongs. Sewing with thread and fastening with metal brads are the methods used. The attractive and sometimes unique means of using leather buttons and other leather fastenings has been supplanted by all manner of metal devices.

In this book the broad term of "braiding" is used throughout much after the manner in which it is used by the Spanish *trenzador* and the craftsmen of Mexico and Latin America in general. Actually braiding means to weave together, to plait, and usually is associated with the so-called flat braid, or the three-thong "hair braid," or the simple braids used in making belts.

For our purpose it will mean the weaving of leather knots, the making of buttons, the working of edge lacing on leather articles, the covering of belt buckles, the appliqued work on leather which was introduced to the American public for the first time in my *Leather Braiding*, and the beautiful one-thong weave which the Spanish *conquistadores* used on their sword belts, as well as many variations of the commonly known round and flat braids.

Leather braidwork has many forms and many applications. You don't make things just to look at and admire, but to use. You combine beauty with utility. This work can be used in making handles for suitcases, briefcases and other leather articles. It adapts itself to use on and is associated with plain or carved or tooled leather work, supplementing and complementing such examples of craftsmanship.

It can be used in covering the handles of canes, umbrellas and tools.

It is, of course, employed in the making of quirts, riding crops, belts and wristwatch straps, dog collars and leashes, hackamores, bridles and reins, leather buttons, buckle coverings and for many, many other practical things.

The rewards of a small amount of work are ample and highly gratifying. There is another thing that should not be overlooked: the practicability of this handcraft for those persons who are convalescing or who are partially disabled or have some permanent injury which confine them to their beds or wheelchairs. The few tools necessary, the small amount of space in which the work can be done and the cleanliness with which it can be executed, make it uniquely adaptable in such cases. Its value in occupational and recreational therapy cannot be ignored.

While this book is primarily for those interested in leathercraft, the methods of braiding in nearly all cases are applicable to strands of many other materials—silk, cotton, plastic, rawhide, catgut or horsehair.

Especial care has been exercised in giving detailed step-by-step instruction methods, both in diagrams and text. It has been presumed that the reader knows nothing of braidwork and wants each move carefully explained.

Many photographs have been included in this book. Some accompany plate instructions and depict step-by-step methods; others show finished articles. Braiding can be considered a universal language and I have included photographs of braidwork from many countries. It is hoped that the excellent examples of leathercraft articles will prove to be an incentive to the reader.

In the years of my study of this subject—in Europe, South America and among Mexicans, Basque sheep herders, cowboys and others—I have picked up many things of value. I have worked out many types of braidwork, which have suggested themselves from the basic principles commonly in practice. Possibly they are not new but many are now shown in print for the first time.

As to Turk's-heads and woven knots the methods employed in illustrating them and how to make them are at least an innovation. By the use of diagram patterns any type of Turk's-head or woven knot, no matter how complicated, can be made by a method which is foolproof.

As a native of Texas, it is sincerely hoped these efforts will arouse interest in a craft which is identified with the tradition of our plainsmen and of our West and Southwest. There are very few museum collections in this country of cowboy handcraft—of braided bridles, hackamores, quirts (cuartas), or reatas, nor even of stamped and carved leatherwork! It is a definite part of our folklore and has a positive archeological and anthropological value.

Fifty years from now many museums will be digging around frantically in an endeavor to assemble a representative collection of the handcraft of the cowboy. But it will have vanished.

RAWHIDING IN THE OLD WEST

Historians of the Old West have dug deep in their search for story material on that period in American history usually termed our true national tradition. In some instances they have not dug deeply enough. One thing they usually fail to turn up, or take for granted or completely ignore, is *Rawhide*.

So many things have been given credit for winning the West, whatever the phrase actually means, that one hesitates to bring forth another. Yet it seems no more than justified, considering the years it has been disregarded, to say that rawhide should take its place in the front rank in the battle that converted the West into a wilderness of steel, concrete, and vapor lanes; main streets and motels, gas stations, hot-dog stands, and billboards.

Anyway, rawhide is itself a tradition—not merely a word. It embodies the story of the Old West from the brushpopper to the cowpuncher, from cowhunts to roundups, from the open plains to fenced-in ranches, from the chaparral country clear up that course of an empire, the Texas Trail. The story is tied together in tough and lasting rawhide.

Certainly the writers have sifted every aspect, artifact, hombre, and animal of the Old West in trying to tie together their stories. The Colt revolver, the Winchester carbine, the Stetson hat, the western saddle, the Bowie knife, the prairie schooner, the mustang, the maverick, the barbed wire—these and many other things have their places in how the "west was won." Rawhide is seldom mentioned—it is often erroneously termed "leather."

As "Indian Iron," the Mormons employed it to lash together the beams of their first temple at Salt Lake City. As "Mexican Iron," or *cuero crudo* the southwestern cowboys used it for making quirts, headstalls, *reatas*, bosals, and reins—and softened it into *latigos*, or saddle tie-strings, and belts. Nothing has been found better suited to cover a saddle tree.

The Apaches shod their horses with rawhide shoes. Indians used rawhide for many things, including drum heads, bow strings, and thongs to bind on their arrows and lance heads. They converted deerskin rawhide into the softest buckskin.

When an iron band broke on the wheel of an old-time prairie schooner, it might be replaced with a rawhide rim. Pioneers used it for gate and door hinges and after treating it with linseed oil employed it for semitransparent window panes.

The fur-trappers, or "mountain men," made moccasins from the smoke-impregnated, and thus unshrinkable, rawhide coverings of their winter lodges.

They say Texas was bound together with rawhide. Texans were known to northern cowboys as "rawhides," because of their custom of repairing everything with this material—from bridles to wagon tongues. A "rawhide" was an affectionate name for an old-timer.

"Rawhiding" in cowboy lingo meant to torture or abuse, or to verbally "ride." It also meant to thrash. It meant as well to work rawhide. Rawhide lumber was cottonwood slabs. There were even "rawhide" ponies.

One of the most unpleasant deaths consisted of being sewed up in a green rawhide skin—one just off the animal—and left in the sun. As the rawhide shrank, in this savage version of the "Iron Maiden," the victim gradually was squeezed to death.

This marvelous power of constriction of green rawhide made it unusually efficacious in lashing together corral posts, ranch furniture, as well as other articles where nails usually were employed. The "jewel box" of the chuck wagon contained an assortment of rawhide strings and pieces for repairs. Slung beneath the wagon itself was the "cooney," a rawhide apron for carrying fuel—usually buffalo or cow chips.

Literature on the subject of rawhide-making is scarce. Most that has been written on this subject is superficial and takes too much for granted. One might conjecture that the apparent basic simplicity of the process needs no explanation. Rawhide just makes itself. The cowboy or Indian skinned his animal, stretched the hide, and then scraped off or shaved off the hair. There was little else to it, except cutting it into strings or appropriate pieces.

Rawhide braiding is another thing. It is here that rawhide work graduates from a mere handcraft to an art. In this area, indeed, there is a downright scarcity of instructive literature. It is practically non-existent. It was to correct this deficiency, as well as to justify in my own fashion my western heritage, that I set about writing books on the subject of rawhide and leather braiding.

My first effort was a story in the *Western Horseman* magazine for December, 1949, called "The Vanishing Craft of Braiding." The response to this was surprising and gratifying. Old-time braiders and many interested in braiding wrote me letters.

I found it heartening to realize that I had not started too late. Nor had I started too early. There were still a few old-time braiders around, a very few. In former days such men were highly secretive, close-mouthed and uncommunicative when it came to their craft. The braiding art was something to be passed on from father to son. A particular woven knot, for instance, was almost the trademark of a braider. He let no one in on the secret of how he made this knot.

Thus I was extremely fortunate in my timing. The rawhide braider, like many who work with their hands, could no longer make a living. His son was not interested in learning this esoteric craft. Everyone now calculated work on a so-much-per-hour basis. When a piece of his work was on view, the rawhide braider—as well as other handcrafters—was invariably asked the annoying question: "How long did it take you?" It might be like asking a doctor, after an intricate operation: "How long did that take you?" Thinking back over his years in school, internship, etc., he could justifiably say, "Twenty years." The old rawhide braider could possibly reply, "That thar piece o' work jest took me seventy-odd y'ars."

Anyway, now he could not make a living from his work and his son was more interested in going to the city and becoming an engineer, so the old rawhide braider was no longer reluctant to explain some of the secrets of his craft. In fact, many I found were most anxious to have this craft preserved in writing.

One man I know seeks out these old-timers and sits at their knee, like the youth of Athens in the presence of Socrates. He once wrote me that he had found Pinkie Bethel high up in the Sierras—a fellow who had been working rawhide for fifty years—and came upon him when he was actually at work braiding.

"I suddenly realized," wrote my friend, Ernie Ladouceur, of Madera, California, "that I had never before seen one of these old-timers actually braiding rawhide. I had seen much of Pinkie's stuff and much of the fancy work of others, but this was the first time I had ever seen one of these expert braiders busy at his craft."

Strangely enough, while Ernie Ladouceur had expected a rebuff, he had found Pinkie Bethel most cooperative in explaining what he was doing.

John Conrad of San Ysidro, California, one of the finest of the professional rawhide braiders, wrote me:

"To most people the word 'rawhide' carries little significance, but to many old-timers like myself, it brings back fond memories of an era in life which will never be forgotten.

"Back in the late Nineties I was a member of a family who had pioneered far from the railhead, out on the California prairies. By our own resourcefulness and the assistance of friendly Indians, we managed to overcome most of our difficulties, and I remember with much gratitude the Indian brave who gave me my first lessons in bronco-busting and cow-punching.

"Living several hundred miles from any place where there were saddleshops I early learned the virtues of rawhide, which I was able to produce in a crude manner. We used it as riding equipment, to string up our bunks, and make the bedrolls more comfortable, also for chair seats and backs, and to lash together rails and posts, because we had no nails.

"From the beginning I have always had a sentimental regard for rawhide, which I feel played as big a part in our pioneer existence as gunpowder. In later years my hobby has been designing and making rawhide articles, still very usable, but considerably more artistic, than those made fifty years ago."

In obtaining a fuller picture of the Old West it is well to widen the scope of research to include the use of rawhide and it is even better to preserve the art of rawhide braiding. This Moorish craft came over with the Spanish conquerors and a knowledge of it would be of great value to anthropologists and to archaeologists. Where you find rawhide braiding you can be certain the Spanish were there in the early days.

There are still rawhide braiders around and they are increasing all the time. Recently Jerry Eastman of the Four Lazy F Ranch, Jackson Hole, Wyoming, wrote me: "I have been working with rawhide for several years now and each year the demand for braided items gets greater. The people in my area seem to be becoming more aware of the beauty as well as the durability of braided rawhide work as well as not minding the price I'm asking for custom work."

Making and Working Rawhide

Leather-braiding Tools

Braided bridle shown on the famous stallion "Fact," which was presented to Averell Harriman by Premier Stalin of Russia. Bridle, made by author, contains more than 500 feet of leather thong.

PLATE 1

Making and Working Rawhide. Some readers of this book will be in a position to make their own rawhide. Others will have to buy it.

Those who wish to work with leather most likely will have to go to a leather dealer or handicraft store to obtain their leather or cut thongs and lacing.

First let us talk about *boughten* rawhide. The kinds of rawhide that can be easily purchased include those used for making drumheads, artificial limbs, and other commercial articles. This prepared hide can be used by the braider, who soaks it in water and cuts it into strings. There is also a product termed "rawhide" which is oil-packed and more pliable. But shy away from a commercial product called "rawhide" that is a greasy, sleazy stuff used for shoe laces. It is no good for braiding.

As to leather, most handicraft or hobby shops carry a commercial type of leather lacing or thonging. This lacing comes in several widths, but the 1/8- and 3/32-inch widths are the most popular. It also is to be had in a variety of colors. Goatskin lacing is stronger and more durable; calfskin is more dressy. Such lacing can be used in braiding. Various types of plastic or composition lacing also may be found in such shops, and I have seen some fancy headstalls and reins made from that material.

Leather, too, can be purchased in skins, hides, or kips. Skins are from the smaller animals like the calf, goat, deer, etc., and hides are from the cow, steer, horse, moose, and larger animals. Kips are from mature, but smaller or undersized animals. From all these, satisfactory thongs may be cut.

Leather-making, or tanning, is a long and difficult process; so it is best to buy your leather. But anyone with a back yard or small outdoor space can make good rawhide. (Douglas Lamoreaux of Winton, Cal., shows how in this section.) Nature does most of the work. It is best to obtain the hide or skin as soon as possible after the animal has been killed, and before it is dried out. This is known as a "green hide." If it has been dried out without being salted or treated with chemicals, it is known as a "flint hide." Flint hides can be used if they have not been dried in the sun, but "salt hides," or those treated chemically, are not good for rawhide strings, except under certain circumstances which will later be referred to. Such hides have lost some of their "life."

In working with the green hide, first stake it out on the ground or other place in the shade for about two hours. Nothing more has to be done, for it will change of its own accord from the green hide to rawhide. In Fig. 1, Plate 1, is shown the proper way to stake out a hide, pulling it in the direction of the arrows so it will "set" as near round as possible.

After it has been staked for two hours it is stiff enough to work with. Trim off the hanging bits of flesh on the flesh side of the hide and cut it into a round or oval shape (Fig. 1). That is, find the center of the hide and make a large circle, or oblong, which will eliminate the legs, neck, and other outside parts.

Cut this disk, or oblong piece, into a strip about 2 or 2½ inches wide by going round and round the circle until you get to the center. This can be done with heavy shears or a sharp knife (Fig. 2). In the thinner portions of the hide, such as the belly, cut the strip slightly wider. When the strip dries it will shrink to about two-thirds of its width.

Be attentive to what is known as the moisture control, that is, if the strip becomes too dry to cut easily, dampen the hide. Then fasten one end of this long strip to a post and, holding it taut with the left hand, shave off the hair with a sharp knife. Do not cut the top or scarf skin as this is the tough part and in it lies the strength of your string.

There are other ways to dehair rawhide. If it is calfskin or deerskin, the hair will usually slip if the skin has been soaked four or five days in running water. But the hair on cowhides and steerhides comes away less easily. These can be soaked in a "milk" of lime and water. Take one part quicklime and fifteen parts water. When the lime has been slaked place the strip in it for four or five days. The hair should then come off easily.

Douglas Lamoreaux suggests that after removing the hair with lime—either slaked or dehydrated lime—wash it in several baths of cool running water and then soak it for twenty-four hours in thirty gallons of water containing three ounces of lactic acid. This will neutralize the lime and make a more pliable rawhide.

In removing the hair, the back of a butcher knife, or an old file with edges smoothed and slightly rounded, are good implements to employ. Stick the point of the butcher knife in a round piece of wood to give a good hand "holt" on that end. In the case of the file, it can be sunk into a groove in a round piece of wood, with about ¼ inch of the edge protruding.

A mixture of wood ashes and water is a good dehairer. The best ashes come from hardwood. Make this into a soupy paste in a tub and soak the hide in it for forty-eight hours. In a pinch you can wet the hide and sprinkle the ashes on the hair side and roll it up. Wrap a damp burlap cloth around it and leave it for a few days. Slip the hair without removing the ashes.

Jim Shaw, of Lander, Wyoming, ran across an old taxidermy book which detailed a couple of ways of removing hair from a hide. Jim passed this information along:

"The usual method of loosening the hair is by the use of lime and red arsenic. These are made into a thick paste and slaked together, by adding a small amount of water. After slaking, more water is added and the mixture is smeared on the hair side of the hide. The hide is now folded together, hair side in. The hair slips in one or more days."

Red arsenic (arsenic disulphide) can be replaced by sodium sulphide and used in the same way. The formula for this would be: one gallon of boiling water; ½ cake of brown soap, shaved; cool and add one heaping tablespoon of sodium sulphide and one pint of dry unslaked lime, the last two to be slaked together and then added to the solution.

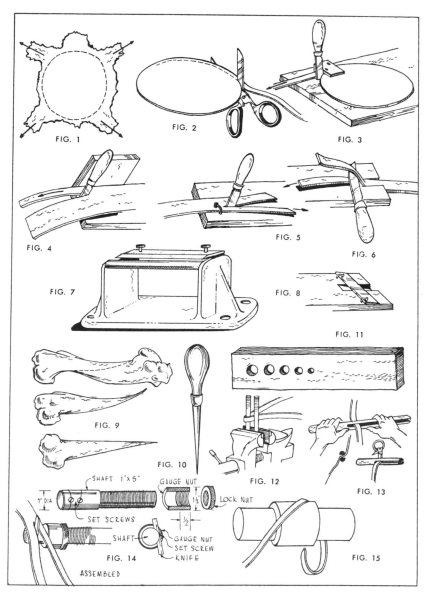

FIG. 1

FIG. 2

FIG. 3

FIG. 4

FIG. 5

FIG. 6

FIG. 7

FIG. 8

FIG. 11

FIG. 9

FIG. 10

FIG. 12

FIG. 13

SHAFT 1" x 5"

GAUGE NUT

1" DIA

1½

LOCK NUT

SET SCREWS

SHAFT

GAUGE NUT
SET SCREW

½

FIG. 14

KNIFE

FIG. 15

ASSEMBLED

PLATE 1. Making and Working Rawhide.

Steps in making rawhide. *A.* Hide spread on ground. *B.* Washing and soaking. Hide soaked in lime or hardwood ash solution to loosen hair. *C.* Putting hide over dehairing post, hair side out. *D.* Pushing or slipping off the hair. *E.* Placing hide in drying frame. *F.* Removing excess flesh and fat from flesh side. *G.* Buffing flesh side. This is done after hide has dried out and can be done by hand. *H.* After cutting hide out of drying frame. *I.* Long strip of hide made by cutting around the hide in spiral fashion, stretched between posts and allowed to dry for several days. This strip is about 2 inches wide. *J.* Cutting strings from long strip. Here machinery is used. But this can be done by hand.

Jim Shaw suggests scraping off the bulk of the hair as soon as it starts to slip, then putting the hide back into the solution with a handful of borax, which cleans the hide. As a neutralizing agent, he favors one quart of chicken manure to a gallon of water, or boracic (boric) acid or lactic acid.

"Another method that is easiest of all, as no solutions are involved," continues Jim, "I learned from an old rawhider in Washington. The only stickler is you have to get the hide with the body heat still in it. If you can do this, fold the hide from each side with the hair on the inside and roll up tightly and tie securely. In a day or two the hair slips and the hide can be scraped and stretched. However, if you have to, you can leave the hair on for several days without damage if the hide is unrolled

Steps in making rawhide *(cont.)*.

every day for an hour or so of airing. This makes good, firm rawhide and it seems to have more life and body than ordinary rawhide. I have an old bosal that was made of an eight-braid without core, yet it has more life than most cored commercial bosals."

After the hair has been taken off, the long strip of rawhide should be stretched between two trees or posts—in the shade— and allowed to dry thoroughly. Leave it strung up for four or five days. When it is dry it is ready to be cut into strings.

If flint hides are used they should be "tempered." After being soaked until there are no hard spots you can rub in saddle soap, using it as it comes from the can, or plain yellow laundry soap. Neat's-foot oil or tallow, if used, make the hide waterproof and hard to dampen for reworking.

Simple as rawhide-making is, there is always something to learn about it. Recently I was told of an old Texas method of making it and I have found it very good. This is a "salt method," but produces a different skin than the salt-cured hide, which is not suitable for rawhide braiding. For instructions on the procedure involved I am indebted to Ed Rickman, who says he learned it from an old Texan named Sonny Strong. Sonny Strong has passed over the Great Divide, but his way of making rawhide lives on.

This is it: When the hide or skin is taken off the carcass and while the body heat is still in it, spread it out flat with the flesh side up and salt it down with 40 or 50 pounds of fine stock salt. This is for a mature hide. For a yearling or calfskin use half the amount of salt. Spread the salt evenly and fold the hide over so the hair side is out and the flesh sides are together.

Leave the hide in a shady, dry place for from a week to ten days. It is important to salt the hide while the body heat is still in it, Rickman emphasizes. So if you do not actually remove the hide yourself, get the person who does the work to salt it down for you. The salt runs the blood and glue out of the hide before it congeals and Rickman feels this is important in keeping the hide pliable.

When the hide has reached the consistency of stiff bread dough after a week or so, spread it out and split it down the back into two parts. Next cut into strips lengthwise. These strips should be about three inches wide. Lay a gunny sack on your knee, take a strip of the hide and, with a sharp knife—we mean sharp!—grain off the hair. Pull the strip toward you as you cut with the knife blade almost flat. Instead of scraping the hair you will be splitting it off at the roots. This takes off the top grain of the hide, and it should be cut off smoothly. Turn the strip over and flesh it down to good solid hide. These fine tissues on the flesh side make the hide hard when dry. Get them off.

Now you can roll the strip up and let it dry for future use, or you can cut it into strings right away. If you are going to let it dry and cut it later you will have to soak it in a can of salt water until it is soft—not soggy, but pliable like leather.

Rickman, instead of splitting his strip, rubs down the flesh side by pulling it back and forth over a shoeing rasp. Place the rasp in a vise and pull the strip of rawhide back and forth across it. This evens the hide throughout its length and no splitting is necessary. However, do not rub the hair side against the rasp—the flesh side only.

This is an entirely different way of making rawhide, and may be considered by many old-timers as unorthodox. I have worked with such rawhide and it is very strong and more pliable than the ordinary kind.

If you wish to use the *Indian method*, then merely let the hide dry out, after being staked to the ground. Indians sometimes dry it in the sun. Soak it two days in running water, remove it, scrape off the hair and flesh, and it is ready for use. Indians save this hair and flesh for making a kind of soup; but I presume we can skip that. The hide is softened by rubbing in the cooked brains and liver. It is made waterproof by smoking it. This is *buckskin*.

If you want to do very fine work with narrow strings, the rawhide strip should first be split to a uniform thickness. In such a case it is run through a splitter. Previous to this it must be soaked in water until no hard spots are felt, and then wrapped in a damp cloth and allowed to mellow for an hour or so. There is a point where rawhide is neither too damp nor too dry and cuts perfectly.

The best type of splitter is that used by harness-makers (Fig. 7). This consists of two uprights about six inches in height and ten inches apart, bolted to a heavy metal base. A thick-backed, thin-edged knife is fastened to the uprights in such a way that it is adjustable and movable· to and from a machined steel roller, which is below it and parallel to it. By adjusting the knife the rawhide can be split any thickness desired. This method is used also for leather thongs, of course.

For a homemade splitter I am indebted to Dan Delaney, an old-time cowboy who works with the Hoodoo Outfit in Daniel, Wyoming. This is shown in Figs. 6 and 8. Cut a notch on the edge of a board—notch slanting down into the edge. Over this notch fasten a knife (Delaney nails on a mower section). Start the strip of rawhide through the notch, flesh side up. By moving the knife forward or backward the thickness may be increased or decreased. An ordinary knife can be held over the notch by pressure of the hand.

With the strip (or "soga", as it was known in the old days along the Border) of a uniform thickness, you now cut it into strings. (It will be noted that the term "strings" is used for rawhide and "thongs" for leather.)

There are several ways of cutting strings. Bill Phillips, of Savona, British Columbia, takes a board of soft wood and nails it to a bench or the floor. Then he drives a No. 7 horseshoe nail (Fig. 5) solidly into the center of the board, with the flat of the nail along the grain. The nail is bent over sharply so that the bent part lies parallel to the board's surface, with enough space between nail and board to accommodate the rawhide. Point of the knife is pushed into the wood with the keen edge against the nail, at a distance from the upright part of the nail equal to desired width of the string. The blade may be set at an angle to bevel the strings as they are cut. This bevel would thus run on the hair side of one edge of the string and on the flesh side of the other. The knife may be moved to make wider or narrower strings.

Also is shown a cutter designed by Doug Lamoreaux which may be clamped in a vise (Fig. 14). It has two slits for placing the blade to cut a beveled edge or a vertical edge. Doug estimates that this gadget can be made for approximately five dollars.

As to beveling rawhide strings and leather thongs, the rawhide usually is beveled on the hair side and the leather on the flesh side. The reason for beveling the rawhide on the hair side is that otherwise the sharp edges curl upward in drying. Beveling prevents this and gives a smooth finish to the braid. A thick thong of leather beveled on the flesh side allows it to lie snug. In some wide thongs, the bevel is on the hair side on one edge and the flesh side on the other. These edges overlap on the alternate thongs.

In Fig. 3 is shown a cutter where the string or thong is made from a small round or disc of leather or rawhide. In such a case, an 1/8-inch thong or string a yard long can be cut from a disc two inches in diameter; a three-inch disc yields two yards, and a four-inch disc three and one-half yards, and so on. In Fig. 4 is another type of homemade cutter for cutting thongs or strings from long strips of leather or rawhide.

Old-time quirt and whip-makers sometimes use a sharp knife with the thumb as a guide in cutting strings and thongs freehand. In this manner they can taper the string or thong by moving the thumb toward the knife. This requires considerable practice.

If rawhide strings are to be softened they should be placed while damp in warm melted tallow or neat's-foot oil. They are then pulled back and forth against a round piece of wood held in a vise. Keep oiling them and working them around the wood as they dry out.

I have found a good way to soften strings, or even *sogas*, is to clamp two sections of a broom handle in a vise, about ¼ inch apart (Fig. 12). Place the string or strip of rawhide around these as shown in the diagram and seesaw back and forth, keeping the string or strip well saddle-soaped. I am partial to saddle soap instead of tallow or neat's-foot oil, as I think the tallow and oil tend to deteriorate the rawhide, especially if it is left in the sun. Instead of saddle soap, good old yellow laundry soap may be used and is just as effective.

In braiding rawhide it will sometimes be found that, when the finished braid dries, the strings have narrowed and daylight can be seen through them. This means they have been improperly tempered or have been worked while too wet. Rawhide workers dampen their strings until they are just workable. Then they rub soap in them. If the string has little of the natural oil left in it the rawhider retempers it. To retemper strings, rub them well with saddle soap (or tallow or neat's-foot oil) and wrap them while damp in a piece of damp burlap and allow them to remain for forty-eight hours. If you use soap you can redampen these strings, while if you temper them with neat's-foot oil or tallow, once they dry out it is difficult to restore them to that pliable condition required for good work. So don't spare the soap.

You won't need many tools for braiding. A good, sharp knife is essential. Most important is a fid, or an instrument which tapers to a thin, rounded point—not a sharp one (Fig. 10).

Fids can be made from bone. In fact, several of your tools may be made from bone—soup bones, or those from the Sunday roast. With a hacksaw and file you can shape a piece of bone nicely. Polish it with steel wool and then some fine abrasive, such as pumice or rotten stone.

I turned out a very fine fid from the leg bone of a sheep. (Cattle men, please forget your prejudices for a moment.) This bone had a slight curve to it and I took advantage of this curve in fashioning my fid. This is shown in the accompanying illustration (Fig. 9).

Another practical gadget can be made from a piece of thick bone, or hardwood. This is a gauge for round braid (Fig. 11). A half dozen holes are drilled through the bone or wood with machine drills—say, starting with a 5/8, graduating down to a 1/16-inch hole. Bevel or smooth edges of the holes on both sides.

A round braid after being rolled under foot, is first drawn through the hole which is closest to its diameter. Then it is drawn through the next smaller hole; then the next smaller one. This evens up the braid and polishes it, and makes it of a consistent diameter throughout.

Several mandrels of various diameters are handy gadgets. They are used in making Turk's-heads and braided knots. One is shown in Fig. 15. This is a piece of broom handle with a leather or rawhide collar. The collar is to keep the knot from slipping while being braided. A face may be cut or filed on each of the four sides and these faces numbered in a clockwise direction from 1 to 4 (Plate 3, Fig. 12). This will help in the instructions which follow on braided knots.

Additional Notes on Making and Working Rawhide. In Queensland, Australia, they still use some old-time methods in making rawhide. Francis Ian Maclean, of Cunnamulla, writes:

"Peg out the hide while the animal body heat is still in it. The hide is stretched drum-tight on the ground with wooden pegs through small slits in the hide and made so it finishes in a circle, or as near as possible. Salt and ashes are laid on liberally to the extent of 10 to 12 pounds to a two-year-old steer hide, and allowed to remain for a few days. Leave the tail of the beast on the hide. The reason for leaving the tail on the hide is that the old drovers and bullock teamsters would tie the hide flesh down behind their wagons and drag it for miles. This method cleansed the fat and other tissues from the hide and helped to 'break' it. If the hide was not wanted for several days salt and fat was rubbed in after the dust was shaken off. Such a hide would keep for a long time if rolled up and left in the shade. This makes terrific rawhide."

He says sometimes bran was used instead of ashes and this imparted a yellow color to the hide. For small skins, like those of rabbits, he spread a paste of baking soda on the flesh side, repeating this for a

9

couple of days. Then he softened the skin by kneading with his hands, or pulling back and forth around a rough piece of hardwood. This gave it a soft and pliable finish.

"I have also seen," he further writes, "a bullock hide placed in a calf yard where four or five calves were locked up. Every night for about a month this hide was turned and believe me it was the best rawhide for ropes and hobbles I ever saw. The urine and dung made a super job."

Milton F. Farley, an old-time buckaroo of Crawfordsville, Oregon, wrote me recently that, after years of trying to find some easy and satisfactory method of thinning and evening rawhide strings, he had learned from an old fellow how to skive them by a very simple and homey way.

"Now, here's what I want you to do," he wrote. "Go to a hardware store and tell the salesman you want a good joiner's plane. When you get it in your hands it explains itself. You turn the screw behind the bit clockwise to close the gap behind the bit. When you turn the screw anticlockwise it opens the gap. If the strings are one inch or smaller I hold the plane in my left hand, pull the string with my right. When the strings are wider, I fasten the plane in a vise. Darn it, Bruce, it's so simple it's silly!"

Milton F. Farley skiving rawhide strings with his joiner's plane. The flesh side is against the blade.

Mr. Farley also came up with a homemade gadget for removing hair from rawhide. It is simply two hacksaw blades mounted between two pieces of wood so the teeth are in opposite directions and protrude about an eighth of an inch. The gadget is held in a vise and the rawhide string is pulled back and forth with the hair side against the blades. I

10

presume the strings should be dampened and well soaped to do a good job. Mr. Farley says it works very well.

Ernie Ladouceur of Madera, California, has a method of sizing sleazy leather which stiffens and glazes it and also makes it waterproof. However, a word of caution. As white gasoline is used in this process, great care must be exercised and it is advisable to do your work out-of-doors.

"I take a quart of white gasoline—the ordinary automobile fuel will not do—and set it in the hot sun to warm good, or in a pail of hot water," Ernie writes.

"I use a quart fruit jar with the lid put on loose. I don't screw it down tight, as vapor pressure may build up and break the glass. I work out-of-doors away from any fire or flame. When the gasoline is warm, I take some Parawax, the kind a woman uses to seal a jar of jelly with, and shave this up with a knife and put in all that the gasoline will dissolve. If there is too much wax, this won't do any harm.

"When the wax is all dissolved, I put in my leather thongs and let them stand in the solution for a couple of hours. After this, I hang them in a sunny, windy place away from any chance of catching fire, and let them dry.

"You will be surprised at what this wax filling will do to a piece of leather. If you treat your leather before you level it, you will be delighted at the ease with which it cuts. You will like the feel of it and how it looks after braiding.

"But be very careful. The fumes from white gasoline travel a great distance and *will ignite from a flame fifty feet away*. These fumes are heavy and flow along the ground or floor."

There are various ways to dye rawhide strings. The ordinary vegetable dyes on the market are good, especially the so-called Easter egg dyes. However, the dye solution should be only lukewarm, not hot, when the rawhide is placed in it.

John Conrad once wrote me that he had perfected a method whereby he could keep the rawhide the same color as the animal's hair. An animal with white hair produced white rawhide and, while he was in business, his pure white rawhide was of the very best. Conrad never explained his method.

To obtain black rawhide, the gauchos of the Argentine take the residue of their native drink, *yerba mate* (sometimes called Paraguayan tea), and place it in water with rusty iron. This produces a jet black liquid in which the rawhide is soaked for several days. The rawhide comes out a bluish black which is indelible. It is dyed throughout, not just on the surface.

This same result can be obtained with a strong solution of tea and rusty iron. Strain off the liquid and soak the rawhide in it for a couple of days. This produces a kind of gunmetal black.

Much fine braiding is done in South America with dried intestines, or what we term catgut. To make catgut, steep the intestine of any animal in water for a day, peel off the outer membrane, then turn the gut inside out, which is easily done by turning a very short piece of it inside out, just as you would turn up the cuff of your sleeve; then, catching hold of the turned-up cuff, dip the whole in a bucket, and scoop up a little water between the cuff and the rest of the gut. The weight of this water will do what is wanted. It will bear down an additional length of the previously turned gut, and thus, by a few successive dippings, the entire length of any amount of intestine, however narrow it may be, can be turned inside out in a minute or two. Having turned the intestine inside out, scrape off the whole of its inner soft parts and that which remains is a fine transparent tube. This, being twisted and stretched to dry, forms catgut.

A fine sewing thread can be made from the outer membrane of intestines. Steep the intestines of any animal in water for a day. Then peel off the outer membrane, which will come off in long strips. These should be twisted between the hands, and hung out to dry. This thread is excellent for sewing rawhide together or for any other purpose.

An excellent example of Argentine rawhide braiding. A *rebenque*, the handle intricate "fid work" or *trenza de alezna*. Collection John Walter Maguire.

12

PLATE 2

Cutting Rawhide in the Argentine. In the Argentine, where this ancient craft of rawhide braiding has been kept alive, the *gaucho* artisan makes braided articles with the simplest of tools. In many cases these articles become acquisitions of museums and prized possessions of ardent collectors—but they are always articles of great utility value.

Continually on the prowl for anything connected with the processing, cutting, and working of rawhide, I came across several practical methods of cutting rawhide strings during a recent visit to the Argentine. One is the nearest approach to using the thumb as a guide that I have ever seen. Another, and the first I shall explain, is ideal for cutting any width string from a round piece of rawhide.

This first gadget is made from a rectangular piece of hardwood (Fig. 1, Plate 2) measuring 2 x 1-3/8 x 7/16 inches. Saw down the center as indicated in Fig. 1. The bottom of the saw-cut is on a slant, deeper on the forward end than on the rear end as shown by the dotted lines (Figs. 1 and 2).

Next cut out a square in the lower part of your guide. This square's size is determined by the width of the knife blade to be used. It should be slightly smaller than the width of the knife. The forward position, too, is cut at an angle as can be seen in Fig. 3. Figure 4 shows how the knife is placed in position. The width of the string to be cut is determined by the position of the knife blade against the groove. The knife should be positioned so the blade turns slightly at an angle toward the rawhide. It is well to file little grooves to hold the back of the knife in place.

The knife should be tightly positioned. With the right hand against the knife blade and guide, and the left hand holding the rawhide, start your string. The rawhide strip should be well-anchored at the forward end, of course.

Unless you are using softened rawhide, it will have to be dampened sufficiently so that it will cut properly. Place it in water a few minutes, then remove and rub in the liquid soap. Wrap it up in a damp cloth and let stand until the rawhide is damp but not flabby. Dampened rawhide reaches a point where it will cut like butter; only experience can teach you when it reaches this point. On very thin rawhide I never use plain water, but a solution of one-part liquid glycerin and four-parts water.

This little gadget I have described is very handy in cutting rawhide from the round. While I did not see this done in the Argentine—and those I talked to had never considered it—I began to experiment when I returned home. The only difference is that instead of holding the knife and guide in the right hand once you have started your cut, you simply pull the string itself. There is no need to worry about the knife dropping from its position as the pull on the emerging string wedges it even tighter into position. The right hand pulls the string and the left hand holds that part of the disc just forward of the wooden guide and

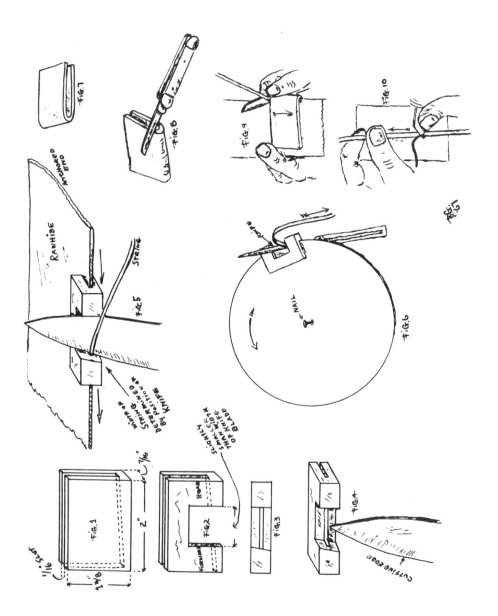

PLATE 2. Cutting Rawhide in the Argentine.

14

the knife. The disc or round of rawhide should be nailed in the center to the edge of a table or other flat surface so that it can turn freely (Fig. 6).

It is astonishing how long a string one can obtain from a disc or round of rawhide cut in this fashion: possibly as much as 100 feet of 1/16-inch of string from a round 12 or 13 inches in diameter. But one word of caution in cutting from the round: the disc must come from a section of the hide or skin that is consistently the same thickness. If part of the disc is from the belly, this portion of the string will come out thinner than the rest.

In making the simpler form of guide to cut strings (Fig. 7), cut a rectangular piece of heavy rawhide and fold it hair side in. Place between the folded parts (damp, of course) a piece of cardboard wrapped in cellophane or waxed paper so it won't stick, weight it down, and allow it to dry for several days. I might explain that folding with the hair side in is practical, as rawhide curls on the hair side when dry. It will curl out of shape anyway if left around, so when not using it, place the cardboard between the folds and keep a weight on it.

Figure 8 shows the position of the knife blade against the groove to determine the width of string to be cut. Push the blade edge into the rawhide slightly, so it will not slip out of position. Figure 9 shows the way to use this guide. The upper part of the rawhide strap is anchored securely.

The gaucho method of "knocking off" the sharp edges of rawhide strings is shown in Fig. 10. With a sharp knife and a piece of cardboard on your knee, this is not difficult. The thumb of the hand holding the knife holds the string closely against the knife blade, and the rawhide string is pulled forward as illustrated.

Martín Gómez, of the Argentine, whose work is in museums and in the hands of collectors, demonstrated for me his method of softening rawhide. The finest rawhide is made from the skins of colts. The skin is staked out in the shade for a couple of hours, then fleshed, and the hair removed—either with a sharp knife or by soaking for a day or two in a solution of quicklime (sometimes in a solution of sodium sulphide), and finally given an alum bath. The method of staking out determines the ultimate use of the skin. If it is to be cut in the round (that is spiraled into one long strap or *soga*), it is staked out to be formed as nearly round as possible. If for broad straps or *lonjas*, it is staked so the pull is from head to tail.

Dehaired, fleshed, and cut into strips (the belly section is the best for very fine strings), the rawhide is then softened. This is done in two stages. First the strip is rolled in a long spiral, with the hair side in, then dampened and rubbed liberally with yellow laundry soap, and beaten with a wooden mallet until the fibers are broken down.

Next, one end is fastened to a post and the strap is pulled many times through a *mordaza*. This is a cylinder of wood with a groove cut in it for two-thirds of its length. By turning the mordaza upward on one pull and downward on the next to offer as much resistance as possible,

15

Martín Gómez demonstrating two steps in softening rawhide. *Top:* Rolled strip is beaten with a wooden mallet until fibers are broken down. *Bottom:* Strap is pulled through a *mordaza* until it is as soft as leather.

the strap is worked until it is soft as leather. While tallow is used on such rawhide, it is the tallow which comes from fat around the animal's heart and liver. Ordinary tallow rots rawhide in time, the gauchos say. No salt is used on the skin as this causes the rawhide "to cry" or sweat in damp weather.

Gómez cuts his strings with a sharp knife, using his thumb as a guide. When he cuts hair-like strings, they curl in the air as he proceeds, and are of a consistent width for their entire length. Sometimes he uses a heavy piece of doubled rawhide with a square cut out of the folded part. Into this square goes the knife, its cutting edge adjusted for the width of the strings to be cut.

After the rawhide is softened it is ready to be cut into thongs. Martín Gómez demonstrating one method of cutting thongs. This step requires a sharp knife. Using his thumb as a guide he can cut strings that are hair-like in width and consistent for their entire length.

The edges of the strings are next beveled on the skin side by placing a knife, at an angle, on a card or piece of rawhide. This is placed on the knee, and the string is pulled against the knife's edge. The thumb acts as a guide.

Sogas, or wide strings cut from the round, mainly are used for making twisted lariats. The soga is softened only with the mordaza, as a *lazo* needs a certain amount of life or spring.

17

A second method of cutting strings or thongs is to use a round or disc of leather, as illustrated in Figure 6, Plate 2. The picture below clearly shows the disc attached to a heavy log and in position so it can turn freely. When using a round it is important to select a section of hide that is consistently the same thickness. A very long thong can be obtained by using a round.

Cutting strings from a round.

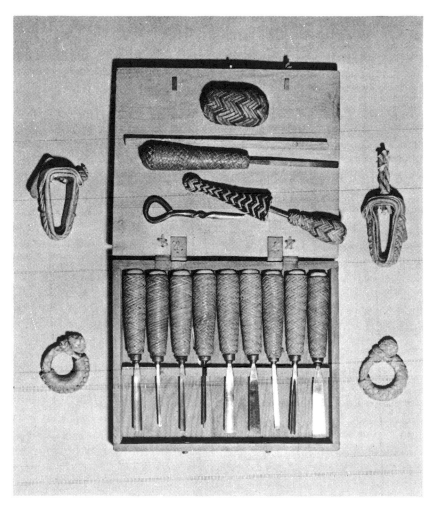

Braid Miscellanea. The box contains a set of wood carving tools, the handles of which are covered with a variety of braided knots made by the author. On the lid at the top is a rock, covered with rawhide braiding, used as a paperweight. Below is a chisel with a braid-covered handle and below this a fid and case—all braidwork by the author. To the left of the fid is a practical metal fid made by Mrs. Mary Fields. To the left of the box at the top is a honda made by Burt Rogers. Below is a honda made by John Conrad. To the right at the top is another honda made by Burt Rogers with a portion of a twisted rawhide *reata*. Below this is a honda with a braided boot made by the author.

PLATE 3

Leather-braiding Tools. In leather braiding and thong work the best tool is the hand. Just as other tools must be sharpened and well cared for, so must this most valued tool; the sharpening in this instance is its development and training, which involves a certain mental process leading to the coordination of eye and hand.

The actual tools themselves are mere projections of the hands. To use tools properly one must become so familiar with them, with their feel, with their application and their purpose that it is possible to use them with the same dexterity as the hand. Most tools can do more harm than good in unpracticed hands.

Some people have a natural born deftness and knack for braiding and thong work; others acquire it only through careful and conscientious study and application—by hard and faithful practice. Yet, taken step by step, and each step carefully and accurately performed, it is, as is any handicraft, relatively simple.

A good knife is important, It may be a pocketknife or the type of knife known as the skiving knife (Fig. 1). Keep the knife sharp at all times.

Figures 2 and 3 show thonging chisels for cutting slits in leather. A lacing needle (Fig. 5), purposely shown over-sized, is necessary for working with small thongs. The revolving punch with tubes (Fig. 4) which cuts holes of six different diameters, is an essential part of the equipment. A drive punch (Fig. 6), which may be had in different sizes, is also a necessary tool, in order to make holes several inches from the edge of the leather, which cannot be made with a revolving punch.

The fid, with a tapering metal part and blunt on the end, is a most valuable tool (Fig. 7). The space marker is a convenience, especially when lacing leather parts together, as it evenly marks the holes through which the thongs must pass (Fig. 8).

To cut belts or wide thongs from skins and hides, a draw gauge is used (Fig. 9). A mallet (Fig. 10) and dividers (Fig. 11) are also necessary.

For making Turk's-heads or woven knots of leather a mandrel is needed. This can be made with six inches of common broomstick. Cement a collar of leather near one end, file the other down on four sides and number these surfaces from 1 to 4 in a clockwise direction (Fig. 12).

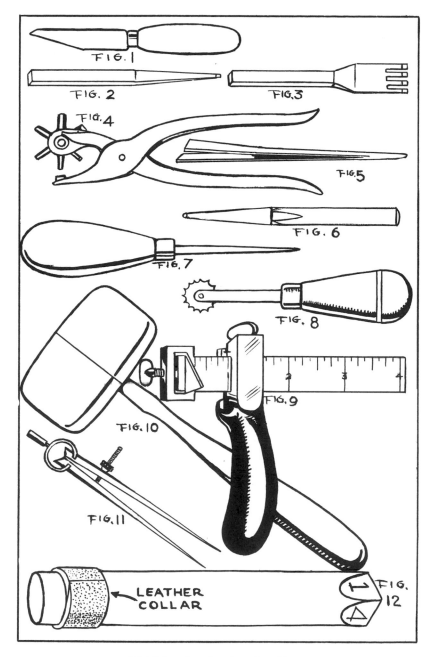

PLATE 3. Leather-braiding Tools.

21

PLATE 4

Thong Cutting. Some braiders prefer to cut their own thongs. These should be taken from that portion of the skin or hide that presents the least spongy appearance. Lay the leather on a hard cutting board and with a straightedge or ruler and a sharp knife cut the thongs, always cutting across the grain in the wood so the knife cannot follow this grain.

Scraps of leather may be cut into discs from four to eight inches in diameter. With a pair of shears, cut around the circumference the width of the thong desired (Fig. 1). After the thong is cut, its spiral shape can be straightened out by stretching it on the convex or inner side of the curve.

Some whipmakers cut their thongs freehand with a sharp knife, using the thumb as a gauge (Figs. 2 and 3). A more practical way is to use a thong cutter constructed as in Fig. 5. Other homemade thong cutters are shown in Figs. 6 and 7.

In cutting thongs it is important that the leather disc have a perfectly even circumference; also that the disc is laid out in the manner shown in Fig. 4, so that. a *leader* is first cut. Make the circle segment for the leader by placing the point of the compass a fraction of an inch above the center of the first circle. Start the leader with a knife or shears.

In cutting a thong, either with a thong cutter or a draw gauge (Fig. 9), *pull only on the thong itself.*

The other illustrations show the uses of a few of the tools already mentioned. Dividers can be used to score a margin on the leather edge (Fig. 8), or to step off spaces (Fig. 10). Fig. 11 shows the use of the four-pronged thonging chisel. Always put one prong in the last hole cut, thus insuring even spacing throughout. Figures 12 and 13 show the use of the space maker and the revolving punch.

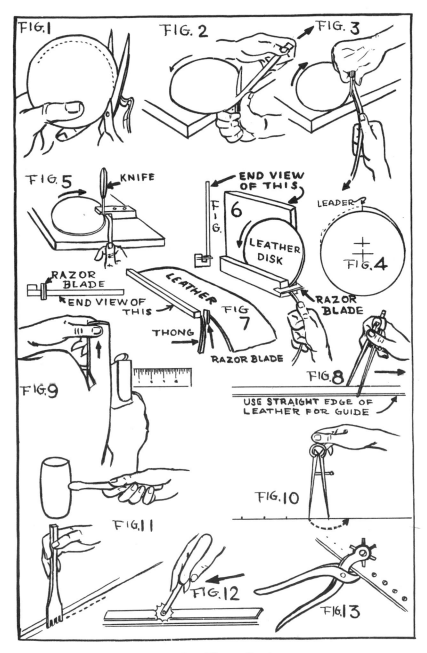

PLATE 4. Thong Cutting.

Two Indian bows with twisted rawhide bow strings. The one on the right is a Pampas Indian bow and the one on the left an Apache bow. The universality of the bow with twisted strings is a puzzle to archaeologists.

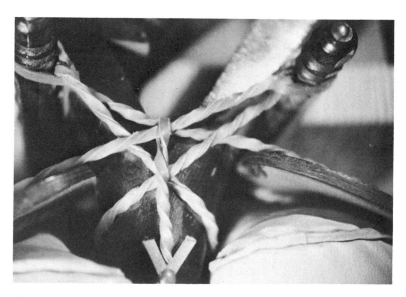

The universal twist braid employed in another practical way. The twist braid is clearly shown in this camel saddle from Arabia.

Twist Braids

PLATE 5

Twist Braids. Twist braiding probably is the oldest form of this craft. No doubt the intertwining of vines about trees and other plants, and often about themselves, inspired ancient man to simulate this braid in making his rope and string from tree fibers, grasses and other suitable materials. Later he used rawhide and found it practical as the torsion in the twisted string created a friction acting against itself to make it considerably stronger than an untwisted string.

Strings on primitive man's bows usually were of a single twisted strand of rawhide. Bows and arrows were used throughout the world, so this weapon can be considered a link between the cultures of ancient races. This belief is strengthened by the fact that twisted rawhide was used almost universally to brace ancient bows.

The simplest form of the twist braid is that of one leather thong or rawhide string (Fig. 1). Take a thong or string of uniform thickness and wet it thoroughly. If leather, it should not be too wet, but allowed to dry until the natural color almost reappears; if rawhide, just damp enough to be workable.

Do not actually twist the leather but roll it upon itself, the flesh side in (Fig. 1). Keep rolling it until it is a hollow tube and then begin gradually to stretch it until the tube narrows and the leather comes together at the spiral lines. While it is still damp, holding the two ends so that the roll does not uncurl, roll it beneath your foot or upon some hard surface with a piece of wood.

The two ends should then be clamped or nailed down to a board and the leather allowed to dry completely. It will retain its twist or roll. The ends may be left flat and attached to boxes for handles, or as shown in Fig. 2, inserted in holes and nailed or fastened inside.

Rawhide twisted in this fashion is used for a variety of purposes—cores for bosals, whips and riding crops. In utilizing such a core for riding crops it is made with a taper. The twist braid first is made from a heavy hide—bull hide or water buffalo hide. When dry it is sanded down to the proper taper. A taper also can be achieved by cutting the string from the back area down to the belly part, for the tape in a twist braid depends upon the thickness of the leather or rawhide and not the width.

Round Braid of Two Thongs or Trick Twist. This may not be new but I worked it out in the following manner: Slit the leather down the center, leaving the two ends closed as in Fig. 3. Dampen the leather, and then, with the hair side toward you, bring one end through to the front, as shown in Fig. 4. Continue pulling the bottom end through from rear to front until the braid is tight and then pull straight.

This braid can be made into a belt, or, by using a small piece of leather, into a wristwatch band, as shown in Fig. 7.

Don't forget to provide for the usual shrinkage—about ½ inch in a wristwatch strap.

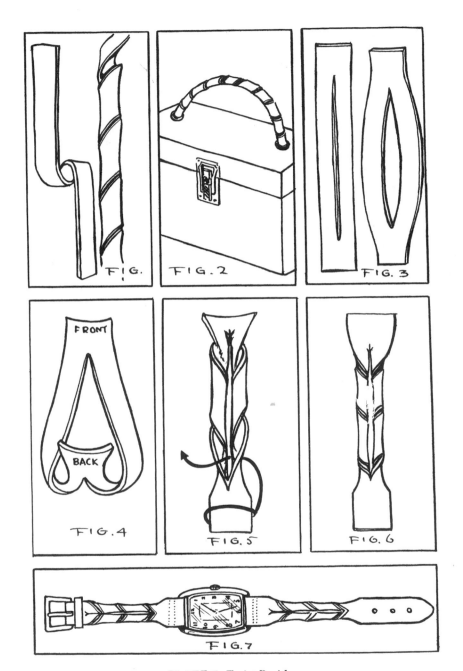

FIG. 1 FIG. 2 FIG. 3

FRONT

BACK

FIG. 4 FIG. 5 FIG. 6

FIG. 7

PLATE 5. Twist Braids.

Twist braid belt of one thong with woven knot for keeper loop.
(See Plate 5, Twist Braids.)

Interesting parts of an old braided headstall, sent to the author by L.H.
Rutter, Hinsdale, Montana. The keeper above has a loop made with an
8-string braid and then woven into a 16-string braid without core. The
16-string flattens out. This braid is illustrated under braided hobbles.

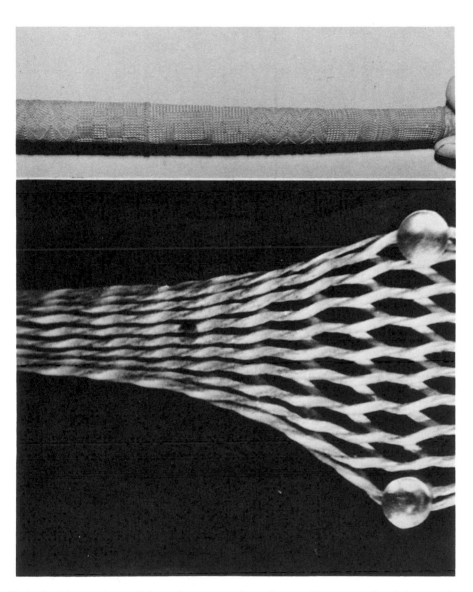

Twist braids can be used in various ways. *Top:* An excellent example of the tops in rawhide braiding. The handle of this Argentine *rebenque* (whip) is covered with *mondonguillo* braid of 48 fine strings. The various twist braids are used to form the intricate pattern. The *rebenque* belongs to Daniel Beritich of the Argentine and was photographed by Luis Alberto Flores of Buenos Aires. *Bottom:* A twist braid belt, the thongs are stretched to show the twist in each individual string.

PLATE 6

Attaching a Honda to a One-string Twist Lasso. The metal honda is fastened to the lasso of one twist as shown in Figs. 1-3. Sufficient string is left untwisted for this purpose. Another method is illustrated in Figs. 4-5. This type of rawhide lasso, still used in Mexico and parts of South America, mainly in Chile, generally is termed *Lazo Chileno*. It is twisted by the same method shown in the photographs where one of two strings is built.

In Fig. 6 is illustrated a sports belt from leather one inch or more in width. Leave a sufficient portion flat at each end—one end for attaching the buckle and the other as the billet where the holes are punched.

Double Twist. This unique twist was shown to me by Luis Alberto Flores of Buenos Aires (Figs. 7-11). Use about ½ inch wide thong or string slightly dampened. String A is given a full twist with the left hand (Fig. 7). Then string B is given a twist in the opposite direction with the right hand, and brought over to the left so that the edges of both strings interlock (Fig. 8). Next, work string A to the right (Fig. 10). These alternate moves are repeated until the desired length is obtained. Stretch and allow to dry. The finished braid is shown in Fig. 11.

Twist of Two Strings. A leather thong or rawhide string is looped over a post (Fig. 12) and with an end in each hand is twisted or rolled in the same direction (here, to the left). The left string can be laid over the right as the left hand twist is made (Fig. 14) or both strings can be twisted independently for the desired length and then brought together and allowed to twist themselves double (Fig. 16).

Twist of Three Strings. This twist braid is made much like the preceding one of two strings. The strings or thongs are placed around a post as shown in Fig. 17. The twist of each individual string is to the left and the left-hand string is brought to the right over two strings. This is repeated until the desired length is obtained. In Fig. 21 one long string is twisted and then looped over the post as shown and allowed to twist itself into a three-string twist braid. The result of both methods is shown in Fig. 22.

Building a Twist-Braid Reata. In building or making a one-, two-, or three-string rope or *reata*, strips about two inches wide are first cut from the round, then stretched thoroughly in a shady place until dry. These long strips are cut into ¼-inch widths, split to the same thickness and slightly beveled on the hair side. Little or no softening is done as a *reata* needs a certain amount of life or spring.

The accompanying pictures, taken in the Argentine, show two strings being twisted in rope-like fashion on a simple machine called a *gancho*, or hook. One part of the machine has three hooks with a windlass-like handle and is immobile. The other has a single hook and handle mounted on a weighted movable platform. The platform moves as the strings are twisted.

It takes three men to properly twist a *reata*. One turns the hook handle one way on the three-hook *gancho*, and another turns the hook handle the opposite way on the one-hook movable section, while the third operates the spreader. This spreader, which has a hole for each string, keeps the twist accurate and tight. (Old-time westerners in America formerly used a jacked-up wagon wheel for the immobile part of their rope-twister and tied the strings to the spokes).

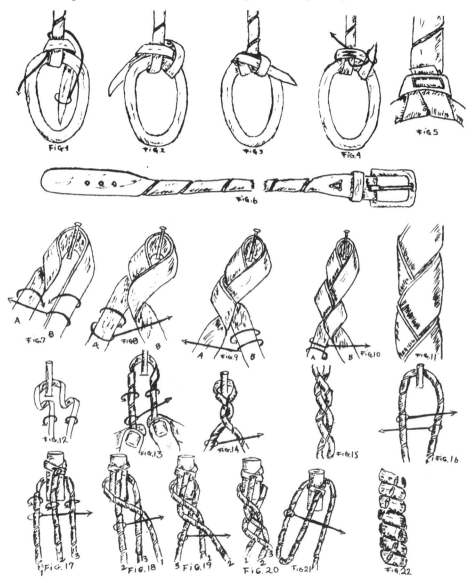

PLATE 6. Attaching a Honda to a One-String Twist Lasso; Double Twist; Twist of Two Strings; Twist of Three Strings; Building a Twist-Braid Reata.

A: Unmovable part of machinery for twisting a *reata*. B: Attaching rawhide strings to the movable part of machinery. C: Beginning the twist from the movable part—one man is turning the handle and the other is using a spreader to keep the twist accurate and tight.

Reata strings are treated first with a paste made from the contents of the animal's paunch mixed with chopped liver. Afterward, tallow from the fat around the heart and liver is rubbed in to keep the *reata* in good shape. Dry saddle soap rubbed in as a paste is excellent.

D: A full crew of three working on a two-string *reata*. Man in the foreground is manipulating the movable section, man in the center is operating the spreader, and the man in the background is turning the handle on the stationary part. E: The finished *reata*. This is of three strings.

PLATE 7

Simulated Four-String Round Braid. This ingenious twist braid is employed to join two or more rings, using only one long rawhide string or leather thong. It can be made any desired length.

Begin as shown in Fig. 1 by looping the string or thong through the top ring, which is held by a nail or post. With the left hand holding the lower ring and two ends of the string, twist to the left until the doubled string forms a twist braid as shown in Fig. 3. String B is passed over string A at the bottom and wound round the basic twist, as indicated by the arrowlines in Figs. 3 and 4.

String B, the working end, is next passed under A at the top (arrowline in Fig. 4) through the ring and then down. It is braided in a sequence of over one, under one, and then over 2, under one at the bottom (Fig. 5). If properly spaced, the path will now be clear for the upward and final pass which will be over one, under one to the top (Fig. 6). The finished braid resembles a four-string round braid, although it actually consists of five strings.

If you wish to join three rings, the same method is used with the result shown in Fig. 7.

The two-ring braid usually is employed on fancy hackamores to replace the fiador. It also may be used as a suitcase handle.

The versatile Fish-scale Braid can be used in a variety of ways. Shown here are three articles covered with this braid. *Left to right:* a bottle, a cigarette lighter and a rock paperweight. The directions for making the Fish-scale Braid are given in Plate 8.

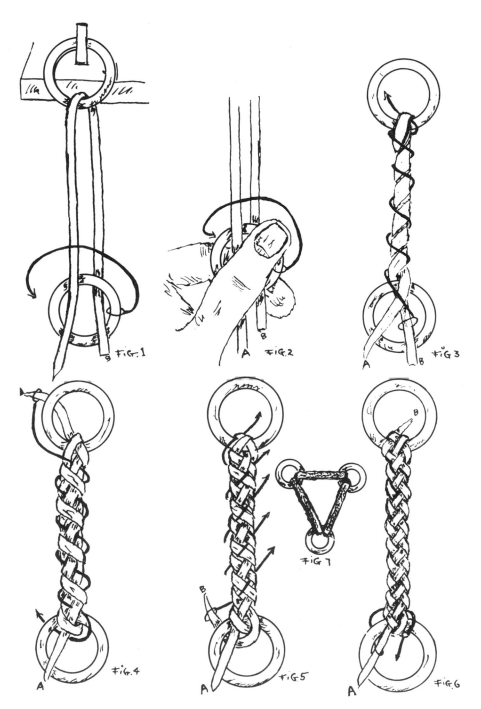

FIG. 1 FIG. 2 FIG. 3

FIG. 4 FIG. 5 FIG. 7 FIG. 6

PLATE 7. Simulated Four-String Round Braid.

PLATE 8

The Fish-scale Braid. This versatile braid was first shown to me by Ed Rickman of Meeteese, Wyoming, as a bosal side button. Later I found it in general use in the Argentine. It can be made to cover almost any object and, combined with the conquistador braid in handle coverings, gives a beautiful effect.

There are several methods of starting this braid. The basic weave, a simple wrapping around is shown in Fig. 1, In the next step, Fig. 2, it is to be noted that the flesh side of the string or thong is always next to the flesh side of the previous links. In Fig. 3 one string is used and it is braided on its own part (Fig. 4). It can also be started on a cord tied around the object to be covered (Fig. 5). In Figs. 6 and 7, where a leather or rawhide foundation is used, the string passes through the holes as shown. And in Figs. 8-11 it is demonstrated how this braid can be started by first twisting the string and continuing as illustrated. The finished braid is shown in Fig. 12.

In the fish-scale braid the pass is always made either under or over. If, for instance, you start by passing under, continue to do so; and vice versa. Since it is difficult to work with a very long string splicing is necessary. In introducing a new string, the end of the working part is skived or thinned about half its thickness for a couple of inches. The new string is skived also on its end. To continue with the new string, start back a couple of passes and braid over the old string. Both ends should be kept beneath the ensuing braid.

To reverse the braid, follow Fig. 13 (top). After passing under with the working end, pass over in the next step. The loop X is formed and all passes are over, even when you get around to the loop. The transition results in the braid shown in Fig. 13 (bottom).

Combination Handle Covering. A smart-looking, yet simple handle covering is shown in Figs. 14-16. First, make a simple twist braid. Then cut a string or thong from rawhide or leather the same thickness as the width; in other words, square. Wet it thoroughly and pull it through a hole made in hardwood or bone, as shown in Figs. 15 and 16. The holes should be graduated and it is better to start with one or two larger than the proper hole and gradually work your string or thong round. This string should be the same diameter as that of the twist braid. They are wrapped around as shown in Fig. 16.

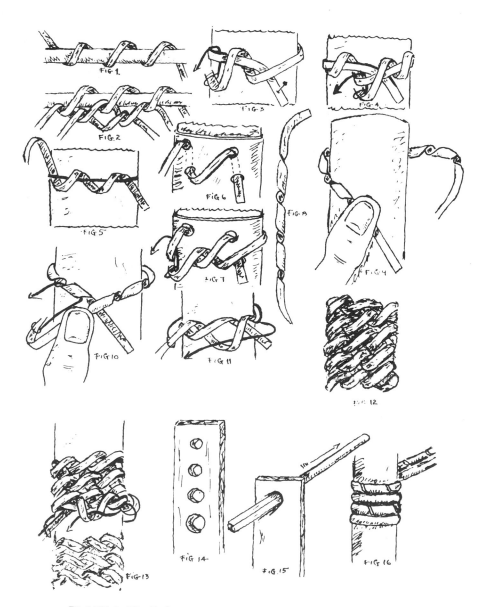

PLATE 8. The Fish-scale Braid; Combination Handle Covering.

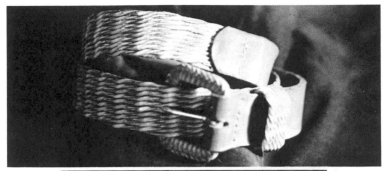

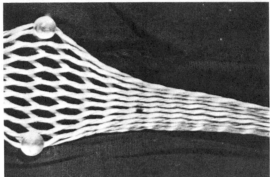

What the author calls the "Fish-scale Braid" is shown here. This twisted
braid can be used for many purposes. *Top:* A belt. *Center:* Belt with
the braid pulled open. *Bottom:* Stone paperweights and a bottle are just
two examples of articles that can be covered with this braid.

38

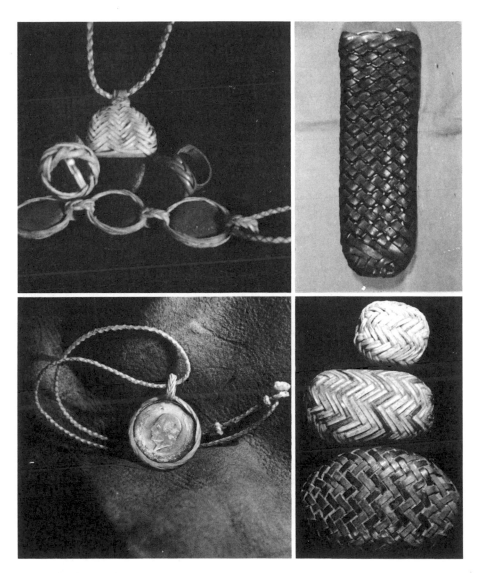

Top, left: The locket with the single stone is made by partially covering a small black stone with a pineapple knot. The locket with three stones uses the Spanish ring knot to link the stones together. The rings, with stone settings, are made like the Gaucho button knot around a mandrel the size of the finger. After the first part of the braid is made, the stone is set inside the top braid and the braid is tightened about it. *Top, right:* Glasses case made with an elongated Turk's-head interwoven with lacing. *Bottom, left:* Mexican coin locket; one Spanish ring knot encircles the coin and a smaller one, made as a link, accommodates the neck rope. *Bottom, right:* Covered rock paperweights of interwoven braid.

PLATE 9

Making a Rock Paperweight. To cover a rock for a paperweight, first make a twist braid in the center of a long string or thong and place it around the center or largest part of the rock (Fig. 1). Using end A, begin a fish-scale braid (Fig. 2). After braiding around several times so the braid is secure, withdraw string B from beneath the braid and start working it in the opposite direction. Continue both braids with A and B. As the rock tapers on the ends, skip each alternate loop in each braid. When the braids have closed on the ends by skipping loops, tuck ends A and B up under several rows of the braid and cut off.

Making a Locket with a Small Pear-shaped Stone or Gem. The stone or gem, say 1¼ inch long and ¾ inch at the widest part, is first partially covered with thin rawhide (Fig. 5). The rawhide is cut so the middle section can be turned in along the dotted lines (Figs. 5-6) and sewed on damp (Fig. 6). In Fig. 7 this loop with edges turned in is passed around a pencil and tied snug. In Fig. 8 the work is reversed to better illustrate the braiding method. Cover the edge of the rawhide with a two-pass Spanish ring knot. Pass a new string through one of the bights of the ring knot. The end B is worked by passing it from the top to the bottom of the next bight. This can be continued for several bights. Then bring the end A back and pass it through the bottom of each bight formed by B. This leaves a loop formed by A which B will pass through when it comes around to that point. This braid with the two ends is continued and as it nears the top where the rawhide cover is tied, it is decreased by passing through every other bight.

A conquistador braid results. This locket is hung on a four-string round braid with a loop in one end and a button worked on the other.

Fish-scale Braid Belt. This is made on a large round object—in this case, a cookie can about ten inches in diameter and 32 inches in circumference. First, tightly weave a three-part elongated Turk's-head around the can (Figs. 9-12). Then introduce independent strings on both edges (A and B in Fig. 13). Don't worry about the ends in this section, marked in brackets designated by X; this part eventually will be covered. Braid A around one way and B around the other using the fish-scale method. Different colored strings can be used for the Turk's-head and the strings A and B. When the desired width is obtained, introduce a thin piece of rawhide (or even cloth, if you like) under the section marked X. Cement it to the braid and to itself, forming a wrapping at this point (Fig. 14). When the wrapping is dry cut it in half, as shown in Fig. 15. One end is used for the buckle and the other for the billet of the belt. Both ends are made from leather folded and cemented.

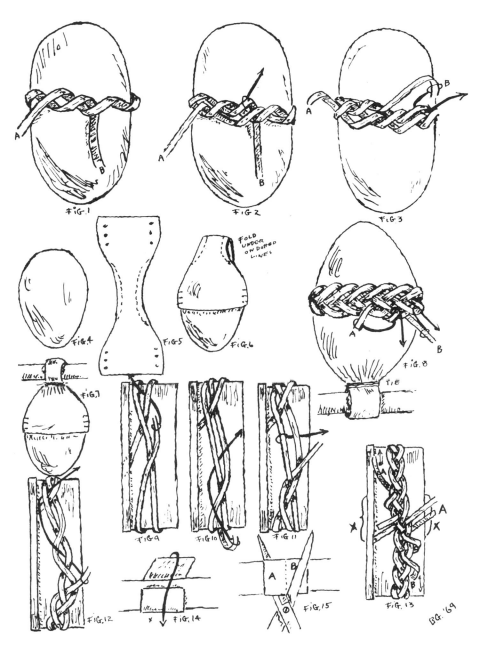

FIG.1 FIG.2 FIG.3
FIG.4 FIG.5 FOLD UNDER ON DOTTED LINES FIG.6 FIG.8 TIE
FIG.7 FIG.9 FIG.10 FIG.11 FIG.13 B.G. '69
FIG.12 FIG.14 FIG.15

PLATE 9. Making a Rock Paperweight; Making a Locket with a Small Pear-shaped Stone or Gem; Fish-scale Braid Belt.

41

PLATE 10

The Conquistador Braid. Here is a remarkable braid which was used by the old-time conquistadores on their sword belts and seems to have been lost somewhere along the line. It is made with one thong. Be sure this thong is of consistent thickness as the braid will not be regular if the thong is thin in some spots and thick in others.

Start with four holes or slits in the leather, evenly spaced and about 1/8 inch from the end. Hold the dress or hair side of the leather toward you with holes upward. Pass the thong through the hole on the left to the back, leaving a small portion of it on the near side, as in Fig. 1. Bring it back to the front and pass it again through the same hole to the rear. Draw it tight, anchoring the end, and bring it forward and pass it through the second hole from front to rear as shown in Fig. 2.

Pass the thong through the third hold (Fig. 3) and then through the fourth hole (Fig. 4). Make the thongs snug.

Introduce the fid under the bight, as in Fig. 5, from the left side upward to the right. Then bring the thong over to the front and draw it through this opening, as in Fig. 6. Draw it up snug, always using as nearly as possible the same amount of pressure on each thong. This will keep the braid consistent throughout.

The next step is shown in Fig. 7, where the thong has passed under the bight of the thong in hole No. 3 and to the rear of itself. The fid already has prepared the next bight to receive the working end of the thong. Continue until the thong has been passed through all four bights. Now start back to the right by passing under the newly formed bight in the second row, as shown in Fig. 8. Figure 9 illustrates a continuance of the sequence. Continue until the thong has passed through all four bights.

Now start back to the left. Thus it goes from left to right, and right to left until the braid is of the desired length. Finish it off by introducing it into four holes of another strap. This makes a fine belt or wrist strap for a watch.

The finished braid is shown in Fig. 10. At first there will be a give to this braid and it may seem elastic. But after it has been worn it will remain at the point to which it has stretched and will no longer be resilient. So allow a little for the give, depending on how tightly the braid has been made.

Wristwatch band made from Conquistador Braid (Pl. 10). Woven ring knots (Pl. 162) used as loop and coverings. Knots next to watch can be made from Headhunter's Knot (Pl. 169).

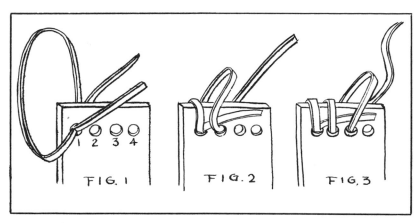

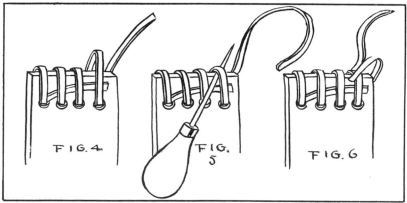

PLATE 10. The Conquistador Braid.

43

PLATE 11

Multiple-string Conquistador Braid. There are several ways of starting this braid, which somewhat resembles the weave in the sailor's Spanish Mat. In Fig. 1 the strings are tied, as shown, completely around the handle, spaced the width of the string. They are then braided, as shown in Figs. 1 and 2. In Fig. 3 a more accurate method to obtain the proper spacing is illustrated. The braid is then continued, as illustrated in Fig. 4.

Figures 5-7 show how this braid can be started from a three-part Turk's-head. This provides a braided start instead of tied string-ends which have to be covered to finish off the braid. Also in Figs. 8-10 a simulated Spanish ring knot can be made as a start—a finished start. Both the Turk's-head and the ring knot can be used to finish the end of the braids.

By continually working your strings in one direction you can obtain a fish-scale braid. Beautiful examples of this multiple-string conquistador braid, as well as combinations with the fish-scale braid, are to be found on gaucho whip handles.

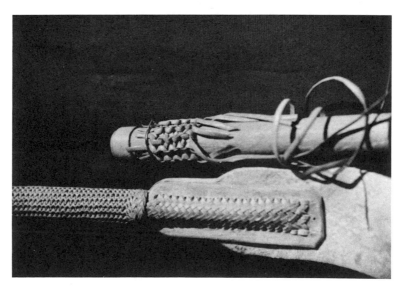

Handle of Argentine *rebenque* covered with rawhide multiple Conquistador braid. At *right, top* is an example of how the author makes this braid.

44

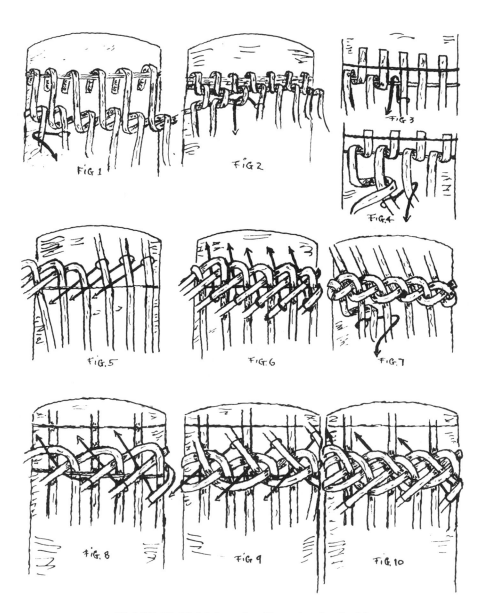

PLATE 11. Multiple-string Conquistador Braid.

PLATE 12

How to Make Braided Twist-Loop Reins. Twist-loop reins are quite common in ordinary strap leather. They are attractive and practical for they do away with buckles and give a double thickness of leather in the loop, thereby minimizing wear at the bit ring.

As long as they are popular and not difficult to make with strap leather, I have worked out a method whereby they can be fashioned from braided rawhide. I hesitate to say that my method or idea is unique, but I can truthfully say that I have never seen reins of this sort.

First, for those who do not know how to make such reins with strap leather, I shall explain how this is done. The same method of twisting the leather loops is used with the braided ones, so by showing the former, I shall make it easier to explain how the latter is done.

Take a 7-foot-long, ½-inch-wide strap and, 2½ inches from one end, slit the strap in the center for 2½ inches (Fig. 1). Fold over the slit part with the dressed side of the leather uppermost and the portion at the top of the slit toward you. With a fid or piece of wood or metal, twist the left loop clockwise one-half turn (follow arrowlines in Fig. 2). Do the same with slit loop on the right (Fig. 3). Pass the long end of the rein through the bit ring and then through the two twisted loops. It is well to have the leather damp. Work the knot tight and the job is done.

This same idea can be employed with three or four slits in the leather (Figs. 6-9).

For rawhide reins, take three 1/8-inch strings about 20 feet each. It is best that these strings first be softened by dampening them, rubbing in liquid soap and pulling them back and forth (flesh side in) around a square piece of wood held in a vise. Work them until almost dry and feel to see if there are any hard spots. If so, resoap them and work some more.

Drive three nails in a board or at the edge of a table (Fig. 10). Double the strings and place the loops over the nails and work down 2 inches in an over-one, under-one 6-string braid (Fig. 12). Then with three strings from each side, braid down two 3-string braids for two more inches (Fig. 13). Join the strings, starting as in Fig. 13, and resume the 6-string flat braid for a couple of additional inches (Fig. 14).

Now, as illustrated in Fig. 14, begin a 6-string round braid. First carry string A on the left and then forward on the right, then under one, over two. Then take string B on the right and around back and forward on the left under two, over one. Continue this sequence, taking the top string on the left around back and to the right and forward under one, over two, and then the top string on the right around back and forward to the left under two and over one.

If you wish 6-foot reins, continue this braid to the last two inches and then finish with a round braid of over one, under one sequence (Fig. 15). This is done by taking the highest string on either side and carrying it around back and forward over one, under one, over one.

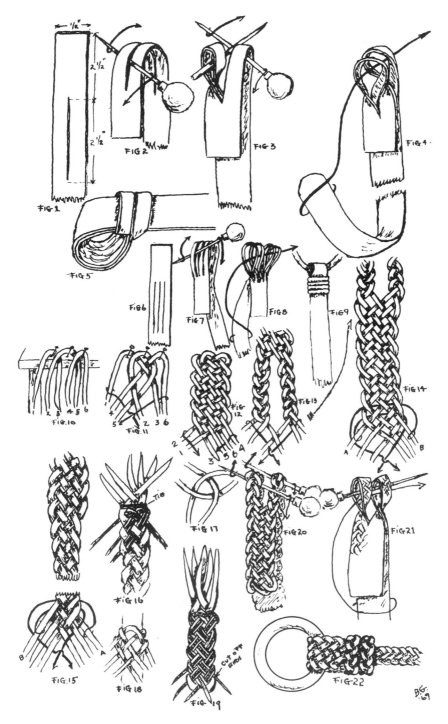

PLATE 12. How to Make Braided Twist-Loop Reins.

47

Work alternate strings and then tie the end of the braid with a piece of twine (Fig. 16).

To permanently secure the braid, take three thin, smaller rawhide strings and introduce them into the original braid, as shown in Fig. 16. Figure 17 shows these newly introduced strings from the top and Fig. 18 shows how they are braided.

This backbraiding is done by following on top of each original string, over and under. Cut the ends flush (Fig. 19) and remove the twine tied around the top of the braid. The interwoven strings will keep the braid intact and will not cause too large a swell so these ends can pass easily through the loops.

Next, double over the two 3-string loop braids (Fig. 20), twist each one-half turn as with the strap leather loops in Figs. 2 and 3. Run the ends of the reins through the bit ring and then through the braided loops (Fig. 21). The final result is shown in Fig. 22.

The twist loops should be damp so they can be gently molded. Allow to dry. It may be necessary to dampen them again should you want to remove the reins from the bit rings.

Such reins are attractive and in harmony with braided headstalls. The reins can be left open or the ends held together with any of the woven button knots.

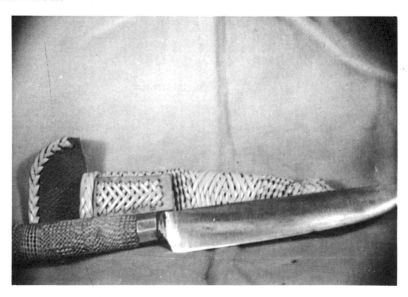

Luis Alberto Flores used a twist braid to cover the handle of the Argentine-type knife. The sheath was made by the author.

Slit Braids

PLATE 13

Slit Braids. By slitting the leather and passing it back through the holes alternately, the effect of a braid is obtained, although it is not a true braid in the usual sense.

An example of this braid may be found in attaching a buckle to a strap. First punch out in the middle of the strap the slot through which the tongue of the buckle goes and introduce the buckle, as shown in Fig. 1. The flesh sides on each portion of the strap face each other.

Make a vertical slit as shown, and indicated as 1, less than the width of the strap itself. Make slit No. 4 in the other part of the strap a little below; then slits 2, 5, and 3. These should be stair-stepped as indicated.

Bring up that portion of the strap indicated as A and pull it through slit 1 from the rear to the front. Then pull the portion shown as B through slit 4 also from the rear to the front. Now again pull A through from the rear to the front. Continue to the end. Don't pull the straps through the slits sideways. Work with the leather damp after it has been thoroughly saddle-soaped.

Figure 2 shows leather or metal conchas as they are fastened to cowboy bridles and saddles by this method.

Figure 3 illustrates a practical application of the various flat braids in making a belt. The braiding starts from the end in which the belt holes are punched, indicated by D. The loose ends are secured in that portion shown as A. Before the braid is sewn in, however, introduce the buckle and the belt loop, illustrated in C. One type of belt loop made from a Turk's-head or woven knot is shown as B. The method of making this will be shown later.

Figure 4 shows how the three-thong inside braid (Plate 14) can be used as a belt, and in this case there are no loose ends to cover or sew in. The five-thong inside braid (Plate 15) also makes a good belt, and either of these braids may be used as wrist loops on whips and quirts.

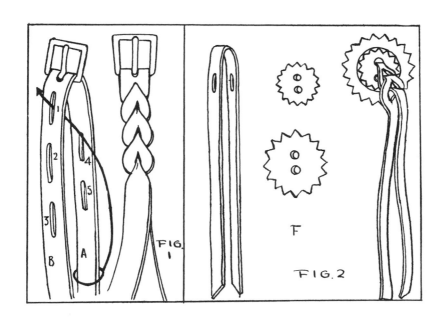

FIG. 1

FIG. 2

F

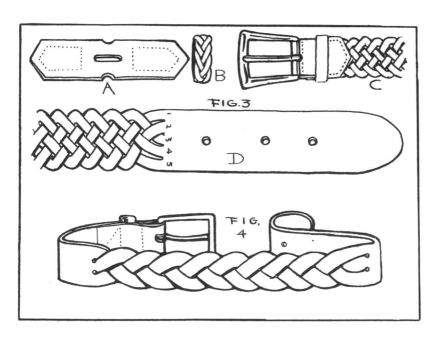

A

B

FIG. 3

C

D

FIG. 4

PLATE 13. Slit Braids.

51

PLATE 14

Three-Part Inside or Trick Braid. This is an ordinary three-part "hair braid" but it is worked inside; that is, the ends of the thongs are not free and are split from one single strap. It is tricky to make and mystifying to the uninitiated.

Lay the strap out in three equal parts and split it the desired length, leaving both ends closed, remembering that there is some shrinkage when the braid is complete, and the strap used in making a belt, for instance, should be nearly one-third longer than the desired length of the belt.

At the ends of the slits punch holes with the smallest tube on the revolving punch. This is to keep the leather from splitting further. Now dampen the leather by saddle-soaping it thoroughly as it is well to braid it while damp.

The first two steps are indicated in Fig. 2. Starting with the right-hand thong, C, place its bight over the center thong, B, then place the bight of the left-hand thong, A, over C. It will be noticed that a reverse or compensating braid is formed at the bottom. This bottom braid must be raveled out, while the top part remains intact.

To make the bottom braid disappear pass the entire bottom of the strap through the opening indicated in Fig. 2. This twists and tangles the thongs as in Fig. 3. The back part or flesh side of the strap will be forward and this should be twisted from left to right until the front side is foremost as in Fig. 4.

Meantime, as shown in Fig. 4, the braiding is continued and thong B is placed over thong A and thong C over thong B. The entire bottom of the strap now is passed through the opening shown in Fig. 4, and when straightened out, the whole work assumes an orderly appearance as in Fig. 5.

In this braid the moves have been made as simple as possible. That is, the bottom end is passed through the braid after each two moves. A "move" is the crossing of a thong over or under another.

In continuing the braid from its status in Fig. 5, place thong C over thong B, then thong A over thong C. Pass through the corresponding opening as was done in Fig. 2. Continue, or repeat, the moves shown in Figs. 3 and 4.

This braid should be made very tight at the top, so that when within a couple of inches of the bottom the braid becomes difficult to continue, the tightness in the upper part can be worked out and the braid distributed evenly throughout.

This braid is popular in making belts. It is also used for camera and shoulder bag straps, handles for quirts and crops and for bridle reins and wristwatch straps. Be sure the original strap is a third longer than necessary, to absorb the shrinkage when it is braided.

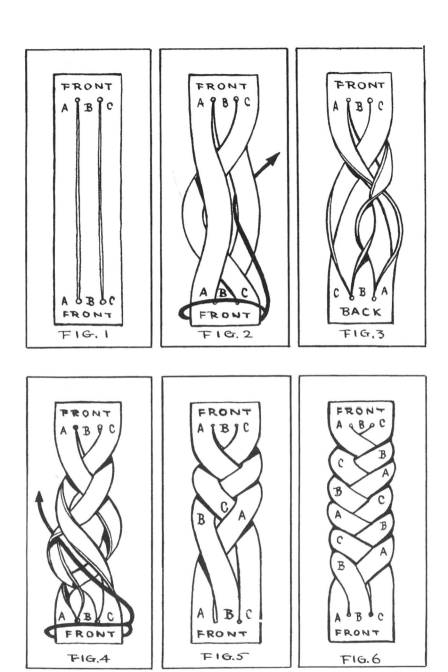

PLATE 14. Three-Part Inside or Trick Braid.

PLATE 15

Five-Part Inside Trick Braid. The five-part trick braid gives a pleasing effect of an over-two-and-under-two sequence. First cut a leather strap as shown in Fig. 1, being sure that the thongs are of equal width.

There is some shrinkage when the strap is braided and allowance must be made for this. For instance, in a strap 1¼ inches wide and eight inches long, cut into five ¼-inch thongs, the shrinkage will be about one inch.

The first step is shown in Fig. 2. Bring the bight of the extreme left-hand thong, A to the right over thongs B and C. Then take the bight of the extreme right-hand thong, E, and bring it to the left over D and A, (Fig. 3). Now bring thong B on the extreme left over C and E to the right (Fig. 4), and pass thong D from right to left over A and B (Fig. 5).

In Fig. 6 two sequences are shown. First pass thong C on the extreme left to the right over thongs E and D. The upper portion of this braid must be held intact, and it will be seen that there have been five different passes. Next, take the bottom of the strap and pass the entire end through the opening between thongs C and D.

The braid should now look like the illustration in Fig. 7. Pay no attention to the tangled condition of the thongs at the bottom and continue to work at the top.

Take thong A on the extreme right and bring it to the left over thongs B and C (Fig. 8). Repeat this operation from each side four more times before the braid is turned from the bottom. For instance, bring the right thong and then the left thong to the center alternately, doing this five times with each thong.

The upper portion of the braid should now appear as in Fig. 9. Take the bottom of the strap shown in Fig. 9 and pass it through the part, as indicated, between thongs C and D. This lower part of the braid will then straighten itself out. Upon examining the top part, which must be held in place while the lower part is passed through, it will be apparent that there are exactly ten steps—that is, the right and left outer strands have been passed inward ten times.

The secret of this braid is that five passes are made each time before the bottom is turned.

When the braid reaches the point illustrated in Fig. 10 begin all over again. Pass thong A over B and C as was done in Fig. 1. When the point corresponding to that in Fig. 6 is reached, turn in the bottom as before. Then continue as in Fig. 7 until the end.

To make it easier to work at the bottom tighten up the braid at the top more than seems necessary. When the braid is completed, loosen it until it is even throughout.

A seven-string (and, in fact, a nine-string) inside braid can be made in similar fashion. In the seven-string braid, seven passes instead of the five in the five-string braid are made, then reverse and continue as shown in the five-string braid, but make seven passes. This results in an over-three, under-three sequence. In the nine-string braid first make nine passes. In this braid an over-four, under-four sequence results.

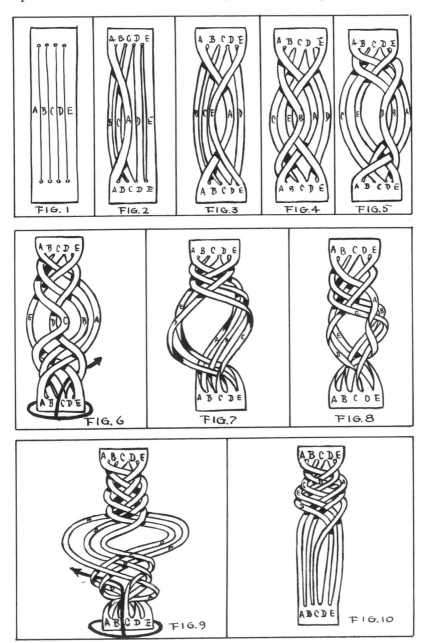

PLATE 15. Five-Part Inside Trick Braid.

PLATE 16

Interweaving the Three-Part Inside Braid. Inside trick braids, even the three-part, have a tendency to narrow in the braided section, while remaining the full width in the uncut portions. This can be overcome in the three-part inside braid by interweaving it with two additional independent strings or thongs. First, as in Fig. 1, introduce string A and interweave as shown by the arrowline. Next (Fig. 2) string B is interwoven as indicated by the arrowline. The final result is shown in Fig. 3. The ends can be tucked under and cemented or sewed down. An over-two, under-two five-part braid is the final outcome.

A Simulated Four-Part Inside Braid. This interweave is valuable when two separate sets of strings are to be joined in four-string inside braid. First the two upper strings are laid over and under as shown in Fig. 4. String A is placed over two and under two, etc., according to the length, as shown by the arrowline in Fig. 4. String B is interwoven under one, over one, as shown by the arrowline in Fig. 5. The result is shown in Fig. 6.

Six-String Inside Braid (not shown in the plate). A regular six-string inside braid can be made by cutting six strings in a strip of leather or rawhide. The same method of braiding is followed as in Plate 13, only the strings are worked in pairs. The same principle can be applied to nine strings worked in sets of three.

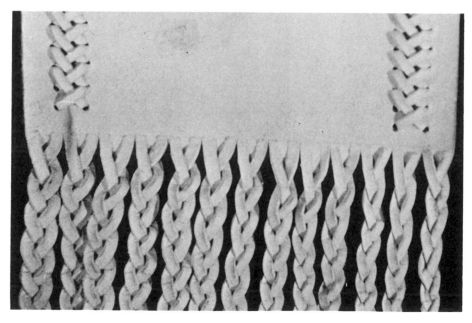

Closeup photo of a braided cincha showing braid and appliqué used to hold fold together. (Plates 23, 24 & 25.)

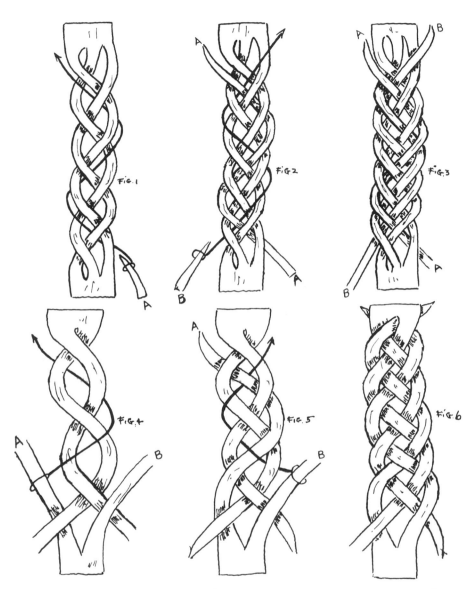

PLATE 16. Interweaving the Three-Part Inside Braid; A Simulated Four-Part Inside Braid; Six-String Inside Braid (not shown in the plate).

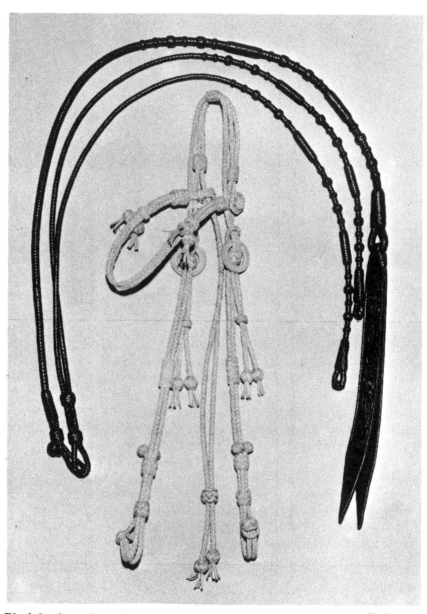

Black leather reins and romal made by Ernie Ladouceur of Madera, California. White rawhide headstall made by author. Buttons are interwoven with a darker shade of rawhide.

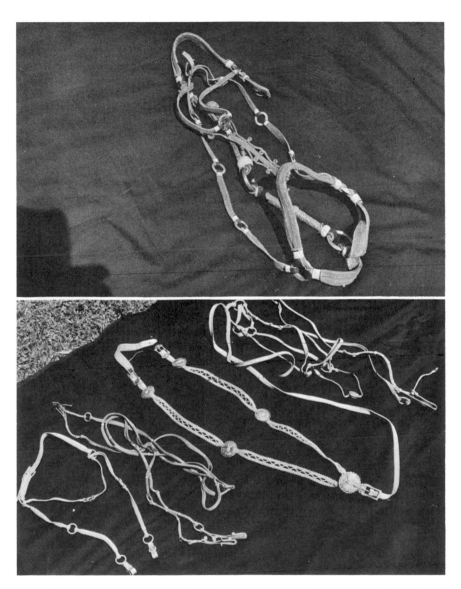

Top: A braided bosal of five rawhide strings. *Bottom (l. to r.):* Headstall, reins, breast plate, and bosal all of braided rawhide with gold ornaments. Collection of John Walter Maguire, Buenos Aires, Argentina.

PLATE 17

Interweaving the Slit Braid. The simple slit braid shown in Fig. 1, Plate 13, can be decorated by interweaving a smaller string as shown in Fig. 1, Plate 17. An interwoven string of a different color will give a pleasing effect.

Heart-Shaped Headstall Front Piece. A single strip of leather or rawhide, thoroughly dampened, can be worked into various designs by this method. The heart-shaped style is the most popular. Three slits are made through the edges as shown in Fig. 2, and numbered 1, 2, and 3. First, end A is passed through slit No. 1 (Fig. 3). Then end B is passed through slits Nos. 2 and 3 (Fig. 4). The braid is carefully adjusted and then tapped with a mallet to finish it. The two top ends are fastened to the browband and the three bottom ends to the noseband.

Four-String Slit Braid. Using two strings of one color and two of another, an attractive slit braid can be made as shown in Figs. 5 and 6. It appears rather complicated but after the start it is quite simple. Other slit braids for ends of reins, reatas, hondas, etc., are to be found under these subjects.

Curlicues or Moñitos. This type of slit braiding offers many interesting possibilities. It is found in profusion in the Province of Buenos Aires, Argentina, and possibly, as the native gauchos claim, it originated there. It is used for headstalls, reins, etc., and is more decorative than useful. The first method is illustrated in Figs. 7-11. The leather (Fig. 2) by slit braiding two narrow pieces of leather or softened rawhide (Fig. 2) and place it (or them) behind the Argentine name *moñitos* is translated as "little tufts" or crests, from the word *moño* which means the tuft or crest on a bird's head. Curlicue is my own interpretation. In the second method the leather or rawhide is doubled so the hair side is out on both sides (Fig. 12). It is slit through the doubled section (Fig. 13). After the ends are pulled through tightly, they appear as in Fig. 14. Tap the slit sections with a mallet to adjust.

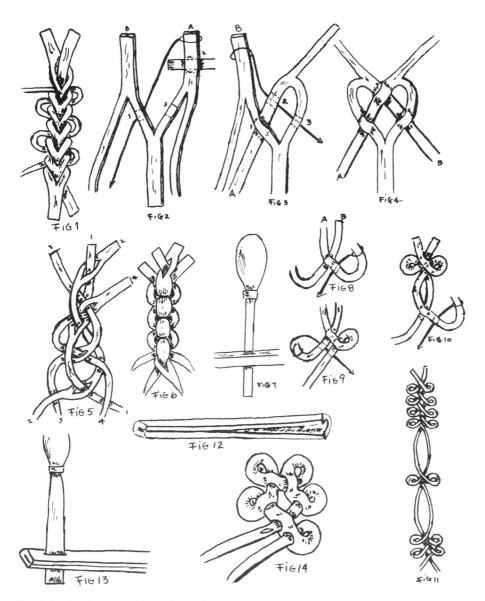

PLATE 17. Interweaving the Slit Braid; Heart-Shaped Headstall Front Piece; Four-String Slit Braid; Curlicues or Moñitos.

61

PLATE 18

Braided Gaucho Belt Fastener. This is a braided version of the famous gaucho *rastra* which is used to fasten the *tirador* or the broad belt of the Argentine cowboy. The *rastra* usually is of silver with small chains on two edges with coins used as buttons. The *tirador* itself is usually inlaid with coins of various denominations.

To make a braided version of the *rastra* take two straps of leather or softened rawhide about 20 inches in length and slit each one 13 inches (Fig. 1). The slitted sections are joined as shown in Fig. 2 and the ends interwoven (Figs. 2-6). Cut the ends of both straps to ¼ inch in width as indicated by the dotted lines in Fig. 5. All six ends are then slit as in Fig. 6 and a Chinese button knot is tied in each (Fig. 6). These buttons are covered with a braided knot, such as the pineapple knot.

It is to be noted that each center is slightly longer than the other two.

To make the *tirador*, or belt proper, cut it a trifle longer than necessary for a snug fit and punch and cut holes in one end and fasten in the buttons. Fit the belt around the waist of the one for whom it is made. Mark on the other end just where the new holes should come. Remove and trim belt and cut holes. The *tirador* can be decorated by any of the appliqué braids. This makes a beautiful woman's belt.

The gauchos found a use for every part of the cow. The lamp shade in the photograph was made from a cow's udder by Alfredo Guyara of the Province of Santa Fe, Argentina.

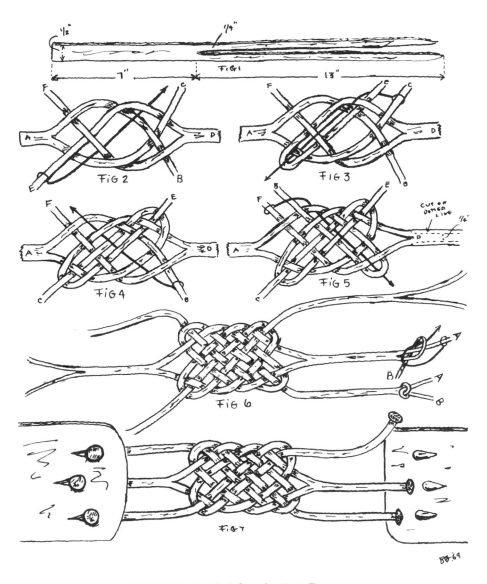

PLATE 18. Braided Gaucho Belt Fastener.

63

PLATE 19

How to Make a Link Belt. Link belts can be bought reasonably in kits or made up by the craftsman. But it is more economical and satisfactory to make your own link belt by utilizing scraps of leather and rawhide. Colored scraps can be used to give a diversified effect.

Make the first link for the buckle end of the belt or hatband (Fig. 1). After this make the keeper loop (or loops) (Fig. 2) by slit braiding two narrow pieces of leather or softened rawhide (Fig. 2) and place it (or them) behind the buckle, as shown in Fig. 3.

Next, make a heavy cardboard template or pattern to use for laying out the links. Make the links for the body of the belt.

The first link in this series is braided in as in Fig. 5. Add in the same fashion link after link until the belt including the billet (Fig. 7) is the desired length. The billet is braided in as in Fig. 8. After cementing together, holes are punched and the belt is complete.

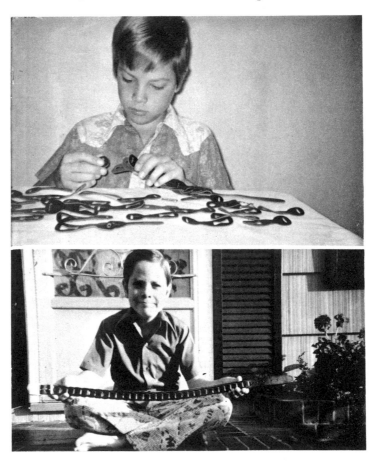

Top: Edward Meyer, Hurlock, Maryland, making a link belt. *Bottom:* The completed belt was made from a Boy Scouts of America kit.

64

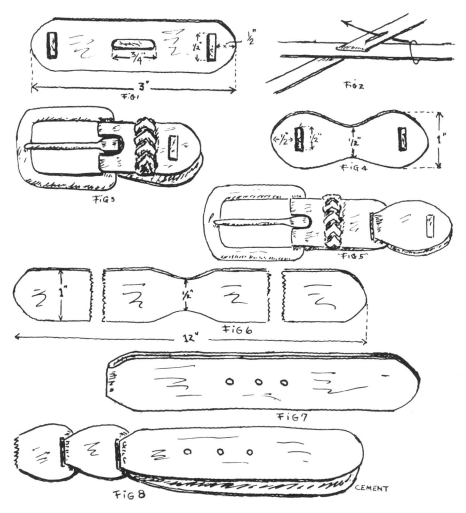

PLATE 19. How to Make a Link Belt.

A finished link belt. Wallets, key hold-
ers, change purses and many other articles can be purchased in kits. These
kits provide children with an excellent
introduction to leather braiding.

PLATE 20

How to Make a Link Breast Collar. The link breast collar is made much like the link belts, but the links are of heavier material and more than twice as large. This also is a good way to utilize scrap leather and softened rawhide.

First make a template or pattern from heavy cardboard (Fig. 1) for the links designated as A. With a metal ring measuring one and one eighth inches inside, start the work as shown in Fig. 2. Figure 3 shows the type of link (B) to be used to finish the links on two other rings. This latter link is split into four strings on one end. After being passed through a hole in the previous link and one in itself is woven into a knot to hold it in place (Figs. 4-5).

Straps are attached to the two upper rings (Fig. 6). One set of these straps is for the horse's neck and the other is to be attached to rings in the saddle.

Argentine gaucho astride horse with a breast collar *(pretal)*. Courtesy of Justo P. Sáënz (h.) from his book *Equitación Gaucha*.

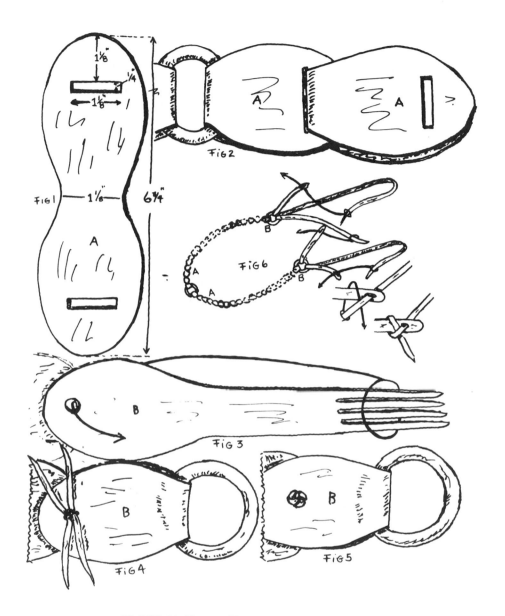

PLATE 20. How to Make a Link Breast Collar.

67

PLATE 21

How to Make a Slit-Braid Hackamore Headstall. With a knife, some leather, and a little patience, you may make yourself a handsome slit-braid hackamore headstall in a few hours. If you are an expert, you can make it in much less time. No metal parts are necessary, and personally, I like this. By using the proper type of braidwork a fellow can do without metal fastenings, buckles, snaps, etc., on any type of horse gear. The gear will be easily adjustable and much more handsome, to my way of thinking. Then there is the satisfaction of making something in which you need to employ a little ingenuity.

To make your headstall, good strap leather is all right, but what is called latigo is better. Real latigo is a vegetable-tanned leather which has been well oiled; but you may use some chrome-tanned latigo. Sometimes you may corral enough good pieces of leather in these so-called repair bundles offered by mail order houses and western outfitters to make yourself a very smart headstall.

You will need four pieces of leather, one-half inch wide and not too thick. One piece will be 18 inches long, another 34 inches, and two 16 inches long.

First take the 34-inch piece, which will form the offside cheekpiece, as well as the headband and part of the nearside cheekpiece. Soak it for a few minutes in water so that it is wet through.

Take a look at Fig. 1, Plate 21. Place the leather around offside part of the bosal, between the side-button and the end of the nose-button; or, if your bosal has a couple of side-buttons on each side, place leather around the part of the bosal between the two buttons. In this drawing, part of the strap is marked A. The other part, B, should be about six inches long. In B, cut a slit lengthwise and about the width of the leather.

In Fig. 1 the arrowline shows how A passes through slit in B. Pull it up tight. Now cut a slit in A as shown in Fig. 2 and pass the end of B through this slit. In Fig. 3, A passes through B. Figure 4 shows this part of the work completed.

Do the same with the short piece—the one 18 inches long—on nearside of the bosal.

Next we will make the browband. Start as in Fig. 5, passing B through A, but leaving a loop of about ¾ inch in the leather. Your *fiador,* or throatlatch (Fig. 10, Plate 54) passes through this loop.

In Fig. 6, A passes through B, shown completed in Fig. 7.

The next step is to attach the browband to the cheekpiece (Fig. 8). Here B passes through A and then A through B, and, finally, B through A again. The work will look like the drawing in Fig. 9. You may make it all a little more fancy with additional slit-braid work, but be sure your straps are longer because there is some shrinkage in this braid.

Attach your browband on the other side. Figure 10 shows two ways of joining these two browband pieces in the center so that they are adjustable.

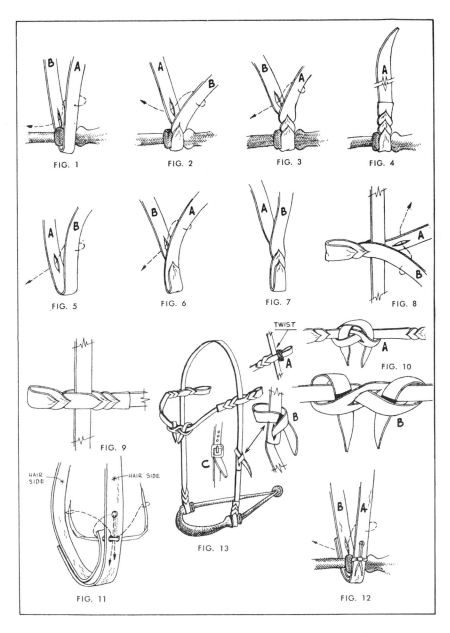

FIG. 1

FIG. 2

FIG. 3

FIG. 4

FIG. 5

FIG. 6

FIG. 7

FIG. 8

TWIST

FIG. 10

FIG. 9

FIG. 13

HAIR SIDE

HAIR SIDE

FIG. 11

FIG. 12

PLATE 21. How to Make a Slit-Braid Hackamore Headstall.

In this type of slit-braiding the flesh side shows in alternate braids. To obtain a more finished braid where only the hair or dress side is out, make your cheekpieces as in Fig. 11. Here two pieces of leather are joined together with a 3-hole fastening. In Fig. 12, it will be shown that A passes through two thicknesses of leather and secures the other end of the splice.

If you observe Fig. 13 at the drawing marked A, you will see how to obtain a similar finished braid on the browband. The loop is formed by holding the leather together with a Turk's-head or Spanish ring knot (Plate 161). Then, behind the cheekpiece, the leather is given a twist so the hair side will be *out* in both pieces.

The completed headstall is shown in Fig. 13. A slit is made in the end of the long cheekpiece and the shorter one passes through it to form the knot you see there. This makes the headstall adjustable. If you are a gadget man you may use a buckle here.

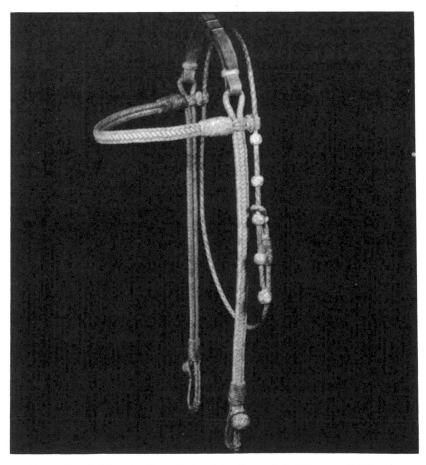

Fancy braided headstall made by John Conrad, Bellflower, California.

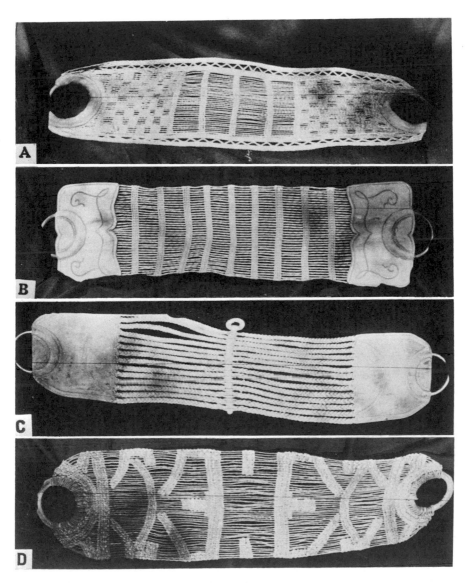

Four examples of cinchas from the John W. Maguire collection. *A:* A cincha of colt's skin beautifully worked. *B:* Intricate-braided cincha which also illustrates how an appliqué braid can be used on the folded end where the ring is enclosed. *C:* This cincha presents something of a puzzle as to the method used to make it but is explained in How to Make a Braided Cincha. *D:* Another example of *trenzados gauchos*, gaucho braid work.

PLATE 22

How to Make a Slit-Braid Headstall. This unique headstall is made basically from one piece of leather or softened rawhide measuring 34 inches by 2¼ inches.

The cuts are shown in dotted lines in Fig. 1. First cut down the center of the strap along the line A for 23 inches. The remainder of the cuts are all from the bottom. Lines marked B and C are cut upward for 30 inches. Lines D and E are cut upward for 28 inches.

Figure 2 shows how this cut strap looks when extended. The two top ends are marked as 1 and 2 and the lower ones as 3, 4, 5, 6, and 7. The closed inner sections are marked 1A and 2A.

In Fig. 3 is illustrated the manner of making a carrick bend with these inner straps. Keeping the hair side of the strap always outward, lay 1A in a loop over itself as shown in Fig. 3. Then the end 2 follows the arrowline and is pulled entirely through along with ends 6 and 7.

For the browband take a small strap 20 inches long, any width you like (Fig. 4) and cut slots in both ends as indicated.

End No. 2 is passed through on the right (Fig. 5). Pull all parts through (Fig. 6) leaving only inside strap 2A. End 6 is next passed through as shown by the arrowline (Fig. 6) and completed as in Fig. 7.

Make the same passes on the left. On the right side No. 7 passes down through the loop at the right of the browband. On the left end No. 3 passes down through the loop of the browband. These two form the throatlatch. End Nos. 4 and 6 are doubled upwards to hold the bit rings as well as the noseband. End No. 5 is attached to the noseband, this noseband is held in place by keeper knots as shown in Fig. 8. At the crown the two ends, Nos. 1 and 2, are tied together as in Fig. 8.

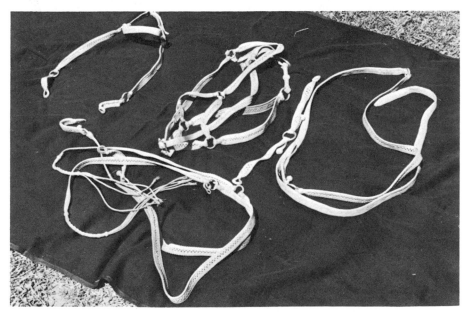

Headstall, bozal, *cabresto* and pair of braided reins. Collection John Walter Maguire.

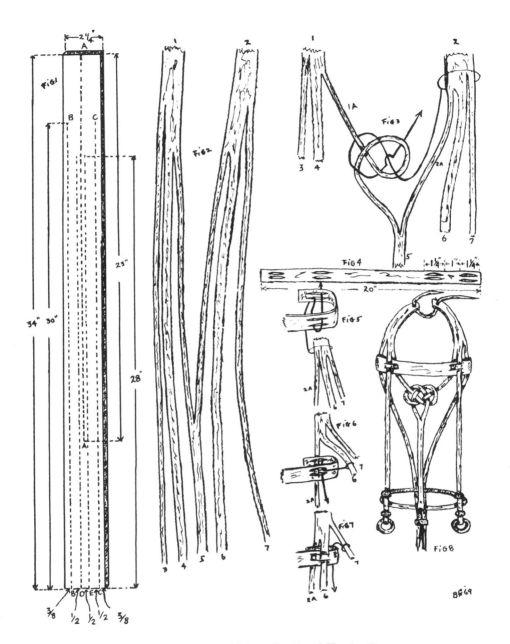

PLATE 22. How to Make a Slit-Braid Headstall.

73

How to Make a Braided Cincha. This unique type of cincha made of softened rawhide, or good latigo leather, is a form used by gauchos on the Argentine pampas. John Walter Maguire of Buenos Aires, owner of the *Estancia Tres Bonetes* in the Argentine, sent me a picture of it some time ago when he generously photographed for me his fabulous collection of *trenzados gauchos*—gaucho braidwork.

In the Argentine practically every piece of horse gear is made from softened rawhide. The softening is accomplished mainly by use of a *mordaza* or *sobrador* a partially slit piece of round wood. The rawhide is pulled back and forth through the slit until the fibers are broken down and it is as pliable as ordinary leather. Cunninghame Graham, who lived in the Argentine and wrote many books about the gauchos and their famous criollo horses, said this softening process was accomplished by beating the rawhide with a mallet.

However, use no oil or oily compound on rawhide—certainly not neat's-foot oil. Saddle soap or glycerin in four parts water is best. Glycerin seems to have an affinity for rawhide and helps soften it.

For those who do not care to soften their rawhide, a good latigo leather or an Indian tan can be used. Cut a rectangular piece some 48 inches long and 5-5/8 inches wide (Fig. 1, Plate 23). Lay off in the middle of this a section of 26 inches, and carefully cut this section into 1/8 inch strings (Fig. 2). This will give you 45 strings.

The next step is to make your inside braid. Starting at one end take three strings (Fig. 3) and begin an ordinary three-string or hair braid. Place the third string over the other two to the left, then bring No. 1 string under No. 3 and over No. 2 (Fig. 4). As you continue your braiding you will find that a similar braid is forming at the bottom. In ordinary braiding this is a nuisance and the complementary braid has to be unraveled at intervals. But here we utilize it. Keep braiding until your upper and lower braids meet (Fig. 5). Place a piece of leather thong through the braid as shown in Fig. 5. It is a good idea here to close up your braidwork, both top and bottom (Fig. 6). You will find the same number of bights in each half. Succeeding three-string braids should have the same number of bights as the first braid. Keep all your braids from unraveling as shown in Fig. 5.

You may or may not want to use 3-inch metal rings on both ends of your cincha. Some riders prefer the use of plain rings as they can tighten a cincha a fraction of an inch. However, you may use a ring and tongue (Fig. 6, Plate 25) or a bar buckle (Fig. 3, Plate 25). Plain rings can be covered with braidwork as shown in Plate 24. Even if you do not use this braiding on your cincha rings, it is a good thing to know for dressing up rings on other gear.

This is actually an eight-string round braid. It must be made with two strings (Fig. 1, Plate 24). Spiral string No. 1 around the ring in a counterclockwise direction (arrowline in Fig. 1, and completed in Fig.

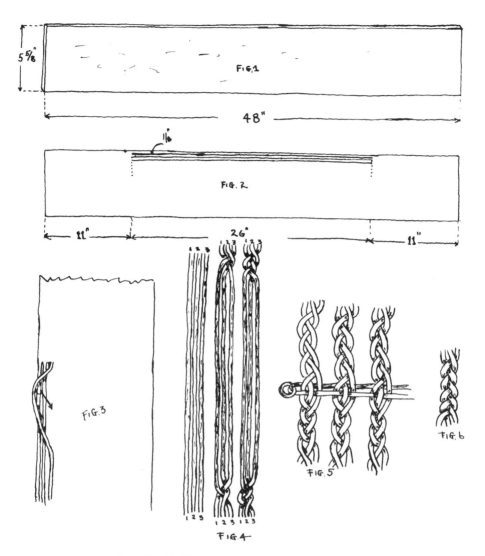

PLATE 23. How to Make a Braided Cincha.

75

2). Next, passing over string No. 1 all the way around, spiral string No. 2 in a clockwise direction, crossing No. 1 both above and below (arrowline Fig. 2 and completed in Fig. 3). On the second spiral we will number these strings respectively 3 and 4—3 being the continuation of No. 1 and 4 the continuation of No. 2. One set of strings will be odd-numbered and the other even-numbered.

String No. 3 (the continuation of No. 1) is wound around, passing over string No. 2 (Fig. 4). String No. 4 is now spiraled around, over one, under one, interlocking all sections (Fig. 5). This completes the first phase and gives us a four-string round Turk's-head over the ring.

Next take string No. 5 (continuation of No. 3) and passing to the left of the original No. 1 string, follow it completely around until it becomes No. 3 and continue following as string No. 7 (Fig. 6). String No. 6 (continuation of No. 4) is now spiralled around the ring twice, splitting strings Nos. 1-5 and 3-7 (Fig. 6). The arrowline shows the splitting process, also as shown in the portion of the string marked "X." (This is merely shown for demonstration purposes, and this portion of the string does not belong in your braid.) The braid is complete in Fig. 7. Figure 8 on the left shows the braid you have just completed. However, if the splitting of pairs is done as shown to the right in Fig. 8 you will obtain a gaucho braid. In one case the "V's" in the braid run lengthwise; in the other, crosswise.

Plate 25 illustrates the method of enclosing the cincha rings. A plain ring is shown in Figs. 1 & 2, and a bar-buckle in Figs. 3, 4 & 5. When using a ring with a tongue (Fig. 6) a hole must be cut in the folded part of the cincha for the tongue.

Between the folded end and the part where the ring is enclosed it is well to hold the leather together with an appliqué braid (Fig. 2). The pull is then on the part held together rather than the inside of the fold.

A satisfactory appliqué of three-strings is shown in Figs. 7-9. Holes are punched through both parts of the leather inside the ring, and the appliqué made as shown.

An appliqué to hold together the edges is more simple, made from one string (Figs. 10 & 11). This also can be used in holding in the bar-buckle (Fig. 4). On this latter ring there usually is a tit or protection which it is well to enclose in a separate piece of leather, shown in Fig. 5. This will keep the tit from punching through the braid. In enclosing the ring with tongue, use the appliqué in two sections—one on each side of the tongue. Be certain the slit for the tongue is long enough to give it proper play.

If this cincha is used on a center fire rig saddle using one cincha or girth—the rider may wish to employ a breast collar, or more properly a martingale. In such case the small strap which separates the middle of the braids in the cincha (Fig. 5, Plate 23) must have a small ring as shown.

Should your cincha be of rawhide, periodically rub in saddle soap, using it as you would a salve. Latigo and Indian tan should be kept clean by frequent use of saddle soap applied with a dampened sponge.

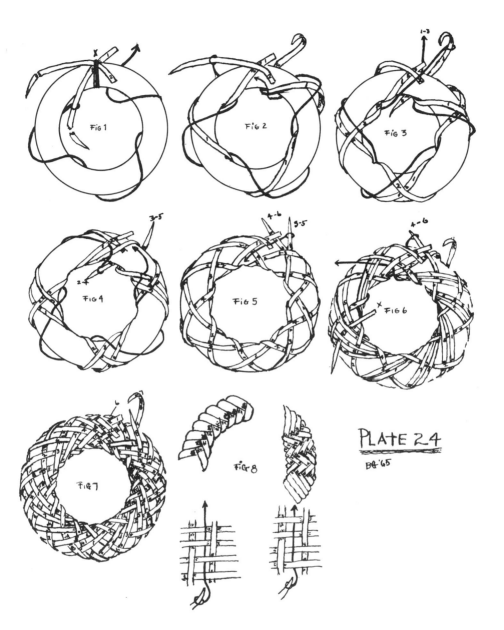

PLATE 24. How to Make a Braided Cincha (Cont.)

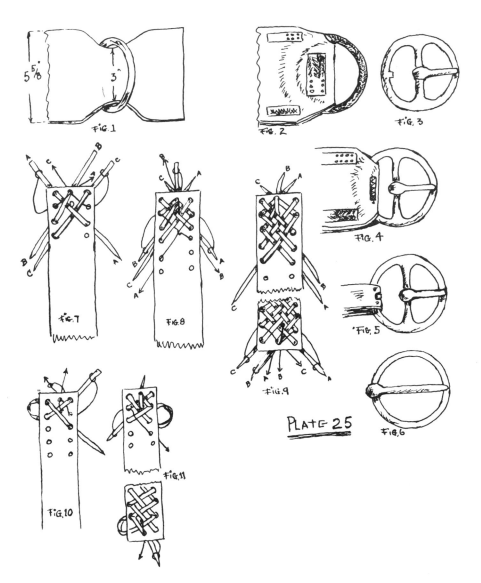

PLATE 25. How to Make a Braided Cincha (Cont.)

78

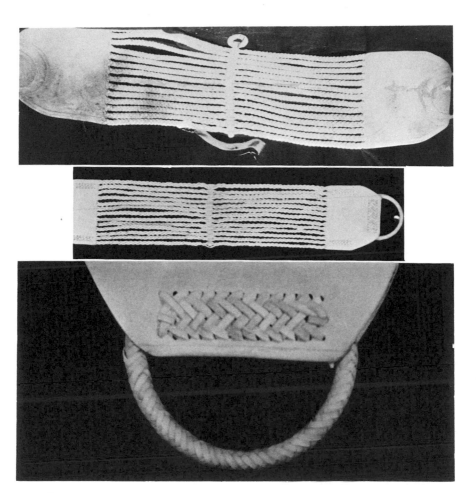

Top: Gaucho braided cincha of softened rawhide in collection of John Walter Maguire of Buenos Aires. *Center:* Braided cincha of white latigo leather, made by author. *Bottom:* Closeup of cincha showing appliqué to enclose cincha ring and braid covering cincha ring. (See Plates 23, 24 & 25.)

PLATE 26

How to Make a Slit-Braid Handbag. This handbag is composed of three major parts: the top, the body and the bottom, with some thonging of varied lengths and widths. No metal attachments are necessary.

The top may be made of any soft, thin leather, such as kidskin, the kind of suede used for linings, or buckskin. Cut it to the specifications in Fig. 2, with eight equally spaced holes in the top part and thirty-one in the bottom part, as well as four on each end.

For the body of the handbag, use 6-ounce leather (Fig. 1), with thirty-one evenly spaced holes on both top and bottom. No holes on the ends are required, as the braiding thong will keep these ends together.

The bottom is a circular piece of leather of the same weight (6-ounce) as the body. Around its edge punch thirty-one evenly spaced holes. To determine the exact diameter of the bottom, divide the length of the body by 3.1416, always taking into consideration the thickness of the body piece. When the body piece is formed into a tube, the inner circumference is less than the outer circumference. As the bottom part fits into the inner circumference it would be well to cut out the bottom and then measure the body part around it before cutting it and before punching any holes.

Next, cut the body piece with vertical slits of one inch in width, beginning ½ inch from the top and stopping ½ inch from the bottom. Remember that in slit braiding of this type the slits must be of an *unequal* number. It might be well to divide the length of the body piece into nineteen equal parts, as it may have been cut a trifle longer or a trifle shorter after being measured around the bottom piece.

Weave a one-inch thong through the slits, beginning several slits to the right of the ends as shown in Fig. 6. Continue around, over one, under one, etc. Cement both ends on the inside. Now lace on the bottom as shown in Fig. 6; next, the top, and then close the ends of the top by lacing and pull through drawstrings, which may be of a small round braid.

The top should go inside the body piece, so here again, it is well to fit it before cutting. Contrasting leathers may be used in this project if desired.

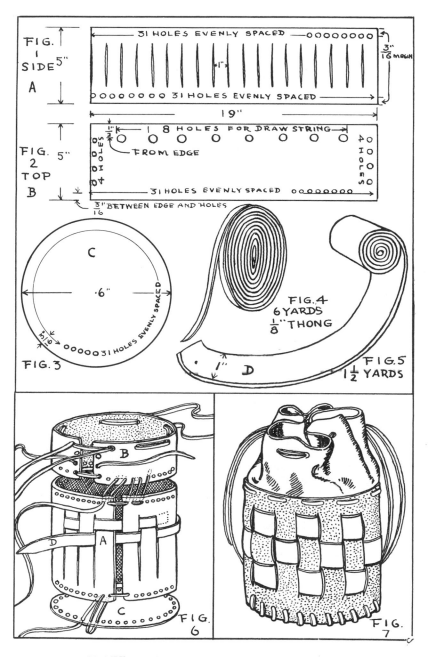

FIG. 1 SIDE 5" A

31 HOLES EVENLY SPACED ——○○○○○○○○
3" ⁄16 margin
←—|—|"—|—→
○○○○○○○○ 31 HOLES EVENLY SPACED ——→

←————————— 19" —————————→

FIG. 2 TOP B 5"

1½" ← 8 HOLES FOR DRAW STRING →
4 HOLES
↳ FROM EDGE
4 HOLES
31 HOLES EVENLY SPACED ○○○○○○○○
3" ⁄16 BETWEEN EDGE AND HOLES

C
·6·
3⁄16
○○○○○ 31 HOLES EVENLY SPACED
FIG.3

FIG.4
6 YARDS
⅛" THONG

·1"· D
FIG.5
1½ YARDS

B
D A C
FIG. 6

FIG. 7

PLATE 26. How to Make a Slit-Braid Handbag.

81

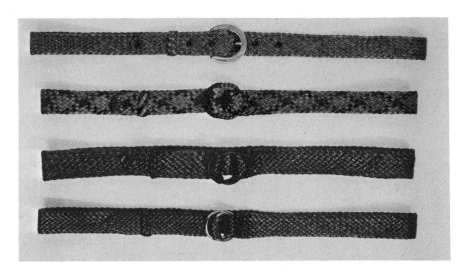

Four belts made by using a flat braid. D.W. Morgan, Austral Enterprises, Seattle, Washington.

Hatband of flat braid showing two-tone work. D.W. Morgan, Austral Enterprises, Seattle, Washington.

Flat Braids

PLATE 27

Two-Thong Flat Braid. Flat braiding is a systematic operation of alternately working from one side to the other. If the right-hand thong is carried to the left, over another and under another, the same thing is done the next time with the left-hand thong, to the right.

Braiding can be done with from two thongs to an infinite number. However, the highest practicable number with which to work seems to be twenty-one thongs. That, at least, will constitute the maximum used in this book.

Some braiders advocate moistening leather thongs and braiding them while damp. This system is very good for the experienced braider, but for the beginner, who might have to tear his braid apart and start over again, it is best first to work with his thongs dry, so that they will not be spoiled for possible rebraiding. Rawhide strings, of course, should be worked damp even when softened.

However, all thongs should be thoroughly saddle-soaped, and the lather rubbed in well. Then, even when dry, they will work easily and the braid can be closed up snugly. An even tension in the braid is important. Try to exert the same amount of pull on each thong and the braid will be uniform throughout.

The first braid will be a two-thong braid, similar to the common so-called chain-knot. Double the thong, place the loop over a peg and then tie an overhand knot, as indicated in Fig. 1.

Bring the end, B, up through the knot, as demonstrated in Fig. 2. The bight of A is next pushed down through the loop formed by B, as illustrated in Fig. 3.

For purposes of clarity the braid is not shown tightened in the drawing. But the next step in Fig. 3 is to pull thong B until it is fairly tight around the loop of A.

Bring the bight of thong B down through the bight of A and pull the end of A until it is tight around the bight of B (Fig. 4). Bring the bight of A through the bight of B and tighten by pulling on B, then the bight of B through A and so on, alternating until the length desired has been braided.

In this braid both the flesh side and the hair side of the leather alternately appears, one being the edge scallop and the other the center portion.

Two one-foot lengths of 1/8-inch thongs will make about three inches in actual braid.

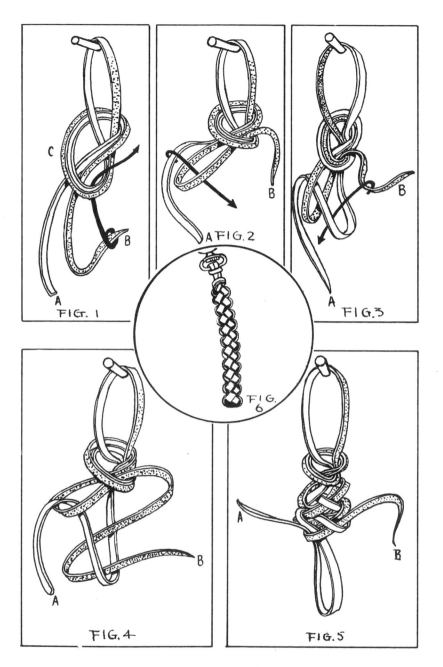

C

B

A

FIG. 1

A FIG. 2

B

B

A FIG. 3

FIG.
6

FIG. 4

A

B

FIG. 5

A

B

PLATE 27. Two-Thong Flat Braid.

PLATE 28

Three-Thong Hair Braid. This braid is known as the hair braid and is one of the simplest and most commonly used of the flat braids. As a general rule it is dismissed, because of its simplicity, with the assumption that everyone knows how to do it. This is not true, and from our standpoint, it is most important that it be done correctly, as it is the key to more complicated flat braids.

As in the majority of flat braids, the extreme right and left-hand thongs are worked alternately toward the center. They follow a definite sequence, in this case, of over-one, under-one.

In all braiding there is a length shrinkage which varies from approximately one-half to one-quarter of the original length. In the case of a three-strand braid, three 1/8-inch thongs of one foot each shrink to ten inches of braid. Figuring on a one-quarter shrinkage would be a good average. Be sure the braiding is snug.

In the beginning, take the extreme left-hand thong, A (Fig. 1), and pass it over thong B; then take the extreme right-hand thong C and pass it over A (Fig. 2). Now bring B to the right, over C (Fig. 3). Bring A from the right toward the left over B (Fig 4). In the next step, pass thong C from the left to the right over thong A; then thong B from the right to the left and over thong C. The thongs are now in their original position, thus completing one phase of the braid. To continue the braid, repeat as before.

Four-Thong Braid. First cross the two center thongs (Fig. 5), C over B. Bring thong D to the left under B and thong A to the right over C and under D (Fig. 6). Now bring B to the left under A, and C to the right over D and under B. Next bring A to the left under C and bring D from the left to the right over B and under A (Fig. 7).

It is best in the beginning to place on the ends of the thongs the letters corresponding to those used here, as indicated in Fig. 5. Follow instructions carefully.

Shrinkage is approximately one-fourth of the original length.

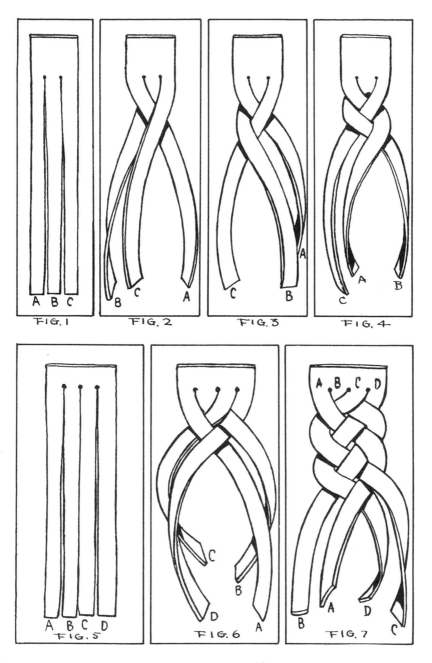

PLATE 28. Three-Thong Hair Braid.

PLATE 29

Five-Thong Braids. To make the five-thong braid in Figs. 1, 2 and 3, first arrange the thongs as in Fig. 1. Now bring thong C, on the left, to the center over thongs D and E as in Fig. 2. Next bring thong B, on the extreme right, to the center over thongs A and C. Continue braiding first with the outer left thong and then the outer right one. In each instance they pass over two thongs. This makes an attractive herringbone braid.

Next we come to the braid shown in Figs. 4 and 5. The first step is to arrange the thongs as shown in Fig. 4. Start working with thong B on the extreme left and pass it to the center over thong E; then bring thong D on the extreme right to the left toward the center, over thong C, under thong A and over B, as illustrated in Fig. 5. In the next step bring thong E in Fig. 5 to the center by passing it over thong D and under thong C. Continue this braid by working alternately from left to right and right to left. This is an over-one, under-one sequence, so one thong is never passed over or under more than once.

Figures 6 and 7 show another variation of the give-thong flat braid. In this case it will be noticed that the center thong, C, becomes a sort of core and runs straight down the center of the braid.

The first step is to arrange the thongs as shown in Fig. 6. It will be noticed that thongs A and E, the two outer thongs, always pass under thong C, but alternate in passing over and under each other. In the case of thongs F and D, they always pass over thong C and alternate in passing over and under each other.

Starting with Fig. 6, take thong D in the right hand and pass it beneath thong A and over thong C. Take thong B on the left and pass it toward the right under thong E and over thong D, at the juncture of D and C. Thong B thus passes over both D and C. Now on the right, thong A is brought to the left over thong B and under thong C. From the left, thong E is brought to the right over thong D and under thong A, at the junction of A and C. Thus E passes under both A and C.

This offers a fine opportunity to use thongs of different colors, or at least to make thong C different from the others.

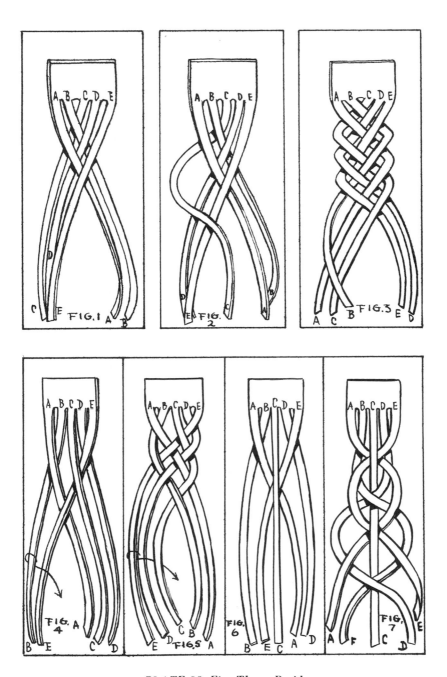

PLATE 29. Five-Thong Braids.

89

PLATE 30

Six-Thong Braids. The first of the braids of six thongs will be the over-one, under-one braid. To begin, arrange the thongs as in Fig. 1. This is done by crossing the two middle thongs, with thong C brought to the right over thong D. Then bring thong B to the right, under D and follow by bringing thong E to the left over C and under B.

Now alternate first on the left-hand side and then on the right, always working the outer thong to the center. Thus, in Fig. 2, thong A is moved over D and under E, and then from the right, thong F is moved under C, over B and under A.

Keep the braid snug and be sure there are an equal number of thongs on each side. When there are four on a side, work the thong on that side, as in Fig. 3. The next move is to bring thong C over B, under A and over D.

Another example of the six-thong flat braid is shown in Figs. 4 and 5. Arrange the thongs as shown in Fig. 4, which is done by moving thong A on the extreme left, to the right, under thongs B and C to the center; then moving thong F on the extreme right over to the left by passing it over thongs E and D and under A.

In this braid the extreme left-hand thong will always pass under two toward the center; the extreme right-hand thong will always pass over two and under one toward the center. Keep the braided part pushed up snugly.

This makes an attractive braid and when finished it will be seen that its sequence is under-two, over-one from the left side, and over-two, under-one from the right side.

The third example of six-thong braiding is somewhat different in that the extreme right-hand thong is used continually. It could just as well be the extreme left-hand thong, but in the illustration the right-hand one has been chosen.

First, as in Fig. 6, take thong F and move it to the extreme left by passing it under thong E, over D, under C, over B and under A. Then take thong E and carry it to the extreme left by passing it under thong D, over C, under B, over A, and under F. Keep the braid closed up snugly. Although the finished braid may seem at first to slant or incline to the left, it will soon straighten out.

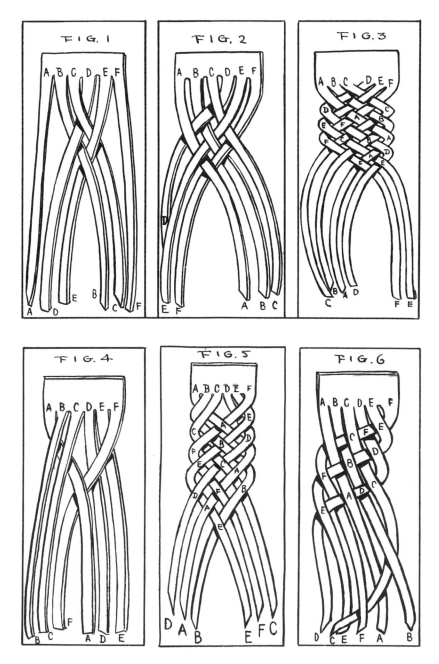

PLATE 30. Six-Thong Braids.

91

PLATE 31

Six-Thong Double Braid. Special attention should be paid to the making of this braid as it furnishes the key to the more intricate and beautiful types of double braids to follow—especially those of nine, thirteen and twenty-one thongs.

Arrange the thongs as shown in Fig. 1. Bring thong A on the extreme left to the right over thong B and thongs C and D. Bring thong F on the extreme right to the left over thongs E and A.

Move thong B to the right by passing it under thong C and over thongs D and F (Fig. 2). It will be noticed in the drawing, which shows the braiding loose so the course of the individual thongs may better be followed, that thong B is under A as well as under C. This may appear to be wrong but it is not; it is thus that the braid is made double. Take thong E on the extreme right, bring it toward the left to the center by passing it under thongs A and B. In this instance it will be noted that E already was under thong F and now it is under all three thongs, F, A and B.

The next step in Fig. 3 reveals further how this braid is made. Now thong C, on the extreme left, is passed over thong D and under thongs F and E. On the right, thong A is passed over B and C.

In referring to the first step in Fig. 1, observe that in working from the left side, the outer thong A first passes over one and then under two. In Fig. 2, the extreme left thong B passes under one and over two, and now in Fig. 3 it passes over one and under two.

On the right-hand side, too, it will be noted that in Fig. 1 the extreme right-hand thong E passes over two; then in Fig. 2 thong E passes under two and in Fig. 3 the extreme right-hand thong A passes over two.

This is the key. Each time alternate on each side. When the first thong on the left is passed *over* one time, it is passed *under* the next time. And the same is true on the right-hand side. When tightened, the braid will be relatively narrower than other six-thong braids but it will be double, as indicated in a side view in Fig. 4.

Seven-Thong Braid. In this braid begin with thong D over thong E; thong B under C and E; thong G to the left over F and under D and B. Pass thong A to the right over C and under E and G. Now pass F to the left over D and under B and A. Continue as in Fig. 5, with each outer thong passing over one and under two.

Nine-Thong Braid. In this braid divide the thongs with four on the left and five on the right. Start by bringing E over D to the left. This can be followed by the drawing. Notice that this braid has an over-one, under-one sequence in the center, but under two each time on both edges.

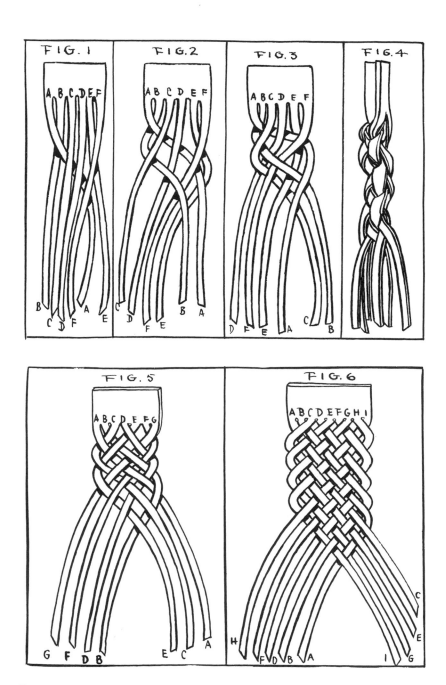

PLATE 31. Six-Thong Double Braid; Seven-Thong Braid; Nine-Thong Braid.

PLATE 32

Variation of Five-Thong Flat Braid. Start this braid as shown in Fig. 1. Then bring thong or string No. 1 on the left to the right side under No. 4 and over No. 5. Now braid the three center strings into a hair braid (Fig. 3). The outside strings Nos. 4 and 3 are braided as shown by the arrowline in Fig. 4.

Again braid the inside strings into a hair braid as in Fig. 3 and shown by the arrowlines in Fig. 5. This sequence is continued, braiding the outside strings every other time, after the inner strings have been braided in a hair braid.

Variation of Seven-Thong Flat Braid. In Figs. 6, 7 and 8, the inside thongs or strings are braided over two and under two—or in a five-thong braid. The outside strings are braided in after two passes inside as shown in Fig. 8.

In Fig. 9 the inside braid is the three-string hair braid and is consistently over one, under one.

Variation of the Nine-Thong Flat Braid. In Figs. 10, 11, 12, and 13 the method of making this braid is illustrated. Another way, not shown, is to work the inside braids into a seven-string braid of over-two and under-two sequence, and then work the outside strings as in the previous braids.

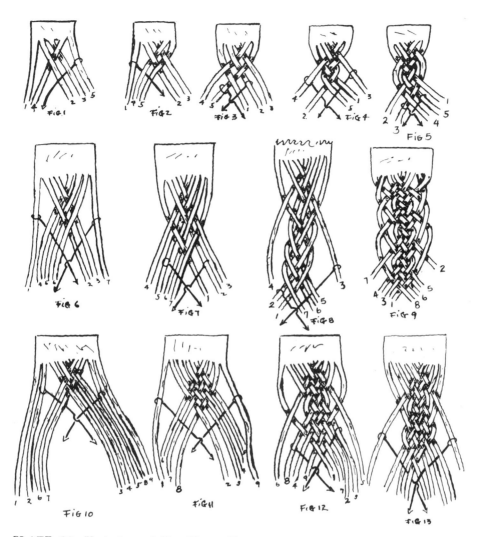

PLATE 32. Variation of Five-Thong Flat Braid; Variation of Seven-Thong Flat Braid; Variation of the Nine-Thong Flat Braid.

95

PLATE 33

Lazy-Man Braid of Six Thongs. In this braid double thongs or strings are worked in the same fashion as single thongs in the three-thong hair braid shown in Plate 28. Thongs 1 and 2, 3 and 4, and 5 and 6 are braided as a single unit. In Fig. 2 this method is illustrated where 1 and 2 are first laid to the right over 3 and 4 and 5 and 6 and brought to the left over 1 and 2 (arrowline). Proceed then as in Fig. 3. The upper double thongs are brought to the center each time.

Lazy-Man Braid of Eight Thongs. This braid is worked as the single four-thong braid also shown in Plate 28, but pairs are used instead of single thongs (Figs. 4 and 5).

Other single-thong flat braids may also be made with pairs in this fashion, also with three strings as a unit, or even more.

Lazy-Man Braid of Ten Thongs. This braid is over one, under one on each edge with the double thongs or strings crossing in the center. It might be called a semi-lazy-man braid. After first crossing the pairs of strings in the center as in Fig. 6, the upper left-hand thong or string (No. 1) is carried to the right and center by passing over one, under two and over two. Working from the same side, string No. 2 is carried to the center over one, under one, and over two (Fig. 7).

Working now from the right-hand side, string No. 10 passes to the left and center over one, under two, and over two (Fig. 8). Then from the same side carry string No. 9 to the left and center by passing over one, under one, and over two (Fig. 9).

Two strings are worked from each side in the same fashion until the desired length of the braid is obtained (Fig. 11).

Many combinations can be used in this lazy-man braid. Do not hesitate to experiment.

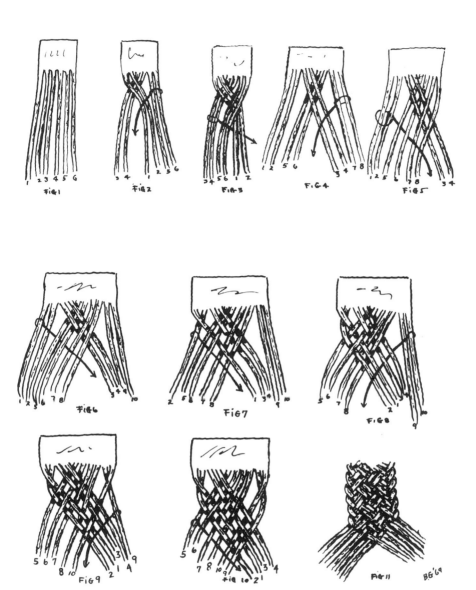

PLATE 33. Lazy-Man Braid of Six Thongs; Lazy Man Braid of Eight Thongs; Lazy-Man Braid of Ten Thongs.

97

PLATE 34

Alternate Seven-Thong Braid. The seven-thong braid shown in Figs. 1 through 4, illustrates the adaptable symmetry of uneven thong or string braids. This can be worked as shown. The left-hand thong in Fig. 1 passes to the right and center under two and over one, and then in Fig. 2 the right-hand thong passes to the left and center under two and over one. The result is shown in Fig. 4. However, the sequence for the thong on each side can be under one, over two (not illustrated).

Alternate Nine-Thong Braid. The same system employed in the seven-thong braid is used in Figs. 5 through 8. In this case the sequence shown in Fig. 5 (after thongs 4 and 5 have been crossed) is to the left over one, under two, over one. In Fig. 6 the thong on the left is worked in the same fashion, and so on. The result is shown in Fig. 8. Variations of this, of course, can also be made, such as over one, under one, over two on each side.

Uneven strings of a greater number can be worked in various combinations.

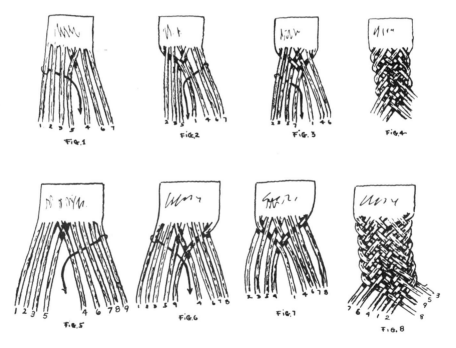

PLATE 34. Alternate Seven-Thong Braid; Alternate Nine-Thong Braid.

An Australian Type Belt. This interesting belt, made of six long thongs with its own loops and buttons for fastening, was described to me by C.W. Halliday of West Australia. The thongs are first doubled and the braid started in the Australian fashion as shown in the lower part of A. After braiding for about three inches the first hole is made by dividing the braid into two three-thong braids for about ¾ of an inch; then the thongs are joined in a six-thong braid for about one inch and again split into two three-thong braids. If you wish more holes in

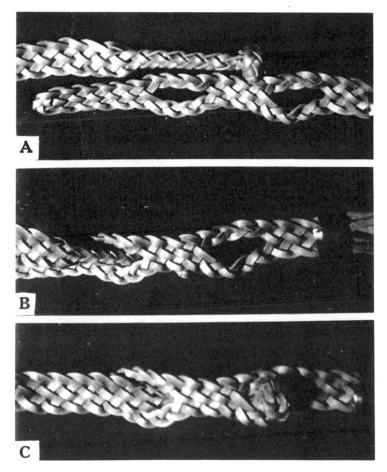

this end, continue as above then continue the six-thong braid for the body of the belt until the desired length has been reached so the button end will pass through two holes. (B shows it passing downward through the first hole and C shows it passing upward through the second hole.)

To form the button end, braid two inches of a six-thong round braid and make your button. Be certain you have enough length to do this. Select any button you desire from the section showing braided buttons.

99

PLATE 35

How to Make an Australian Type Belt. In Australian braiding all flat braids are started as shown in Figs. 1 and 2. The thong A-B is middled and given a twist in the center, as shown in Fig. 1. This twist is to keep the hair or dress side up in both thongs. Then thong F-D is introduced as shown. Next thong E-C is placed in as indicated. The end D is brought down in an over-one, under-one sequence. The end F is woven downward under one, over one, and under one (thong D, Fig. 1).

Thong end C is next brought down over thong end B and under F (Fig. 2). Thong end E on the left is woven downward under thong end A, over thong end D and under thong end C. Also in Fig. 2, indicated by arrowlines, the regular six-thong braid begins—over one, under one on the right, and under one, over one, and under one on the left. This is continued until the desired length of the belt is obtained.

In Fig. 3 the braid is introduced through the buckle as shown, entering from the top (the back of the buckle is illustrated here). In Fig. 4 the braid is secured to the buckle by back braiding. Each thong is passed back, following its own part, as shown. This back braiding can be continued to the center of the six-braid and each end cut off flush. Then two braided keeper knots can be made behind the buckle.

However, in Fig. 6 I have made these keeper knots from the ends of the braid itself. In the lower three thongs, A, B, and D, two are on the left side and one is on the right side. B and D are crossed as shown with the hair side out and A passes over B, under D, back over B and under D. At the top two strings are on the right-hand side, E and F, and one, C, is on the left-hand side. C passes over E, under F, and back over E. All this is shown in Fig. 6.

Taking the lower strings once more, the body of D is pulled beneath D to form a loop, as shown by the arrowline, and then A passes over B and under D. At the top, the body of F is drawn beneath E to form a loop and C passes beneath F and over E. This is continued until a tight three-thong hair braid is formed. Before tightening and tucking the ends beneath the braid, the billet should be slipped through these keepers to see that sufficient room is allowed for it. The finished belt is shown in Fig. 8. This belt is made with six strings, but more even-numbered thongs may be used. Australian belts usually are from 12 to 16 thongs.

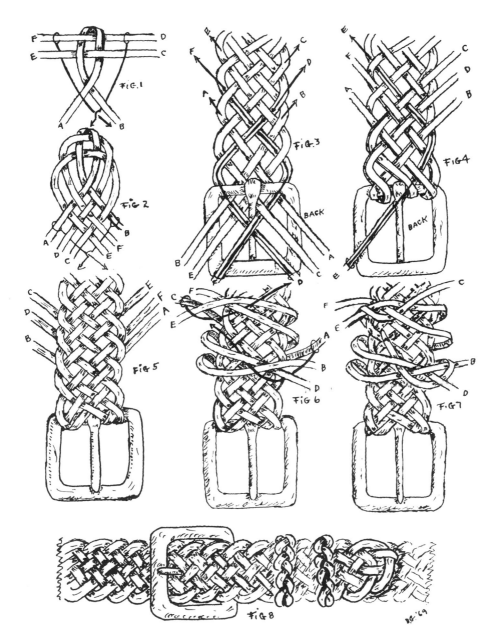

PLATE 35. How to Make an Australian Type Belt.

PLATE 36

How to Make a Braided Belt. In this belt the thongs or strings first are attached to the buckle as shown in Fig. 1. There are six thongs and these are braided in an over-one under-one sequence until the desired length is obtained.

Shown in Fig. 2 is the start of the method of finishing off the billet end of the braid. As indicated by arrowlines, end A is passed upward beneath three thongs. Then end B is brought upward under three thongs. The result is shown in Fig. 3.

In Fig. 4 the underside of the braid is illustrated. Each thong is now brought upward flesh-side-to-flesh-side with its own part. When the ends are all brought toward the center of the braid they are snipped off. Figure 5 shows the finished end.

Figure 6 illustrates a three-thong inside braid to be used as a keeper. Two of these should be made, and sewed closed under the billet.

How to Make a Cinch Ring Belt. The cinch ring belt, using two D-rings, is started at the billet end in the same fashion as the Australian method shown in Plate 35. However, after braiding about six inches the braid is turned over so the flesh side of the thongs are uppermost. Then each thong is twisted so the hair side is uppermost and the braid continued. The reason for this is that when the billet is passed through the rings as shown in Fig. 7, the flesh side of the thongs is next to the rings and the hair side or dress side is uppermost. The billet is secured by a braided keeper or loop as in Fig. 6. The ends holding the two D-rings are back-braided as in Plate 35.

How to Make a Belt with Its Own Keeper. With six strings—that is, three strings or thongs middled—braid a three-thong hair braid as shown in Fig. 8. After joining all strings, in a six-string over-one, under-one sequence for a few inches, place in the buckle as shown in Fig. 9. Then pass the braid through the loop as illustrated by the arrowline in Fig. 9. After adjusting the loop the braid is continued. The billet end is finished as in Figs. 2-4.

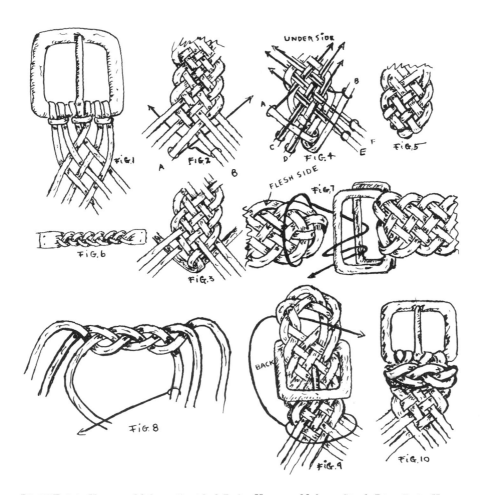

PLATE 36. How to Make a Braided Belt; How to Make a Cinch Ring Belt; How to Make a Belt with Its Own Keeper.

103

A closeup of two fancy whip handles. Courtesy: D.W. Morgan, Austral Enterprises.

Round Braids

PLATE 37

Round Braid of Four Thongs. The four-thong round braid is made with or without a core. When using a core, which may be rope, rounded leather or any desirable round object, arrange the thongs as in Fig. 1. The combined width of the thongs should be the same as the circumference of the core. If the core measures one inch around, each thong should be ¼ of an inch in width.

Very thin leather may be used in this type of covering, as the leather is subjected to no strain when in use. If thick leather is used, it is well to bevel the edge on the flesh side so that the braid will lie snug. Rawhide strings are beveled slightly on the hair side.

Some braiders work with their thongs thoroughly damp. I usually apply saddle soap and allow the thongs to dry. In working with damp thongs the pulling often stretches the leather and the thongs get narrower as they proceed downward.

In Fig. 1 the two thongs in front are crossed, bringing thong 1 to the right over thong 2, and carrying thong 2 toward the left.

Bring thong 4 around to the rear, following the path shown in the arrowline in Fig. 1. Figure 2 shows thong 4 on the left, having passed beneath thong 3 and over thong 1.

The arrowline in Fig. 2 shows the path of thong 3. Bring it around to the rear and back again to the front, passing under thong 2 and over thong 4 (Fig. 3).

Thong 2 is worked next. It follows the course of the arrowline in Fig. 3, going around the rear and back to the front under thong 1 and over thong 3.

There are always two thongs on each side. Work alternately with the outer or upper ones, passing to the rear and following the sequence of under one thong and over the next.

Keep the braid carefully closed up as the work progresses. Unless the same amount of pull is used on each thong, it will show in the finished braid.

Continue to the end as shown in Figs. 4 and 5. Then tie down the thongs.

When the braid is completed, apply saddle soap and roll it under your foot on the floor or some other hard surface. Don't be afraid to exert a little pressure as this will smooth down the braid and bring it closer together.

Cowboys often smooth and polish braid that is made without a core (Figs. A, B, C and D) by drawing it through a series of holes in hard wood or bone, each hole being smaller than the previous one, with the sharp edges of the holes beveled.

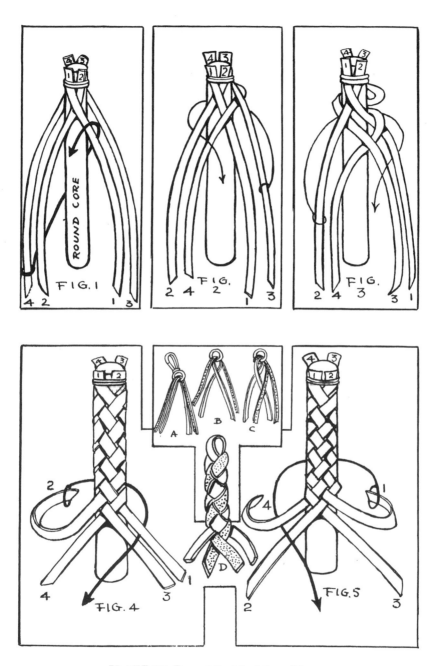

PLATE 37. Round Braid of Four Thongs.

107

PLATE 38

Turk's-head Terminal for Round Braid. There are cases where it may be desirable to finish off a round braid with a handsome knot, instead of merely tying it down. It is then that the Turk's-head terminal knot is used.

When a core has been braided over, continue the braid beyond the core and then arrange it so that the thongs appear as in Fig. 1.

Pass thong 1 around the rear as shown in Fig. 2 and turn thong 3 so that the flesh side is toward you. Thong 1 should also be turned so the flesh is toward you as in Fig. 3.

Lash the thongs together in this order and turn the ends upward to make the braiding easier (Fig. 4). The thongs are now separated as shown in Fig. 5, with the flesh sides of all of them upward.

Fold thong 2 over thong 4, leaving a bight in 2 near the spot where it is lashed, as shown in Fig. 6. Then fold thong 4 over both thongs 2 and 1, also leaving a bight in thong 4, as shown in Fig. 7.

Pass thong 1 over thong 4 and thong 3. Then thrust thong 3 over thong 1 and through the bight in thong 2 as indicated by the arrowline in Fig. 8. The thongs are now arranged as pictured in Fig. 9. The hair or smooth sides of all are upward.

Continuing in the same direction, which in this case is counterclockwise, pass thong 1 around and to the outside of the bight of thong 2 and up under thong 2 and thong 3. This thong emerges in the center of the braid as indicated by the arrowline in Fig. 10 and shown in Fig. 11.

Pass thong 4 around and outside of the bight of thong 3 and then up through the center, under thong 3 and thong 1. Next move thong 2 in the same fashion and finally thong 3. Work the knot tight but be sure to press it back on the braid or it will be inclined to slip upward.

The protruding thongs may be cut off close to the knot or trimmed evenly and left. Saddle-soap the knot, mold it gently and it will remain in this shape after it dries.

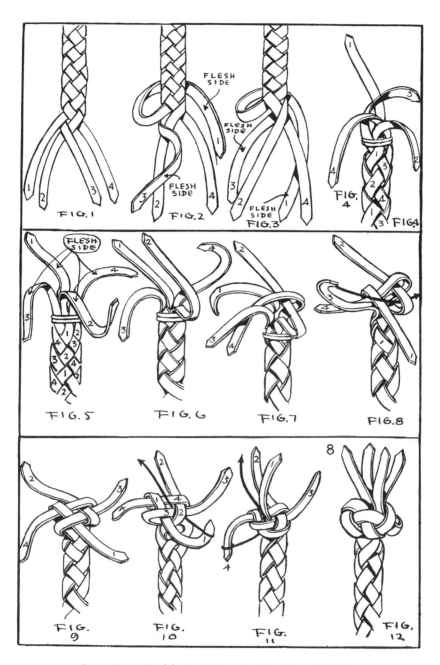

PLATE 38. Turk's-head Terminal for Round Braid.

109

PLATE 39

Round Braid of Six Thongs. It is not often practicable to employ a round braid of more than four thongs without a core. Therefore, in making the round braid of six thongs, a core is used. This may be a rope, rounded leather or other material, or possibly a hard twisted rawhide core such as that used in riding crops and other whips. (For reins, no core is needed.)

The combined width of the thongs should be the same as the circumference of the object to be covered.

Arrange the thongs as shown in Fig. 1. This is to be a braid in which the sequence is over one thong, under one thong and over the next, or what is usually termed the basket weave.

In making this braid there are always three thongs on one side and three on the other.

First bring thong 2 to the left and over thong 1, inclining thong 1 to the right.

Bring thong 4, which belongs to the right-hand group, around to the rear over thong 5, under thong 6 and over thong 2, to return to its original side, as indicated by the arrowline in Fig. 1 and shown in Fig. 2.

Pass thong 5 around to the rear and to the front where it goes over thong 3, under thong 1 and over thong 4, to return to its original left-hand side.

Continue the braid in the same manner to the desired length, always working with the extreme left-hand or extreme right-hand thong. Remember—to the rear, then to the front and over one, under one and over one.

Another method of braiding with six thongs is shown beginning with Fig. 7. Here, as before, the thongs are grouped three on a side.

First cross thong 2 to the left over thong 1. Then bring thong 5 froward under thong 6 and over thong 2, indicated in the arrowline in Fig. 7 and shown in Fig. 8.

Bring thong 4 forward under thong 3, and over both thongs 1 and 5 (Fig. 8). Now start working the thongs around the rear.

Bring thong 3 on the right around the rear and forward on the left under thongs 6 and 2 and over thong 4 and return to its original side, as indicated by the arrowline in Fig. 9 and shown in Fig. 10.

On the left, bring thong 6 around the rear and forward to the right under thong 1 and over thongs 5 and 3 (Fig. 10).

Remember that in this braid the thongs on the right pass around back to the front under two and over one, while those on the left pass around and under one and over two. Continue this sequence until the end. The finished braid is shown in Fig. 13.

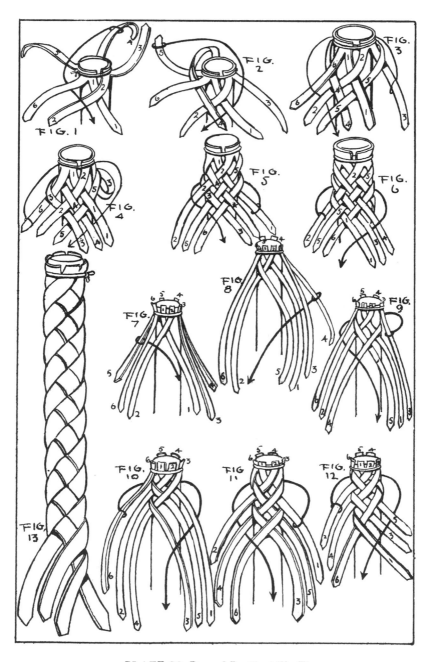

PLATE 39. Round Braid of Six Thongs.

PLATE 40

Herringbone Braid of Eight Thongs. For the eight-thong herringbone braid, fasten the thongs at the top of the core as indicated in Fig. 1. When working with so many thongs it is difficult to space them around the core. The best way to do this is first to lash down thong 1 and pass the thread or string completely around the core; then place thong 3 in position and pass the thread over it and around the core; then thong 5, and so on. Another method is to apply some fast-drying cement around the core at this point, attach the thongs and finally tie them down.

Divide the thongs so that there are four on the right-hand side and four on the left-hand side. In these illustrations, those on the right are indicated by even numbers and those on the left by odd numbers.

Bring thong 7 of the left-hand group around the rear and to the front, under thongs 8 and 6, over thongs 4 and 2 and back on its original side. This is shown in Fig. 1 and the course of thong 8 is also indicated by the arrowline. This thong goes around the rear and back to the front under thongs 5 and 3 and over thongs 1 and 7.

The sequence is always the same in this braid. Bring the rear-most thong on either side around the core, under two and over two.

In Fig. 2, thong 8 is shown in position and the arrowline indicates the path of thong 5 on the other side. It goes to the rear and then forward on the right-hand side under thongs 6 and 4 and over thongs 8 and 2.

Follow the diagrams and by way of practice, number the thongs as shown and check the work by the diagrams, seeing that each thong rests in the place indicated.

Keep the braid up snug, rub in saddle soap thoroughly when finished and roll it beneath the foot. When almost dry, polish with the heel of the hand, one of the best methods of brightening up leather. This is an attractive braid and is widely used on quirts, riding crops and other whips.

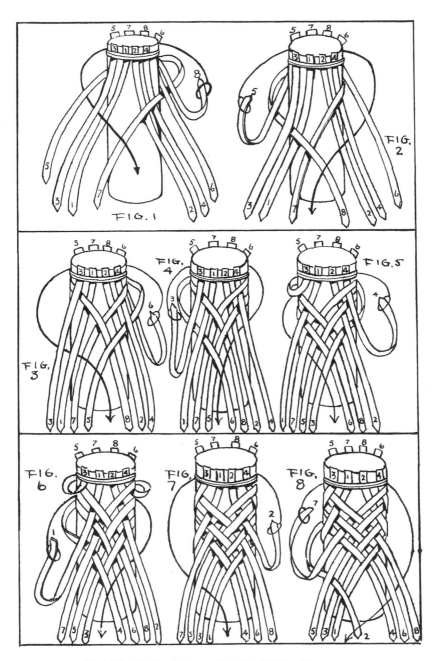

PLATE 40. Herringbone Braid of Eight Thongs.

113

PLATE 41

Back Braid of Six Thongs. First, make the foundation of this braid by braiding down with six thongs in a round braid of an over-one, under-one sequence. The braid should be made loosely, that is, the spaces between the thongs should be approximately the width of a thong.

When the skeleton braid is worked to the desired length, divide the thongs, with three on the right and three on the left. In Fig. 1 notice that where the two middle thongs cross, thong 4, which inclines to the right crosses over thong 5, which inclines to the left.

Take the upper left-hand thong, No. 6 in this case, and pass it around to the rear, over the thong on the extreme right (No. 3), under the next (No. 1), and up alongside and to the right of No. 4. This thong will parallel No. 4 to the very top. (The move explained is indicated by the arrowline in Fig. 1.)

Bring the next highest thong on the left (No. 3) around to the rear and under the one on the extreme right (No. 3) and up alongside and parallel to thong 1 (indicated by the arrowline in Fig. 2). Bring the last thong on the left (No. 5) around and parallel with thong 3, passing under thong 6, as did No. 3 (indicated by the arrowline in Fig. 3).

Figure 4 shows these thongs in their proper positions.

In Fig. 5 the braid begins. Pass thong 4 to the right, over two thongs and under two thongs. As the sequence will be over-two, under-two, remember that from now on all working thongs will pass over two thongs and under two thongs.

In Fig. 6 the work is with thong 3, which passes up to the right, over two and under two. In Fig. 7, pass thong 1 which is on the right around to the rear and up in the same relationship as the previous two—over two, under two.

This will be the sequence to remember in passing the last three thongs on the right—always over two and under two, until they reach the top. Those on the left passed upwards parallel to the thongs on their left—those on the right in the over-two, under two sequence.

Thus, although only six thongs are used, the equivalent of a twelve-thong braid is obtained.

To tighten this braid, start working down with those thongs which are fastened at the top and when the bottom is reached tighten them upwards. This gives a finished end at the bottom.

Made in this manner, a twelve-thong braid of the herringbone pattern is achieved. The V's in the braid run up and down. To make a gaucho-type braid where the V's run horizontal or around the braid, start with the back braid at Fig. 5, go under two instead of over two, and repeat with the remaining two thongs.

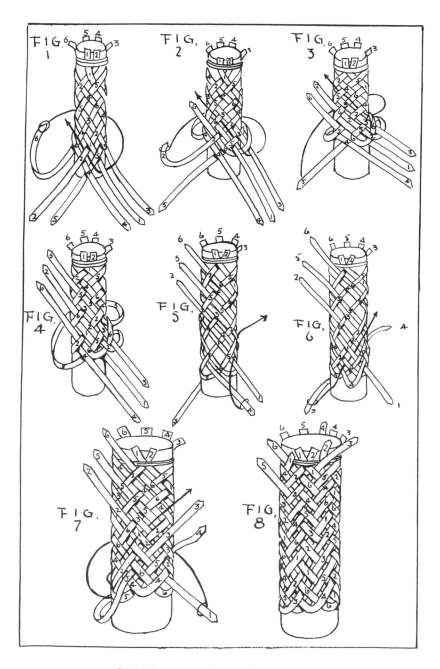

PLATE 41. Back Braid of Six Thongs.

115

PLATE 42

Back Braid of Eight Thongs. By braiding down the core with eight thongs in a basket weave—over-one, under-one sequence—and then at the bottom braiding back up in an over-two, under-two sequence, a sixteen-thong braid is obtained. The bottom presents a finished end which does not have to be covered.

Start by arranging the thongs as shown in Fig. 1. Begin the basket weave by crossing thong 1 to the right over thong 2 and incline thong 2 to the left. Bring thong 7 around to the rear, under 8, over 6, under 4 and over 1, as indicated by the arrowline in Fig. 1 and shown in Fig. 2.

From the right-hand group of thongs, take No. 8 and bring it to the rear under 5, over 3, under 2 and over 7, indicated by the arrowline in Fig. 2 and shown in Fig. 3. Continue braiding down, first from one side and then the other, until the work has progressed to the point illustrated in Fig. 5, or in other words, until the desired length of the finished braid is reached. Leave a space between thongs just the width of a thong.

To begin the back braid, take thong 5 on the left, pass it to the rear and then forward under 6, over 4, under 7 and then up along the right side of thong 8, following exactly the same course as thong 8, which in the first step would bring it under No. 2. This is indicated in the arrowline in Fig. 5 and shown in Fig. 6.

The other thongs on the left are braided accordingly as shown up to Fig. 9. Now, to begin the second phase of the back braid, bring thong 8 to the right, over 5 and 1, under 3 and 4, and over 2 and 6.

Note that the diagrams in Figs. 10, 11 and 12 show all the braiding crowded to the front. This is done merely to illustrate the work in greater detail; actually, the core is turned as you proceed.

Thong 1 is worked next (Fig. 10). Pass it over thongs 3 and 4, under 2 and 6 and over 7 and 8 (Fig. 11). Pass thong 4 over thongs 2 and 6, under 7 and 8 and over 1 and 4. Pass thong 6 over thongs 2 and 8, under 5 and 1, over 3 and 4, and so on.

The thongs working up toward the left, follow exactly the thongs to their left; those inclining up to the right maintain an individual over-two-under-two sequence.

To tighten this braid, begin at the top where the thongs are lashed down. Work down one set at a time—that is, those slanting downward to the right, and follow them back to the top. Then tighten those inclining to the left, all the way to the bottom and back to the top.

To make this into a gaucho braid, start at Fig. 9 and go past No. 8 under two instead of over two and continue the same over-and-under sequence. The remaining three thongs are also first passed over two instead of under two, and so on.

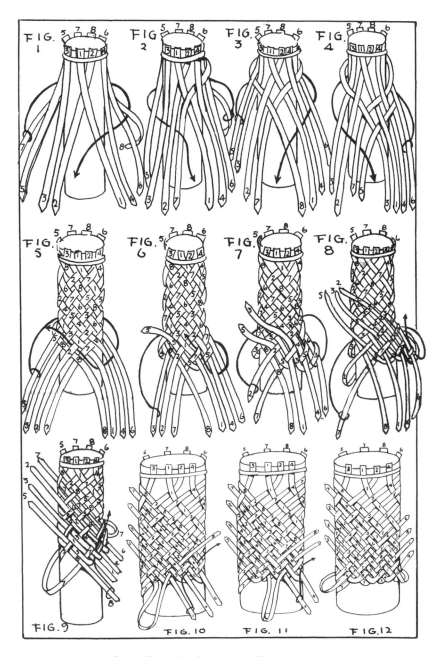

PLATE 42. Back Braid of Eight Thongs.

117

PLATE 43

Eight-String Round Gaucho Braid. In Plates 41 and 42 directions for making the gaucho braid of twelve and sixteen thongs have been given. This braid is distinguished by the fact that the V's run around the braid instead of up and down.

This effect can be obtained also by straight-braiding instead of by back-braiding. In Fig. 1 we start with eight strings or thongs. After crossing the four middle thongs as shown in Fig. 1, carry thong No. 8 around back and to the front, under two and over two.

The sequence now is: No. 1 on the left is carried around and forward over one, under two, over one (Fig. 2). Next No. 6 on the right is passed around back and forward over two and under two (Fig. 3). No. 2 on the left passes in back and forward under one, over two, under one (Fig. 4). The finished braid is shown in Fig. 5.

The important thing about this braid is that the sequences repeat after every four passes. For instance, to continue from Fig. 4 the sequence is: (same as in Fig. 1) right thong around and under two, over two; (same as in Fig. 2) left thong around and over one, under two, over one; (same as in Fig. 3) right string around and over two, under two, and (same as in Fig. 4) left thong around and under one, over two and under one. Thus, repeat the sequences after four passes.

Twelve-String Round Gaucho Braid. After crossing the six center strings as shown in Fig. 6 the string No. 1 on the left is carried around and forward over three, under three. The sequence in this braid repeats after six passes. This is it: Right to left (Fig. 7) under two, over three, under 1; left to right (Fig. 8) over one, under three, over two; right to left (Fig. 9) over three, under three; left to right (Fig. 10) under two, over three, under one; right to left (Fig. 11) over one, under three, over two. Figure 12 shows the completed braid, as well as the beginning of the next set of sequences (as in Fig. 6). Continue on for five more of this set, and then repeat.

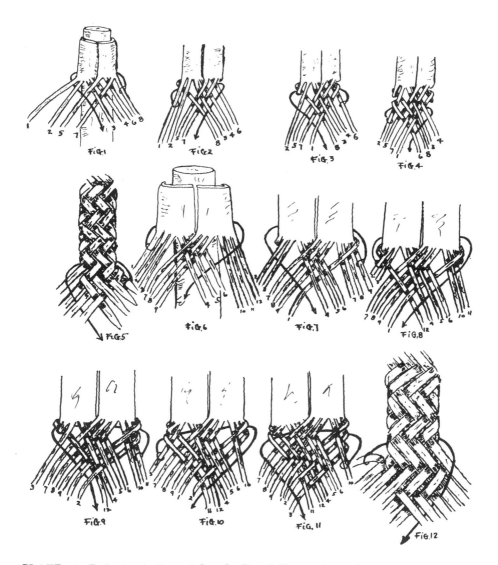

PLATE 43. Eight-String Round Gaucho Braid; Twelve-String Round Gaucho Braid.

PLATE 44

Round Braid of Twelve Thongs. In making the round braid of twelve thongs, lash the thongs around the top of the core as shown in Fig. 1. The total width of the twelve thongs should be the same as the circumference of the core. In these drawings a little space is left between the thongs to make it easier to follow the process of braiding.

In this case the six thongs on the left are given the uneven numbers, 1 to 11 and those on the right are even, 2 to 12. Each thong will return to its own side, always advancing at each step from the thong in the rear to the one in the front of its group, or "going to the head of the class."

The braid is alternate—work first one side and then the next. The sequence is the same on both sides—over two thongs, under two thongs and over two thongs.

First, bring thong 11, the rearmost of the left-hand group, around to the rear, pass it over thongs 12 and 10, then under thongs 8 and 6 and finally over thongs 4 and 2, returning it to its side. This is shown in Fig. 1.

Also in Fig. 1 is indicated the path of the next thong (No. 12) from the right-hand side. Bring it to the rear, around and to the front, pass it over thongs 9 and 7, under thongs 5 and 3 and finally over thongs 1 and 11.

The next move is from the left side: Take thong 9 around to the rear and pass it over thongs 10 and 8, under thongs 6 and 4 and finally over thongs 2 and 12.

This is indicated by the arrowline in Fig. 2 and shown in Fig. 3.

Continue this braid, working from the right side and then the left side, and follow the sequence of over two, under two and over two.

Figure 7 shows the result, with the braid loosely woven, of arranging black or colored thongs on the left side. This gives a pleasing pattern. Other patterns may be worked out by using thongs of different colors, and alternating the colors on each side.

As the work progresses keep the braid snug and exert the same amount of pull on each thong. Saddle-soap thoroughly and roll beneath the foot until the braid has a smooth surface.

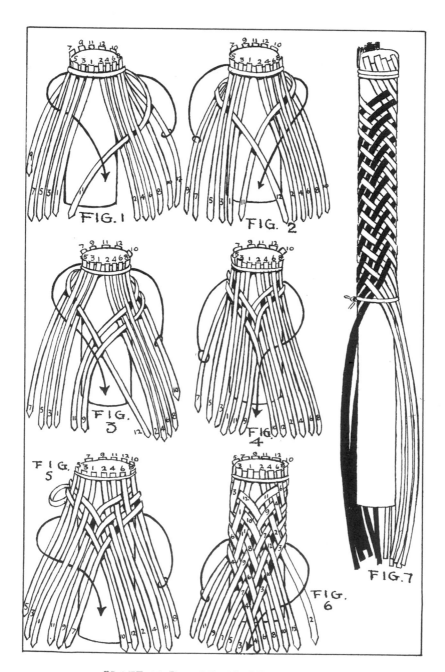

PLATE 44. Round Braid of Twelve Thongs.

PLATE 45

How to Make a Rawhide Bosal; The Core. Down in the Mexican State of Sonora they had a habit of breaking a horse when he was young and, so that the bars of his tender mouth might not be injured by a bit, the Mexicans used the *jaquima* (hackamore).

The trick item in hackamore gentling is the bosal. It is a noseband of rawhide which has a double function. It serves to cut off the horse's wind when the nose button of the bosal presses against his nose. But, more important, the back or hind part of the bosal in coming up, touches the horse's chin. This teaches the bronc to react.

So a bosal, properly fitted, should be rather loose with the front part up, and the lower, or back part, dropping down at an angle. In making a bosal loose it can be adjusted to a smaller size when the *mecate* (McCarty) or reins are attached. The number of wrappings around the lower end determine the tightness of the bosal.

The standard bosal measures twelve inches from the inside of the nose button to the inside of the heel knot (Fig. 6, Plate 51). Now, in speaking of these things it is best to name the parts of the bosal and how to make it, which is our job.

Most bosals are made on a core, either of steel cable or twisted rawhide, whichever is preferred. Some are made without cores. But if made with a core, the core is braided over. This is commonly an 8-string square braid (one with four faces), or on fancier bosals, a 12- or 16-string braid. This core and the braid covering it form the noseband proper.

In the center of the noseband is the nose button, a long braided knot about seven or eight inches in length. It might be braided over a tapering swell, made by wrapping the noseband at this point before the nose-button knot is put on. This swell may be made with waxed twine. Sailors call this work "mousing." But many nose buttons do not have this swell or "mouse."

On each side of the noseband are one or maybe two side buttons. These serve to hold the headstall in place where it is attached to the noseband on both sides.

At the point where the noseband ends come together is the heel knot—a large round, or almost round knot. The heel knot keeps the ends together, adds some weight to the bosal at this point, and keeps the *fiador* (Theodore) and *mecate* (McCarty) in place. (See illustration of an assembled hackamore, Fig. 10, Plate 54).

The first thing is to select your core, if you want one. This may be a piece of telephone guy wire from 3/8 inch to ½ inch in diameter; a four-string piece of braided rawhide; a twisted rawhide core, or a length of braided "spot cord" rope. As the nosebands of bosals vary from 3/8 inch to 1 inch in diameter, select your core with this in mind. The average bosal noseband, when the braid is on, is 5/8 inch in diameter.

I would say a twisted rawhide core is the best. It should be made from the best of your rawhide. Take a ½ inch strip, two yards in length. Be sure it is the same thickness throughout its length. Then wet it, not too much—just so it is as pliable as 12-minute spaghetti, with no hard spots in it. Rub in a lot of ordinary yellow laundry soap or saddle soap. Laundry soap is cheaper and just as good.

Now twist the strip upon itself with the *flesh side in* as shown in Figs. 1 and 2 in Plate 45. Twist it until you have thirty-four inches; then pull it and twist it some more until it is tight throughout its entire length. Nail it down by the ends on a board and let it dry (Fig. 3). When it is almost dry place another board on it, or use your foot, and roll it on the board underneath, without moving the nails or loosening it. Roll it back and forth a little. This will smooth it out. Let it remain here a day or so. This is your core.

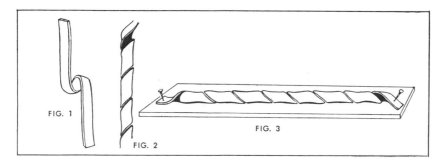

PLATE 45. How to Make a Rawhide Bosal; The Core.

The braider finds a use for every part of the animal. A bull's pizzle with a natural twist can be used as a core for a whip. (See Plate 74, How to Build a Bullwhip.)

123

PLATE 46

Eight-String Square Braid over Core. This braid is made over a core. Measure circumference of the core. Divide this by eight. This will give you the width of each string. Say the core is one inch in circumference. Each string will be 1/8 inch wide.

Tie down your strings at one end of the core. Leave about eight inches of strings above the point where you tie down. This is not shown in Fig. 1, Plate 46, but is necessary, since these loose strings will later be utilized.

Start braiding as in Fig. 1. First bring string No. 1, which was on the left side, around to the back, under two strings and over two, to return it to its original side. Arrowline shows how string No. 8 on the right is brought around to the back and then toward the front, under two and over two.

In Fig. 2, the highest string on the left, No. 5, is brought around to the back and forward under two and over two. The arrowline indicates its path.

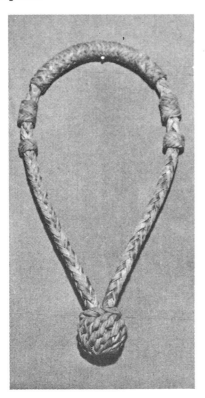 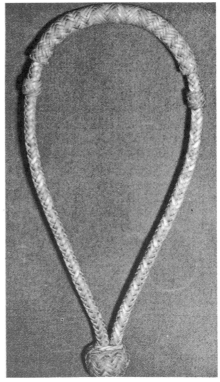

Left: Homemade type of bosal made by L.H. Rutter, Hinsdale, Montana. Very rugged. Noseband braided without core. Note heel knot, made by continuous crowning, like sailors make boat fenders. *Right:* Bosal made by author. Braided over twisted rawhide core. Heel knot is over three, under three braid. (See Plate 45.)

In Fig. 2, the highest string on the left, No. 5, is brought around to the back and forward under two and over two. The arrowline indicates its path.

Then, on the right, the highest string, No. 6, is carried around to the back and forward under two and over two. Continue in this manner, alternately working the highest string on each side, until you have braided full length of the core.

There should be eight or more inches of free string at this end also, after you have tied down the end of your braid.

There is a shrinkage in braiding. It is well to play safe. Make your strings twice as long as the finished braid.

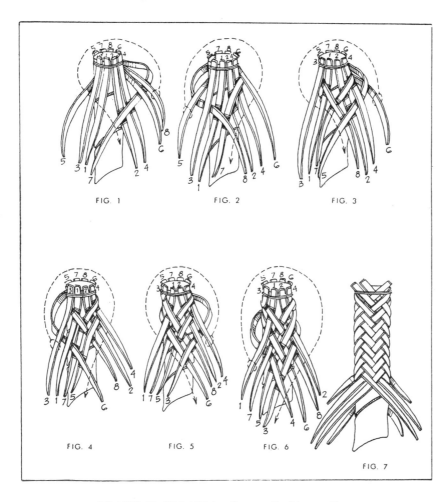

PLATE 46. Eight-String Square Braid over Core.

PLATE 47

Eight-String Square Braid Without Core. For those who do not use a core—and I must say I've seen plenty of good bosal nosebands without cores—the braid shown in Figs. 1, 2, 3, and 4 in Plate 47 may be used. This is made with eight strings, each ¼ inch wide, and, as it is necessary to have some working ends—on both ends of the braid—each string should be about two yards long.

We begin in Fig. 1. In this drawing the strings are spread out to better illustrate the sequence. But they should be tied together, leaving about eight inches at the top.

Arrange the four center strings as shown in Fig. 1. Then bring string No. 2 around in back and forward over the two front strings, as shown. In Fig. 2, the No. 7 string on the right is carried around to the back and then under one and over two, as shown (it actually is under two). In Fig. 3, the No. 1 string on the left is carried around back and forward under one (actually under two) and then over two. After this work the upper string on each side alternately, bringing it around in back and then forward under two and over two.

Exert the same even pull on all your strings; don't let them turn on you, and keep your braid up tight.

Make the braid thirty inches long. Now hang it up with a weight on one end and let it stretch and dry. When it is almost dry, take it down and roll it under your foot on a flat surface; not too hard, but enough to even the braid. This braid has four square faces. Let it dry for a couple of days, with the weight still on it.

When using this braid around a core you can make a 12-string one by coming around under three and then over three; or a 16-string braid by passing under four and over four, or under two, over two, under two, and over two, on each side.

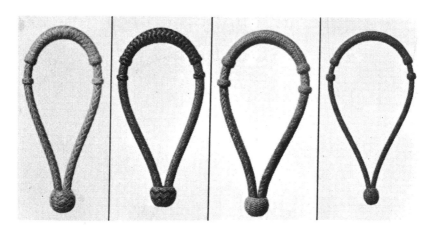

Bosals made by John Conrad, Bellflower, California. Steel cable cores.

A word again about dampening your strings before using them. Most braiders get their strings too wet. Then, when the braid dries, the strings seem to loosen and show daylight in the work. Have the strings just damp enough so there are no hard spots; then soap them well with laundry soap or saddle soap. Moisten and soap the working ends as they dry out.

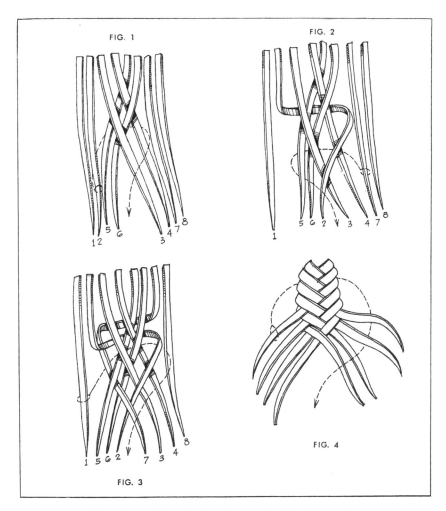

PLATE 47. Eight-String Square Braid without Core.

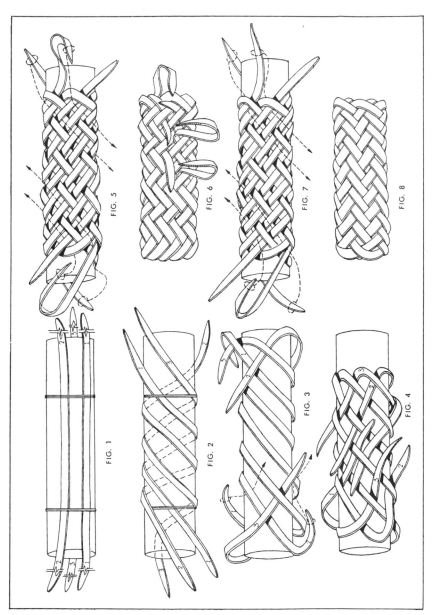

FIG. 1

FIG. 2

FIG. 3

FIG. 4

FIG. 5

FIG. 6

FIG. 7

FIG. 8

PLATE 48. The Nose Button.

128

PLATE 48

The Nose Button. There still are some old-time rawhide-braiders around. I have located possibly a score or more of them who are busily making fancy quirts, bosals, reatas, headstalls and other articles of horse gear. In almost all cases they are "retired" cowboys or buckaroos.

It would not be far-fetched to say that these fellows are the very last of the Old West, survivors of former days, still doing things as they were done in the long ago.

These old-timers have many ingenious tricks in making braided knots. Take the long nose-button knot for a bosal, for instance. There are several ways to make the nose-button knot. One is with a long string of rawhide. The knot is so long, however, that it becomes awkward in working with a lengthy string. A simpler way is with a multiple-string knot, or one which is made by several strings. This is a variation of what I have called the Cowboy Knot later in this book.

Take a look at Fig. 1, Plate 48. You place from three to six strings on the middle part of the noseband and tie them down the length the finished button is to be—say eight inches. (Three strings are shown in these drawings for simplicity; you might use more.) Make each string about a yard long. The way to determine the width of the string is to: measure the circumference of the noseband. Say it is one and one-half inches around. In this knot three strings are going to pass back and forth, until they form six bights on each. If you were braiding down, one bight would mean two strings, because you use both ends. So with six bights you are actually using twelve strings. With twelve 1/8-inch thongs you can cover a circumference of one and one-half inches. So three strings of 1/8 inch will cover this noseband. In other words, figure the number of bights or scallops on a woven knot and double it to obtain the actual number of strings you will use.

In winding your strings around the noseband, as shown in Fig. 1, the dress of hair side of the strings is *out*. In Fig. 3 start your braid. On the left-hand side bring each working end over one string and under one as shown. On the right-hand side bring each string under one and over one. These working ends spiral back at right angles to those they pass over and under.

Keep passing over one and under one until the strings from each side meet. You will notice in Fig. 4 that string No. 1 on the left meets string No. 1 on the right. After the ends of the strings have come together in this fashion, keep working towards the opposite ends, this time doubling the strings.

When you reach the stage shown in Fig. 5, bring back the ends on the left under two and over two, splitting the doubled pairs as shown. On the right, the ends come back over two and under two. When the ends meet, as in Fig. 6, cut them off and tuck them in the braid. Don't have all pairs of ends coming together in the same part of the knot. Scatter or stagger them so that the finished knot is uniform.

129

This gives you what I call a Gaucho Braid. The V's in the braid run around the knot. In the next braid (Fig. 7), which I call the Herringbone Braid, the V's run, or point, the length of the knot.

To make the herringbone braid, start back at Fig. 5, but pass the working ends as shown in Fig. 7. This time the ends on the left go over two and under two. Those on the right go under two and over two. Finished knot is shown in Fig. 8.

You may combine these two braids on your nose button, making it more fancy. On each end make two tucks with the gaucho braid, and finish the inside with the herringbone braid. Where the two braids join there will be an alternating over-one, under-one sequence, but as this is regular it does not detract from the knot. This makes an attractive button—"very cowboy."

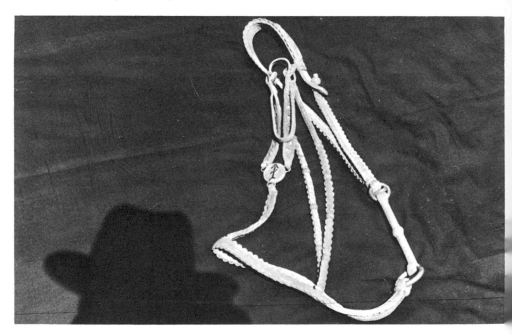

A beautiful bosal of colt's rawhide. Mr. Maguire's cattle brand is on the silver center. The braid is called *trenza pampa*. Collection John W. Maguire.

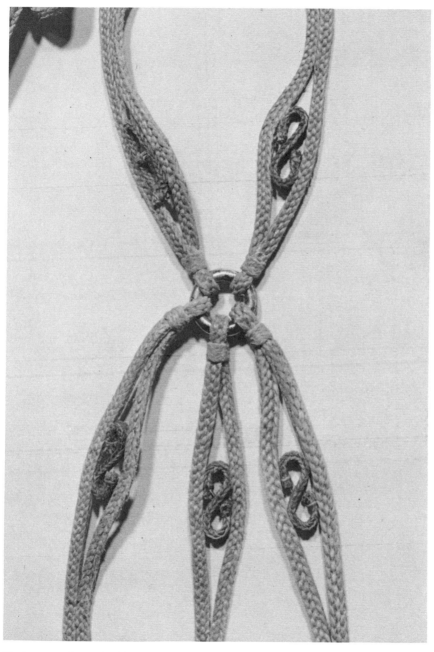

Hackamore from the Edward Larocque Tinker collection, The Hall of the Horse men of the Americas, The University of Texas.

PLATE 49

The Side Button. Side buttons on a bosal are for the purpose of holding the hackamore headstall in place and there may be either one or two to a side. If the nose button is short, make two. The space between the buttons, or between one button and the end of the nose button is the width of the leather in your hackamore headstall.

The Spanish ring knot (Plate 161) can be used, but you may like this one better.

I have shown this button worked around a mandrel with a leather collar to better illustrate it. You may work it directly on the noseband. It is made from one long string, 1/8 inch wide. Play safe and use a string about a yard long. I might add that old-timers work their knots so that there is no need to go back and re-tighten them. This is a good thing to practice and saves string. When you have once properly made your button, it is on good and tight; so you have no need to rework it.

In these drawings the mandrel is numbered on four sides from 1 to 4 clockwise: No. 1 is the front; No. 3 is the back.

Start in Fig. 1 from the front and pass up and around the mandrel and then back on the right side and up again to go under the standing part. In Fig. 2, the working end goes around and then down to the right, over one, and then up to the top where it passes under one and over one.

In Fig. 3, the mandrel has been turned slightly to show how, in the third move, the working end passes at the bottom—over one and under one. Then at the top (Fig. 4) it is under one, over one, under one.

Fig. 5. Bottom: over one, under one, over one. Fig. 6. Top: under one, over one, under one, over one.

Fig. 7 shows the completed skeleton knot, working end coming up alongside the standing end. Braiding of the knot—or Turk's-head—has started here and it will be seen that the working end passes up on the right of the standing end. At the top it passes under two, bringing it over to the other side of the standing end.

Fig. 8 is the back view. Still following the standing end, the working end passes over it as well as another string and under one to the top.

Fig. 9. Top: the sequence is under two, over two, under one. Fig. 10. Bottom: over two, under two, over one. Fig. 11. Top: under two, over two, under two. Fig. 12. Bottom: over two, under two, over two. Fig. 13. Top: under two, over two, under two. Then pass around to the front and up alongside standing part.

The completed knot is shown in Fig. 14. It can be increased to over-three, under-three sequence by following around again and splitting the pairs.

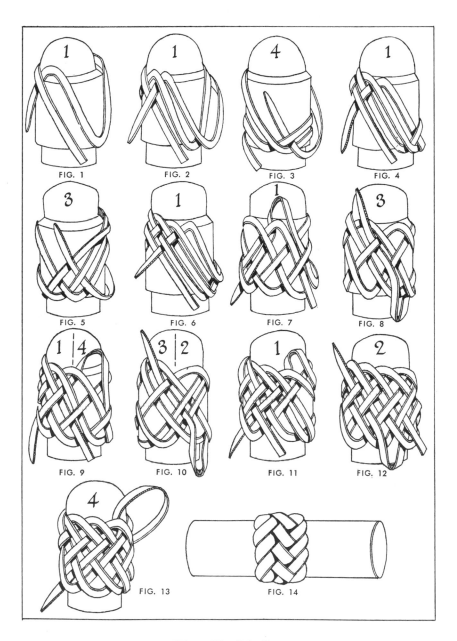

PLATE 49. The Side Button.

133

PLATE 50

The Heel Knot. The final knot on the bosal is the heel knot. But first the ends of the bosal must be joined together so that the inside measurement, from the inside of nose button to the point where ends are joined, is approximately twelve inches. You may want your bosal longer or shorter—but average size is twelve inches.

In joining the ends together you make a foundation knot. There are several ways to make this knot. The ends can first be tied and then secured with the knot shown in Figs. 9, 10, and 11 of Plate 77. You can use four or six strings, making sure that a half of them comes from each of the ends. This forms a foundation knot.

However, one of the best ways of securing the ends and making your foundation knot is shown in Figs. 1 and 2 of Plate 51. Ends are brought together and tied. Then, at the point where they are tied, you make a Spanish ring knot (Plate 161) or a side-button knot (Plate 49.) Make either of these knots with ¼-inch-wide string but not too tight.

You will recall that, when you braided the noseband, you left eight inches of loose strings on each end. Moisten these strings. Each string is then brought back and through the ring knot or side-button knot, as shown in Fig. 1. There are sixteen strings in all and all are passed back and through the knot and pulled tight. Arrange them in regular order; then cut them off flush with the knot.

Best covering I know for this foundation knot is one I call the Pineapple Knot. It is one of the most practical knots in braiding. As the bights or scallops on each edge are staggered toward the center, the knot closes on the end when tightened and, in fact, will close on both ends and completely encompass a spherical object. The pineapple knot can be interwoven to make it larger, yet its outside bights remain the same in number, enabling it to close over the head of a quirt, bottom of a heel knot, or other round or semi-round object. It is the King of Braided Knots, and you will find many uses for it. The Argentine gauchos use it to cover buttons and call it the button knot.

Take a look at Plate 50. We start out by making a four-bight, five-part Turk's-head, which is completed at Fig. 7. This is then raised to a six-bight, seven-part Turk's-head and is completed at Fig. 11. (In case you wish a larger Turk's-head, use the same key in raising it to an eight-bight, nine-part Turk's-head.)

In Fig. 11 we start braiding or interweaving. (Drawings show this knot made on a mandrel, but you can make it directly on the heel-knot foundation of your bosal.) The working end passes along to the right of the standing part, as shown by the arrowline; and then over to the left under two strings at the point where they cross. In Fig. 12, passing down, the working end follows the string on its left. The sequence is over one, under one, over one, under two.

Fig. 13. Going up: over one, under one, over one, under three, splitting parallel strings.

Fig. 14. Going down: over one, under one, over one, under three (splitting two parallel strings).

Fig. 15. Up: over one (not seen in the drawing), under one, over one, under three.

Fig. 16. Down: over two, under one, over one, under three.

Fig. 17. Up: over two, under one, over one, under three.

Fig. 18. Down: over two, under two, over one, under three.

Fig. 19. Up: over two, under two, over one, under three.

Fig. 20. Down: over two, under two, over two, under three.

Fig. 21. Up: over two, under two, over two, under three.

Fig. 22. Down: over two; under two, over two, under three, which brings the working end up alongside its original starting part. The finished knot is shown in Fig. 23, not tightened.

This knot can be made with 1/8-inch strings. If it does not completely cover the foundation knot you will have to enlarge your Turk's-head, or, better yet, you can enlarge the knot by interweaving in an over-three, under-three sequence. See Plate 51.

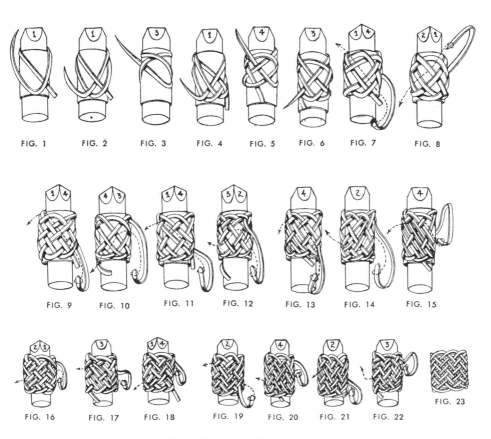

FIG. 1   FIG. 2   FIG. 3   FIG. 4   FIG. 5   FIG. 6   FIG. 7   FIG. 8

FIG. 9   FIG. 10   FIG. 11   FIG. 12   FIG. 13   FIG. 14   FIG. 15

FIG. 16   FIG. 17   FIG. 18   FIG. 19   FIG. 20   FIG. 21   FIG. 22   FIG. 23

PLATE 50. The Heel Knot.

135

PLATE 51.

The Heel Knot (Cont.). By using the pineapple knot and increasing the sequence you can cover any size foundation knot at the heel of your bosal. For instance, after placing on the over-two, under-two pineapple knot detailed in Plate 50, you find it does not completely cover the foundation knot, you can go around it again, to make it larger, with an over-three, under-three sequence.

The key to increasing the sequence in this knot is shown in Figs. 3 and 4, Plate 51. In Fig. 3, the working end which, in the previous explanation, came up alongside its original part, is shown here.

The working end now passes up along on the right of its original part and, at the top, goes under two, as shown by the arrowline in Fig. 3. It now follows down alongside the string above it and then, at the bottom, it passes under four. This is shown by the arrowline in Fig. 4.

In continuing up, the working end passes over two, under two, over two, and under three, splitting two parallel strings in the previous weave.

From this point, the sequence is:

Down: over two, under two, over two, under five, splitting parallel strings.

Up: over two, under two, over two, under three (again splitting two parallel strings).

Down: over three, under two, over two, under five.

Up: over three, under two, over two, under three.

Down: over three, under three, over two, under five.

Up: over three, under three, over two, under three.

Down: over three, under three, over three, under five.

Up: over three, under three, over three, under three.

Down: over three, under three, over three, under five.

This brings the working end alongside the starting portion of the string in this last weave. The knot is complete.

With this key you may increase your knot still more, or by using a different colored string, produce a contrasting pattern. If you use a different colored string for each interweave you can produce a very fancy knot, indeed.

I have seen this knot on some old work where it had an over and under sequence of nine—that is, a string would pass over nine others and under nine.

In Fig. 6 is shown the completed bosal. The swells at each end of the nose button are made by placing the nose-button braid over two three-part Turk's-heads (Figs. 1 to 8 in Plate 161). Swell or taper of the nose button is made by "mousing," as described in the first part of this explanation of how to make the bosal.

In Fig. 7 is another type bosal, called a tie-down bosal. The core of this is an endless cable and the bosal is usually about pencil-thickness. If made without a core, the ends are spliced together beneath the part covered by the nose button.

Take your time in making your bosal. The finished product looks difficult, but when you follow each step carefully it is simple. You may work out ideas of your own in the process, as, for example, making the nose button of leather thongs instead of rawhide strings.

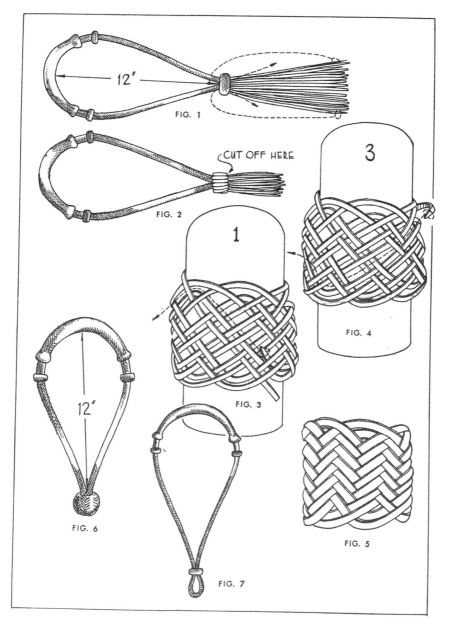

PLATE 51. The Heel Knot (Cont.).

137

PLATE 52

How to Make a Braided Hackamore Headstall. A fancy headstall can be made entirely of braid. By the use of woven knots it is made adjustable to fit any horse's head. Such a headstall is used with a pencil-width bosal.

This headstall (Fig. 14, Plate 52) consists of the following parts:

One metal ring 1-3/8 inches outside measurement, covered with braidwork (marked A in Fig. 14).

Two long braided "rounds" 40 inches each for the offside cheekpiece, headpiece, and part of the nearside cheekpiece, (B).

One braided "round" 24 inches for the lower part of nearside cheekpiece, (C).

Two braided "rounds" 24 inches each for the browband, (D).

Woven knots of various sizes.

This headstall can be made with a four-string braid, illustrated in Plate 77, with or without a core. If used with a core, this core should be braided cord. The eight-string braid shown in Plate 46 can be used over a core. Measure circumference of the core and then divide this by the number of strings to be used in your braid. The result will give you the width of each string. For example, if the core is an inch in circumference and you use eight strings, each string will be 1/8 inch in width.

When latigo or leather thongs are used it is best to employ a core. If you use rawhide strings, no core will be necessary and the best braid for this purpose is shown in Plate 47—the eight-string braid.

With or without the core, make your thongs or strings about double the length of finished braid to take care of shrinkage, and leave enough unbraided on each end to tie a foundation knot for your covering or woven knot.

We will start with the metal ring. In Fig. 1 is shown the first step in covering this with a Spanish type edge-braid of two loops. The end B should be about two inches long. Working end A is passed through the ring as shown, and then brought forward over B and through the ring once more. In Fig. 2, the working end A is brought back and passed beneath the crossed strings X, and between the strings and the outer rim of the ring. The working end in this instance does not pass through the ring.

In Fig. 3, the working end passes through the ring and, in Fig. 4, is brought back once more beneath the crossed strings—but not through the ring. Braid is continued in this manner until it covers the ring and is near the starting point.

To join the braid after it has been made around the ring, look at Fig. 5. Standing end B has been pulled out as shown. Working end A passes through the ring and up in back through the same loop which contains B. The working end A next passes underneath two crossed strings and then down through the loop containing B, through which A previously passed. Now draw your braid tight and cut off ends A and B flush with the braid.

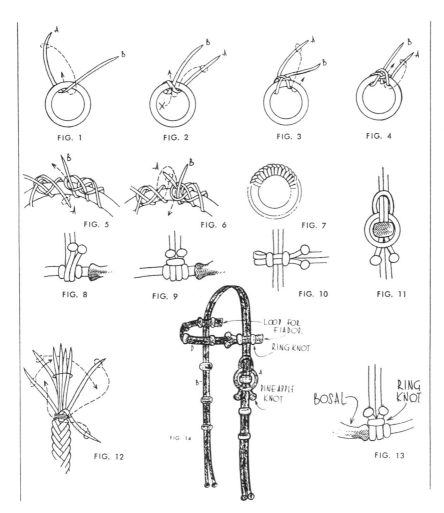

PLATE 52. How to Make a Braided Hackamore Headstall.

In our drawings the braid is shown very loose, so that details can be more easily followed. The covered ring is shown in Fig. 7.

In Fig. 12 is shown how the ends are tied for the foundation knot. Four strings are used for this purpose. Details of this knot are shown in Figs. 9 and 10, Plate 77, or you may use the knot shown in Figs. 9, 10, 11, and 12 in Plate 78. Cut your ends off flush with the top of the knot.

The woven knot which covers this foundation knot is the pineapple knot, shown in Plate 50. The pineapple knot is used also in the other woven knots shown on the finished headstall. However, the Spanish ring knot (Plate 161) is best for the smaller knots on the browband and those fastening the cheekpieces to the bosal.

The knot at the point of adjustment on the nearside cheekpiece should be smaller than the inside of the metal ring.

139

PLATE 53

How to Make a Braided Bridle Headstall. If a horse could laugh, he would express much amusement over some of the baubles and gaudy trinkets his owner puts on bridles, saddles, and other riding gear.

Still, the average animal does not appear too happy about this heavy, out-of-character "horse jewelry." Many of them seem downright sad, especially when they are carrying a saddle that requires two men to place into position, or wearing a bridle bearing all sorts of metal doodads that would weigh down any proud horse's head.

A few expensive and carefully selected conchas and buckles may not be out of place on ordinary occasions, and perhaps a horse "diked" out like a dowager at the opening night of the opera is *de rigueur* in a parade or on a movie set, but for my part I like leather carving, saddle-stamping, and braidwork as decoration for horse gear at all times.

A decorative bridle headstall can be made entirely of braidwork. No metal fastenings of any kind are needed. If you want it particularly fancy you may use several colors in your rawhide strings or leather thongs.

This bridle headstall is similar to the braided hackamore headstall with the exception that there are two cheek-headpiece adjustments instead of one—one on each side—a throatlatch, and cheek-bit loops. Here are the specifications:

	Length when braided	Number and width of strings	Length of each string	Total
Throatlatch (1)	4 ft. 6 in.	8 3/32 in.	9 ft.	72 ft.
Browband (2)	2 ft. 2 in.	16 3/32 in.	5 ft.	80 ft.
Headpiece (2)	2 ft. 6 in.	16 1/8 in.	5 ft.	80 ft.
Cheekpiece (2)	3 ft.	16 1/8 in.	6 ft.	96 ft.
Cheek-Bit Loop (2)	9 in.	16 1/8 in.	18 in.	24 ft.
				352 ft.

There will be some 28 buttons, or woven knots, which will require an additional 84 feet of string. So the grand total for making the headstall will be about 436 feet of rawhide string.

The braiding will be the 8-string square, as shown in Plate 47. In case you use leather thongs, and braid over a core of braided rope, use the braid shown in Plate 46.

Follow the instructions for making the braided hackamore headstall, only in this case use two braid-covered metal rings instead of one, and also make your throatlatch and cheek-bit loops (Fig. 1). In making the latter, the cheekpieces ends are first joined together with a foundation knot (Figs. 9-12, Plate 78), then covered with a woven knot (Plate 50).

There are several ways of making the headpiece-cheekpiece adjustment. One is with metal rings as shown in Fig. 3; another is by braiding over a short, stiff piece of rawhide and placing a button on each end, as shown in Fig. 4. In Fig. 5, there is neither the ring nor the crosspiece, and the adjustment is made with two woven buttons or knots as shown.

If you wish to make a bridle head from strap leather, follow the details in Fig. 9.

The cheek-bit loop is made from strap leather also. On one end cut four thongs, cutting back several inches. Then make a foundation knot as shown in Figs. 9 and 10, Plate 77, or in Figs. 9, 10, 11 and 12, Plate 78. Cover this with the pineapple knot (Plate 50). The ring knot which holds the loop to the ring is slipped down close to the button, where it passes through the slit in the leather and holds it in place.

When using leather thongs the ends can be finished off with *tassels*, or, as the cowboy says, frills. Cut your frill as shown in Fig. 6 and then wrap it around the end of the "round." Sew it and lash it. Then cover with a pineapple knot.

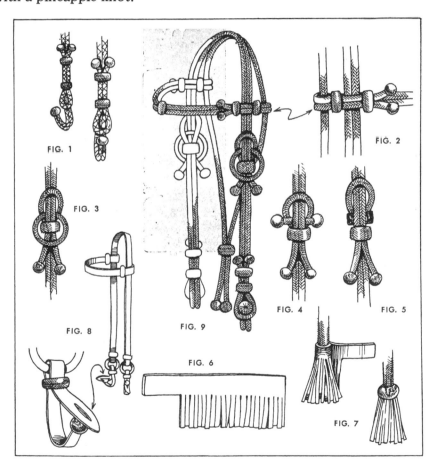

FIG. 1

FIG. 2

FIG. 3

FIG. 8

FIG. 9

FIG. 4

FIG. 5

FIG. 6

FIG. 7

PLATE 53. How to Make a Braided Bridle Headstall.

141

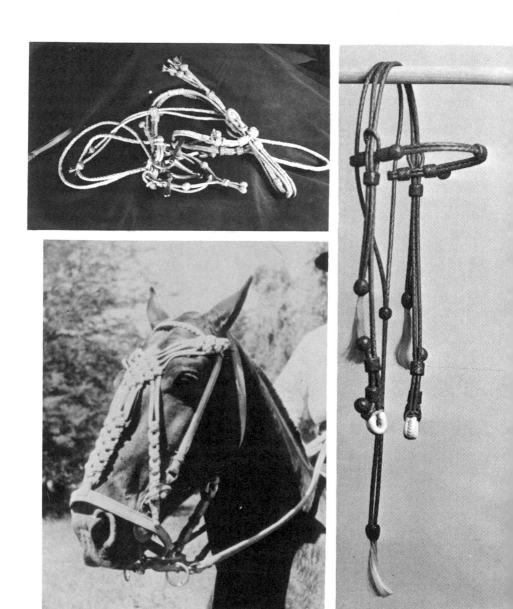

Top, left: Braided rawhide headstall, reins and chin strap made by the author. *Bottom, left:* Fancy headstall used in the Argentine. *Right:* Black leather braided headstall made by Burt Rogers, Spearfish, South Dakota. The headstall has white horsehair tassels.

142

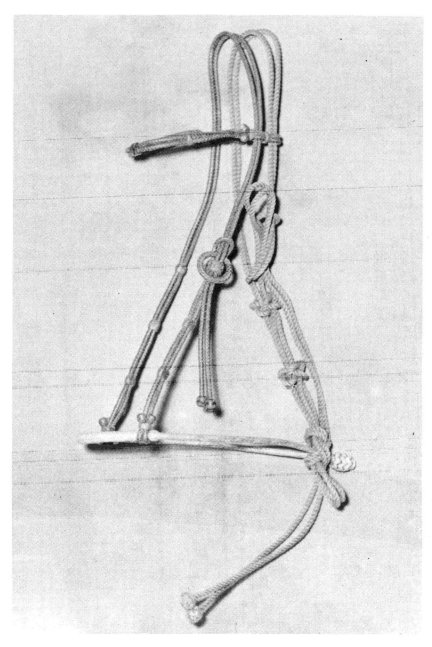

Completely rigged hackamore made by Duff Severe, Pendleton, Oregon. Braided headstall, pencil type bosal.

PLATE 54

Rigging the Hackamore. The Western hackamore pretty well illustrates the influence of the Mexican *vaquero* on the American cowboy and buckaroo. Not only is the idea of its use Mexican—and we mean *Mexican* as adapted from the Spanish *conquistadores*,—all names for parts of the hackamore coming in a picturesque jargon from the Mexican.

Hackamore originally was *jaquima* (hah'-key-mah). The cowboy twisted it around to suit himself and when he got through with the word it was "hackamore." The bosal comes from *bozal* and so has remained almost in its pure form. The "Theodore" and "Theodore Knot" come from the word *fiador* (fee'-ah-dohr). Many believe this safety device, or throatlatch, with its intricate knot got its name from *Theodore Roosevelt*, but, considering the liberties the cowboy took with other Spanish and Mexican words, he undoubtedly merely converted *fiador* into "Theodore." Then there is the *mecate* (may-kah'-tay), or hair rope used as reins and lead-rope. The cowboy calls this "McCarty."

The hackamore, and I call it this to mean headstall, fiador, bosal and mecate, is handy gear around a ranch or any place where horses need to be gentled. Its use is one of the oldest in breaking horses and has long been popular in the West, particularly in California. Others more expert than myself can explain the value of the hackamore method in teaching a horse to neck-rein.

We have made the different parts of the hackamore, namely, the headstall and the bosal, so now it must be properly rigged.

The first thing is to make the double hackamore knot. It is interesting how writers on knots and rope work have explained the hackamore knot as used by the cowboy. They claim that this knot—also known as the bag, bottle, jug, and beggarman's knot—after being made, may be loosened up and used as a sort of halter, or headstall. Let us forget all this nonsense and see just how the hackamore knot is actually fashioned and used.

First, it must be tied double. Take fourteen or fifteen feet of good braided cord—No. 10 Sampson spot rope that resembles clothesline is the best. Double it. About three feet from the bight marked A in Fig. 1, Plate 54, start your knot by laying it out as shown. Follow the arrowline in Fig. 1; then follow the arrowline in Fig. 2. Straighten out your rope carefully so that it does not overlap in the knot and leaves about two inches of the double bight D above the knot. Bight A below the knot should be about eighteen inches in length.

This is the knot that secures the lower end of the fiador to the bosal. In Fig. 4, it will be noted that the knot is loosened and the double bight D has been withdrawn. Through the space, push the nose button of the bosal, as shown by the arrowline. Then bring bight D down through the space between the noseband and back through the loops in the knot it formerly occupied. Tighten it as shown in Fig. 5, leaving two inches of bight D below.

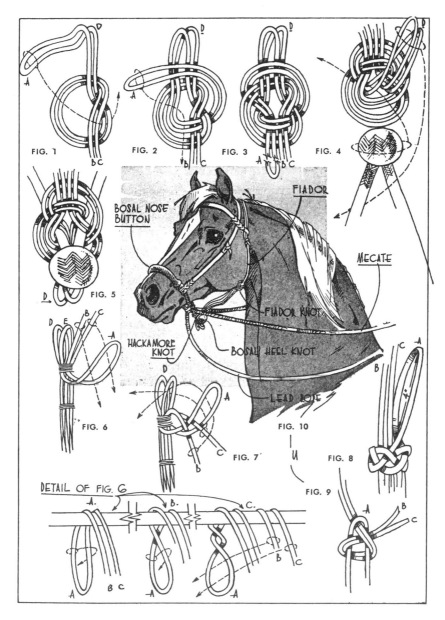

PLATE 54. Rigging the Hackamore.

The fiador knot is started about six inches above the double hackamore knot. Remember there were two ends, marked B and C, and the bight marked A. These are tied together as shown in Fig. 6, bight A being turned down to form the two bights, D and E.

The secret of making this knot is the twist given to bight A, when it is brought forward beneath the part where it is tied. To better illustrate this I have shown the steps in this twist in Figs. 11, 12, and 13. Be sure to arrange the rope in this fashion in tying the knot according to the diagrams in Figs. 6 and 7.

Bight A should be about 4 inches long when the knot is completed (Fig. 8). In tightening the knot after Fig. 7, seize the ends B and C and the bight A, remove the tie-string, and work the knot until it looks as in Fig. 8. Its position on the fiador is seen in Fig. 10. In Fig. 9 is the simple knot used to fasten the ends of the fiador.

PLATE 55

That "Ole" Fiador Knot. The fiador is the toughest of all horse gear knots to tie. Many letters have come from readers who say they have found it impossible to tie the fiador.

Possibly more cuss words have been wasted on this "ole" fiador knot than on all the one-cow stampeding Brahmas, balky jackasses and ornery bronco gizzard-poppers and gut-twisters put together.

The fiador, or Theodore, can almost be labeled "the knot that nobody can tie." Of course, there still are some old-timers who can whip up this knot, and some have their own private way of doing it. But even these fellows are becoming fewer, and that is too bad, because the fiador is the one typically horseman's knot. Most all other knots can be traced to sailors and sailing ships—but not the fiador. It came hundreds of years ago from the Argentine Pampas and up through Mexico and into the Southwest—and it came on horses and not on ships.

Today, a very small percentage of the horsemen who use the hackamore with the fiador tie this classic knot themselves—either it comes with the rig when they buy it, or they purchase it from a saddle shop or mail-order house with the knot already tied. Should these riders transfer the fiador from the hackamore to another, they are careful not to upset or capsize the knot.

So, for those who want to tie the fiador to *use* it, or those who simply want to learn to make it for the satisfaction of helping to keep alive a part of the Old West, we believe a simple, foolproof way has been worked out.

In showing how the fiador is made, we have also described again the making of the two other knots that go with it—the hackamore knot, which secures the heel knot of the bosal, and the sheet bend or tie knot, by which the fiador is adjusted and fastened. By doing all the knots together, their relationship to each other can be illustrated more clearly.

The hackamore knot should be made first. Take 15 feet of sash cord and middle it, forming the loop or bight A in Fig. 1. With 3 feet of the doubled cord—from B to A in Fig. 1—start the knot as shown, working

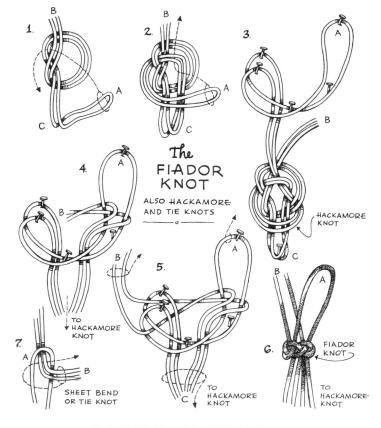

PLATE 55. That "Ole" Fiador Knot.

with the loop A. In Fig. 2 the final pass is made as indicated by the arrowline. The double bight C at the bottom should be about 2 inches. The bight A should extend above the knot about 13 inches, as this will be a part of the fiador knot.

Now, take a board and hammer and six nails (Fig. 3). The distance between the bottom nail and the top nail should be about 1 foot, and between those on the right and those on the left, about ½ foot. You don't have to be too exact about placing the nails, as they are merely to hold the rope turns apart.

Secure loops C of the hackamore knot over the lower nail. Then, working with loop A as shown in Fig. 3, pass it around the nails, as shown, being careful about crossing the strands, and finally loop it over the top nail. Next, work the two ends marked B as shown in Fig. 4. Complete the knot as shown in Fig. 5. Take the loop A and the ends B in one hand and the loops C in the other and remove the rope from the nails and draw the hands apart, tightening the knot. With a little coaxing, the fiador knot will emerge as shown in Fig. 6.

The fiador knot should be about 6 inches above the hackamore knot, but this must be adjusted to suit the horse's head. The manner of making the tie knot is shown in Fig. 7.

Some expert fiador knot makers may grumble that this "ain't the right way" to tie this knot, but, "what thee hackamore!"—the result is the same.

PLATE 56

The Hackamore Reins and Lead-Rope Knot. The hackamore reins and lead rope are made from one long twisted horsehair rope, known in Mexico as the *mecate*. As with other horse-gear terms from below the Border, the cowboy has changed this to suit himself. He calls it *McCarty*.

The *mecate* is 22 feet long and varies from 3/8 inch to 5/8 inch in diameter. Some are ¾ inch in diameter.

At one end of the *mecate* is a tassel known as *la mota*.

The first step is to determine the length of the reins. This is usually done by holding the bosal knot and the doubled *mecate* in one hand and then stretching the other hand out to form a bight which will be the reins. This measurement is termed a *brazada*, or the distance from hand to hand when the arms are extended. Another way is to place a bight of the *mecate* in the saddle seat and measure to the position of the bosal heel knot—both bosal and saddle on the horse, of course.

In Fig. 1 is shown a portion of the bosal with the hackamore knot tied. The hackamore reins and lead-rope knot is tied just forward of the hackamore knot. Take that portion of the *mecate* with the *mota*, or tassel, and wrap it around the left cheek of the bosal, as shown. This section of the *mecate* is marked B. Take the other section, marked A, and lay it over the right cheek of the bosal, as shown.

The arrowline indicated the next turn of A.

In Fig. 2 the previous turns are shown, with the arrowline showing the next turn of that section, marked A. Notice the turn is made beneath the reins.

In Fig. 3, the final turns are made, as indicated by the arrowline. Notice that A, which is the lead-rope, passes through the two bights of the hackamore knot. Figure 4 shows the completed knot. It is loose and should be pushed up snug against the hackamore knot.

More turns can be taken with section A, if desired. By these turns, the bosal can be adjusted to fit the horse.

The inside measurement of the bosal from the heel knot to the nose button usually is twelve inches. This is the size you will receive from a dealer if you do not specify a definite measurement. If you build the bosal yourself for a particular horse, you will of course make it to fit that horse's head.

The turns taken with section A as described above close the sides of the bosal near the heel knot. Thus if your bosal is too large for the horse on which it is to be used, you take a sufficient number of turns to

148

close it up at this point and thereby reduce it in size. However, the bosal should not fit snugly, but loose enough so that the heel knot drops well below the plane of the nose button. Take great care to adjust your bosal correctly.

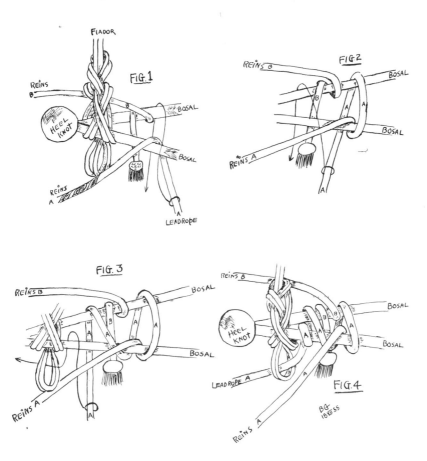

PLATE 56. The Hackamore Reins and Lead-Rope Knot.

PLATE 57

How to Make a Pair of Braided Reins. Reins are of two general types—open and closed. In the old days the Texas cowboy favored open reins, while the California buckaroo was partial to closed reins.

The open ones are not joined together at the saddle-end, so, if the rider is thrown, he is in no danger of becoming entangled in them. Also, when a horse is grazing, his reins would not get caught in the brush. But the chief point was that, when the cowboy dismounted, he merely let his reins drop to the ground, so that, if the horse tried to get away, the animal would step on the reins' ends and stop himself.

Closed reins usually have a long flexible quirt, or *romal*, attached at the saddle-end (Plate 63).

If using leather thongs in making your reins, I suggest that a core be used. In such case measure around the core and divide this measurement by eight—if using eight thongs. Thus if a core measures one inch in circumference, use eight 1/8-inch thongs. Core should be of braided rope, 9 feet long. Thongs should be twice that length.

Braiding with leather or latigo thongs will be slightly different than with rawhide. With leather thongs, braid the middle part of your closed reins as shown in Fig. 1, starting braid at A and finishing B. Then braid the two sections from A to C and from B to D. This break may be wrapped tightly with waxed twine and then covered with a braided knot (Fig. 2).

Open reins may be braided in the same manner. The approximate length of these is 7 feet.

Rawhide reins usually are braided in their entirety. That is, there is no break in the braid. If the completed reins are to be 9 feet long, use eight 1/8-inch strings, each 18 feet in length. No core is necessary. Use the eight-string braid shown in Plate 47.

Rawhide reins are shown in Fig. 3. Turn back each end to form a loop about one inch long. Lash down the ends and cover this part with the Cowboy Knot shown in Plate 59.

You may scatter as many knots along the lower ends of these reins as you desire. But be sure you have the same number and same kinds on each side. Larger knots may be the cowboy knot (Plate 59) or the pineapple knot (Plate 50); smaller ones, the ring knot (Plate 161); or the bosal side-button knot (Plate 49).

In Fig. 4 is shown the way they can be placed. In the old days when horsemen used a "Spade Bit" or a heavy "Mexican Bit," these knots served a purpose. They covered weights for balancing such bits—wicked instruments in unpracticed hands.

In either the leather or rawhide reins a braid-covered ring (Plate 52) about one inch in outside diameter can be enclosed in the loops on the ends of the reins. Chains are then used to connect the reins to the bit. Such chains prevent a horse from working the reins' ends around to his mouth and chewing on them.

However, a rein-bit fastener can be made from a leather or rawhide strap (Fig. 5). The button knot on the end of the strap is made by

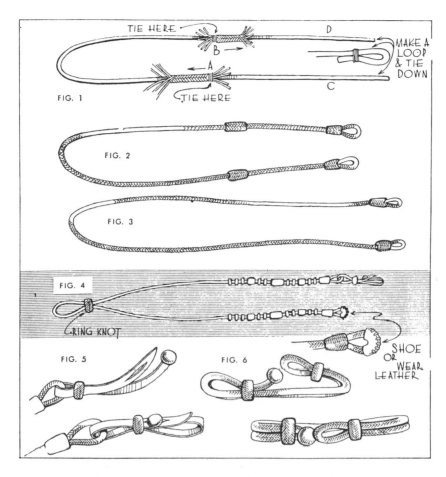

PLATE 57. How to Make a Pair of Braided Reins.

slitting it into four parts and then forming an end knot, as shown in Plate 77. This knot can be covered by a pineapple knot. The "keeper knot" is a ring knot (Plate 161).

A more fancy rein-bit fastener can be made of braided rawhide (Fig. 6). You will, of course, need two such fasteners, and each should be braided 9 inches long. This braid is then doubled, the ends braided into a single knot (Figs. 9-12, Plate 78), and then covered with the pineapple knot. Now place two ring knots on each fastener, as shown.

Loops on the ends of the reins can be fitted with wear-leathers or shoes. This is illustrated in Fig. 4. Such a wear-leather is the same as that detailed in Plate 77.

151

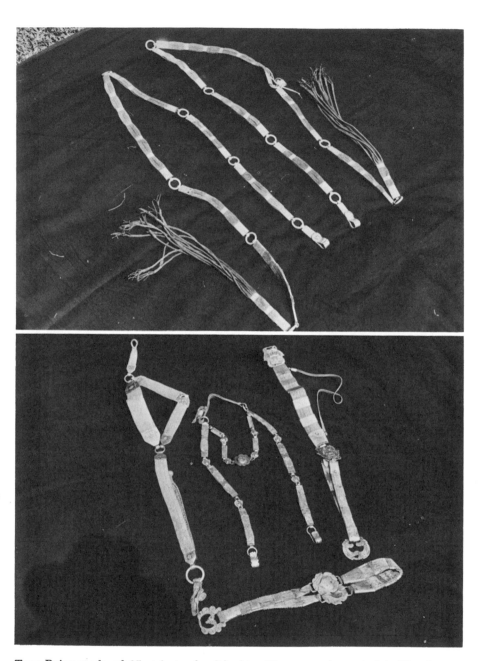

Top: Reins made of 65 strings of colt's skin. They were presented to Maguire as a wedding present in 1940 by a famous collector, A. Barreto. *Bottom:* Three *fiadores* (collars) and one headstall (center) of braided rawhide. Collection of John W. Maguire.

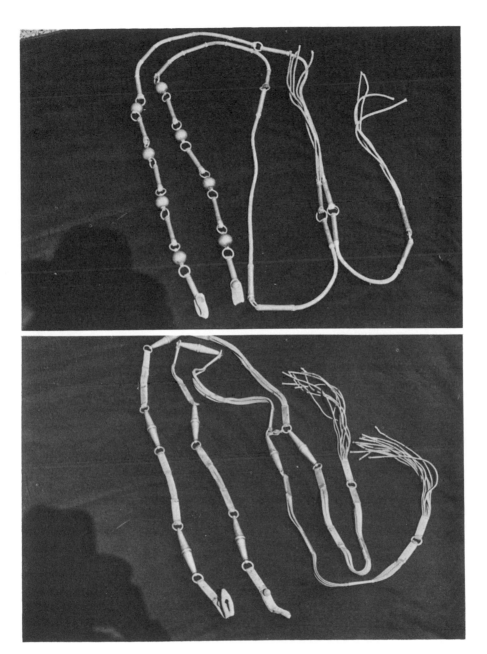

Top: Braided rawhide reins with silver ornaments. *Bottom:* Pair of reins of 75 strings with silver ornaments; made in 1845 for Colonel Martín Santa Coloma of the Rosas Army, Argentina. Collection of John Walter Maguire, Buenos Aires, Argentina.

153

PLATE 58

How to Secure Rein Knots. Small knots which are made on braided reins and braided quirts are spaced an exact distance apart and they should remain that way during the life of the article. However, when such knots are made with one string, it is difficult to keep them in place, however tightly they may be braided.

In Fig. 1 is shown the start of a simple knot made on a four-string round braid. As can be seen, the standing parts of the strings are first inserted beneath the braid. The working ends of the strings are crowned clockwise, as indicated by the arrowlines.

In Fig. 2, the strings are crowned in reverse, as shown by the arrowlines. Next, in Fig. 3, the two working ends, A and B, pass under two, and in Fig. 4, have passed over two and now upward under two. The knot is completed. The ends are cut off. This knot will not slip.

In Fig. 6 is shown the beginning of the same knot on an eight-string braid. Four strings are used here, but the sequence of each string is the same as that of the previous knot.

A knot of the "head-hunter" variety is shown in the next sequence. The braid around which the knot is made is not shown, but the ends are inserted here as before explained.

In Fig. 7, the strings have been crowned. The arrowline shows how string A is brought around and parallel to string B. In Fig. 8, string B is now passed around and over A and under its own part, as shown by the arrowline.

String A passes up over one, under one (not shown).

Next, in Fig. 9, string A passes down under two, over two (one being the standing part B), and under one. String B passes down under two, over two (one being the standing part A) and under one. In the next sequence (not shown) string A passes up over two and under two alongside the standing part A.

This is an attractive knot of over-two, under-two sequence, and, though made of but two strings, it has four bights. The finished knot is shown in Fig. 10.

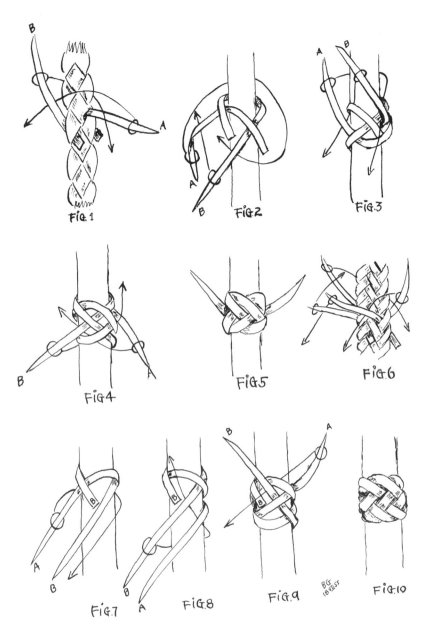

PLATE 58. How to Secure Rein Knots.

155

PLATE 59

The Short Cowboy Knot—Gaucho Weave. Now and then a knot turns up which demonstrates the ingenuity of old-time braiders. Such a knot is the one I have named the "Cowboy Knot." I have never heard it called that; in fact, I have never heard it given any name but "knot," or possibly "multiple-string knot." So, as likewise with many other braids and woven knots, I have taken it upon myself to give this knot a "handle."

The knot can be made with one long string or thong. Plates 167 and 167A show the knot which I have termed. "Double Gaucho Knot of Two Passes."

The advantage of making it with several strings—especially when working with rawhide—is that the braider can work the knot tight from the start and there is little adjustment to be made after it is woven. Then, too, shorter strings being used, there is no need of continually pulling one long string through the knot as the work progresses.

While I have specifically labeled this "The Short Cowboy Knot," it can be made any length. Thus it can be used in fashioning the nose button on a bosal and for many other purposes.

In Fig. 1 the knot is started with four strings or thongs. You may use as many as you like—I have simply used four by way of illustration. These strings are tied down at the standing ends, as shown, the flesh side against the core.

I might add here that more experienced braiders do not tie down these ends. They simply hold them down with the thumb until secured as the braid progresses. The former method, however, is recommended for the beginner.

The next step, indicated by the arrowlines in Fig. 1, is to "crown" all the working ends. This means that each end passes beneath the thong to its left. Thong D passes beneath thong C; thong C beneath thong B; thong B beneath thong A, and thong A passes around the back of the core and to the front under thong D.

The crown is tightened and the tied-down ends are then adjusted so they are evenly spaced around the core. Sequence is the basket weave, or over one, under one. This is shown in Fig. 2.

After the thongs have been passed under one, over one, under one, over one, you spiral or wrap them down for the length you wish the knot. In this case they have been wrapped around once.

In Fig. 3 you start working from the bottom. If you turned the work upside down, you would see that you "crown" the thongs again. If it is held upright, the term is to "wall" them. Anyway, each thong at the bottom passes beneath the one to its left. It is then brought up, over one, under one, until it meets the standing end (the tied-down part). Each thong will systematically come out at the proper place; that is, will join with the proper standing end. By this I mean that it should meet it in such a way that you can parallel it on the right side (Fig. 4).

In Fig. 5, all working ends have been brought to the top and each is on the right-hand side of its standing end. Then, as shown in Fig. 5 by

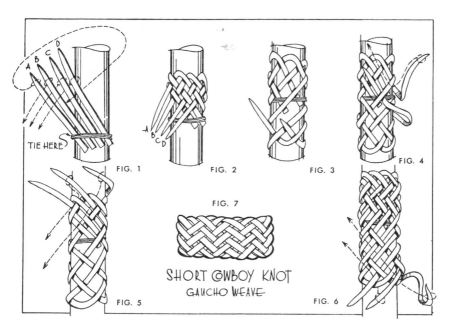

FIG. 1 FIG. 2 FIG. 3 FIG. 4

FIG. 7

SHORT COWBOY KNOT
GAUCHO WEAVE

FIG. 5 FIG. 6

PLATE 59. The Short Cowboy Knot—Gaucho Weave.

the arrowlines, the working end passes down under two. Each working end brought to the top makes this same pass. Parallel thongs, or pairs, are split by the working end as it proceeds downward. Then it begins to follow parallel to the thong on its left to the bottom of the knot.

At the bottom (Fig. 6), each working end is brought up under two at the edge. Working ends are then passed upward in an over-two, under-two sequence, splitting the parallel pairs until they join the over-two, under-two sequence at the top. The knot is now finished. Ends are cut off and tucked. The finished braid is shown in Fig. 7.

This produces a braid where the V's point around the circumference of the knot. I term this a gaucho weave. The herringbone weave, in which V's point toward the ends of the knot is illustrated in same class of knot in Plate 64.

It might be added that a knot one inch long can be made with four 1/8-inch strings each 10 inches long. This would give a finished knot with 13 parts and 8 bights or scallops.

PLATE 60

How to Make the Santa Ines Reins and Romal. A detailed description and drawing of these famous reins and romal was sent to me by Harry Schipman, Jr. of Las Cruces, New Mexico. Mr. Schipman is a well-known artist and writer of western and cowboy lore. He acquired his valuable reins and romal in California some years ago and considers them the *pièces de résistance* of his fine collection, for these beautiful reins and romal truly are collectors' items.

To make the reins take twelve softened rawhide strings and middle them. Then divide them into three parts of four strings each. Start braiding each set of four strings into a four-string round braid for approximately 26 inches. Now introduce a small core and joining all twelve strings into a twelve-string round braid work down for twenty inches. Make a small loop and interbraid or splice the ends into the main twelve-string braid. It might be a good idea before closing the loop to introduce a small metal ring in it so that a chain can be attached to connect with the bit.

Go back to the start and braid three independent four-string round braids for another 26 inches and then over a core join the ends and braid down 20 inches and form the loop on this side. The entire length of the three four-string braids is 56 inches.

The parts where the bit loops are spliced back into the braid are covered with a long woven knot, with two Spanish ring knots, one at each end of the long knot. The other braided knots are scattered along the reins as illustrated in Mr. Schipman's drawings. He says that all types of braided knots known to braiders in California are represented. Under the braided knot section of this book you will find enough variety to suit your tastes. Most of the knots are worked over a foundation to make them stand out.

The romal with lash and loop is 49 inches long. It is joined to the middle of the reins by a braided keeper. Different shades of rawhide can be used for the braided knots.

Should you desire a finer and richer set of reins and romal make the larger braids with 18 strings, say 1/16 of an inch in width. The three braids at the center can be of six strings each.

The length of these reins when closed is less than four feet. Silver chains to connect the reins to the bit usually are used. However, the twelve-string braid on each side can be lengthened twelve or more inches. But chains are more appealing to the California buckaroo.

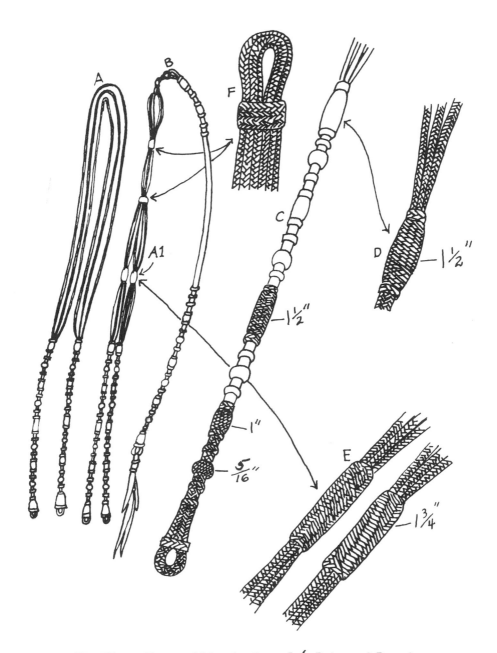

PLATE 60. How to Make the Santa Inés Reins and Romal.

PLATE 61

How to Make a Braided Ear-Head. The ear-head or ear-headstall is a light, serviceable headstall and has long been popular with riders. Ear-heads come in several types, some with a split in the headpiece which allows the headstall to go over both ears of the horse, some with throatlatches, but usually with one slit on the right side for the horse's ear. Most are made of strap leather. Few attempts have been made to braid an ear-head—in fact, I personally have never seen one.

The ear-head presented here is braided throughout and adjustable by woven knots to fit any horse's head. The entire head, with the exception of the two cheek-bit loops to hold the bit rings, is made from one long braided piece. The braid on the ear-head proper and the loops, as well as the weave of the knots, is planned so that a pleasing contrast in design can be obtained throughout.

The first step is to select a core over which the braid will be made. If thin calfskin strings (or thongs) are used, the core can be of braided sashcord 3/16 inch in diameter. If thicker latigo leather is employed, the core should be smaller. Deep-sea fish line is ideal.

This core should measure 11 feet in length. Over it we will use a six-string round braid. Six 1/8-inch strings are tied to the core at one end as shown in Fig. 1, Plate 61. The uneven numbers given the strings are on the left and the even ones on the right. The left strings are all one color—the three on the right are another color. Black and natural color are good combinations. So-called Indian tan and yellow latigo give a pleasing effect.

In tying your strings (or thongs) see that string No. 5 on the left is tied over No. 6 on the right. The braid begins by bringing No. 2 on the right side around the back and then forward under strings Nos. 1 and 3 and over No. 5 (Fig. 1). Next carry No. 1 around back to the right and under No. 4 and over Nos. 6 and 2. This is the sequence of the braid throughout. Strings on the left are carried around back and then under one and over two. Those on the right are carried around back and then under two and over one. The completed braid is shown in Fig. 7.

There is a shrinkage of at least a third in your strings in braiding. Braid to cover a core 11 feet long would require strings of 16 feet in length. Splicing of the strings may be necessary. This is done by beveling one string on the hair side and the added string on the flesh side. The strings are cemented together with a good adhesive. I find a casein glue very good for this purpose. One under the trade name of "Elmer's Glue" will cement latigo. The bevels on the strings should be long and the spliced part should be made so that in continuing the braid it will fall beneath one or more other strings.

When your braid is complete, a tassel of "frill" is fastened to each end. Cut your leather as shown in Fig. 8, then wrap around the end of the braid and sew on securely. A woven button knot to be detailed later will be placed over this sewn part.

The cheek-bit loop—you will need two—is shown in Figs. 14-15. The same braid as that on the ear-head proper is made over the same size

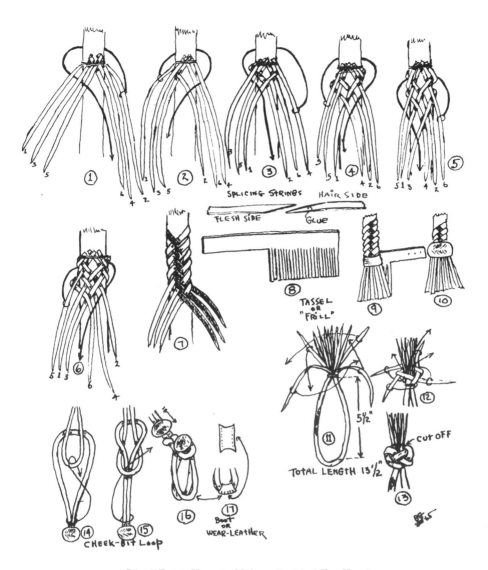

PLATE 61. How to Make a Braided Ear-Head.

core. The core in this instance should be 13½ inches in length. In tying your strings to one end of the core, leave at least five inches above and in finishing the braid, leave another five inches at the end. The braided section is then tied together as shown in Fig. 11, forming a bight of some 5½ inches, with your unbraided strings above the tie. Select two from each braided portion and tie these in the foundation knot shown in Figs. 11-13. The remaining eight strings in the center are cut off flush above the knot. Over this foundation knot will be woven a button knot to be demonstrated later.

161

PLATE 62

Method of Building an Ear-Head from 11-foot Braided Rope (Figs. 1-3). Tie a square knot (be certain it is not a granny knot) as shown, leaving a bight 40 inches long above (or below, whichever is convenient in tying). The next step is to grasp this bight in the middle and bring it down in *front* of your square knot, forming two bights on either side. These two bights form the cheekpieces and the remainder of the braided rope forms the throatlatch. Here it would be well to temporarily tie up the ear-head at the places where the woven knots will be formed—shown in Fig. 3. Tease out a portion of the rope, A, to form the loop which goes over the horse's right ear. Even up the other sections and by adjustment you can give your horse a preliminary fitting.

All that remains now is to weave your 13 knots. I have selected the pineapple knot for this purpose (see Pineapple Knot). It is one of the best and most versatile of woven knots and the weave can be increased to cover any circumference, while the ends can be drawn to fit snugly over any cylindrical object. By using a contrasting color in your interweave you can follow the pattern in your ear-head braid. The larger knots should be made with 1/8-inch strings and the smaller with 3/16-inch strings. With the exception of the ends of the cheek-bit loops and the ends of the throatlatch, these knots should be made over a collar of strap leather sewed in a cylinder around your ear-head braid with the skin side of the leather inside. Draw the collar tight enough so that it can be slipped, but not slip of its own accord.

All that remains now is to place the cheek-bit loops—Figs. 14-17, Plate 61. Both should have a boot or wear-leather, preferably made of rawhide. Reins can be made with the same braid as that of the ear-head.

How to Make a Headstall of One Long Braid. This interesting braided headstall is patterned after one made for me by Don Alfredo Guraya, Carcarana, Province of Santa Fe, Argentina, a superior braider and true gaucho. Using a four-string or four-thong round braid work it into fifteen and one-half feet in length. Drive nails into a board as shown in Fig. 4, Plate 62 and starting with the section marked A, wrap the braid around the nails. The sections are marked from A to N. The measurements of each section are given in Fig. 4. Next where the nails are placed tie the braids together and cover with woven knots as in Fig. 7. In the cheekpieces and browband the braids are separated and after working a braided knot on a doubled piece of rawhide and leather (Fig. 5), introduce the ends through the braid. Work two braided knots as shown in Fig. 6 to hold these interior knots in place. The crown is formed by a piece of soft leather or rawhide as shown at the top of Fig. 7. The finished headstall is illustrated in Fig. 7.

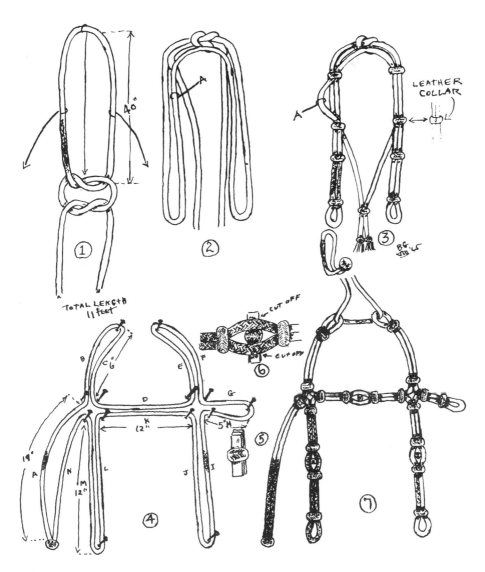

Labels within the figure:

40"

A

LEATHER COLLAR

L

A

① ② ③ BG VIII 65

TOTAL LENGTH 11 feet

B
C 6"
D
E
F
G
19"
A
N
M
12"
L
J
I
K
12"
5" H
④ ⑤

CUT OFF
CUT OFF
⑥

⑦

PLATE 62. Method of Building Ear-Head from 11-foot Braided Rope (Figs. 1-3);
How to Make a Headstall of One Long Braid.

163

PLATE 63

How to Make a Braided Romal. The *romal*—ramal, or romel, as it is sometimes written—is a long flexible quirt or whip attached to the saddle-end of closed reins. This romal is about 3 feet in length with a lash of 10 inches or more.

In Fig. 1 is shown a fancy romal, with knots scattered along its lower end, and a braided lash. This is a type made by John Conrad, of Bellflower, California. It may be made without the decorative knots and braided lash, its utility value being thus unaffected.

To make the romal, take four 1/8-inch-wide rawhide strings, each 12 feet long. Middle them and at this point work them into a four-string round braid (Plate 86), sufficient for the loop shown at the top of the romal. Now bring the eight strings together and braid them down in an 8-string braid without core (Plate 47) for 3 feet 6 inches. This will give you enough at the bottom for turning braid back to form an eye or loop. Braid is lashed down where the eye is formed and this part covered with a woven knot.

You have a variety of woven knots from which to choose in decorating your romal. In Plate 64 is shown the cowboy button knot, which may be used for the longer knots at the top and bottom of the romal and that in the center of the other knots along its lower end. The braided lash is detailed in Plate 65.

To attach the romal to the reins you can use either of the two types of fastenings shown in Figs. 2 or 3. The one in Fig. 2 is illustrated more fully in Plate 57.

In Fig. 3 the fastening is made directly on the end of the romal. A short length is braided and a button worked on the end. This is lashed to the end of the romal as shown. The loop for the button is made by turning back the end of the romal and lashing it down; then covering it with a woven knot. However, in an eight-string braid, you can make two four-string braids into the button and loop ends.

If a D-ring fastening is desired, it can be made as shown in Fig. 4. Here the D-ring is slipped through a strap lashed to the braided end of the romal. It is shown stitched down in the illustration, but it is better to bring the end back and lash it down on the romal end, covering it, of course, with a woven knot. Types shown in Figs. 3 and 4 are used by Duff Severe of Pendleton, Oregon.

In Fig. 5 is shown a romal sent me by Tom Dorrance, of Joseph, Oregon. The handle is made of a round piece of wood, 6½ inches long and 7/8 inch in diameter. A hole is bored up in its lower end into which the braid is slipped and secured by pegs or nails driven in crosswise. Handle is covered with a long woven knot. This may be the cowboy button knot with pineapple-knot weave, as explained in the text with Plate 64. Such a braid will close on the top of the handle. Or you may use the lone star knot, shown in Plate 86.

Near the top of the handle a hole is bored through. Braid on the handle is pushed aside and a wrist loop of four-string braid is passed

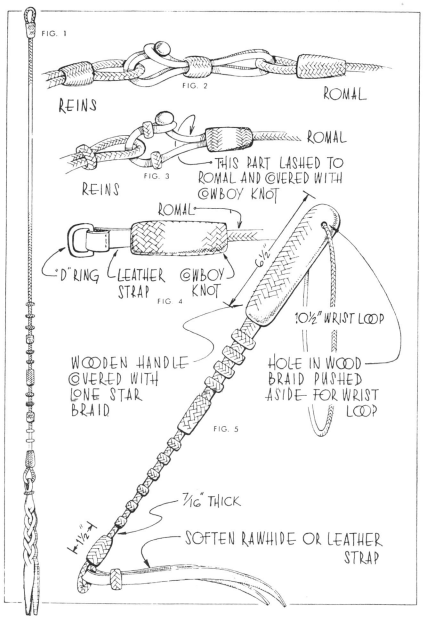

FIG. 1

FIG. 2

REINS

ROMAL

FIG. 3

REINS

ROMAL

THIS PART LASHED TO
ROMAL AND COVERED WITH
COWBOY KNOT

ROMAL

D" RING   LEATHER   COWBOY
STRAP   KNOT

FIG. 4

6½"

10½" WRIST LOOP

WOODEN HANDLE
COVERED WITH
LONE STAR
BRAID

HOLE IN WOOD
BRAID PUSHED
ASIDE FOR WRIST
LOOP

FIG. 5

7/16" THICK

1½"

SOFTEN RAWHIDE OR LEATHER
STRAP

PLATE 63. How to Make a Braided Romal.

through it. The place where the ends of the braid are tied together is worked into the hole.

This romal has a slight taper. The body is made of a twelve-string braid (see text with Plate 47). In this case your strings are cut to a taper. At the bottom, the braid is turned back to make a loop or eye. The lash is either leather or softened rawhide.

PLATE 64

How to Make the Cowboy Button Knot. This is a knot similar to that shown in Plate 59, but here the weave is the "herringbone" instead of the "gaucho." It may be made any length desired and may be used for the nose button on a bosal, as well as for many other purposes.

In the illustrations, I have used four strings to show how this knot is made. More strings may be used if desired. Just follow the same sequence as shown in the drawings.

And this brings up an important point. I have been asked on numerous occasions just how one figures out the width and number of strings required to cover a certain circumference with a woven knot.

Let us take this knot with four strings. When the knot is completed it will have eight bights or scallops at both top and bottom. We will consider only those at the top. A bight or scallop means that both ends of the string are used for braiding. This would give us a braid of sixteen strings. So we can apply the same simple principle to this as we do to round braids (Plate 46).

Thus, if the part you want to cover with a braided knot is 2 inches in circumference and you are using a sixteen-string braid, this would mean that each string or thong should be 1/8 inch wide. There are sixteen 1/8 inches in 2 inches. If the core were one inch in circumference, you would use 1/16-inch strings.

However, where there is an over-two, under-two sequence, you have considerable leeway and do not have to figure exactly. The knot will adjust itself satisfactorily to somewhat larger or smaller circumferences.

Beginning with Fig. 1, the strings are spiraled around the core as shown. The standing ends may be tied down, but, as I explained in the previous cowboy knot (Plate 59), most workers simply hold them in place with the thumb until they are covered with the braid. Better tie them down.

String No. 4 passes down over No. 3 and under No. 2. String No. 3 passes over No. 2 and under No. 1. String No. 2 will pass over No. 1 and under No. 4. String No. 1 passes around in back and over No. 4 and under No. 3. This can better be seen in Fig. 2.

The weave is carried down as in Fig. 3 and then in Fig. 4 the working ends are spiraled around the core approximately the length of the braid desired.

The same sequence is followed at the bottom as at the top. Working ends are passed upward over one and under one (Fig. 4).

Braid is carried upward until the working ends join with the standing ends. It will be seen in Fig. 5 that String No. 1 comes up alongside the RIGHT of the standing end of No. 4. String No. 4 is to the RIGHT of standing end No. 3, and so on.

Working ends pass to the top, parallel to the strings on their left. In Fig. 6, the working ends pass beneath the crossed strings at the top, as shown.

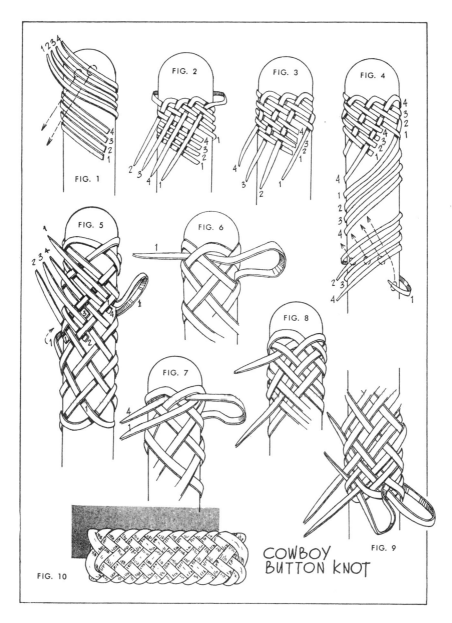

FIG. 1
FIG. 2
FIG. 3
FIG. 4
FIG. 5
FIG. 6
FIG. 7
FIG. 8
FIG. 9

COWBOY
BUTTON KNOT

FIG. 10

PLATE 64. How to Make the Cowboy Button Knot.

Follow the sequence illustrated in Figs. 7 and 8. At the bottom, the working ends pass over three strings and go upward again, splitting parallel pairs (Fig. 9). This is continued until they come out at the beginning of the herringbone braid at the top, where they are cut off and tucked in.

The finished knot is shown in Fig. 10.

167

This knot can also be made with a pineapple-knot braid by bringing the working end up the *left* side of the standing part and then passing beneath the crossed strings, as shown in Plate 50. The pineapple braid will close at the top and bottom and so is the best for covering the tops of quirt handles.

There are, of course, several other ways to make such knots where more than one string is used. Each old-timer appears to have his own particular method. The end result is the same, but the manner of arriving at this end result is different. One such method consists of actually braiding on the skeleton knot and then interweaving. For instance, four strings are secured on the part to be covered. These are braided down, over one, under one, in a four-string round braid The strings are then crowned and worked upward, each alongside of its nearest string. The top strings are crowned and in working downward each splits a pair of parallel strings. This produces in the end the same knot before described.

Author demonstrating to Martín Gómez, famous Argentine braider, how to make a typical American cowboy knot.

168

PLATE 65

How to Make a Braided Lash for the Romal. If you wish a fancy braided *lash* for your romal take a strip of rawhide—or a piece of strap leather—24 inches long and ¾ inch wide. If rawhide is used, soften it before you start braiding.

Braid to be used is that known as the "Trick Braid," or "Inside Braid." It is a puzzle to many. On seeing it for the first time, it is hard to believe the braid can be made without its working ends being free. It is often used on belts and wrist loops for quirts or riding crops.

Mark the middle of strip and measure off 1½ inches each way from this center. At these points slit the strip into three ¼-inch parts, cutting down on each side for about 6 inches. This is shown in Fig. 1.

Place the two slit parts of the strip together, the flesh sides together, as in Fig. 2.

In Fig. 3, beginning of the inside braid is shown. However, for simplicity, only one side of the rawhide strip is shown. In actual braiding, you braid both sides together at the same time.

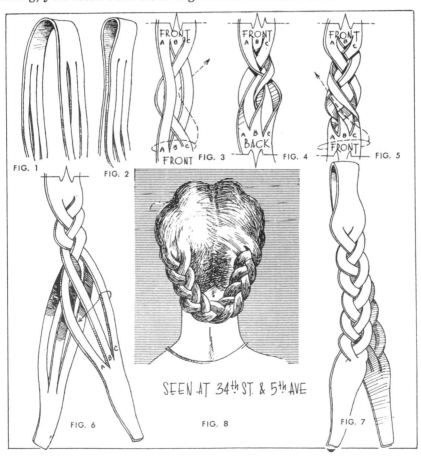

PLATE 65. How to Make a Braided Lash for the Romal.

Starting with the right-hand thong (or *thongs*, as you will be braiding two at once) marked C, place its bight over the center thong (B); then bring the bight of the left-hand thong (A) over C. It will be noticed that a reverse or compensating braid is formed at the bottom. This bottom braid must be raveled out, while the top part is to remain as it is.

To make this bottom braid disappear, pass the entire bottom end of the strip through the opening indicated in Fig. 2. This will twist and tangle the thongs as shown in Fig. 4, but do not mind this. Back part of the strip will be forward and should now be twisted from left to right until the front side is foremost (Fig. 5).

After this twist, be sure that thong B is over thong A, and thong C over thong B, as shown in Fig. 5. Now pass the lower end up and through the opening, as shown in Fig. 5. Braid will appear as in Fig. 6. Both parts are shown here braided together.

From this point you start braiding each strip independently. First step is shown by the arrowline in Fig. 6. Refer back to Fig. 3 and continue through Fig. 5. Turn the work over and braid the other strip in the same fashion.

The finished lash is shown in Fig. 7. The ends are tapered and top part of the lash also is tapered. In working this through the loop in the end of the romal, you either make your loop after braiding on your lash, or slip it in position through the loop before you start braiding.

You will notice, in looking at the romal in Plate 63, that a Turk's-head or ring knot is worked over the upper end of the lash to make it fit snug on the loop. This is mainly for decoration, however, as the double braid in your lash will hold it on the romal loop.

In Plate 65, Fig. 8 is shown a curious example of feminine hairdressing. I have been able to work out many types of intricate braids, but must admit that for once I am stumped. I cannot figure this one out—but, of course, there are a lot of things about women's gear which have always been a puzzle to the male species.

After seeing the picture of the girl whose hair was done in back with a trick inside braid, C. W. Halliday, of West Australia, wrote me that as a young man he had seen an old Afghan of Afghanistan with his chin whiskers and mustache braided together in a similar fashion. He sent a rough sketch (see drawing below).

170

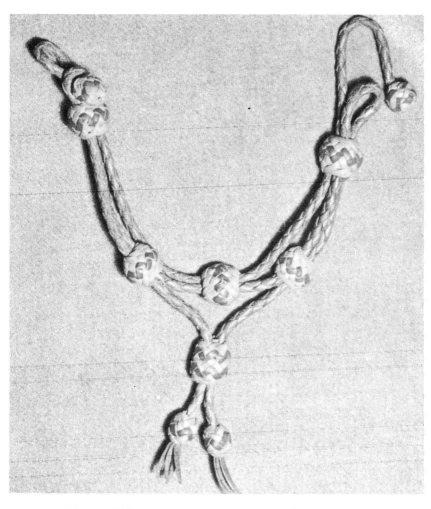

Braided rawhide curb strap made by author from design sent by
Joe De Yong, Hollywood, California. (See Plate 66).

PLATE 66

How to Make a Braided Curb-Strap. One of the finest examples of the braider's art I ever encountered was a beautiful rawhide "curb-strap" in the form of an excellent pen-and-ink drawing sent me by Joe De Yong, artist and writer, who had found it in Arizona. From this drawing I could see the strap as well as if I held it in my hand.

Joe De Yong, friend of the late Will Rogers, and protege of Charles Marion Russell, the cowboy artist, had been scouting for authentic western horse gear in connection with a movie. Joe has been technical adviser for many famous western movies.

The braided curb-strap, shown in Fig. 1, is a tricky bit of gear that is completely adjustable by means of a series of woven knots.

At first glance it is hard to determine just how it is put together; but the strap is fairly simple, once you have studied it. Its simplicity makes it all the more artistic.

I made up this strap from two 15-inch lengths of eight-string braid (Plate 47). The rawhide strings were 3/32 inch in width. On each end of the braid I first worked a foundation knot, as for the San Juan honda shown in Plate 78. These foundation knots were covered with small pineapple knots (Plate 50).

It will be seen that the braid A terminates in an end button at the upper right and lower left. At the upper left it forms a loop. Braid B terminates in an end button at the upper left and the lower right. At the upper right it forms a loop. The two braids cross under the woven knot in the upper center.

After making your two lengths of braid, tie them together at the points where the woven knots will be. Then use whatever decorative knots you wish. I used the pineapple knot in all cases. First I placed a small ring knot (Plate 16) on the braid and covered this with a pineapple knot.

This curb-strap when closed should measure about 10 inches in length. It is used, of course, with either the American or Mexican curb-bit and goes well with a braided headstall and reins.

Another type, termed a Mexican controller bit-curb, is shown in Figs. 2 and 3. In the center of the strap is a rawhide braided knot which works against the tender part of the horse's chin, thus making its use highly effective. The strap is of latigo, fastened with buckles. Details and measurements are shown in Figs. 2 and 3.

The rawhide knot is made of ¼-inch strings. It is hardened by several coats of lacquer or varnish. Several types of knots may be used, but the pineapple is the best. Make it over a foundation such as the ring knot.

172

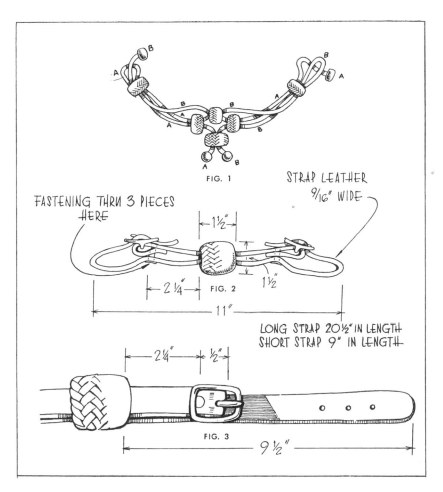

FIG. 1

STRAP LEATHER
9/16" WIDE

FASTENING THRU 3 PIECES
HERE

1½"

2¼"   FIG. 2   1½"

11"

LONG STRAP 20½" IN LENGTH
SHORT STRAP 9" IN LENGTH

2¼"   ½"

FIG. 3   9½"

PLATE 66. How to Make a Braided Curb-Strap.

PLATE 67

How to Make a Running Martingale. There are two types of martingales—the running and the standing. Here we deal with the running martingale which consists primarily of three pieces: the reins piece which has two rings through which the reins pass; the neckpiece, the belly piece. A braid-covered ring holds all the other pieces together. This is made as in Figs. 1-3. Take an iron ring with an inside diameter of two inches, and after crowning two pieces of leather or softened rawhide thong or string as in Fig. 1, place the ring in the position indicated in Fig. 2 and begin wrapping the ends as shown. After each end is wrapped around the ring it is brought up through the center knot and braided into a terminal knot, Fig. 3.

Start independent braids of four-string round on two rings about 1½ inch inside diameter (Fig. 4). After braiding each down thirteen inches join the braids into an eight-string flat braid (Fig. 5). Braid for six more inches, then divide the braid into two four-string flat braids for about an inch, join again and bring the loose ends over and around the braided ring, through the braided slot and tie in a terminal knot, Figs. 5, 6, and 7. This completes the reins piece.

The neckpiece or neck strap is in two sections. First middle your strings and braid a four-string round braid into a loop, join the braids into an eight-string flat and braid for 18 inches and fasten to the ring as in Fig. 7. The other section with the adjustable knots is started as eight-string round braid for several inches and then woven into an eight-string flat braid for 39 inches and also fastened to the ring. The belly piece attaches to the girth or cincha of the saddle and is started at the loop end, using adjustable knots that can be lengthened or shortened. Terminal knots may be covered with fancier braided knots and sliding knots can be Spanish ring knots or other braided knots over a collar.

How to Make a Standing Martingale. This is made in the same manner as the preceding one, except instead of a rein piece there is a piece of about 23 inches that leads to the noseband.

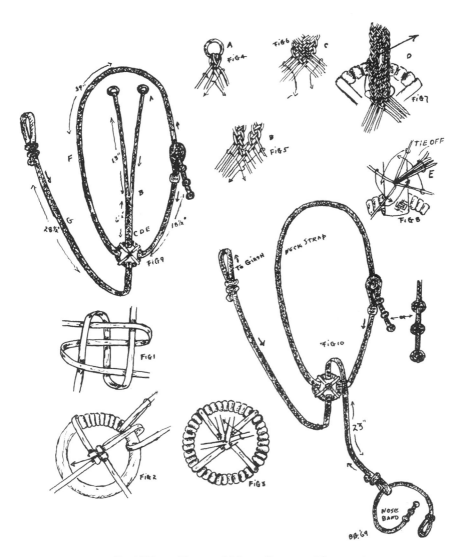

PLATE 67. How to Make a Running Martingale.

PLATE 68

How to Make a Multiple-Ring Button. More than one ring can be used to make the ring button. In Fig. 1 two rings are used, a smaller one inside a larger one.

The strings are first crowned as previously shown. In Fig. 1 the braid is started from the center to the outer ring, wound around in a clockwise direction, brought inward to the middle ring and wound in an anticlockwise direction. The strings should be close together. In the drawings they are separated sufficiently so the sequences can be clearly illustrated.

Each string, after completing its anticlockwise turns about the inner ring, is brought up through the center knot (Fig. 1).

In Fig. 2 a different start is given. Here the string first makes a turn about the inner ring and then goes about the outer ring as shown. This method provides more support for the inner ring which is skipped in the first pass in Fig. 1.

Figures 3 and 4 show the method of braiding a three-ring button. In Fig. 3 the first pass is to the outer ring. In Fig. 4 the first pass encircles all three rings. In Fig. 5 is shown how the two-ring button can be employed as a decoration on a belt.

How to Make a Ski-Pole Basket. The braided ring button can be used to form a ski-pole basket of rawhide. The materials needed are a ski pole, a 5½-inch aluminum ring, as well as two strips of rawhide, ½ inch wide and four feet long.

The two rawhide strips are first middled and laid along the pole a few inches where the button is to be and braided down in a four-string round braid. The aluminum ring is then positioned and the ring button made as previously explained. The strings (after passing through the center alongside the pole) are then brought upward and worked into a

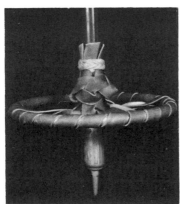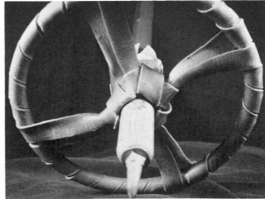

Left: Side view of basket showing ends held by Spanish ring knot. *Right:* Bottom view of basket.

176

terminal knot. The ends can either be cut off flush, or held with a Spanish ring knot.

The rawhide ring button is varnished before use so that the rawhide will not be affected by dampness.

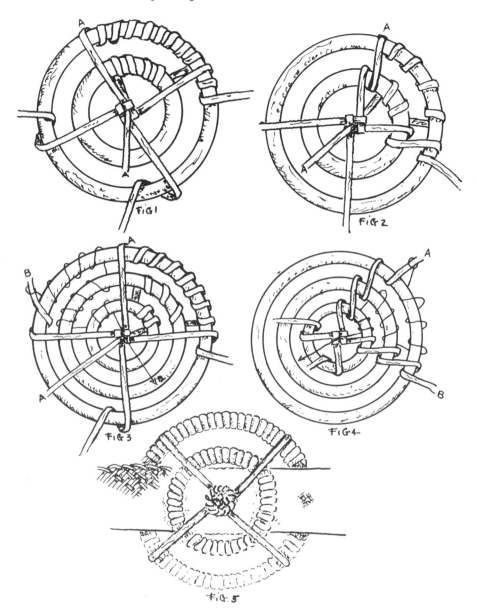

PLATE 68. How to Make a Multiple-Ring Button; How to Make a Ski-Pole Basket.

177

PLATE 69

Uses of the Ring Button. I first saw this braided ring button on a gaucho headstall during a visit to the cattle auction pens of Gibson Brothers of Buenos Aires, Argentina. It was used in this instance as an ordinary button on the throatlatch. Since then I have found many uses for this unique and practical button.

The same button can also be utilized as a drawer pull (Figs. 7 and 8) and as regular buttons on a leather jacket or shirt (Fig. 9).

By using a small ring and very fine thongs or strings in a four-string round braid, it can be worked into cuff links (Figs. 10 and 11). A terminal knot is made on each end of the four-string braid and this is covered by a pineapple knot. The interwoven strings of the pineapple knot can be of a contrasting color.

Figures 12 through 17 show how this ring button can be made with Spanish edge braiding. Two strings are first middled and made into a crown knot as shown in Fig. 12 and tightened as in Fig. 13. Place the ring over the back of this knot, Fig. 14. The first string A is brought underneath the ring and twisted as in Fig. 14. This twisted section is held in place while the edge braiding continues to the right—or clockwise. After the braid covers one-fourth of the circumference, the next string is braided in, as in Fig. 15. When the braid has been made completely around the ring it will be seen how it is finished through the first twisted loop (Fig. 16). After passing through the center knot, all ends are made into a terminal knot and covered with another braid, if desired.

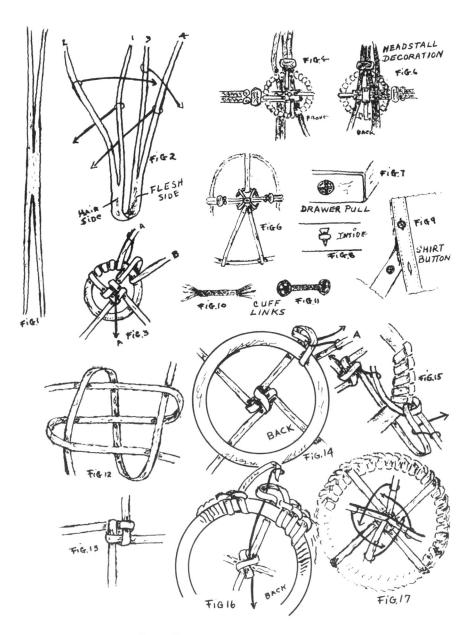

PLATE 69. Uses of the Ring Button.

179

PLATE 70

How to Make a Braided Quirt. The quirt, or short, loaded whip, found hanging from every western saddle horn, is one of those cowboy artifacts that differ according to locality. Various sections of the West have their different types of the whip and a close student of such matters can fairly well tell what part of the country a rider hails from by the quirt he carries.

Like other articles of cowboy gear, the quirt has its origin in Mexico, where they call it *cuarta* (kwar'-tah). Some American cowboys term it a "quisto."

A simple quirt, combining most of the best features of all types, is shown in Fig. 1.

The foundation, or core, is made of tapered strips of rawhide or leather, about 17 inches long, lashed together as shown in Fig. 2. If rawhide is used, dampen it before lashing together, roll it under foot when lashed, and then hang it up to dry, with a weight on its lower end.

Now place over upper end of the core a small piece of rawhide or leather, such as shown in Fig. 3. This is lashed on as in Fig. 5. Next lash on the wrist strap, which can be latigo or other type of leather, or softened rawhide. The strap is shown in Fig. 4 and in process of being lashed on in Fig. 5. Both wrist strap and covering can be lashed on at the same time, using waxed twine and passing beneath alternate ends as shown. Such a type of lashing will clinch them on tight.

Usually the flat part of the wrist strap is at right angles to the edges of the lash at the other end. Remember this in putting on your lash.

In case you wish your quirt handle weighted, insert a short metal bar in its upper end, pushing it down into the core. You may have to cut out some middle sections of the core so that, when the metal bar is in place, the outside diameter does not swell.

Just below the ends of the wrist loop and the covering, lash on eight rawhide strings (or leather thongs if you are working with leather). Combined width of these strings should be equal to the circumference of the core at this point. Use strings twice the length of the finished braid. They should be, in this case, about 34 inches long. Better to have too much than too little. Braid down with the eight-string braid (Plate 46) until the end of the core is reached. Take a look at Fig. 7. Here the two upper strings on either side which are circled, are left as they are. You will not work with them any more. Take the four lower strings and make a four-string round braid (Plate 77). This is illustrated in Fig. 8. Braid down about 3 inches and then fold braid back to form a loop. Tuck the ends into the eight-string braid and lash them down tightly. Cut off all ends flush, including the four that were not used in the four-string braid.

Slip your lash (Fig. 9) through the loop and secure it with a ring knot (Plate 161). Upper and lower parts are covered with the long cowboy knot, shown in Plate 64.

Saddle-soap the entire quirt and, while it is damp, roll it beneath the foot to even the braid.

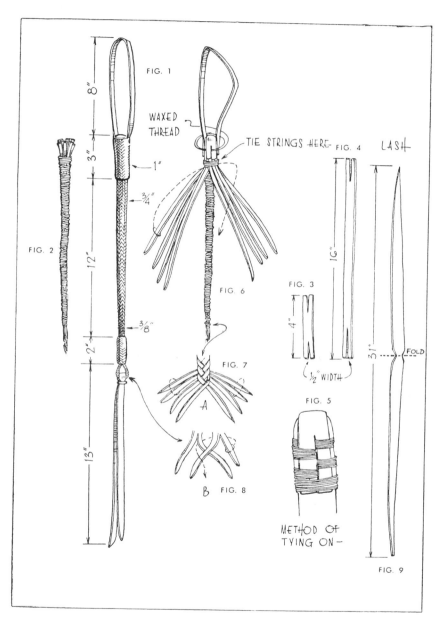

FIG. 1

WAXED THREAD

1"

3/4"

3/8"

FIG. 2

8"

3"

12"

2"

13"

TIE STRINGS HERE

FIG. 4

LASH

FIG. 6

FIG. 7

A

B   FIG. 8

FIG. 3

16"

4"

(½" WIDTH)

FIG. 5

METHOD OF TYING ON—

31"

FOLD

FIG. 9

PLATE 70. How to Make a Braided Quirt.

181

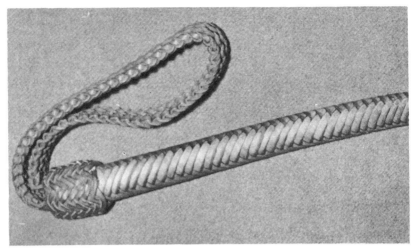

Braided quirt from the Texas-Mexico border, owned by author. Knot on the handle is same type of braid as shown on Arabian knife and Argentine *rebenque.*

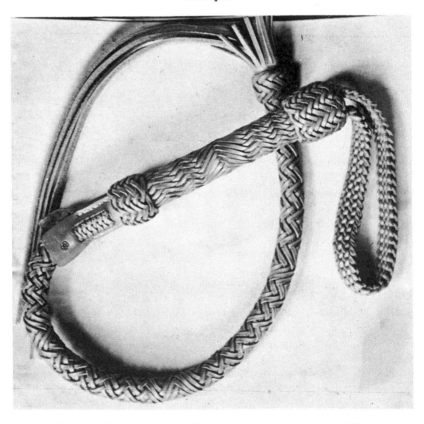

Quirt made by author with an Argentine *rebenque* motif.

Jesse Wilkinson of Paso Robles, California, standing beside an exhibit of some of his beautiful braidwork. Jesse is among the last of the great braiders. He was 72 when this picture was taken and had been doing rawhide braiding for some sixty years. "I can still do it fairly well," he writes modestly. Photograph by Stevens Studios, Paso Robles.

PLATE 71

Another Braided Quirt. The first step is to make the core or filler of the quirt. Take a piece of leather, preferably 8-ounce leather, which is about 1/16 inch in thickness, and cut it as shown in Fig. 1.

Dampen the leather thoroughly and nail the narrow end to a piece of board as shown in Fig. 2. Roll or twist it in a clockwise direction, so that the flesh side is innermost (Fig. 3). This type of twist braid is demonstrated in Plate 5.

When the core has been twisted tightly, stretch it and then nail the wide end to the board and leave it to dry (Fig. 4).

Next, make the wrist strap by braiding together three 1/8-inch thongs (Figs. 6 and 7). Braid tightly, using the method illustrated in Plate 28. Cut the lash, also of 8-ounce leather, with a horizontal slit in the center (Fig. 10).

The core should be completely dry before covering. Cut off the parts through which the nails have been driven. Insert a spike nail in the top (Fig. 5) to stiffen the handle part. Cover this nail top with a small strip of leather, bringing the ends down on the handle, and lash them there. Next, attach the wrist strap, lashing it to the sides of the top of the handle between the ends of the strips which covered the head of the spike nail. Directly below the ends of the wrist strap, lash the six 1/8-inch thongs which will be braided over the entire core (Fig. 8).

The braid for the quirt is the six-thong back braid shown in Plate 41. Carry the braid just a trifle beyond the end of the core at the bottom before starting to braid it back. When the braid is back at the top, lash it down and continue wrapping the twine around the ends of the braid as well as around the ends of the wrist strap, until a bulge is formed for the knob of the handle.

Cover this bulge with a Turk's-head made with ¼-inch thonging, a pattern for which is given in Fig. 12. Insert a sheet of carbon paper underneath this pattern and over a piece of heavy brown paper. Trace the pattern, transferring it to the brown paper. Cut flush at the right-hand side and then roll up the paper so the lines on both ends come together. Place pins in the loops marked with an X. Lay the standing end of the thong at the point marked *starting point*, and hold it there with a light rubber band. Then follow the lines around with the working end, always passing *over* each intersection of thongs except those marked with a *circle* in which case pass *under*.

Remove the Turk's-head from the pattern by withdrawing the pins, and tighten it over the knob on the handle. Dampen the lash, insert the end of the quirt through the slit and then pass the ends down through the center of the braid (Fig. 9) and pull tight.

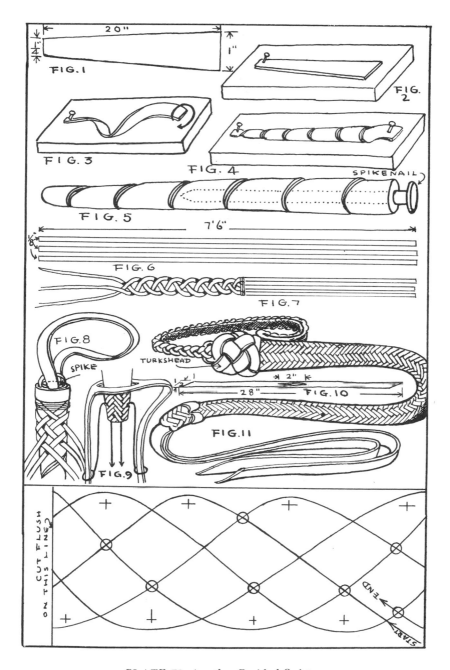

PLATE 71. Another Braided Quirt.

185

PLATE 72

How to Make a Mexican Quirt. This quirt, or *cuarto*, is characteristic of the type made in the Colima district of Mexico. The finished quirt is shown in Fig. 1 and has an overall length including wrist loop and lash of 35 inches.

The core of the handle which measures 11 inches is made from dampened rawhide scraps, tapered and lashed together in a bundle and hung up to dry with a weight on the bottom end. Insert a small round stick through the top as shown in Fig. 2. This is for the wrist loop hole.

Four types of rawhide quirts.

Cut a rawhide strip as shown in Fig. 3 leaving the center portion uncut and with seven strings on each end, both sets about 18 inches each. The dotted line on the uncut portion indicates where the rawhide will be folded inward to form the loop for the lash.

Braiding is started from the bottom (Fig. 4). Place another round stick over the bottom of the core as in Fig. 5. The beginning of the fourteen-string braid is illustrated in Fig. 5 and continued in Figs. 6, 7, and 8. The sequence on each side is over two, under three, and over two on each pass.

Continue this round braid to the very top of the core, tie down with waxed thread or wire, and cut the ends off flush.

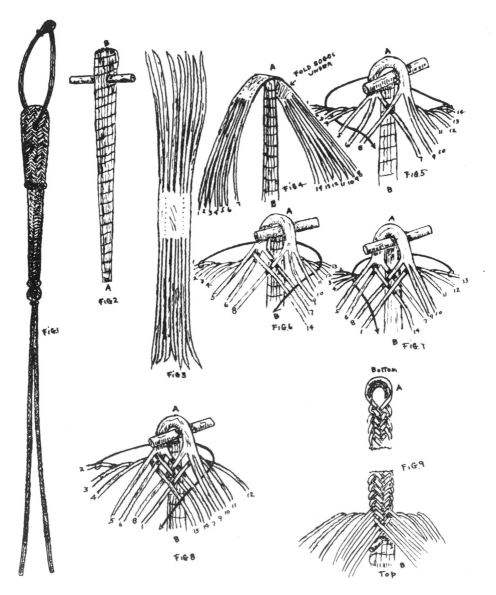

PLATE 72. How to Make a Mexican Quirt.

187

PLATE 73

How to Make a Mexican Quirt (Cont.). The tricky and unique part of this quirt is the handle braid. Take two pieces of thin rawhide and cut each into eight strings 1/8 inch wide. Leave about an inch or more at one end of each piece. Mesh the two pieces, flesh side to flesh side (Fig. 1). Place the meshed strings over the head of the quirt core (Fig. 2). Mold the rawhide down and start the braid as in Fig. 2. After braiding this one section as shown in Fig. 3, braid the strings opposite in the same fashion. Keep your braid tight.

Tie off strings Nos. 5, 6, 7, and 8 on the left and Nos. 9, 10, 11, and 12 on the right. Begin the next step by braiding the strings shown in Fig. 5 in an under-two, over-two sequence. Arrowlines in Figs. 4 and 5 show the course of string No. 13. Figure 6 shows string No. 13 in place and the arrowline indicates where string No. 4 goes. After eight passes, turn the core around and braid those strings which had been tied off. Keep working the braid, section by section, down for about four inches (Fig. 7).

This handle braid covers not only the uncut ends at the top but also is made over the body braid. The ends of the handle braid can be formed into a Spanish ring knot of two or three passes (Plate 161) or tied down and covered with a woven knot.

Next take two one-inch-wide pieces of rawhide, each piece 36 inches long, and cut as shown in Fig. 8. The three-inch uncut end is rolled inward as you make your four-string round braid. Worked damp it will retain its shape when dry. Braid this lash for about 18 inches in a four-string round braid and then change for several inches to a four-string flat braid. The two flat braids are joined or spliced as shown in Fig. 12. This lash is passed through the quirt loop, middled, and the two braided parts are held together with a woven knot as shown in Fig. 1, Plate 72.

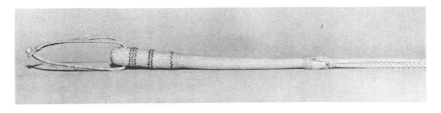

Perfection in rawhide braiding. A Mexican quirt owned by the author braided with 1/32-inch rawhide strings. The black interweaving is done with black horsehair.

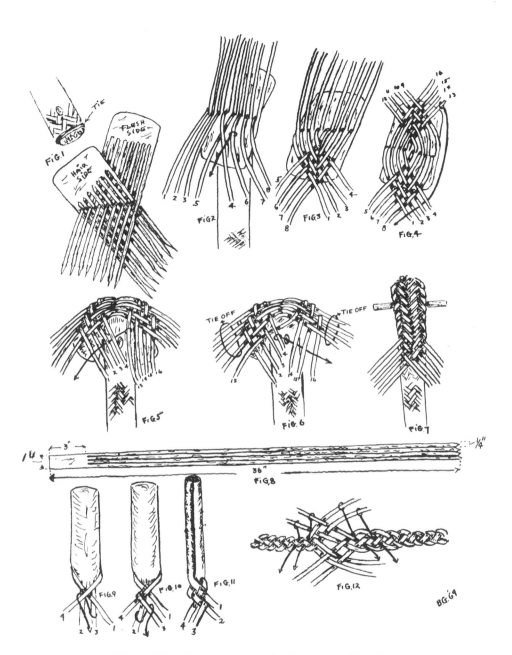

PLATE 73. How to Make a Mexican Quirt (Cont.).

189

PLATE 74

How to Build a Bullwhip. The bullwhip, glorified today by whip artists on the stage, and favored by enthusiasts who like to hear the sharp crack of the popper, by others for decoration, and by some as a utility article, comes in many forms. One major characteristic is a stiff handle. The bullwhip's companion, the blacksnake whip, has a flexible handle, where the braid usually is over a core of small shot sewed in a tapered canvas or buckskin bag.

A good bullwhip properly made does not need a great deal of weight in the middle. The one detailed here is unweighted, but the wooden core handle can be bored out at the top and lead or a piece of metal inserted. The body of this whip is braided over a braided rawhide core—a leather braided core can be used. Rawhide, however, will give weight, balance and "life" to the whip. For an unusual core see the photo on page 123.

Take a round piece of wood, 14 inches long and about ¾ inch in diameter, and rasp it to a taper, as shown in Fig. 1, Plate 74. Make a shoulder 8 inches from the top so that when the rawhide or leather core is placed on, the entire handle has a uniform taper. Cut the core strings from a 4-foot piece of rawhide (or leather) which is the same width at the top as the circumference of handle at that point. Nail it to a board and cut the four strings as shown in Fig. 2.

Tack the core on below the shoulder (Fig. 3), then work on a four-string round braid (Figs. 3 and 4). When the end of the wooden core is reached, insert a leather string or small sash-cord core which is braided around until almost to the lower tip of the whip. No need to fasten the end of this core—just start braiding over it as shown in Fig. 5.

Next cut twelve strings as long as possible, approximately 1/4 inch in width, or with the total width of the strings equal to the circumference at the top of handle. In making this whip the same width string will be used throughout, as it is difficult for many to cut long tapered strings. The taper will be achieved by the trick of dropping two strings at intervals. So that your strings lie snug, it is well to bevel each one on the hair side on one side and the flesh side on the other.

Arrange the strings at the top of the handle and tie them down—six to a side. Start the twelve-string braid as illustrated in Fig. 6. First the upper left-hand string is brought around back and forward, under three and over three. Then the upper right-hand string goes around back and forward, under three and over three (arrowline, Fig. 6).

This twelve-string braid is continued down for about two feet and then two strings are discarded or dropped. In Fig. 7 these strings to be discarded are marked with "X's." Then you go into a ten-string braid (Fig. 8). The sequence is—the right-hand upper string is brought around back and forward under three and over two (also passing over the shortened discarded string on the left marked "X"). Then the upper left-hand string is carried to the rear and forward, under two and over three (also passing over the shortened discarded string marked "X" on the right side (arrowline, Fig. 8). These discarded strings are passed over

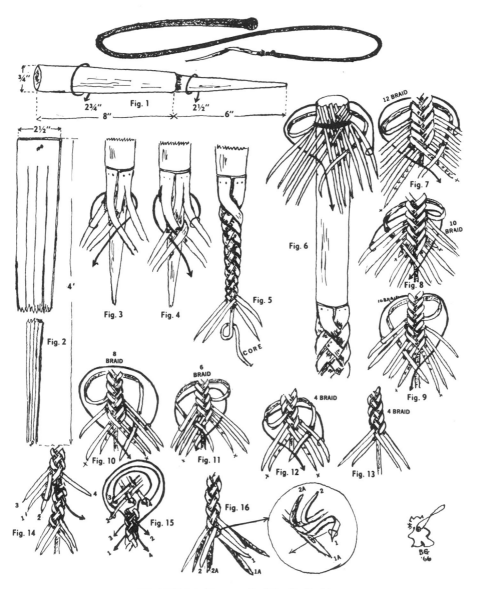

PLATE 74. How to Build a Bullwhip.

each time for several braids until "lost." It might be well to skive or thin their ends.

After braiding for a couple or more feet, two more strings marked "X" in Fig. 9 are shortened and discarded. An eight-string braid is continued as in Fig. 10. Upper strings are carried to the back and forward, under two and over two (Fig. 10). The next strings to be dropped are marked with "X" in Fig. 11. This is the beginning of the six-string braid. Here the sequence is: Right upper string around back

191

and forward, under two and over one (covering, of course, the discarded string). Left upper string around back and forward, under one and over two (covering also the discarded string). The final four-string braid starts in Fig. 12 where the two strings to be dropped are marked "X." The sequence from then on is—upper strings on each side are carried alternately around back and under one and over one (Figs. 12 and 13).

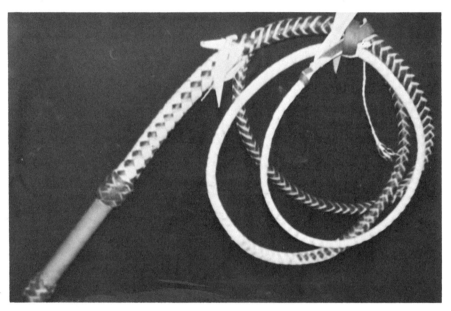

Ten-foot bullwhip with weighted revolving handle, made by J.M. Bucheimer Co.

In Figs. 14 through 16 is shown the method of splicing the braid, if necessary. First make a four-string braid around the core and push it up snug under the original braid. Continue the original braid down, weaving it into the lower braid as shown in Figs. 14 and 15. The strings of the original braid are on top of those of the other. To keep from having too much swell here, it would be well to thin or skive the ends of the strings of the original braid. In Fig. 16, after working down three or four inches, the ends of the original braid are passed through slits in the lower strings and "lost" beneath as the lower braid is continued. Slit each lower string at a point where it will be covered by a string.

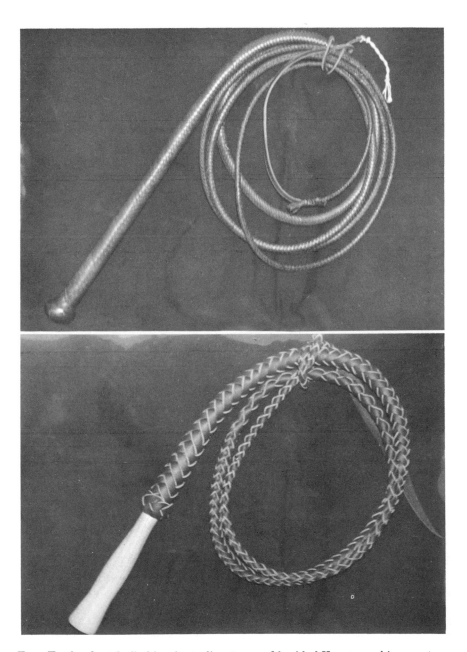

Top: Twelve-foot bullwhip, Australian type, of braided Kangaroo skin, courtesy of D.W. Morgan, Austral Enterprises. *Bottom:* Eight-foot bullwhip made up from a kit sold by the Tandy Leather Company.

193

PLATE 75

The Aztec Button for the Bullwhip. On the left side of Plate 75 is shown the approximate lengths of the different braids. The next step is to make the button for the top of the handle. The "Aztec Button" goes well here as it closes completely on top. Start making it on a mandrel, Fig. 1, Plate 75. Pass the working end around, over the string in front and under in the back. Do this three times (Fig. 3). If a larger knot is required, pass around over and under four, or under and over five or more times.

Fig. 4, going down: under one and over three (in case of four passes, it would be under 1, over 4, etc.). Fig. 5, up: over 1, under 3 (in four passes it would be over 1, under 4, etc.). Fig. 6, down: over 1, under 1, over 3. Fig. 7, up: under 1, over 1, under 3. Fig. 8, down: over 2, under 1, over 3. Fig. 9, up: under 2, over 1, under 3. Fig. 10, down and up: over 3, under 1, over 3 and around (arrowline) under 3 alongside the standing part. The knot is removed from the mandrel and placed over the end of the handle, which has been amply wrapped with string and glued to form a bulge, and then tightened (Fig. 11). The top of the knot looks like the drawing in Fig. 12.

Next secure the cracker or snapper to the end (Fig. 13). The cracker is a half-inch-wide thong, 14 or more inches in length, slit at the upper end (buckskin is ideal). Bring the braid through the slit, then half-hitch one string as shown in Fig. 14. Half-hitch a second string over everything as shown in Fig. 15 and so on until all four strings are

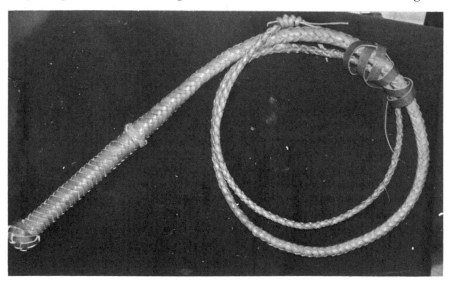

Ten-foot bullwhip made by author of yellow latigo leather over rawhide core. How to make this whip is explained in the text for Plate 74. The small Spanish ring knot on whip shown above is not necessary.

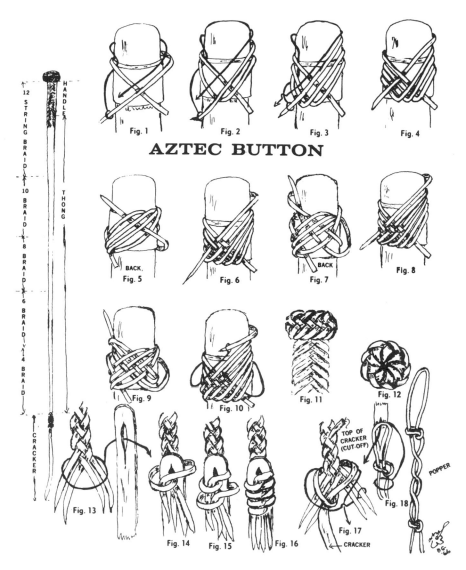

AZTEC BUTTON

PLATE 75. The Aztec Button for the Bullwhip.

hitched on. Another method is to trim the upper part of the snapper to about ¼ inch in width and use it as a core for a short distance, then hitch it over the braid as shown in Fig. 17. Also hitch one or two strings as shown in Fig. 17.

All that remains is to place on the popper a doubled piece of string or nylon cord, made as in Fig. 18. Its upper loop is placed over a slit in the end of the cracker and the end of popper brought through from the rear to the front through the slit. The knot is drawn tight—and the whip is ready for business or noise!

195

PLATE 76

How to Make the Tamale. Anyone who has braided several long strings of rawhide, or another type of thong, is aware that as the work proceeds, the loose ends begin to form into a braid of their own. This reverse braid must be unraveled from time to time and the result is that the strings usually become knotted and tangled.

To avoid this, when working with long strings, braiders usually form them into what is called the *tamale*. This is a coil so fashioned that the braider can draw out from the center the quantity of string needed without destroying the shape of the tamale or causing it to collapse. Use of the tamale circumvents a lot of time and trouble.

There are several ways to make this tamale. Mrs. Mary Fields, wife of Glen (Slim) Fields, of Bonanza, Oregon, has allowed me to demonstrate the method she uses in making the tamale. It might be added that building a reata is all in the day's work for the comely and energetic Mary Fields. Not only that, but she skins her cow, cures her hide, cuts it into strings and braids everything from headstalls to reatas. A fascinating series of pictures show Mary Fields at work on a reata.

"It takes seventy-five feet of string to make fifty feet of rope," she writes. "Don't believe it takes quite the whole seventy-five feet, but I learned a long time ago what happens if you get your string too short!"

She has had much experience with rawhide, and offers a bit of advice: "I never knew there was so much difference in hides until I made a dozen or so ropes. I had been told that the only kind of hide for a rope was a hide from some old cow that just gradually dwindled away. Well, I was frankly dubious about this until I finally got hold of one like that. I could sure tell the difference. It cut up so even and was so waxy and clear looking and braided without stretching. Now I try to get that kind of hides for all my ropes."

Now to make the tamale. Tie one end to a nail, as shown in Fig. 1. Bring the string down over the palm of the left hand, then, by turning the hand over and in the other direction (Fig. 2), the string is brought up the back of the hand. The working part of the string, held in the right hand, is then looped around the standing part, as shown in Fig. 2. Turn the hand again, as in Fig. 3, with the thumb down and double the string across the back of the hand. Continue as in Figs. 4 and 5 until all of the string is used except enough needed to wrap it around the middle of the tamale and tie it, as shown in Fig. 6. The working end, the part secured to the nail at the start, will now feed out as needed.

A second method, which can be used with smaller strings, is also shown.

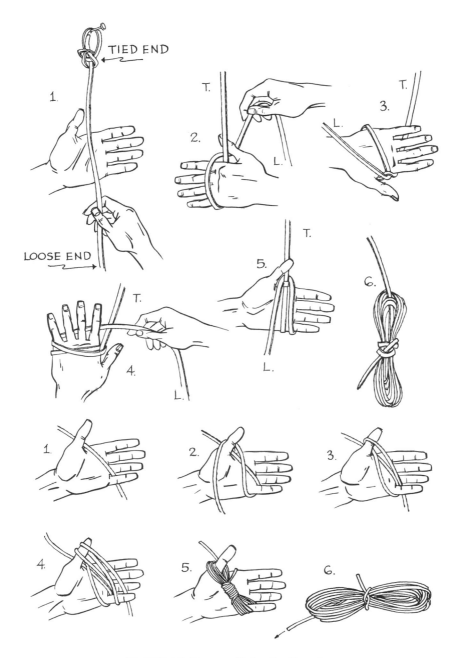

PLATE 76. How to Make the Tamale.

197

PLATE 77

How to Build a Reata or Rawhide Rope. In Mexico the *reata* (ray-ah'-tah) may be of sisal or maguey fiber, or of twisted or braided rawhide. But, in the western section of the United States, *reata* means a braided rawhide rope as distinguished from a fiber rope, It is from "la reata" that the cowboy obtained his word "lariart." Some Mexican slang concerning the *reata* is to be heard along the Border, too. To be *muy reata* is to be valiant, and when a man is called *uno bueno reata*, it means he is a gay dog with the ladies.

The *reata*—sometimes written *riata*—can be made with either a four-string or an eight-string braid (Plate 46). The eight-string is fancier and considered *muy brava*, but it is less satisfactory as a working rope. It is more for show. Reatas are from 40 to 85 feet in length, some even longer. They come in several diameters. The 3/8-inch is called light; the 7/16-inch is termed medium; the ½-inch is heavy; and the 9/16-inch is extra heavy. These diameters are determined by the diameter of the core and thickness of the rawhide strings.

In Fig. 1 we start braiding a four-string reata over a core which is either a long rawhide string or a sash cord. Remember that the total width of the four strings should equal the circumference of the core. The strings should be one-half longer than the finished length of the reata—needless to say, of the best quality rawhide.

Lash the strings around the core as shown in Fig. 1. To start, as shown in Fig. 2, pass string No. 1 around to the rear and back to the front on the right, under string No. 4 and over No. 2. In Fig. 3, string No. 4 is carried around to the rear and to the front on the left, under string No. 3 and over string No. 1. Continue this braiding sequence to the end, keeping your braid snug and tight.

In Fig. 5 is shown one method of finishing off the "bitter end," or the end opposite the honda. The braid is arranged as shown and a slit is made in strings Nos. 4 and 2. No. 1 passes through the slit in No. 4, and No. 3 through the slit in No. 2 (Fig. 6). Then two slits are made in strings Nos. 1 and 4 (Fig. 7). Strings Nos. 2 and 3 are passed through these slits, as shown by the arrowline in Fig. 7 and completed in Fig. 8. Or, after the step in Fig. 6, strings Nos. 1 and 4 and strings Nos. 3 and 2 can be slit-braided by themselves (see Plate 21).

A simple honda can be made by taking a strip of rawhide ¾ inch wide and rolling it together, so that it has an inside diameter of two inches (Fig. 9). After shaping it, punch a hole in the bottom, the hole to be the diameter of the reata braid. Pass end of the reata through as shown in Fig. 9. The four loose ends now are tied in a terminal Turk's-head, as shown in Figs. 9 and 10. The loose ends are cut off flush with the top of the knot (Fig. 11).

The reata should be well saddle-soaped and rolled under foot, or between two heavy boards. Some use melted tallow. It is softened by working it back and forth around a smooth post. Don't spare the elbow grease.

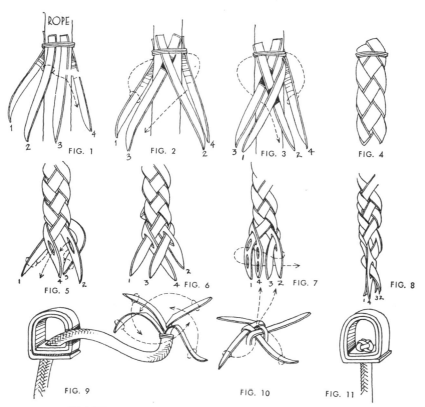

PLATE 77. How to Build a Reata or Rawhide Rope.

Rawhide twisted lariat or, more properly, *reata*. In the center are three types of rawhide hondas for lariats.

PLATE 78

How to Make a San Juan Honda. The *San Juan honda* which was developed in Sonora, Mexico, is a very fancy but practical honda for the reata. It has a replaceable boot, or wear-leather, as will be shown.

The first step in making this honda, or eye on the working end of a reata, is to first middle four ¼-inch-wide rawhide strings, each about 24 inches long.

When they are middled lay them one on top of the other. In Fig. 1 it will be seen that the top string, or string No. 1, passes down through slits in strings Nos. 2, 3, and 4. Then string No. 2 passes down through slits in strings 3, 4, and 1. Next string, No. 3, passes down through strings 4, 1, and 2. In Fig. 2, is seen the flat side of this slit-braid; in Fig. 3, a three-quarters view.

A still more fancy method of making this braid is shown in Fig. 4. The strings are laid one on top of the other as before, but are slit-braided, so that when viewed on the edge (Fig. 6) they will look like a four-string braid. In this braid, string No. 2 first passes down through a slit in string No. 3. Then string No. 3 goes up through a slit in string No. 1; No. 4 through No. 2; No. 1 through No. 4 (Fig. 5). Pass thus until the original top string is on the bottom and the original bottom string on top, and then begin over. The flat side of this braid is shown in Fig. 7.

The next step is shown in Fig. 8. Take a round piece of wood about ½ inch in diameter and wrap the slit-braided part around it. Now work with all eight strings, making an eight-string braid as shown in Plate 47. Braid down about four inches, or enough to form an inside eye of 1½ inches when the working ends are pushed up through the slit-braided eye, as shown in Fig. 9.

Tie together the four center strings as in Fig. 9. Then work the other four into a terminal knot. First *crown* the strings as shown in Fig. 9. Then *wall* them, or pass each string upward alternately (Fig. 10). Each string now is again passed upward through the center, as shown in Fig. 11. All eight strings are cut off flush with the top of the knot (Fig. 12).

You might find it simpler to place on your boot, or wear-leather, before pushing the braid up through the small eye and tying the terminal knot. However, the *boot* is shown in Fig. 13. By cutting it concave on its ends, the part that bends in the inner section of the eye will not buckle.

The boot is pinched together on the outside of the honda, holes are punched through both edges, and it is laced together with a rawhide string. Boot is shown in place in Fig. 14, designated as A. The part B is where the end of the reata is fastened on. Reata is folded around and the four working ends are tucked back into original braid. This is then covered with a woven knot, a suitable one being the cowboy knot in Plate 59.

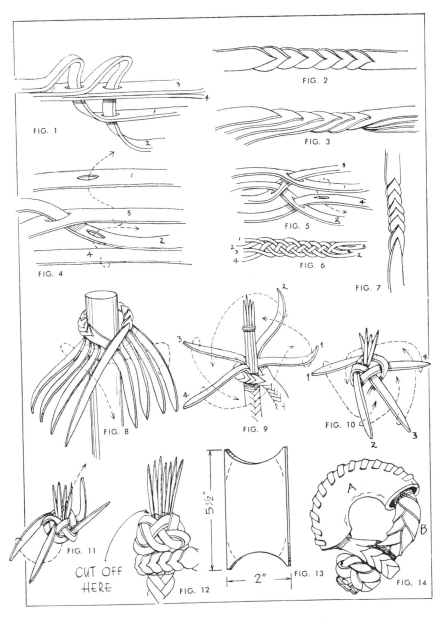

PLATE 78. How to Make a San Juan Honda.

Reatas are built and not made and Mrs. Mary Fields is an expert, from making her own rawhide to braiding the rawhide rope.

The accompanying series of photographs showing the various steps required to build a reata demonstrate the lady's ability.

Top: Shaving off the hair. *Bottom:* Cutting string with a draw gauge.

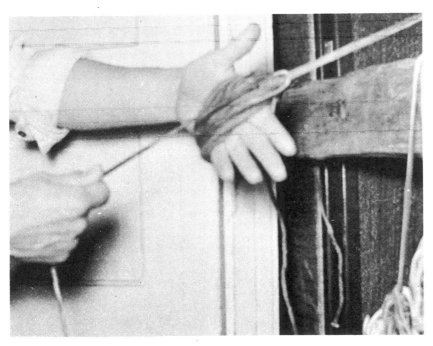

Top: Fleshing—splitting the rawhide string. *Bottom:* Making a tamale.

203

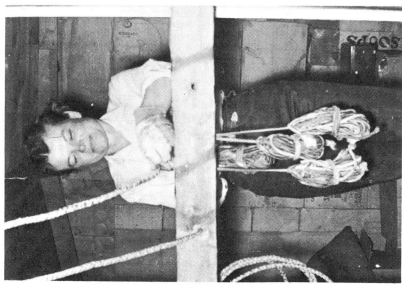

Left: Braiding—the fingers are cut out of the gloves. *Right:* Pulling over the peg.

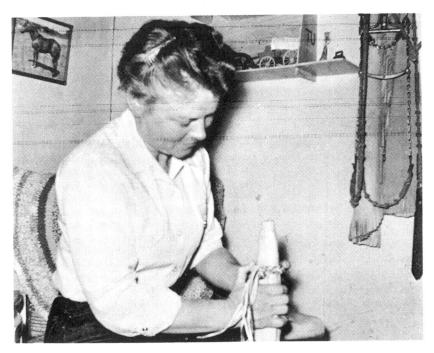

Top: Breaking in the *reata* by pulling it through holes in a post. *Bottom:* Shaping the honda over a stick.

PLATE 79

How to Tie the Reata to the Honda. In Plate 79 is shown one of the methods of securing the reata to the honda. The fastening knot is actually a five-part four-bight Turk's-head, but made with four strings. The same method can be used in making a longer Turk's-head, but the five-part Turk's-head is sufficient.

Leave about 8 inches of the reata unbraided. Place it on the honda, as shown in Fig. 1, so that two strings come up on one side and two on the other.

The strings are now crowned about three-quarters of an inch up from the honda. Crowning means that string A is laid over string B in a counterclockwise direction; string B then is laid over string C; string C is laid over string D, and string D is passed through the bight made in string A.

The result is shown in Fig. 2. Also, in this diagram it will be seen that the arrowline indicates that string A passes over one string (C) and then under string D. In a similar manner, string B passes over string D and under string A. String C passes over string A and under string B. String D passes over string B and under string C.

This sequence is shown in Fig. 3. Now each string passes over one and then completely under the knot to come out at the top. The ends, shown in Fig. 4, may be cut off, or they may be spliced back into the honda for several inches to give the knot more strength.

By referring to the short cowboy knot (Plate 59) and the cowboy button knot (Plate 64), other and fancier sequences can be worked out.

A Brazilian *reata* in the Tinker collection at The Hall of the Horsemen of the Americas, University of Texas.

206

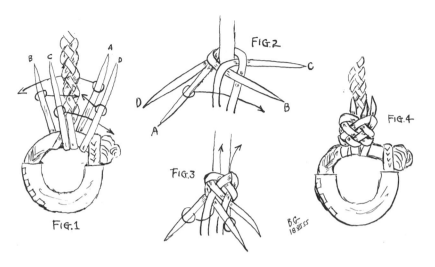

PLATE 79. How to Tie the Reata to the Honda.

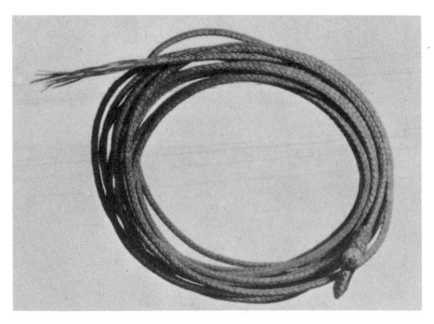

Braided rawhide *reata,* or *lariat,* with San Juan honda, made by John Conrad, Bellflower, California.

PLATE 80

The Saddle-Horn Tie Knot. There is a difference in using the rawhide rope, or *reata*, and the hempen rope. The California buckaroos, who are partial to the rawhide rope, are known as "dally men." The term "dally" comes from the Mexican *dar la vuelta*, "to give a turn." In other words, the dally men turn the bitter end—or end opposite the loop—in a counterclockwise direction several times around the horn of the saddle after throwing the rope. The rawhide rope user "dallies" his rope because a rawhide rope cannot stand the sudden strain when the cow is "busted" on the other end, and by "dallying," the rope is allowed to give or slip a trifle.

The Texan and those of his school who use the hempen or fiber rope, makes the rope fast around the saddle horn and so is termed a "tie-man." Rodeo cowboys are "tie-men," too.

There are various ways of tying a rope to the saddle horn, but Roy Harmon, of Las Cruces, picked up a practical knot for "tying" at the Socorro Rodeo and has passed it along to the author. Roy says this knot was shown him by a rodeo cowboy, Bill Rush, of Lovington, New Mexico.

"The knot is primarily used by rodeo cowboys to fix their rope to the saddle horn in such a manner that it can be easily removed," explains Roy. "It's really a slip knot. The ordinary knot used by cattlemen and working cowboys is tied in the end of the rope and, after heavy stock have been roped and dragged, the knot often tightens so that it is hard to untie. But with this one, the rope can just be slipped off the horn."

To make this knot, take a string or thong of rawhide or latigo, whichever is preferred, about 3/8-inch wide and 24 inches long.

In Fig. 1 is shown the lariat in position to receive the knot. The working area is indicated by the C. Commence the braid as shown, bringing the end of the string marked B around to the front, and then the one marked A around and over B.

In Fig. 2, the string-end A has passed over the string-end B three times in the front and twice in the rear (Fig. 3).

It will be noticed in Fig. 3 that when the string-end A is brought to the rear, it is then crossed under B. Now spiral A upward, crossing it over all sections of the string, as indicated by the arrowline.

This latter step is shown in Fig. 4. Also, the arrowline in Fig. 4 indicates how B passes beneath its own part. The arrowline in Fig. 5 indicates how B is worked upward, interlocking the braid.

The finished braid is shown in Fig. 6. The saddle-horn knot is shown in place in Fig. 7.

This knot can be made any length and can be used for bosal nose buttons and other coverings. It may, of course, be interwoven with the gaucho or herringbone braid.

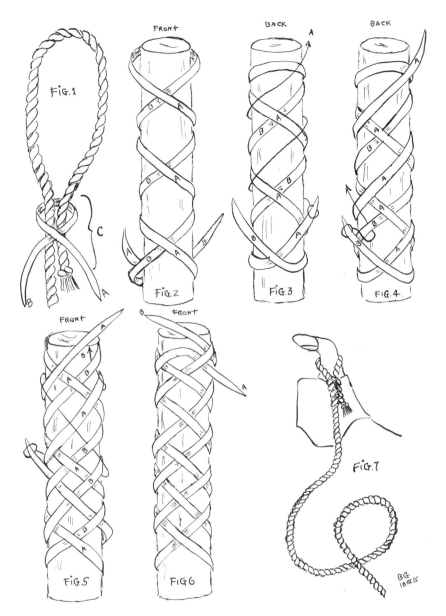

PLATE 80. The Saddle-Horn Tie Knot.

209

PLATE 81

How to Make a Mexican Swivel Honda. Some time ago Art Reuter, of Norco, California, wrote me the following letter:

"Where can I find out how to braid a rawhide honda? You show the folded type in your book but I would like to know how to make the other. I have a real use for this as I rope steers and use a nylon rope and I think you will agree with me it's virtually impossible to tie a honda straight up in one of these ropes. This braided one, of course, swivels and really does the trick. I saw one that was made in Mexico, but did not see it long enough to figure out how it was made."

Mr. Reuter enclosed a sketch showing how the honda looked. I sent him my ideas on how this honda was made. However, the complete details of how it is built are as follows:

First take four ¼-inch-wide rawhide strings each a little more than a foot in length. Middle them and braid a four-string round braid about five inches long (Figs. 1 and 2). Next take a round piece of wood slightly larger than the diameter of the rope to be used with the honda, bend the four-string round braid over the top as in Fig. 3. It is a good idea to mark in ink on the ends of the strings the numbers as shown in Fig. 3.

The ends of the strings are then braided into an eight-string round braid around the mandrel or piece of wood, arranging them first as shown in Fig. 3. String No. 2 on the right is carried around to the rear and then forward under strings 1 and 3 and over 5 and 7. In Fig. 4 string No. 1 on the left is carried around back and forward under strings 4 and 6 and over 8 and 2. The braid is continued in Figs. 5 and 6.

The next step (Fig. 7) shows strings 7, 3, 4 and 8 turned upward and secured so they will remain out of the way for the time being. Then begin a four-string round braid with strings 5, 1, 6 and 2 (Fig. 8). Start with string No. 6 on the right. Carry it around to the back, then forward on the left side under string No. 5 and over string No. 1. This four-string braid is continued in Figs. 9 and 10. In Fig. 11 string No. 1 is brought around from the left side to the rear and up on the right directly under string No. 6, up over string No. 5 and alongside and to the right of string No. 2. This is the beginning of the back-braid.

String No. 5 (Fig. 12) also on the left is passed around back and brought forward on the right and up alongside string No. 6. In so doing it passes under its own part. Working with the two strings on the right, Nos. 2 and 6, first pass No. 2 upward, over two and under one, as shown by the arrowline in Fig. 13. String No. 6 passes around back and up, over two and under two, as shown by the arrowline in Fig. 13.

Strings Nos. 1, 5, 2 and 6 in back-braiding will, by a sequence of over and under two, meet the ends of strings which have previously been turned upward and tied out of the way. In other words, by continuing the back-braid, string No. 1 will meet string No. 8; string No. 2 will

210

MEXICAN SWIVEL HONDA

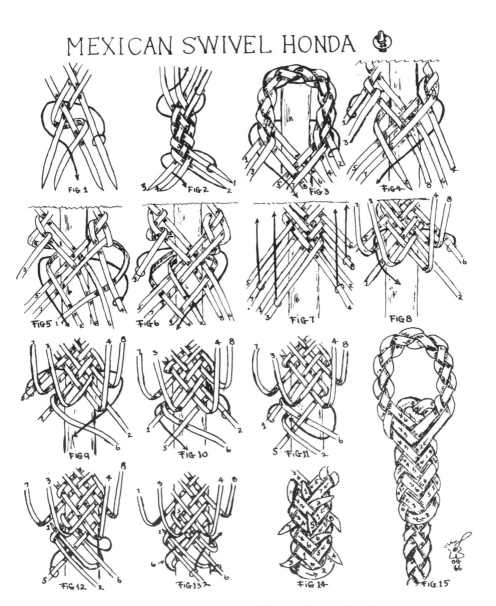

PLATE 81. How to Make a Mexican Swivel Honda.

meet string No. 7; string No. 5 will meet string No. 4 and string No. 6 will meet string No. 3 (Fig. 14).

The meeting points should be scattered and the ends of the strings cut off and tucked under the cross strings. The completed honda is shown in Fig. 15.

211

PLATE 82

How to Make a Mexican Swivel Honda (Cont.). The terminal knot should be made by first pushing the rope end up through the round braid of the honda to allow sufficient length for tying the knot (Fig. A). Starting with end No. 1, lay it to the left over No. 2; No. 2 passes over No. 1 and No. 3; No. 3 over No. 2 and No. 4; No. 4 over No. 3 and No. 1 (Fig. B). Next, end No. 3 passes around No. 1 and up in the center under No. 1 and No. 4; No. 4 around No. 2 and up under No. 2 and No. 1; continue this sequence as shown in Fig. C. Tighten your knot as shown in Fig. D and cut the top ends off flush.

This sequence is for a four-strand rope. If more strands are in the rope, follow the same instructions as for the four-strand.

It is well to add a wear-leather to the loop part of the honda whether the rope is of rawhide or of fiber. Cut your rawhide or leather piece as shown in Fig. E. Make it slightly wider than the circumference of the honda loop braid. Then sew it on as shown in Figs. E and F.

Another way to make this swivel honda is shown on Plate 82, Figs. G-J, with the completed honda in Fig. M. Middle four strings and braid down as in Fig. G. Join the ends and make an eight-string braid as illustrated in the same figure. All strings are next back-braided and brought up beneath the loop and cut off flush. This gives a sixteen-string round braid for the swivel part.

In Figs. K-M is another type of wear-leather I learned from an old braider in Colima, Mexico. It is simple and can easily be replaced when necessary.

Author (left) with an old braider from Colima, Mexico. In seven trips to Mexico, he was one of few old-time braiders the author was able to locate.

212

TERMINAL KNOT ᵃⁿᵈ WEAR LEATHER

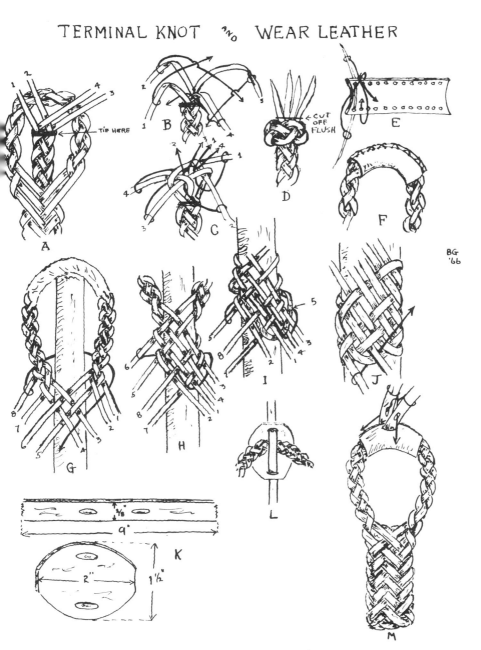

PLATE 82. How to Make a Mexican Swivel Honda (Cont.).

213

PLATE 83

How to Make a Second Type of Mexican Swivel Honda. This interesting and decorative honda was explained to me by Ed Rickman, Meeteetse, Wyoming. Ed discovered it, badly chewed up by pack rats, among some old gear owned by his father. With the aid of his wife, Mary Jane, a competent artist, Ed sent me some drawings and details.

Take a strip of rawhide measuring 30 inches by three inches and cut as shown in Fig. 1. With the hair side toward you bring the end, where five strings have been cut, over through the rectangular hole, as shown by the arrowline in Fig. 1. When this move has been completed as shown in Fig. 2, the dress or hair side of the rawhide is on the inside. In Fig. 3 dotted lines show how the rawhide is folded at the edges and a five-string, over-two, under-two flat braid is started.

In Fig. 4 the fold over and the braid have been completed around the honda. Three of the strings have been brought through the three small holes around the center hole. The fourth string is brought through the beginning of the braid and the fifth string is tucked under and cut off.

A round stick slightly larger than the rawhide rope to be used is inserted in the center hole, through the braid beneath and pressed down to the bottom inside of the honda. A four-string round braid is made around the top of the stick for a couple of inches—more or less, according to taste—and then back-braided from the top down and the strings cut off flush.

While the honda is damp, it can be molded over a shaped stick and allowed to dry. The reata is then introduced from the top and the holding knot made as previously explained.

Three types of rawhide hondas. *Left:* San Juan honda (Plate 78); *Middle:* Mexican Swivel honda (Plate 84); *Right:* Mexican Swivel honda (Plates 81 and 82).

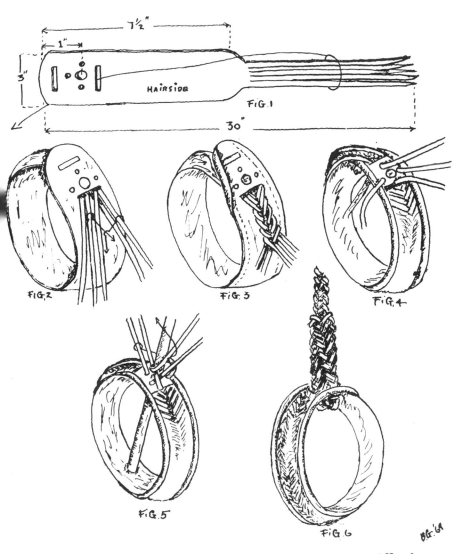

FIG. 1

HAIRSIDE

FIG. 2

FIG. 3

FIG. 4

FIG. 5

FIG. 6

BG '69

PLATE 83. How to Make a Second Type of Mexican Swivel Honda.

215

PLATE 84

How to Make a Third Type of Mexican Swivel Honda. Some years ago the late Burt Rogers of Spearfish, South Dakota, one of the great rawhide braiders, sent me one of these hondas. Later he also sent the metal ring bolt and hook for molding it. Burt said that while the honda was of the Mexican type, he had learned how to make it from an old Indian.

There is a certain similarity in this honda and the one of Ed Rickman. Rickman's type also can be molded in the shape of this honda by using the metal ring bolt and hook used for this one.

Cut your rawhide, which measures 26 inches by 2-7/8 inches, as shown in Fig. 1. The sides A and B are then folded inward so that the holes come together. Then, as in Fig. 2, the long end with the cut strings is folded over as shown in Fig. 3. Hold this together with a fid as illustrated. In Fig. 4 the five-string flat braid is started. To keep this braid in its proper position on the outside of the honda, the first layer of rawhide is cut as shown in Fig. 5, and the braid passes through this slit (Fig. 6). Two or more slits around the outside of the honda can be made.

In Fig. 7 the braid has passed entirely around, and the ends are drawn through the holes indicated in Fig. 3. A terminal knot is made to fasten the braid in place.

The gadget for shaping the honda is detailed in Fig. 9. This consists of a ring bolt, a couple of nuts and washers and leather pads. The finished honda is shown from the side and front in Figs. 8 and 10, respectively. In Fig. 11 the method of shaping and drying it with the ring bolt and hook is illustrated. Let it dry for several days and it will always hold its shape.

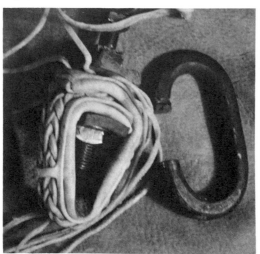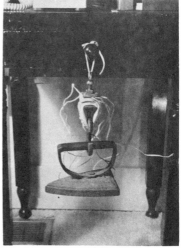

Left: Implements for shaping honda, made for the author by the late Burt Rogers. *Right:* Shaping and drying honda.

Other fancier braids and knots can be employed on this honda. On one which Burt Rogers sent me, the strings were twisted instead of braided.

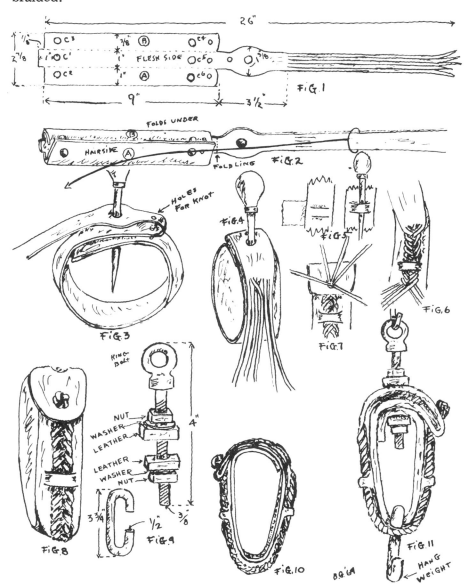

PLATE 84. How to Make a Third Type of Mexican Swivel Honda.

PLATE 85

How to Make a Braided Riding Crop. A riding crop usually is made over a twisted rawhide core. This core is 23 inches long and tapers from ½ inch in diameter at the handle end to ¼ inch at the other end (Fig. 1). Such cores are commercially made and may be bought from whipmakers, rawhide manufacturers, and some handicraft supply stores.

The core, however, may be of rattan or elm root, or a tough flexible switch from the quince tree. Prize crops are made from the bull's pizzle sanded down.

The first step is to lash on the wrist strap. This may be made from a flat braid or merely a strap 5/8 inch wide. It can be tied on at the top of the handle, as shown in Fig. 5, or five or six inches down on the side of the core, as illustrated in Fig. 6. Best method of lashing on the strap is shown in Figs. 2 and 3. Split the strap on each end; then alternately pass the turns of waxed twine over one part and then the other, as shown in Fig. 3. The loop should be about 6 inches when on the crop.

Other end of the core is fitted with a short leather piece fastened on in the same manner (Fig. 4). The shape of this end leather can be as you wish, either like that shown in Fig. 4, or those shown in Figs. 7 and 8.

If the wrist loop is at the end of the handle, you can start your braid at the very top and carry it down to the smaller end, using the eight-thong braid shown in Plate 46, or the 12-thong as detailbd in the text accompanying Plate 47.

If the handle end is to be braided differently from the body, there are several types of braid to select from. One of these is shown in Figs. 9, 11, 12 and 13. This is made with a strip of leather six inches long and wide enough to encompass the core at this point. Slit the leather four times, as shown in Fig. 9, so that you have five strips of the same width. Lash it on at the top (Fig. 11) and with a different colored thong pass around over one, under one, spiraling down as illustrated in Figs. 12 and 13.

Same effect can be achieved with thongs, as illustrated in Figs. 14, 15, and 16. Figures 17 and 18 show a method of making a handle-covering with Spanish hitching.

After the handle part is braided, the remainder of the core is covered with a braid as described. Woven knots are used to cover all places where braids join or where ends are lashed down (Figs. 5, 6, and 8). Where the wrist strap is used on the side (Fig. 6), an attractive braid for the handle is shown in the next plate, 86.

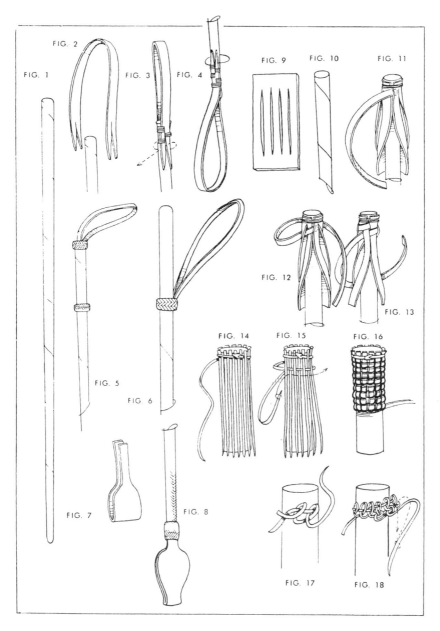

FIG. 1 FIG. 2 FIG. 3 FIG. 4 FIG. 9 FIG. 10 FIG. 11 FIG. 5 FIG. 6 FIG. 12 FIG. 13 FIG. 14 FIG. 15 FIG. 16 FIG. 7 FIG. 8 FIG. 17 FIG. 18

PLATE 85. How to Make a Braided Riding Crop.

219

PLATE 86

The Lone Star Braid. I am not anxious to revive the old argument as to whether the first cowboy came from Texas or California. However, the oriflamme of the Texan, the Lone Star, is a popular decoration on cowboy gear from coast to coast. So we might say the Lone Star is the trademark of the cowboy.

This five-pointed star may of course be made with silver and other metal, or by leather carving and stamping. But it also can be worked out in braiding. I've been able to do it with a two-toned braid, as well as with a Spanish woven knot (Plate 87).

The braid can be used as a handle-covering for a quirt, riding crop, romal, cane, or umbrella. This is the way to make it:

Take ten rawhide strings or leather thongs whose combined width is slightly less than the circumference of the core to be covered. Five of these strings will be white and five of a darker shade. Lash all ten strings or thongs, with the colors alternating, at the bottom of the handle to be covered, and with their flesh sides next to the core. This is shown in Fig. 1. Next the strings are spiraled up around the core to the top, where they are also lashed down.

Lashing at the bottom is later covered with a woven knot. However, in the case of the romal (Plate 59), where a finished braid is desired on the bottom, you will follow the same method as you do at the top. The way of starting this is shown in Fig. 2. Ends at the bottom are carried upward and join with those coming down from the top.

But to continue the sequence at the top: Bend down all the white strings, as shown in Fig. 3. With the darker ones make a crown knot (Figs. 3, 4, 5, and 6). In Fig. 7 we are looking down on this crown knot, which rests on top of the core.

In Fig. 6, the down braid is started. First work with the dark strings. It will be noticed that string No. 2 passes over string No. 6 and under string No. 8. Observe this carefully. Weave the other dark strings in like manner, over one and under one, and your work will appear as in Fig. 8.

Next weave the white strings. In Fig. 8, we see that string No. 7 is brought up and over dark string No. 2; then beneath the cross formed by dark strings Nos. 8 and 4. When you have worked with all white strings in this fashion you will see that each one passes beneath three other strings—two dark and one white.

Keep your braid up snug with the star part now formed resting exactly on top of the core. You start braiding down now with all ten strings—over two and under two. The herringbone effect in this braid is shown in Fig. 10. In Fig. 11, looking down on top of the braid, you can see the five-pointed star, with the white strings forming the background. By working carefully, after removing the upper binding, the star knot can be closed completely at the top.

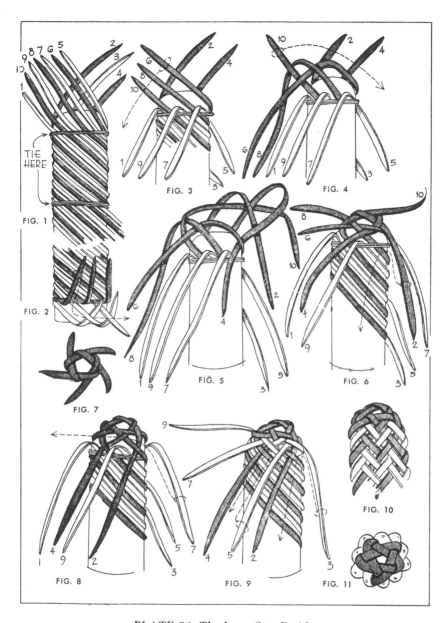

PLATE 86. The Lone Star Braid.

221

PLATE 87

How to Make the Lone Star Knot. The Texas Lone Star Knot is a decorative button knot or a finishing knot on the end of a piece of braid or a quirt handle. It is an appropriate one for the button knot on the hobbles in Plate 142.

For clarification, the knot here is shown made on a mandrel having a leather collar. The mandrel is divided into four areas, or sections, numbered clockwise from 1 to 4, section 1 being the front and that marked 3 the back.

The foundation knot is a 6-part, 5-bight Turk's-head. Its five bights or scallops provide the design for the five-pointed star.

Start as in Fig. 1. Pass the working end of the rawhide string or leather thong around the top of the mandrel and then down on the right side and over the standing part as shown.

In Fig. 2 you are looking at the back part of the mandrel. Here the working end passes beneath the bight at the top.

Now bring your working end to the front, as in Fig. 3, and beneath the standing part and over the part on the left. In Fig. 4 we are again at the back. Sequence is over one, over one.

Fig. 5. Pass down: over one, under one, over one.

Fig. 6. Pass up: under one, over one, under one.

Fig. 7. Down: under one, over one, under one, over one.

Fig. 8. Up: over one, under one, over one, under one.

Fig. 9. Down: over one, under one, over one, under one, over one.

Fig. 10. When you pass under one to the left of the standing part, the skeleton or foundation knot is complete. While in these drawings we continue with the same string, showing it in a different tone, to obtain the star effect in interweaving, it is necessary to begin at this point with a different colored string. The sequence will be under one, over one, under one, over one, following along to the left of the standing part.

It might be pointed out that the weave here is the same as that of the pineapple knot (Plate 50) at the top; at the bottom it differs in that the bight is formed on the outside of the knot instead of inside.

Fig. 11. Under two. Fig. 12. Over one, under one, over two, under one.

Fig. 13. Over one, under two (splitting a pair). Fig. 14. Over two, under one, over two (crossed strings), under two.

Fig. 15. Over one, under two (crossed strings). Fig. 16. Over two, under two, over two (crossed strings), under two.

Fig. 17. Over two, under two (crossed strings). Fig. 18. Over two, under two, over three, under two.

Fig. 19. Over two, under three. Fig. 20. Over two, under two, over three. Working end is now passed under one (or two to make it more secure) at the starting point of the interweave.

Knot is removed from the mandrel and placed in its permanent position. It is tightened until the top closes. Side view and top view are shown in Fig. 21.

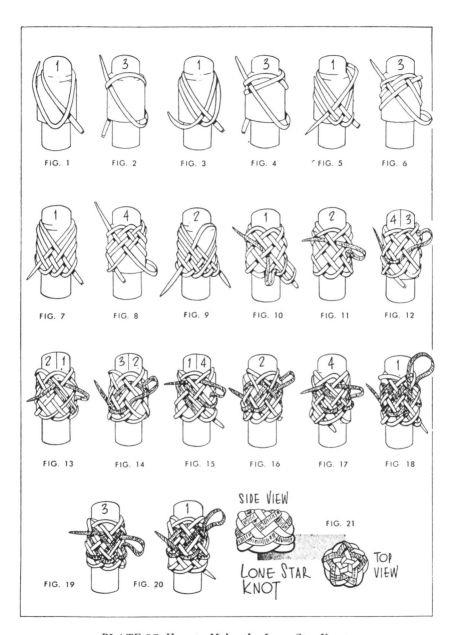

FIG. 1 FIG. 2 FIG. 3 FIG. 4 FIG. 5 FIG. 6

FIG. 7 FIG. 8 FIG. 9 FIG. 10 FIG. 11 FIG. 12

FIG. 13 FIG. 14 FIG. 15 FIG. 16 FIG. 17 FIG 18

FIG. 19 FIG. 20 FIG. 21

SIDE VIEW

LONE STAR
KNOT

TOP
VIEW

PLATE 87. How to Make the Lone Star Knot.

PLATE 88

How to Make a Riding Crop with the Lazy-Man Braid. In this Lazy-Man Braid the strings or thongs are worked in parallel sets, instead of singly. The skeleton of an over-one, under-one sequence can first be made and then followed around to parallel the basic braid. While this is necessary in increasing the size of Turk's-heads, in straight round braiding the strings can be worked in sets of two, three, four, or more.

Some striking effects can be obtained by using strings of differing colors and by varying the sequences.

The finished riding crop is shown in Fig. 1. The braid is made around a twisted rawhide core. In Fig. 2, 12 strings are used. Arrange them, if contrasting colors are used, as shown in Fig. 2 and after the first pass you will have six strings of one color on one side and six of the other color on the opposite side. This braid is continued down for several inches (Figs. 3 and 4).

In Fig. 5, it will be noted that only one string is worked at a time—string No. 4 passes around back and forward, under three and over three. In Fig. 6, string No. 11 passes around back and forward, under three and over three. Having worked this braid for the desired length, you can switch as in Fig. 7, where string No. 7 passes back and then forward, over two, under two, and over two. In Fig. 8, the right-hand string No. 6 passes back and then forward, over two, under two, and over two. In Fig. 9, three strings are worked as a unit. They pass around back and forward, under three and over three. The same sequence is illustrated on the other side in Fig. 10. Vary these different sequences as often as you wish.

Figures 11, 12, and 13 show how to make the wrist loop, also using strings of contrasting colors. Leave sufficient unbraided string at each end and fasten these down to the top of the core by lashing them as in Fig. 18. The wrist loop should be put on before beginning the braid on the handle and this braid will then cover the lashed-down sections.

The end leather of the crop can be attached as shown in Figs. 14, 15, 16, and 17. It is lashed on as described in Plate 85. The Lazy-Man Button (described in Plate 179) is used at the top and bottom. In Fig. 19 is shown a method of attaching the end leather by braiding it upward from the bottom of the core.

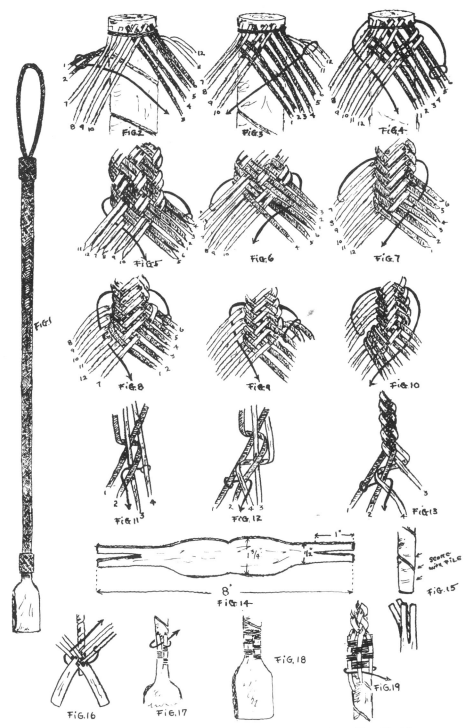

FIG.1
FIG.2
FIG.3
FIG.4
FIG.5
FIG.6
FIG.7
FIG.8
FIG.9
FIG.10
FIG.11
FIG.12
FIG.13
FIG.14
FIG.15
FIG.16
FIG.17
FIG.18
FIG.19

PLATE 88. How to Make a Riding Crop with the Lazy-Man Braid.

225

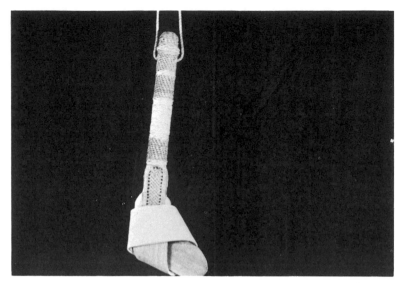

Argentine *rebenque* or heavy quirt.

Top: The butt of an Argentine stock-whip. *Bottom:* Hanging from this breast-plate is a medallion with the initials of Edward Larocque Tinker, in The Hall of the Horsemen of the Americas, The University of Texas.

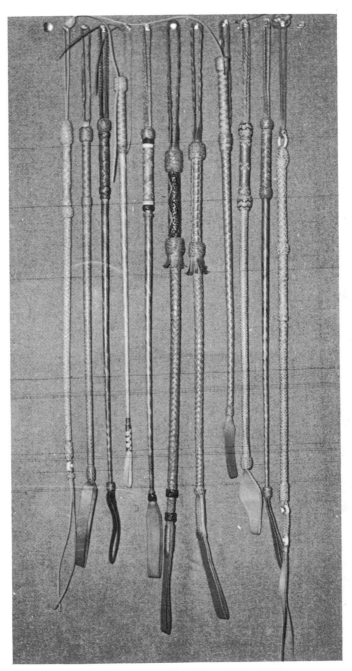

Collection of riding crops owned by author.

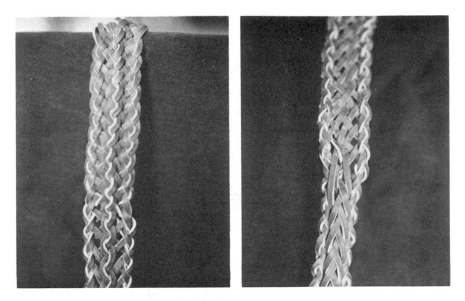

Left: Crocodile ridge braid of three simulated flat ridge braids and continued down where two outside ridges are of simulated round braid. *Right:* Crocodile ridge braid with ridges on each side.

Left: Crocodile ridge braid with ridges on both sides. *Right:* Crocodile ridge braid with one center ridge of over-two, under-two sequence.

Crocodile Ridge Braids

PLATE 89

The Crocodile Ridge Braid. This beautiful braid, made with one, two, three or more ridges on a flat-type braid foundation, is used for many purposes. It is quite popular in parts of Australia and extensively used in Argentina where it is termed *lomo de yacare* (back or ridge of the crocodile). As a flat-type braid it is used for belts, headstalls, reins, hobbles, etc., and as a round braid, for handle coverings. It can be worked into button knots of various kinds. It is an attractive utility braid and its variations challenge the ingenuity of the creative braider.

The flat braid, with which we shall deal here, is best made with an even number of strings or thongs. The six-string crocodile ridge braid beginning with Fig. 1 is started by bringing string No. 5 to the left over No. 4; then string No. 3 to the right over No. 5 (arrowline). The secret of this braid is now shown in Figs. 2 and 3. String No. 2 is carried to the right and, with a slight twist to keep the dress side outward, it passes under Nos. 3 and 5 and is then brought back to the left over No. 3. In Fig. 3, string No. 6 passes to the left over string No. 4 and then, with a twist, under strings Nos. 2 and 3; then carried back to the right over string No. 2.

This same sequence is repeated in Figs. 4 and 5; over one, twisted under two and then back toward its origin over one. The completed braid is shown in Fig. 6.

The next sequence is of eight strings or thongs. In Fig. 7 string No. 4 is brought to the right over string No. 5; then string No. 3 passes to the right and then, with a twist under strings Nos. 4 and 5 and finally brought back over string No. 4. Always work strings on alternate sides. In Fig. 8, string No. 1 passes to the right under string No. 5; over string No. 3; then twisted under strings Nos. 2 and 7 and brought back over string No. 7. The arrowline in Fig. 9 shows the same sequence—under one, over one, twisted under two and back over one. Follow this sequence on each side until the desired length of braid is reached. The completed braid with its center ridge is shown in Fig. 10.

A ten-string braid is shown in Fig. 11 with a sequence of over one, under one, twisted under two, and back over one. This braid is shown completed in Fig. 12. It can also be made by a sequence of over two, under three, and back over one.

In all examples illustrated here the braid is rather loose, so it can be followed better.

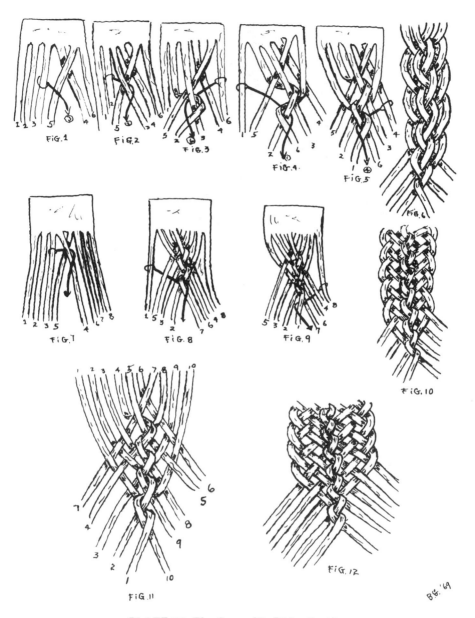

FiG.1 FiG.2 FiG.3 FiG.4. FiG.5 FiG.6

FiG.7 FiG.8 FiG.9 FiG.10

FiG.11 FiG.12

BG.'69

PLATE 89. The Crocodile Ridge Braid.

231

Crocodile ridge braided belt made from 1/8" commercial lacing, started with a flat braid used by Australians. Made by author.

PLATE 90

Double-Center Crocodile Ridge Braid. Instead of passing back over one string in the center, you can pass back over two or more to then make the ridge. In this plate ten strings are used.

The start of the braid is shown in Fig. 1. Braid the inside strings Nos. 4, 5, and 6, as shown. In Fig. 2, the double ridge begins where string No. 7 passes to the left beneath three strings, then twisted and brought forward and to the right over two strings.

In Fig. 3, string No. 3 passes to the right beneath four strings, twisted and brought forward and to the left over two strings. String No. 8 is worked in the same sequence from the right (Fig. 4).

Figure 5 illustrates the path of string No. 2 by the arrowline. It passes to the right, over one string, under four, and twisted and brought back over two. The same sequence is observed in Fig. 6 where string No. 9 passes over one, under four, twisted and brought back over two.

In Fig. 7, the left outside string No. 1 passes to the right, under one, over one, under four, twisted and brought back over two. The same sequence is observed in Fig. 8 where string No. 10 passes to the left, under one, over one, under four, twisted and brought to the front over two.

These passes on each side are continued until the braid is of the desired length. The finished braid is shown in Fig. 9.

232

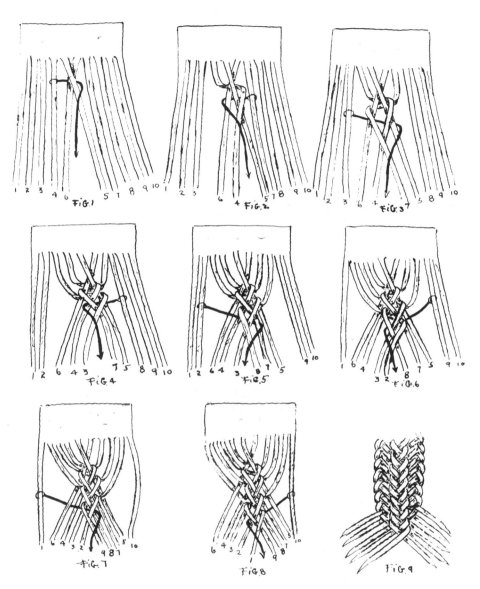

PLATE 90. Double-Center Crocodile Ridge Braid.

233

PLATE 91

Half-Round Center Crocodile Ridge Braid. In this braid the center ridge gives the impression of being the same as a four-string round braid.

Start the braid with eight strings as in Fig. 1. It will be noted that string No. 6 is given a full twist as in the regular four-string round braid, and that string No. 3 also is given a full twist (Fig. 2).

In Fig. 2, string No. 7 is brought to the left (arrowline), over one, under wo, twisted a half turn and then back to the right, over one. In Fig. 3, string No. 2 passes to the right (arrowline), over one, under two, twisted and back over one.

In this braid strings Nos. 3 and 6 always remain in the center and never pass to the edges. They are always braided in the same manner as in a regular four-string round braid. After one pass by each of these strings the outer strings are braided in as explained.

Studying this carefully will prove a valuable key to other crocodile ridge braids to follow.

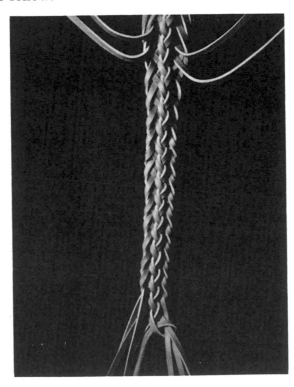

Crocodile ridge braid with one center ridge.

234

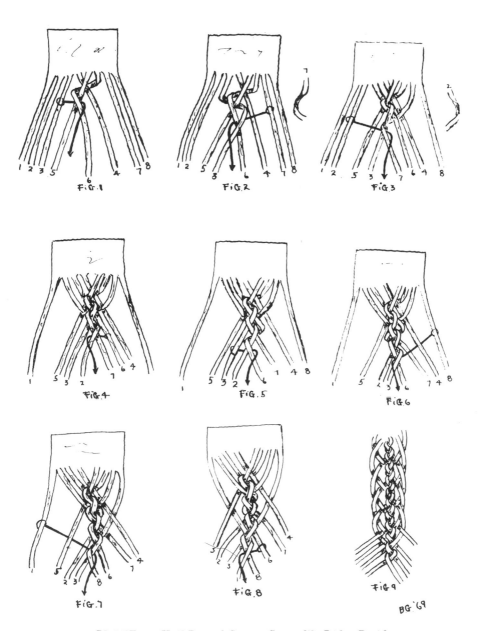

PLATE 91. Half-Round Center Crocodile Ridge Braid.

235

Crocodile ridge braid belt, started at billet end in Australian fashion and then worked into crocodile ridge with one center ridge.

PLATE 92

Crocodile Ridge Braided Belt with Round Center This belt is started with four light-colored strings and one black string. They are middled, giving ten ends. It is begun in the Australian fashion described in Plate 35.

First the sequence is a simple flat braid, over one, under one. When sufficient braiding has been done for the billet of the belt, and the two black strings cross in the center as shown in Fig. 1, the center round braid begins. Strings Nos. 4 and 7 (both black) always remain in the center, as explained in the previous braid. They are worked with a full twist as in a four-string braid, while those brought in from the outer edges are given a half twist. Thus the center braid always is half black. The center braid is made after passes from one string on each side.

A few inches from where the buckle is to be positioned revert back to the simple over-one, under-one flat braid, using all strings. Back weave at the buckle-end as previously explained.

Crocodile Ridge Braid of Two Outer Half-Round Ridges. This braid is made with eight strings, four black and four natural color, the colors alternating as in Fig. 5. Once the braid has started, two black strings remain always on one side and the two others always on the opposite side. Thus strings Nos. 3 and 1 remain on the left side, while Nos. 8 and 6 remain on the right side. As previously explained, these strings are worked with a full twist as in the four-string round braid. The natural colored strings pass from side to side and, after the start, are given only a half twist. Figure 9 shows the finished braid, purposely drawn loose so the braid can be followed.

236

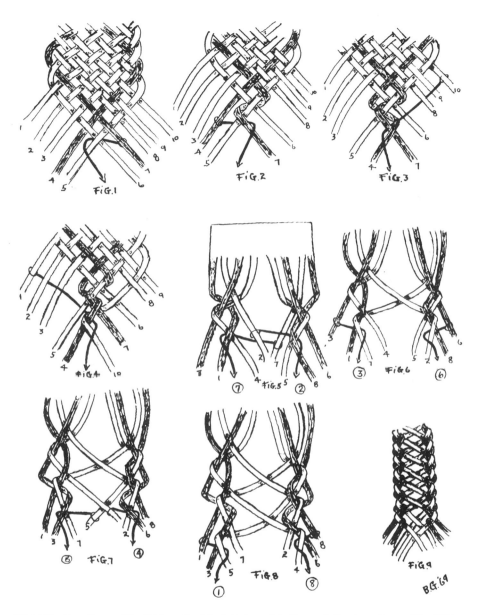

FiG.1 FiG.2 FiG.3

FiG.4 FiG.5 FiG.6

FiG.7 FiG.8 FiG.9

BG.'69

PLATE 92. Crocodile Ridge Braided Belt with Round Center; Crocodile Ridge
Braid of Two Outer Half-Round Ridges.

237

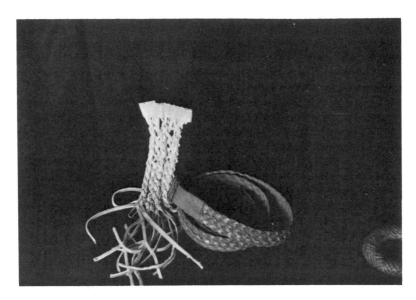

Crocodile ridge braid with three ridges—12 strings.

PLATE 93

Crocodile Ridge Braid of Three Ridges. The two outer ridges of this braid are half-round, while the center ridge is made with the half twist. Of course there is no limit to the number of ridges that can be made in a braid; all that is required are the strings and a lot of patience and ingenuity.

This braid is made with ten strings. The ridges on the edges are made with two passes each, while the ridge in the center is only one pass each—one from each side. Two contrasting colored strings can be used on the sides for after the braid is started they will remain on their respective sides. The finished braid is shown in Fig. 5.

Crocodile Ridge Braid Finished on Both Sides. This beautiful braid was described to me by Don Luis Alberto Flores, of Buenos Aires, who learned it from an old-time Argentine braider. It is much like the previously described braids, but with the exception that each string is given a full twist as shown by string No. 1 in Fig. 6. The unfinished or flesh side of each string is completely hidden when the braid is made tight.

In this case we have used eight strings. More can be employed if desired, remembering that they must be of an even number.

238

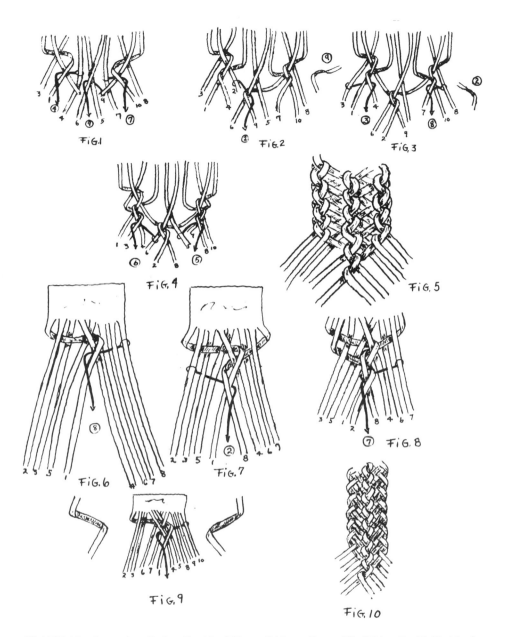

Fig. 1

Fig. 2

Fig. 3

Fig. 4

Fig. 5

Fig. 6

Fig. 7

Fig. 8

Fig. 9

Fig. 10

PLATE 93. Crocodile Ridge Braid of Three Ridges; Crocodile Ridge Braid Finished
on Both Sides.

239

PLATE 94

Crocodile Ridge Button. The Crocodile Ridge Button is appropriate when used with other types of this braid. First make a running five-part, four-bight Turk's-head, which is explained later under the section on Turk's-heads. The Turk's-head is shown in Fig. 1.

In Fig. 2 it has been capsized or turned upside down as the braiding in of the second Turk's-head will be on what is now the bottom of the first. In Fig. 3 the start of the second Turk's-head is shown from the back. The new string goes up, under one, over two and under one and brought around under the standing part. It then passes under two, over two and under one. Here its course is followed by the arrowline, which passes around, forward and over the standing part and under its own part. This second Turk's-head is exactly like the first, only when woven the point of intersection with the other is under two and over two and under two (Figs. 5, 6, and 7). When completed and tightened, it appears as in Fig. 8 with the ridge ringing the circumference.

Crocodile Ridge Braid Handle Covering. Cut your strings from a strap as shown in Fig. 9. The width of the strap should be wide enough to encompass the circumference of the handle. Take the set of six strings on the left and braid them down in an over-one, under-one sequence. Then string No. 7 passes to the right under string No. 6, down over strings Nos. 6 and 3 and under string No. 3, as shown in Fig. 9.

Also in this figure is illustrated the course of string No. 12 which passes around and to the front under string No. 1, over strings Nos. 4 and 1 and under string No. 4. Now braid strings Nos. 8, 9, 10, and 11 as shown in Fig. 10. After this, interlock the top strings with the previous braid as shown in Fig. 11. String No. 10 passes under two, over two and under one. On the other side string No. 9 passes under two, over two and under one. Continue thus until you have braided the required length.

In Fig. 12 the same method is used with 14 strings. The seven-string braid is first made in the front and then the edges are interlocked with the strings of the other braid. After interlocking strings Nos. 8 and 14, braid strings Nos. 9, 10, 11, 12, and 13 in the same manner as shown for the front braid. Finish off both ends with the button described above.

Crocodile ridge braid, four ridges used in handle covering.

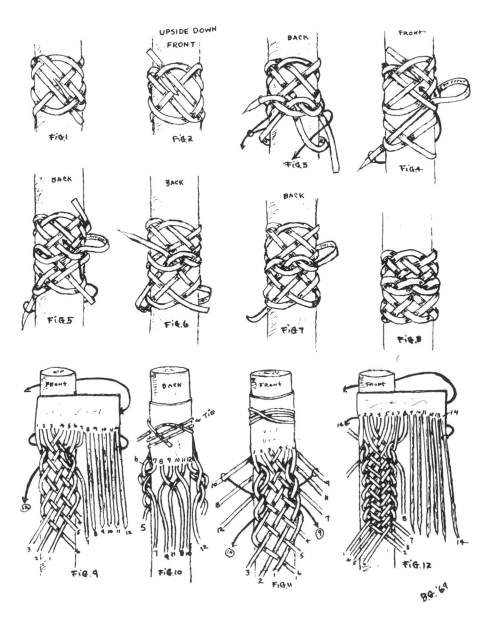

PLATE 94. Crocodile Ridge Button; Crocodile Ridge Braid Handle Covering.

PLATE 95

Crocodile Braid Button No. 2. This button is made with two knots, which I call the Ginfer Knot. One edge has an under-two, over-two sequence and the opposite edge has an over-one, under-one sequence. I shall have more to say about the Ginfer knot later under Braided Knots.

In Fig. 1 the working end of the string marked B is passed around twice, as shown. Going up the back it goes under one, over one (Fig. 2). In Fig. 3 it passes down under one, over two, and in Fig. 4 the sequence upward is over one, under one, over one.

Coming down again in Fig. 5 the sequence is over one, under one, over two, and in Fig. 6 going upward it is under one, over one, under one, over one. Fig. 7 shows the final pass downward of under one, over one, under one, over two. It is then tucked up alongside the standing part A.

This knot, like the one in Plate 94, is then capsized as shown in Fig. 8 and the interlocking braid is made on the over-one, under-one edge. The standing part of this new braid is marked C and the working end is marked D.

The interlocking sequence is the same as in the previous knot. But as you continue, you must make another Ginfer knot (Figs. 9, 10, and 11). The finished knot is shown in Fig. 12.

The advantage of the over-two, under-two sequence on the ends is that they can be made to close more effectively on the top—or bottom. This is the knot used in the crocodile ridge braid hobbles as keeper knots. These hobbles are explained in Plates 98 and 99.

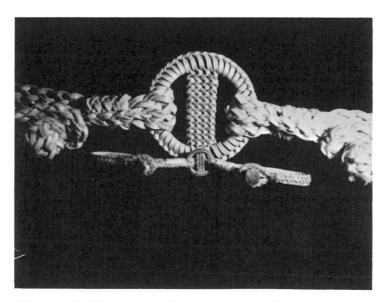

Miniature hobbles shown with regular size hobbles designed by
Don Hilario Faudone of Argentina.

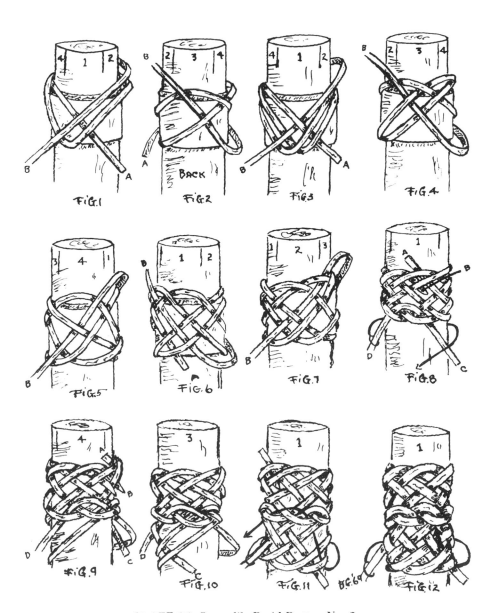

FIG.1 FIG.2 FIG.3 FIG.4
FIG.5 FIG.6 FIG.7 FIG.8
FIG.9 FIG.10 FIG.11 FIG.12

PLATE 95. Crocodile Braid Button No. 2.

243

PLATE 96

Crocodile Ridge Round Braid of One Ridge. In the first three figures this braid is shown made without a core so that the detail may be more easily followed.

To start, as shown in Fig. 1, string No. 3 is laid over string No. 4. The arrowline indicates the course of string No. 7 which is brought around back as in any round braid, passed under string No. 2, then over the same string and under both strings 4 and 3 and then with a half twist is brought over string No. 3 to the left. This pass is shown completed in Fig. 2 and the arrowline indicates the course of string No. 1.

When made over a core or around a mandrel as shown in Fig. 4, the same sequence is observed. This gives a ridge down one side (Fig. 8), but in the back the braid is a plain over-one, under-one sequence (Fig. 7).

To make two, three, four or more ridges on a round braid, the strings are arranged as shown in Fig. 9. In this instance we will make three ridges. First make a four-string flat braid of over-one, under-one sequence, tying off the other strings as indicated in Fig. 9. In Fig. 10 the flat braid of section 1 is completed and the start of interlocking section 2 begins. As the interlocking process proceeds, the flat braid must also be made (Fig. 10). It will be noted that the first pass of the interlocking braid (Fig. 10) passes under one, over two, and under one (string No. 7). Thereafter the sequence is under two, over two, under one (string No. 8).

After section 2 has been braided into section 1, section 3 is simultaneously braided into both section 1 and section 2 (Fig. 11). This means, of course, that now the strings encompass the mandrel.

A belt made using the crocodile ridge braid.

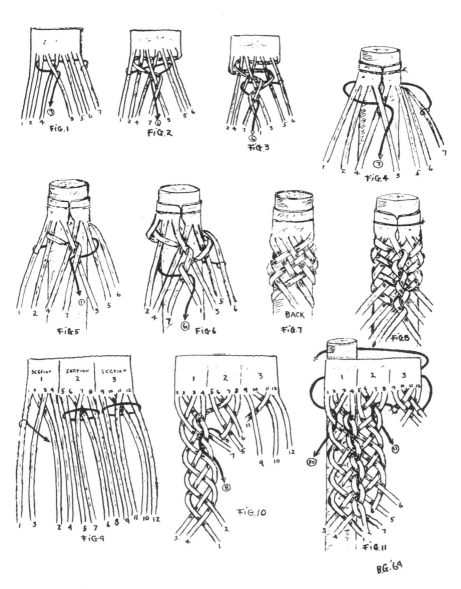

PLATE 96. Crocodile Ridge Round Braid of One Ridge.

245

PLATE 97

Crocodile Ridge Braid Reins The first three figures in this plate are the same as those found in the previous plate. However, the core should be very small. After the braid is the length desired, the core is slipped out and the braid carefully tightened on itself. This makes a unique braid where the front, side and back are all different (Figs. 3, 4, and 5). This braid and the one that follows can be made into reins.

In Fig. 7 the round braid is made with an over two, under two, right down the front. This, too, can be made over a very small core which is withdrawn after the braid has reached the required length and then carefully tightened upon itself. Figures 8, 9, and 10 illustrate that this also has three different sides.

Crocodile Ridge Appliqué Braid. This is a four-string appliqué and is made like the regular appliqué with the exception that a ridge is formed down the center. Starting with Fig. 11, it will be seen that string No. 4 on the right passes under two, is given a half twist, and comes back to its own side, over one.

String No. 1 on the extreme left passes under strings Nos. 4 and 3, and then with a half twist returns to its own side, passing over string No. 4. The sequences are the same on each side with the exception that before passing beneath two crossed strings the working string passes over one.

All such types of appliqué braids can be worked with the crocodile ridge braid. The center ridge, too, can be of an over-two, under-two sequence.

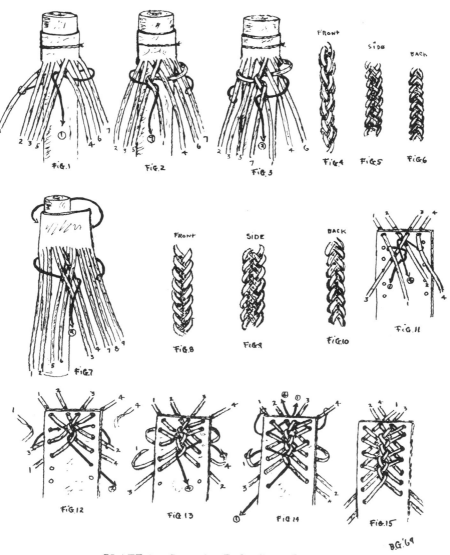

PLATE 97. Crocodile Ridge Braid Reins.

PLATE 98

Mousing a Braided Ring with the Conquistador Braid. The first use I saw of this moused ring was on a pair of miniature hobbles presented to me by Don Hilario Faudone, Sunchales, Province of Santa Fe, Argentina. These tiny hobbles, worked with rawhide strings about the thickness of thread, are about 5¼ inches long and the inside diameter of the ring is less than ½ inch. Don Hilario is considered one of the foremost braiders in the Argentine, where there are many such craftsmen.

I call this process mousing for want of a better name. It is similar to work done by sailors and they use the term "mousing."

The moused ring is used on hobbles throughout with variations of the crocodile ridged braid. The braid around the ring is the Spanish-type ring covering of two loops. The braid within (or "mouse") is the conquistador braid.

The Spanish-type ring braid is started in Figs. 1, 2, 3, and 4. In Fig. 5 the string for the conquistador braid is caught by one of the loops as shown, flesh side to flesh side. In Fig. 6 the conquistador braid is once more imprisoned but before the braid is tightened the conquistador string is formed into a loop, passing beneath its own part and through the ring braid. The braids were linked together when string C formed a loop before it was tightened. This is done in each loop for four passes. Now begin to work the conquistador braid in the opposite direction in the same manner as explained under this braid. When the conquistador braid has been made almost to the bottom of the ring, work the ring braid around, once more imprisoning the conquistador braid (Fig. 10). In Fig. 12 this phase of the work is completed and the ring braid is continued on around to the start. Here it is joined as shown. Figure 16 shows the final result.

It is possible in making this combination to first work the ring braid entirely around, and then insert the loops for the conquistador braid. Since the braid has to be tight, I find this a more practicable method.

This decorative braided ring with conquistador braid can be used in other things besides hobbles.

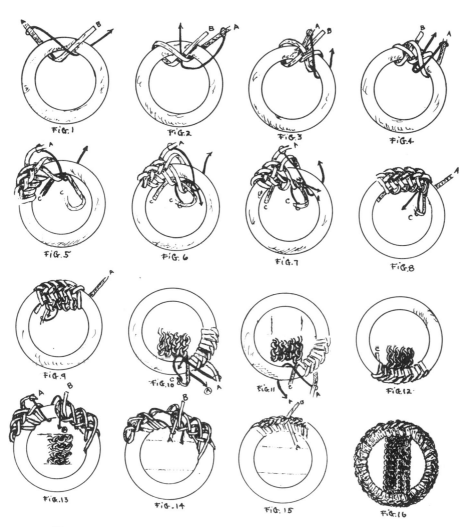

Fig. 1   Fig. 2   Fig. 3   Fig. 4

Fig. 5   Fig. 6   Fig. 7   Fig. 8

Fig. 9   Fig. 10   Fig. 11   Fig. 12

Fig. 13   Fig. 14   Fig. 15   Fig. 16

PLATE 98. Mousing a Braided Ring with the Conquistador Braid.

249

PLATE 99

How to Make Crocodile Ridge Braid Hobbles. To start these hobbles, designed by Don Hilario Faudone of the Argentine, take five softened rawhide strings or latigo thongs, each about 48 inches long. Middle them and begin a five-string crocodile ridge braid. That is, start your braid in the middle part of the five strings.

Figure 1 shows the start of this braid. The three strings on the left, Nos. 1, 2, and 3, are all worked with a full twist as in a round braid, while the two on the right, Nos. 4 and 5, are given a half turn. After braiding thus for five inches, make the braid into a loop and join all 10 strings (started in Fig. 5). This braid is continued in Figs. 6, 7, 8, 9, and more fully shown in Fig. 10.

The ten-string corcodile ridge braid is made for 8½ inches and then three outer strings on the left are tied off temporarily and four on the right, as shown in Fig. 11. The three remaining strings in the center (or the ridge strings) are worked for 1¾ inches in an independent three-string braid or hair braid (Fig. 12). The strings on the right and left which had been tied off are worked in a seven-string braid, over-three, under-three sequence, as indicated by the arrowlines in Fig. 12. After braiding the seven strings for 1¾ inches (the same length as the three-string braid) the two braids are joined (Fig. 13) in the ten-string crododile braid for two inches. This section is then introduced through the braided ring (Fig. 14) and once more the three-string braid is made independently for 1¾ inches, as is the seven-string braid (Fig. 15). But before they are joined, a braided knot or Turk's-head is made around the two seven-string braids (shown by arrowlines in Fig. 15 and completed in Figs. 16 and 17). This secures this section of the hobble to the braided ring.

Now join the top three-string braid and seven-string braid for a distance of an inch or so. Tie off six central strings and then work around them a terminal knot. Cut off all strings flush and cover this terminal knot with a braided knot—pineapple knot or other knot that will close on the top. Use either of the knots in Plates 94 or 95 as keeper knots for your loops, after having completed the other side of your hobbles.

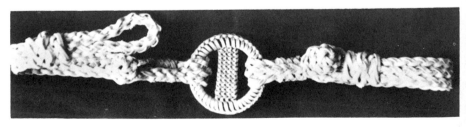

In crocodile ridge braid hobbles like those designed by Don Hilario Faudone of Argentina and made by the author, use the directions for either Plate 94 or 95 to make the braided knots.

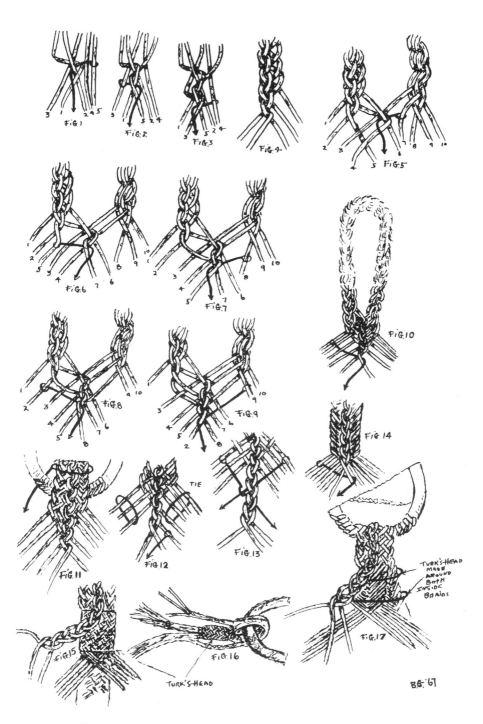

PLATE 99. How to Make Crocodile Ridge Braid Hobbles.

251

Quirts and whips in the author's collection. Left to right: Paraguayan *arreador* (cattle whip—the long one which circles the sides and tops of the others); California quirt (made by Ernie Ladouceur); Mexican quirt; South Dakota quirt (made by Burt Rogers); Texas quirt; New Mexico quirt (made by Roy Harmon); Argentine quirt; California quirt (made by Ernie Ladouceur).

Square, Rectangular, Spiral, Oval and Triangular Braids

PLATE 100

Square Braid of Four Thongs. This braid is made with four thongs but the same principle can be used with three, or with a greater number. It is based on the so-called Sailor's Crown Knot, and is used in making lanyards, watch fobs, dog leashes, and in covering quirt handles, as will be shown later.

Begin as in Fig. 1, showing two thongs of which both ends of each are used. Place the thongs so that the working ends are interlaced as illustrated. The white thong shows end B at the left and end B1 at the right. The back thong shows end A at the top and end A1 at the bottom.

Fold thong B over to the right and thong B1 to the left (Fig. 3). Bring thong A down over thong B and through the bight of thong B1; carry thong A1 up and over thong B1 and through the bight of thong B.

The braid in this second stage, before it is tightened, looks like the diagram in Fig. 4, and after it is tightened it is like that in Fig. 5.

In the previous move, the white and black thongs were worked clockwise, but in the third stage of this braid the reverse is true. The white and black thongs are both moved in a counterclockwise direction.

Bring thong A downward and carry thong A1 upward. Pass thong B over thong A1 toward the left and through the bight of thong A; carry thong B1 to the right over thong A and through the bight of thong A1. This is indicated by the arrowlines in Fig. 6, while the tightened braid is shown in Fig. 7. Continue in this fashion, first clockwise and then counterclockwise.

To finish the braid, tuck the black thongs downward over the last bend and into the braid (Fig. 8), and do the same with the white ones. Or the braid may be finished with the terminal knot, as shown in Plate 38. In this braid the hair side of the leather is first on top and then on the under side. It is not too noticeable when the thongs are colored.

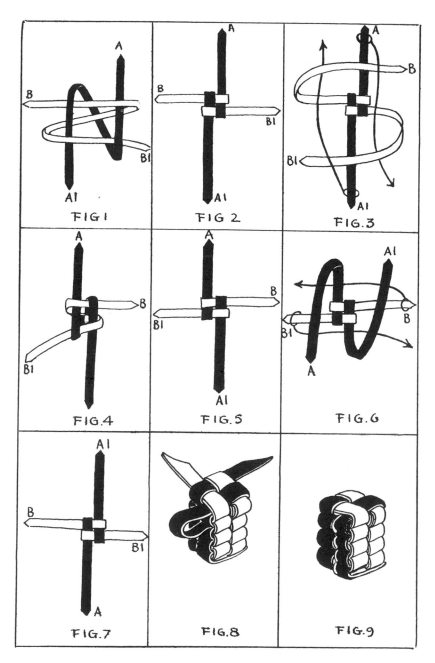

FIG 1 FIG 2 FIG.3
FIG.4 FIG.5 FIG.6
FIG.7 FIG.8 FIG.9

PLATE 100. Square Braid of Four Thongs.

255

PLATE 101

Rectangular Braid of Six Thongs. Arrange your strings or thongs as shown in Fig. 1. While there are six working ends, actually only three thongs are used. Thong A and B are laid in the loops of E and F, and C and D, as shown.

The working end A crosses over from the left to the right (arrowline in Fig. 1 and shown in Fig. 2). In Fig. 2 the working ends D and F are laid over A and B as illustrated, the thongs inclining to the right.

In Fig. 3, interlace working end B in an over-one, under-one, over-one, under-one sequence (arrowline in Fig. 3 and shown completed in Fig. 4). Carefully tighten up your braid as shown in Fig. 5.

The next move is to lay thongs A and B back over the braid as shown. The arrowline in Fig. 6 shows that end C passes over A and under B. End D comes down over B and under A. End E passes over A and under B. Then end F comes down over B and under A.

To continue, strings A and B are laid across and the other strings worked in the same sequence. The front of this braid appears as in Fig. 7 and the side as in Fig. 8.

A cube can be formed with eight strings (Fig. 9). After laying in strings A and C, and B and D, the braiding proceeds as in Figs. 10 and 11.

The objection to such braids is that the flesh side of the leather or rawhide alternates on the outside with the skin side. The flesh side can be dyed a contrasting color and this gives a pleasing effect. Or all such braids can be made in the spiral twist, which follows.

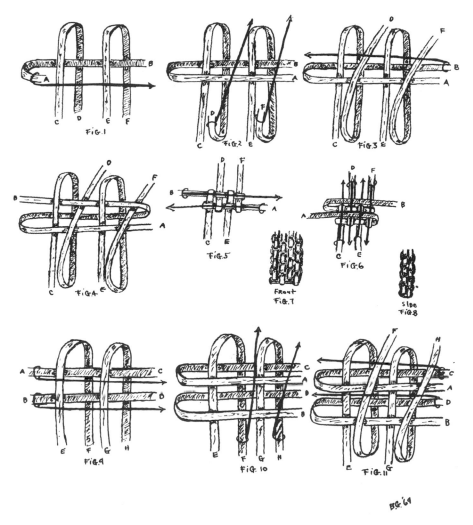

BG. 69

PLATE 101. Rectangular Braid of Six Thongs.

PLATE 102

Spiral Braid. This braid is also worked on the principle of superimposed crown knots. While the previous braid gives a vertical effect in the pattern, this one gives a spiral effect.

It may be worked with six thongs, over a core, as will be shown later, but when four thongs are used, no heart or core is necessary.

The first step is the same as for the square braid in Plate 100. The result is shown in Fig. 1.

Take thong B1 and fold it over thong A1, indicated by the arrowline in Fig. 1 and shown in Fig. 2. Next, fold thong A1 over thong B1 and thong B, as indicated by the arrowline in Fig. 2 and shown in Fig. 3. Carry thong B over thong A1 and thong A, indicated and shown in Figs. 3 and 4, respectively.

In the last step of this stage, take thong A and pass it over thong B and through the bight of thong B1, indicated by the arrowline in Fig. 4 and shown in Fig. 5.

The second phase, starting with Fig. 6, is executed in exactly the same fashion. Note the work moves continually in a counterclockwise direction. However, if the start is clockwise, keep on working that way.

The completed braid is shown in Fig. 7.

Spiral Twist Braid. The spiral twist braid starts exactly as the spiral braid, shown in Fig. 1. In the next step, however, where B1 crosses to the right over A1, give the thong a half twist so that the smooth side remains uppermost (Fig. 8).

Bring thong A1 over thongs B1 and B and twist it so that the smooth side is up and the flesh side is in contact with the thongs beneath (Fig. 9).

The same twist is given each thong. Thus, when the braid is completed, the smooth side of the thong is exposed. In the diagram showing the finished braid (Fig. 12), the twists are emphasized; however, if it is worked carefully and each twist brought down close to the point where the thong emerges, the braid will present a finished appearance.

These braids may be used to make attractive and durable leashes, lanyards and bathrobe belts.

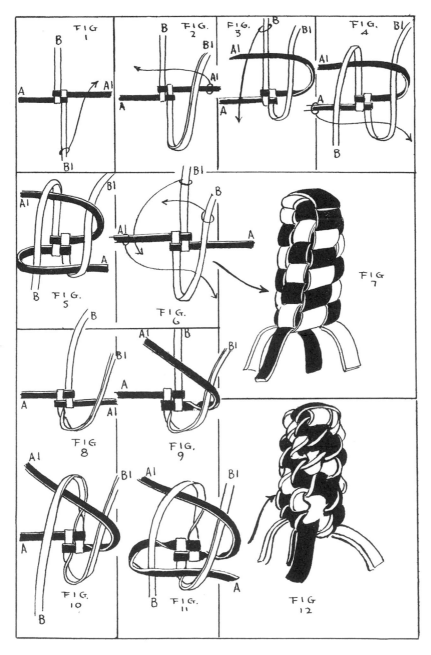

PLATE 102. Spiral Braid.

PLATE 103

Square Braid of Eight Thongs. While this beautiful braid is to all appearances a flat braid, after it is finished and molded it becomes a square braid with four corners and four faces each showing exactly the same weave. It is of South American origin, where it is used mainly on bridles.

Cut a strip of leather into eight thongs of equal width, or lash together eight thongs. The entire procedure is the same as in flat braiding, but on the order of the 13- and 21-thong double braids.

Group the thongs four on each side. Start with the right-hand thong, No. 8 in Fig. 1, and bring it to the left center under the three nearest thongs, 7, 6, and 5. Then bring the extreme left-hand thong, No. 1, to the right center over the three nearest thongs, 2, 3 and 4, and under thong 8. These steps are shown in Fig. 1.

Next bring thong 7 (on the extreme right) to the left center over the three nearest thongs, 6, 5 and 1. This is indicated by the arrowline in Fig. 1 and shown in Fig. 2.

In the fourth step, bring thong 2 from the left to the right center, under the three nearest thongs, 3, 4 and 8, and over 7. This is indicated by the arrowline in Fig. 2 and shown in Fig. 3.

Now thong 6 (on the extreme right) is brought to the left center under the three nearest thongs. This is the key to this braid.

Remember that the extreme right-hand thong alternates by going under three in one move and then over three thongs in the next; the extreme left-hand thong alternates by first going over three thongs and under one thong, then under three thongs and over one thong.

When the braid is of sufficient length, press on the edges to open them up, and in order to adjust the braid so it will be perfectly square, tap it lightly with a mallet on all four sides. This makes all sides the same width and of the same weave (Fig. 7).

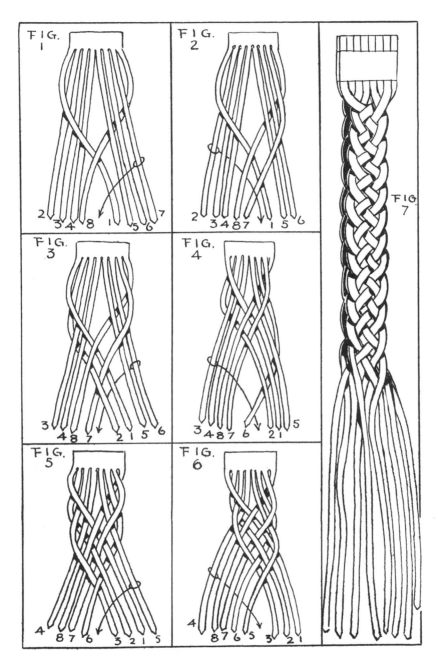

PLATE 103. Square Braid of Eight Thongs.

PLATE 104

Thirteen-Thong Braid. This and the braid to follow are the most beautiful of the flat braids. The key to both may be found in the braid of six thongs in Plate 30. Always remember to alternate over and under on each side; for instance, when the thongs are passed *over* on one side, they are passed *under* on this side the next time.

Divide the thongs seven on the left and six on the right. As each thong is worked from the outside, it comes only to the center.

Begin with thong 4 and pass it to the right over thongs 5 and 6, and under 7. Then pass thong 9 to the left under 8 and 4. Take thong 3 to the right over 5 and under 6, 7 and 9. Bring thong 11 on the right to the left under 10, 8 and 4, and over 3. Pass thong 2 on the left to the right under 5 and 6, and over 7, 9 and 11. Bring the extreme right-hand thong 13, to the left over 12, under 10, over 8, under 4, over 3 and under 2.

This preliminary, which appears somewhat intricate, is not absolutely necessary, but it closes the braid at the top so there is no loss of leather.

Now, take strand 1 on the extreme left and pass it over 5, 6 and 7, and under 9, 11 and 13.

On the right, take thong 12 and bring it to the left under 10, 8 and 4, and over 3, 2 and 1. The extreme left-hand thong is now No. 5. Previously the extreme left-hand thong No. 1, was passed *over* the three nearest it. Now alternate—and this is the secret of the double braid—by passing it *under* the three nearest—that is, 6, 7 and 9, and *over* 11, 13 and 12. On the extreme right, bring the outer thong, No. 10, to the left center by passing it *over* (the one before on this side went *under*) 8, 4 and 3, and *under* 2, 1 and 5.

On the left, pass over three and under three to the right center. On the right, pass under three and over three to the center. The braid is consistent from now on. Remember to alternate the passes on each side. Keep the braid snug and the thongs in order.

By placing the thongs in a drawer and closing it on them at the beginning, they can be kept side by side. If necessary, use paper clips and small pieces of paper and attach each number to the thong.

Flat Braid of Twenty-one Thongs. The principle outlined above is carried out in the twenty-one-thong braid (Fig. 2). Divide the thongs with eleven on the left and ten on the right. To avoid confusion from the start, bring thong 1 on the extreme left to the right center by passing it over the nearest five and under the next five. Then from the right, bring No. 21 to the left center by passing it under five and over five. Next on the left, pass under five and over five and so on.

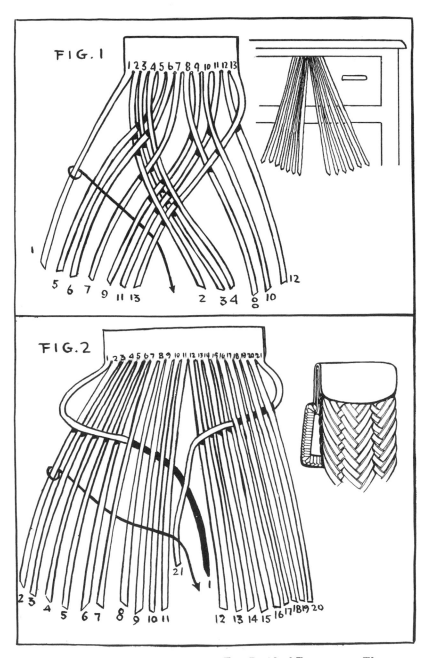

PLATE 104. Thirteen-Thong Braid; Flat Braid of Twenty-one Thongs.

PLATE 105

Double Braid with the Crocodile Ridge. Before we leave the double braid, I would like to say that it is characteristic of the Argentine, Uruguay, and the southern part of Brazil. The gauchos term it *trenza patria*, or native braid. I have never seen it combined with the crocodile ridge braid, or *lomo de yacaré*, but in this instance it works into a beautiful, rich braid.

This braid is made with 12 strings. First cross string No. 6 over string No. 7 to the right (Fig. 1). String No. 1 on the extreme left is brought to the center, under two, over two, and with a half twist under two and back toward its own side (also Fig. 1 arrowline and completed in Fig. 2). String No. 12 on the extreme right passes over two, and under four, and with a half twist to keep the dress side of the string out, back towards its own side.

In Fig. 3, string No. 2 passes over two and under four and with a half twist is brought back towards its own side (arrowline in Fig. 3 and completed in Fig. 4).

In Fig. 4, string No. 11 passes under two, over two, and under two and with a half twist is brought back to its side (arrowlines in Fig. 4 and completed in Fig. 5).

This same sequence is observed as the braiding continues. First, a string passes under two, over two, and under two. Next, the same string passes over two and under four—repeated, of course, in the same sequence on the opposite side.

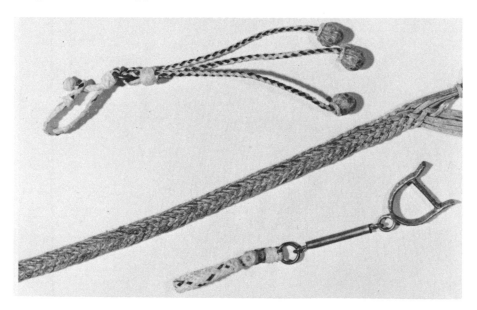

A piece of twelve-strand Argentine braiding, the *trenza patria*, flanked by a set of miniature boleadoras and one miniature stirrup. From Dr. Tinker's collection. The Hall of Horsemen of the Americas, at the University of Texas.

The completed braid, doubled and with the crododile ridge, is shown in Fig. 6.

While the double braid is usually made with an uneven number of strings, when combined with the crocodile ridge, an even number is employed. With a little patience, various sequences and combinations can be made, even a double ridge down the center.

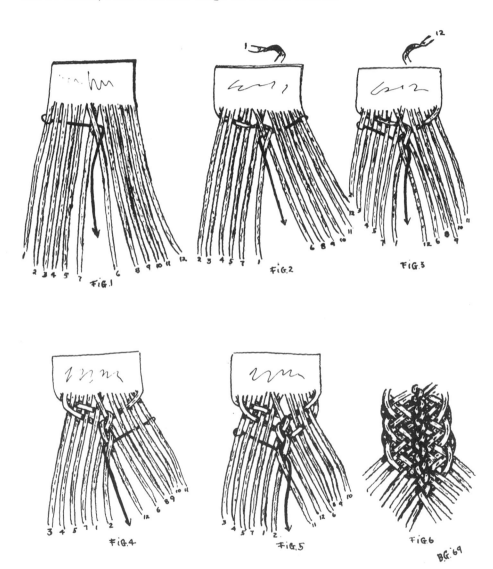

PLATE 105. Double Braid with the Crocodile Ridge.

PLATE 106

Oval Braid of Nine Strings or Thongs. By using the double braid, or *trenza patria*, an attractive oval braid may be obtained. This braid makes a fine pair of reins, and with this in mind I have made it with two separate pieces so one piece can be used for the buttonhole and the other for the button.

Cut your rawhide or leather as shown in Fig. 1. One piece has five strings and the other four. These are meshed together as shown in Fig. 2. Starting with string No. 5 on the right side, pass it over one string and under three to the center (arrowline, Fig. 2). In Fig. 3, string No. 6 on the extreme left passes over one, under three. In Fig. 4, string No. 4 on the right passes under one and over three (arrowline). String No. 7 on the left under one, over three. Alternate the braid thus: one time passing under one, over three and the next on that side over one, under three.

The section marked B (Fig. 5) instead of being cut as in the previous sections can be four long strings or thongs. A suitable hole can be made in section A, and the strings of section B braided in a four-string round braid with a terminal knot on the end. In Fig. 6, you can see how this braid looks on the sides and Fig. 7 gives an idea of its oval shape. In Fig. 8 is a similar braid made of ten strings.

A double braid with the V's of the braid running horizontally is made with ten strings, as indicated in Figs. 9, 10 and 11. The finished braid is shown in Fig. 12.

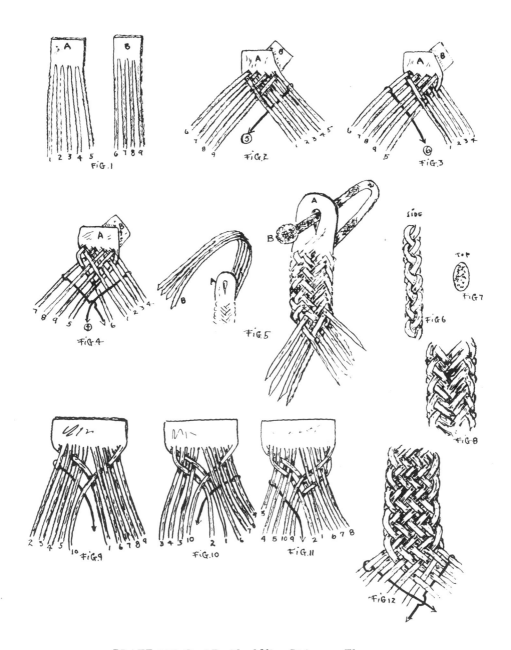

PLATE 106. Oval Braid of Nine Strings or Thongs.

267

PLATE 107

Half-Round Braid of Six Strings or Thongs. This braid is round in front and flat in the back. Start as in Fig. 1, where first string No. 3 is laid across string No. 4, and then string No. 1 on the extreme left is brought around back under three strings and then forward over one.

This sequence is repeated alternately on the right and left until the desired length is braided.

The same effect can be obtained in a larger braid by using eight strings as shown in Fig. 7. These braids are made without a core.

In Plate 142 is shown a sixteen-string round braid which when flattened appears to be a double braid. By using this method with six strings, a flat braid may be obtained as shown in photograph A. To do this take string No. 1 in Fig. 1 and pass it around completely under five strings and back over three. Then string No. 6 in Fig. 2 is passed to the rear under all strings and back over three. When the braid is completed and the strings or thongs still damp, press flat. This is, of course, more effective with rawhide. (See photographs on Page 270.)

Triangular Braid of Twelve Strings. This unique braid is made by first braiding, without a core, twelve strings in a round braid of an over-two, under-two sequence. When the braid is completed and the rawhide still damp take a pair of flat-nosed pliers and press firmly together three corners of the braid, to produce a triangular effect.

Mr. C. W. Halliday of Subiaco, West Australia, wrote me that he had seen this braid on a pair of reins and no one could figure it out. About the same time Don Luis Alberto Flores of Buenos Aires wrote an article in *El Caballo*, the horse magazine of the Argentine, that he had seen a six-sided braid of reins made from eighteen rawhide strings. Such braids are rare and usually create considerable comment.

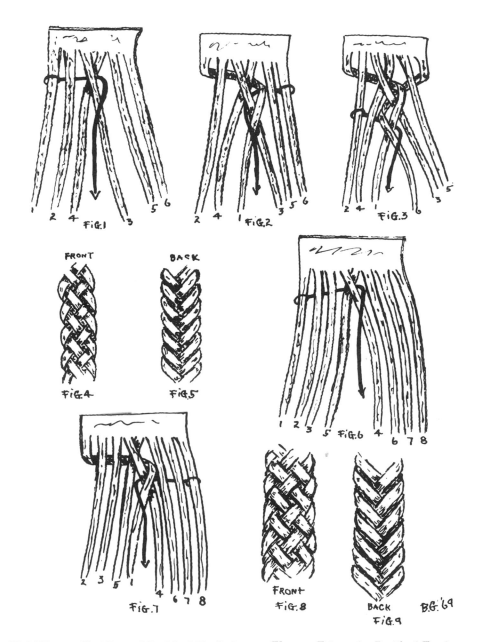

PLATE 107. Half-Round Braid of Six Strings or Thongs; Triangular Braid of Twelve Strings.

269

Round braids of various numbers of strings and without a core can be molded into a variety of shapes. Shown in photograph A is a dog collar made from a sixteen-string braid which has been pressed flat while damp. It resembles the double braid or *trenza patria* of the Argentine.

In photograph B, the center braid is a mashed-together six-string round braid of over-three, under-three sequence.

In B (l. and r.) are two triangular braids which are made from twelve-string round braids—without a core, of course. The sequence of the round braid is over two, under two. The edges are pressed together with flat-nosed pliers while the rawhide still is damp. Few braiders know this trick with rawhide round braids.

In the Argentine, the Providence of Tucuman to be more exact, where braids with as many as six edges are made, they are used for reins and designated "Tucuman reins."

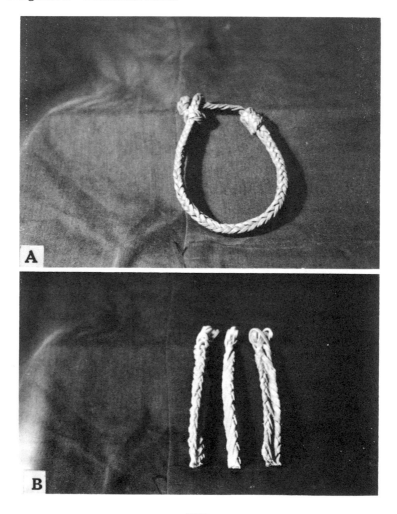

Buttons

PLATE 108

Roll Button. This type of button is undoubtedly the most primitive of leather buttons. It is made very easily and is most practical. In South America the old-time gaucho used one of these buttons in place of a stirrup, hooking the button between his first two toes.

To make this simplest type of button, take a strip of leather, say ½-inch or ¾-inch wide, taper it to a point and, about an inch and a half back from the point, make a horizontal slit as long as the leather is wide (Fig. 1). Dampen the leather, then turn the point inward and pull through (Fig. 2) and the button is complete (Fig. 3).

I saw one of these buttons on the flap of a German Luger holster in World War II. It had seen much wear but was as serviceable as ever.

This type of button may be applied as a belt fastening as shown in Figs. 4, 5 and 6. It is passed through the slot while disengaged and then the button is formed when the tongue of the belt is in place. It can be used thus for all sorts of fastenings.

To make another type of roll button, taper a small strip of leather, wet it and then roll it up from the widest end (Fig. 7). When it is rolled about two-thirds of the way, cut a slot directly through the roll, pass the pointed end through (Fig. 8) and draw it tight (Fig. 9).

This button can be used on pocketbooks, boxes, etc., by leaving a long enough pointed end so that it can be fastened by the three-hole method as shown in Fig. 11.

A leather thong doubled and passed through four holes as shown in Fig. 10 serves as a fastener. To unloosen the button, pull on the pointed end.

The method of using this button as a clasp for a box is shown in Fig. 12. It is also good on leather hunting jackets, or wherever a button or clasp is needed.

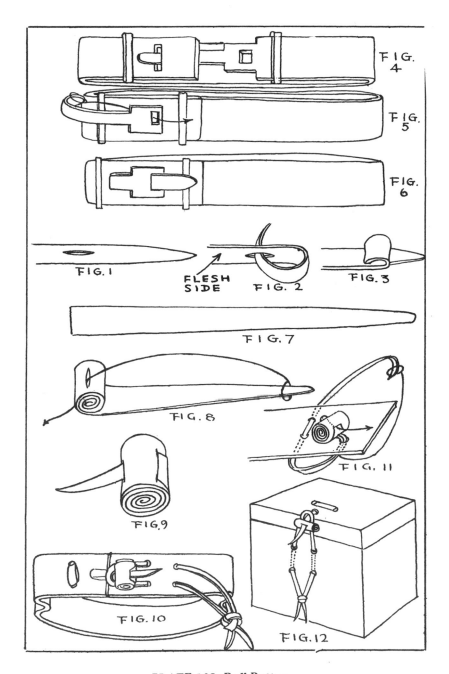

FIG.
4

FIG.
5

FIG.
6

FIG. 1

FLESH
SIDE   FIG. 2

FIG. 3

FIG. 7

FIG. 8

FIG. 11

FIG. 9

FIG. 10

FIG. 12

PLATE 108. Roll Button.

PLATE 109

Two-Thong Turk's-head Button. This is the same type of knot that is used by cowboys in tying the ends of their reins together. Made with a short thong of 1/8 inch in width, it is a practical button.

The first step is shown in Fig. 1 where the thong is doubled with the flesh sides together. Loop the end of thong B as shown and bring it around under A. Next, place A across the loop formed by B. Pass thong B over A and through this loop (Fig. 2).

Bring thong A around underneath and up through its own loop as indicated by the arrowline in Fig. 3. The loose knot is shown in Figs. 4 and 5. Tighten it by pulling easily on both ends of the thongs. See that the ends of the thongs have the flesh sides together.

The ends may be cut off flush with the knot or left to facilitate pulling the knot through the buttonhole.

Three-Thong Turk's-head Button. This knot is made in the same manner as the Turk's-head terminal knot for round braid in Plate 38. In this case three thongs are used. Cut the leather with a tapered end. Split the larger end into three thongs, A, B, and C (Fig. 7).

Begin the crown knot as shown in Fig. 8 by folding the extreme right-hand thong, which is C, over thong B and behind thong A. Next, fold thong B over thong C and in front of thong A. Now fold thong A over thong B and in between thongs C and B at their base, as indicated in the arrowline in Fig. 9.

Pass thong C around the base of thong A and up through the center. Then carry thong B around the base of thong C and up through the center. Pass thong A around the base of thong B and up through the center. These steps are indicated by the arrowlines in Fig. 10. The finished knot is shown in Fig. 11.

To attach this button, cut three holes as shown in Fig. 12 and pass the end X down through the left-hand one, then up through the right-hand hole, down through the middle one and up through the left-hand hole, as indicated by the arrowline in Fig. 12. This end also passes up through the center of the knot and forms one of the ends as shown by the arrowline in Fig. 13. The ends may be trimmed or left, as desired. Attached in this manner, the button will remain firmly affixed indefinitely.

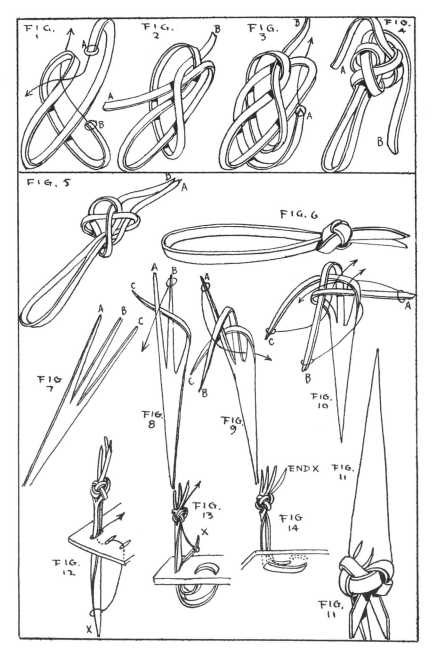

PLATE 109. Two- and Three-Thong Turk's-head Button.

PLATE 110

Chinese Button Knot. The basis of this knot is that which sailors term a carrick bend. Lay the thong over a mandrel as shown in Fig. 1, or around the hand. Twist thong B (on the right) into a loop as shown in Fig. 2 with the bight over thong A.

Bring thong A under thong B and in an over-one, under-one sequence, as indicated by the arrowline in Fig. 2. Figure 3 shows the completed carrick bend.

Bring the end of thong B up through the center on its own side as indicated by the arrowline in Fig. 3. Thong A follows a similar course on its own side, as shown by the arrowline.

Remove the loose knot from the mandrel, or the hand, and bring the two ends together, with their flesh sides touching. Begin to tighten the knot carefully, first taking up the bight which originally was around the mandrel. The knot now appears as shown in Fig. 4. Tighten it gradually, always holding the two ends together until finished, as shown in Fig. 5.

Diamond Button Knot. The diamond button knot starts in the same way as the Chinese button—with a carrick bend. The difference is in bringing up the ends through the center of the knot.

In the case of the diamond button knot, instead of passing thong A up through the center on its own side, bring it around as indicated by the arrowline in Fig. 6 and up on the side of thong B, passing under B. Carry thong B around to the side of thong A, pass it under thong A and up through the center.

The bight around the mandrel is the top of the button. Keep the flesh sides of the ends together and work out the slack until the knot becomes tight. This is a more attractive knot than the Chinese button knot.

Both can be made with a 1/8-inch thong, or wider if desired.

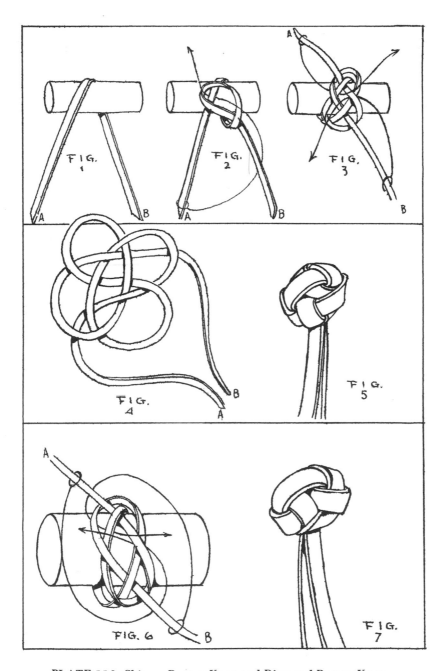

PLATE 110. Chinese Button Knot and Diamond Button Knot.

277

PLATE 111

Round Button of Four Thongs. To make this button take a piece of leather of ordinary thickness, 14 inches long and ¼ inch wide. Split in half 6 inches from each end, making four 1/8-inch thongs (Fig. 1).

Fold the leather with the flesh side in and make a crown knot as shown in Fig. 2. (This is made the same as shown in Fig. 1, Plate 100, under square braids.) Here the thongs are designated as A, B, C and D.

Next, with the thongs designated as A, B, C and D, make a wall knot, which is a crown knot done from underneath; in other words, pass thong A under thong B, thong B under thong C, thong C under thong D, and thong D under or through the bight of thong A. See Fig. 3.

Draw up this wall knot so that it rests below the first, or crown knot. Now make another crown knot as shown in Fig. 4. This one is carefully worked down on top of the other two knots and appears as in Fig. 5.

The braiding or weaving process now begins. The sequence is over-two, under-two, as shown in Fig. 5, where the awl passes under two thongs to illustrate the course of thong C.

Pass thong C down over the two thongs below it and then up under two, the second of which is thong D. Then pass thong D down over the two below it and up under two, the upper one of which is thong A; thong A down over two and up under two, the top one being thong B; thong B downward over two and up under two, the upper one being thong C, which already has been tucked in place in the first move of this step.

The top of the knot now will appear as in Fig. 6. The thongs on top are in the form of a square. If an awl is inserted down in each corner, it will go clear through the knot alongside the folded part of the leather. In Fig. 6 is shown the path of thong D. Working in a counterclockwise direction, or to the left, arrowlines indicate the paths of the other thongs. Pull them down through and cut them off underneath.

This button also can be made with three, six or eight thongs.

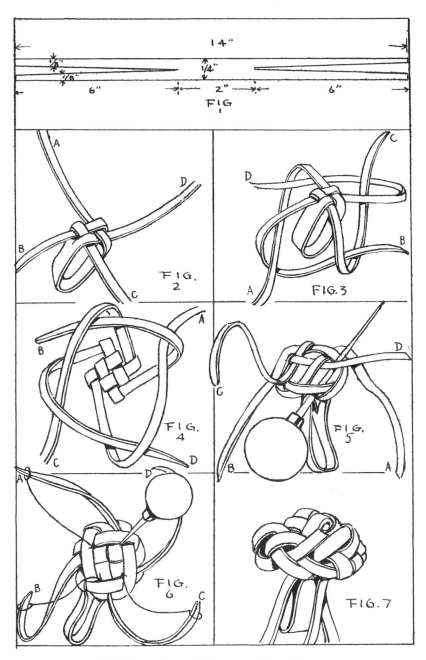

PLATE 111. Round Button of Four Thongs.

PLATE 112

Gaucho Knot Button. When finished, this button, made similar to the preceding one, resembles the gaucho knot of two passes.

Cut the leather or rawhide as in the round button of four thongs (or strings) in Plate 111. The first two passes are identical with those in Plate 111, shown here in Figs. 1 and 2.

In Fig. 3 is shown the braiding procedure for all four strings. This is indicated by the arrowline showing how string No. 3 passes over one and under one. The other three strings are braided in the same fashion. This is shown in Fig. 4.

Figure 4 also illustrates how the strings are doubled—that is, string No. 1 passes down and under one string, parallel to the string on its right. String No. 3 also passes down under one string, paralleling the string on its right. The other two strings are woven in the same way.

The positions of the strings are illustrated in Fig. 5. The next move is the splitting of pairs, as shown by the arrowline marking the course of string No. 1. It passes upward under two, splitting a pair of parallel strings, then over two and under two, coming out at the very top.

The effect achieved is shown in Fig. 6. To complete this braid, each string is passed down through the entire knot, as shown by the arrowline showing the course of string No. 2. The string-ends are then cut off, and the button is complete.

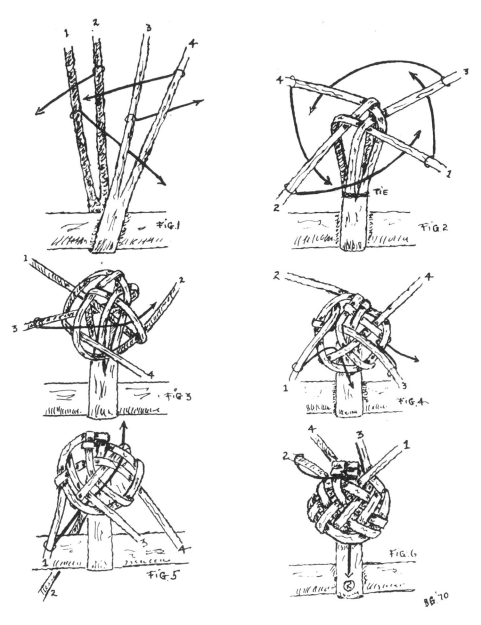

PLATE 112. Gaucho Knot Button.

281

PLATE 113

Eight-Thong Round Button. This is comparable to the round button of four thongs shown in Plate 111. However, it is made with eight thongs or strings.

First middle your thongs or strings and made a four-string round braid sufficient to form a loop around a mandrel of the desired circumference (Fig. 1). Then tie the eight strings together tightly next to the top of the mandrel. Select two strings from each group and tie these four strings at the top, as shown also in Fig. 1. With the other four strings make a crown knot (arrowlines in Fig. 1).

Having completed this crown knot (Fig. 2), make a wall knot as shown also in Fig. 2, and indicated by the arrowlines. This results in the braid shown in Fig. 3. Each string is then brought down in an under-two, over-two sequence (arrowlines in Fig. 3). In Fig. 4 the arrowlines show the path of each string upward—under two.

Untie the four strings which have until now been kept apart. Form them into a crown knot, and bring each end down through the knot itself. Do not pull these ends more than necessary as they might pull through the crown knot. Cut off all ends.

Gaucho Knot Button of Eight Thongs. This is similar to the button in Plate 112, but made with eight strings or thongs. As in the eight-thong round button, start by middling your strings, braid them into a four-string round braid, tie all strings next to the mandrel, and then tie four strings at the top, two from each set. Next, make a crown knot around these tied-off strings with the other four strings. Now, instead of making a wall knot, pass each string over the next and under another. All this is shown in Fig. 6. The wall knot is now made, as shown by the arrowlines in Fig. 7 and completed in Fig. 8. Each string, now already having gone under one at the bottom, passes upward over one, under one, and over one (the top). The sequence of each string downward is: under two, over two, under two, and over two at the bottom. Then under two going upward and the end cut off flush. The finished button is shown in Fig. 9 after the tied-off strings have been crowned and passed down through the knot as in the previous button.

Herringbone Button of Eight Thongs. In making a herringbone braid, all steps in the previous button are completed until Fig. 8. The sequence after the strings have passed beneath the bottom string is: over one, under one, and passing over three strings at the top and going down, split the first pair downward—in other words, go beneath. Next, split the next pair of strings by passing upward, over two, and split the final pair downward. The strings are then cut off. The top crown is made with the tied-off strings and passed through the knot and cut off as previously explained.

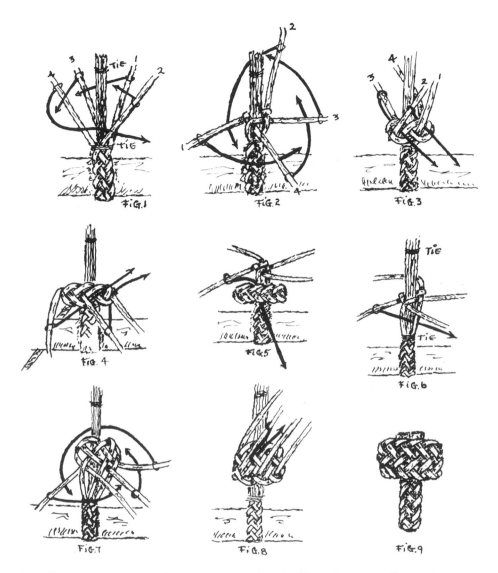

PLATE 113. Eight-Thong Round Button; Gaucho Knot Button of Eight Thongs; Herringbone Button of Eight Thongs.

283

PLATE 114

Square Button of Four Thongs. The square button of four thongs is started in the same way as the round button of four thongs described in Plate 111. Use the same length of leather, cut in the same fashion as indicated for the round button and shown again in Fig. 1.

Fold the leather at the uncut part with the flesh sides inward (Fig. 2). Make a crown knot as shown in Fig. 3, working the thongs toward the left or counterclockwise. Tighten the knot as shown in Fig. 4.

The next knot, which is a wall knot, or crown knot made from beneath, is worked clockwise, or to the right, as shown in Fig. 5. This is important—the crown knot is worked to the *left* and the wall knot to the *right*.

The wall knot is drawn up snug just at the base of the crown knot.

The braiding or weaving of the knot is the next step. Start with thong D as shown in Fig. 7. Work this thong to the right and pass it back and down behind its own part as shown in Fig. 7. The same applies to the other three thongs. For instance, carry thong A to the right and down behind its own part; repeat likewise with thong B and thong C.

All the thongs now point downward.

The final step in making this button is illustrated in Fig. 8. Work the thongs toward the right and upward. Pass each around and over the one next to it and up through the knot, as shown and indicated by the arrowline in Fig. 8. Thong B thus is brought over thong C and up through the knot. Thong C, in turn, passes over thong D and upward. And so on.

The ends may be cut flush with the top of the knot or pointed and left protruding.

This makes a very attractive button.

Additional buttons can be found under Hondas; the Ring Button, and various braided button coverings, such as the Pineapple Knot, etc.

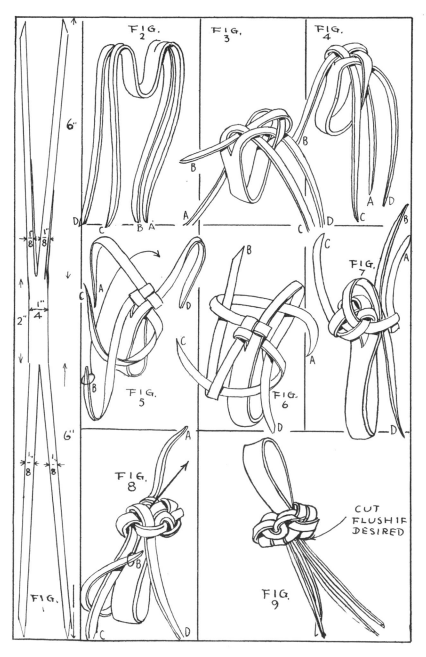

PLATE 114. Square Button of Four Thongs.

285

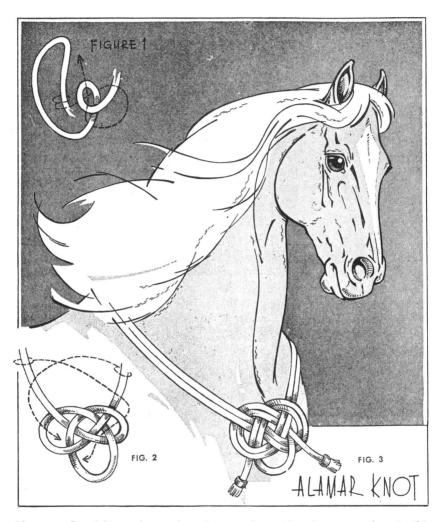

Alamar, a Spanish word meaning *gimp,* or decoration, is a name given to this knot or weave by the Spanish caballero who used it to "dike" out his caballo for parades and state functions.

Edge Braiding

PLATE 115

Spanish Edge-Lacing of One Loop. Edge-lacing serves two purposes. It joins the edges of two or more pieces of leather and provides a decorative finish to the work by covering the raw edges.

Use a lacing thong about four and one-half times the length of the edge to be covered.

Before making the holes or slits on the edges, it is best to thin down these edges with a skiving knife, tapering them on the flesh sides. Then carefully cement them together. In making the holes or slits, take into consideration the width of the lacing to be used. A simple rule is that if a lacing of 1/8 inch is used, space the holes 1/8 inch apart and also 1/8 inch from the edge.

In the Spanish edge–lacing, as well as in other types, it is more convenient to work from the left to the right. Run the lacing through the first left-hand hole from the front until only about ¼ inch of the end is left (Fig. 1).

Now insert the lacing back through the same hole, beneath the projecting end and draw tight (Figs. 2 and 3). The end is thus held fast. Before the loop is closed, apply a small amount of cement. Always work from the front.

Now carry the lacing through hole No. 2 (Fig. 3) and bring it around to the front again; this time it passes through its own loop (Fig. 4).

This loop and working part of the lacing always come together flesh side to flesh side. Tighten the first loop as shown in Fig. 5. Pass the lacing through hole No. 3, around to the front, through the loop, tighten the loop and proceed to the next hole. The finished lacing is shown in Figs. 7 and 8.

To insure·even lacing, always try to exert the same amount of pull each time. When finished, lay the work on a hard surface and gently tap the lacing down with a mallet. This distributes it and makes it lie flat.

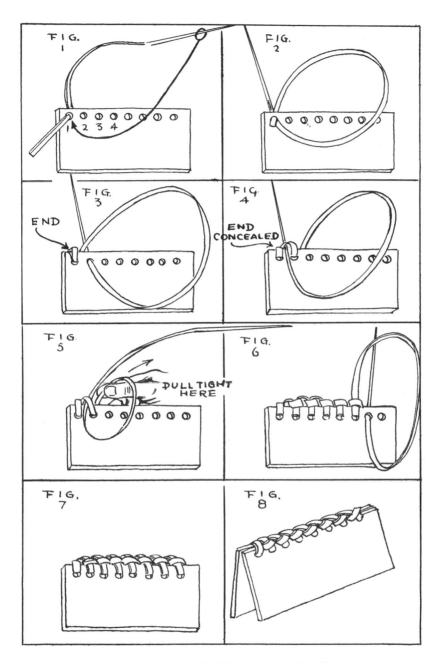

PLATE 115. Spanish Edge-Lacing of One Loop.

PLATE 116

Splicing. In edge-lacing it is best to work with short lengths of lacing thongs and to splice on additional lengths as required. This will eliminate the trouble of continually pulling through a lengthy lacing, which not only is bothersome but also narrows down the lacing toward the working end.

In splicing, bevel both edges of the lacing (Fig. 1). Bevel the working lacing on the flesh side, the other on the smooth side. Thus the top edge of the spliced lacing passes through smoothly (Fig. 1). Touch with some quick-drying cement, either rubber or Duco, and press together. Be careful in using Duco for if it comes in contact with the finished side of the leather, it will eventually leave a light spot as the rest of the leather darkens.

Joining. Sometimes the lacing will run entirely around, as on the edges of a billfold, and in such a case it can be joined together so that it will not be noticeable. In Fig. 2 the lacing on the right represents the start. It has gone completely around and has been brought up to the point indicated on the left. In beginning the lacing which has to be joined, do not fasten down the standing end A but leave a couple of inches free, as shown in Fig. 2.

Withdraw the end A entirely from hole No. 2 and insert end B only through the first piece of leather, allowing it to come up between the two layers as shown in Fig. 3.

Take end A and bring it from the rear forward through the loop of end B and then from the front to the rear through its own loop (Fig. 4). The next step, not shown in the sketch, is to bring end A from the rear forward through hole 2, but only through the one layer of leather and up alongside end B. Tighten the braid, touch a little cement between the two ends, down as far as possible, cut them off and tuck them in. It will be impossible to see where this lacing has been joined.

To end a lacing that is not to be joined, follow the procedure illustrated in Figs. 6 and 7. This will provide a knot which will hold fast.

In going around corners with any type of edge-lacing, always pass through the corner hole two or three times to space the lacing on the outer edge as shown in Fig. 8.

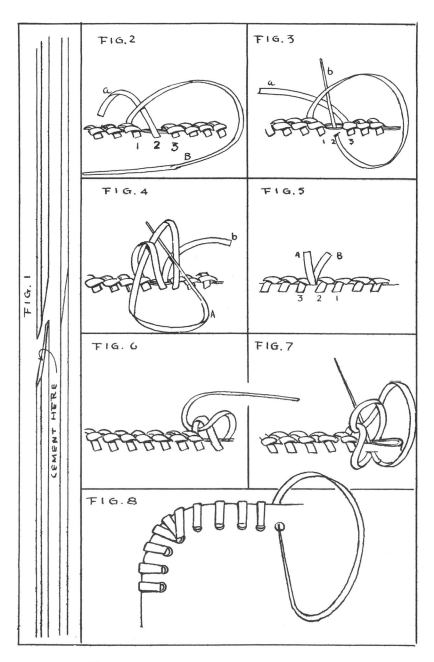

PLATE 116. Splicing and Joining Edge-Lacing.

291

PLATE 117

Spanish Edge-Lacing of Two Loops. Use a thong about six times the length of the edge to be covered.

Start with the standing end in the back, held down by the thumb between the first and second hole. Then pass the thong from the front to the rear through hole No. 1 as shown in Fig. 1. Bring the thong forward again and pass it through hole No. 2 from front to rear, also shown in Fig. 1.

Bring the thong to the front again, and this time, instead of passing it through a hole, carry it beneath the two loops formed on the top as shown in Fig. 2. Tighten the work by pulling at the two points indicated in Fig. 3. Always try to exert the same tension so that the lacing will be consistently even.

After passing the thong under the two loops, bring it to the front again and this time pass it through hole No. 3 as shown in Fig. 4. Bring it to the front and pass it under the two loops as shown in Fig. 5. Tighten by pulling upon that portion of the thong indicated in Fig. 5.

The sequence now is through hole No. 4 from front to back and then under the two loops on the top; tighten (Fig. 6); then through hole No. 5 and under the two loops; and so on.

Joining Spanish Edge-Lacing of Two Loops. Where the edge-lacing goes completely around as on a wallet or billfold and comes back to the starting point, finish the work by joining the braid. When this is done properly it is difficult to tell where the braid ends or begins.

Note in Fig. 7 at the starting point the standing end is shown in dotted lines. The standing end is withdrawn through the starting hole and the loops through which it had passed. It is shown protruding from hole No. 2 in Fig. 8.

The braid has come completely around and the working end is shown in Fig. 9 just to the left of the starting hole. Pass it through this hole from the front, up through the loop to the right, and under the intersection of the two loops to the left, as indicated by the arrowline in Fig. 10. Then pass it back over its own part, down through the right-hand loop and into the same hole in which is the standing end (Fig. 11).

When binding together two pieces of leather, tuck both ends inside between the two pieces and the braid is complete.

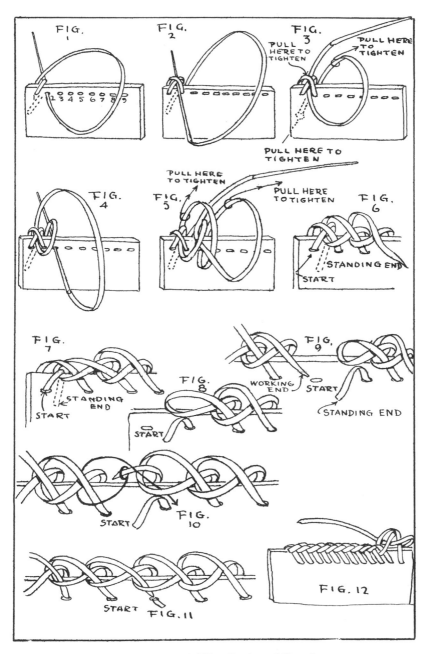

PLATE 117. Spanish Edge-Lacing of Two Loops.

293

PLATE 118

Spanish Edge-Lacing of Three Loops. For this edge-lacing, use a thonging lace about 7½ times the length to be worked. Start by passing the thong from the front to the rear through hole 2 and folding the end over the edge to the back between holes 1 and 2. This end is shown in dotted lines in Fig. 1.

Next, bring the working end to the front and pass it through hole 1 and to the front again and through hole 3. Do not draw the loops tight.

There are three of these loops on the edge of the leather. Now pass the working end through the three loops from the front to the rear (Fig. 2), bring it forward and pass it through hole 4 from the front (Fig. 3).

Tighten the start of the braid by drawing on it in the same sequence it was made and in the same direction, but leave the last three loops slightly loose so the working end can pass through them easily. The original end, shown in dotted lines, should be secured beneath one of its own parts.

In Fig. 4 the working end is shown passing through the second set of three loops. Bring it to the front and then down through hole 5. Continue the braid in this way until the finish, when it is tapped lightly with a hammer or mallet to make it lie smoothly.

Two-Tone Spanish Edge-Lacing of One Loop. If a two-tone effect on edge-lacing is desired, use two thongs of different colors. In the illustration we will designate thong A as white and thong B as black. Always work from the front to the rear. First introduce thong A through hole 1 and then thong B through hole 2. Bring thong A to the front and through hole 3 (Fig. 6).

Now pass thong B through the loop of thong A from the front to the rear and to the left of its own part, as shown in Fig. 7. Bring it forward and through hole 4, as shown. Pass thong A through the loop of thong B and to the left of its own part, and bring it forward and through hole 5 (Fig. 8). Continue this until the end, first working with one thong and then the other. The standing ends at the beginning can be folded over and secured in the rear beneath their own parts.

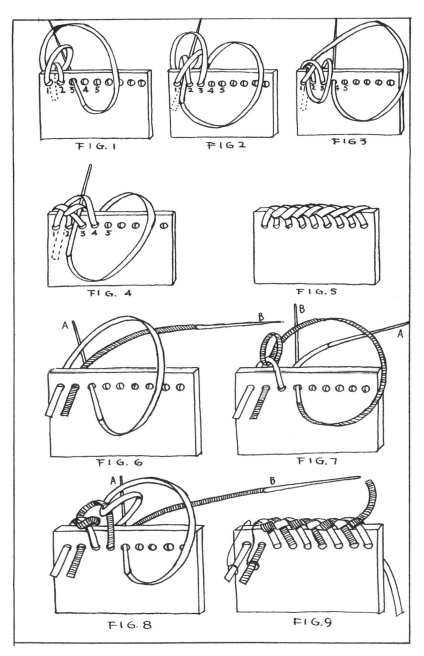

FIG. 1 FIG 2 FIG 3

FIG. 4 FIG. 5

FIG. 6 FIG. 7

FIG. 8 FIG. 9

PLATE 118. Top: Spanish Edge-Lacing of Three Loops.
Bottom: Two-Tone Spanish Edge-Lacing of One Loop.

295

PLATE 119

Round Braid Edge-Lacing. This edge-lacing resembles the four-thong round braid, except that it is made with one thong. There are several methods of making this beautiful edge-lacing. Here we will consider the first:

Start with a thong at least seven times the length of the edge to be covered. Space the holes the same as the width of the lacing and punch them this same distance from the edge.

Pass the thong through hole 1 from the front; forward and through hole 3 from the front; the same through hole 5 (Fig. 1); then 7 and finally 9. If the edge-lacing is longer, keep on passing the thong to the right through every other hole. Leave an extra hole (hole No. 10) at the end as shown (Fig. 2).

Now to start working back. From hole 9 go back through 7 as indicated by the arrowline in Fig. 2. Continue back toward the starting point until hole 2 is reached. Pass the end through hole 2, as indicated by the arrowline in Fig. 3.

In the next step, work towards the right, passing the thong through holes 4, 6, 8 and 10 (Figs. 4 and 5).

Now the actual braid begins. The working end of the thong is in the rear of hole 10. Bring it forward over its own part and under the next thong.

This step is indicated by the fid in Fig. 6. The thong follows the same course. Carry it through hole 8 (Fig. 7), and in the rear pass it under the thong to the left of it, as can be seen in Fig. 8, then over the next and under the next (Fig. 8). The awl is shown passing through hole 6 in Fig. 8, which will be the course of the thong. On the other side, pass it under one, then over one on top and under one in the front. Continue until it joins the standing end which is in hole 1.

This braid lies flat and entirely covers the raw edge of the leather. It has many uses on saddles, pistol holsters, knife sheaths, etc.

A very practical watchband in kangaroo hide. Courtesy: D.W. Morgan, Austral Enterprises.

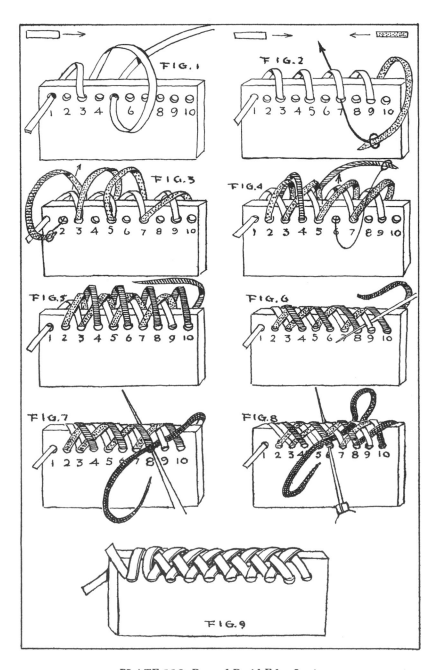

PLATE 119. Round Braid Edge-Lacing.

297

PLATE 120

Round Braid Edge-Lacing (Second Method). Here is another way to make the four-part round braid edge-lacing of one thong Start as in Fig. 1 by passing the thong through hole 1 from rear to front; then over the edge to the rear and forward through hole 4.

In the next step, also shown in Fig. 1, bring the working end to the left and forward through hole 2 from the rear to the front.

In Fig. 2 the working end is shown passing over the edge and through hole 5 from rear to front. Up to this point the working end of the thong has been passed over its own parts. However, in Fig. 2 the arrowline indicates how the working end in the next move passes to the rear over its own part and beneath the loop of that part of the thong over hole 4.

Bring the working end of the thong forward through hole 3 as shown in Fig. 3. The fid, with its end beneath the thong which emerges from hole 4, is also shown in Fig. 3.

After passing the working end beneath the thong at hole 4, carry it over the edge, to the rear, and forward through hole 6 (Fig. 4). Pass it over its own part and under that part of the thong illustrated by the course of the fid in Fig. 4.

Next, bring the working end from the rear to the front through hole 4, which is already occupied by a section of the thong (Fig. 5). Pass it beneath the section of the thong which emerges from hole 5, as shown by the fid in Fig. 5. Now move the working end to the rear and forward through hole 7. Pass it over its own part and under a section of the thong as in Fig. 4, and then through hole 5 to the front—and so on until the finish. The sequence is always over one, under one. If the original standing end has been left long it can be worked forward to close up the braid at the beginning, following the over-one, under-one sequence.

Round Braid Edge-Lacing (Third Method). By using four thongs, all of different colors, or two of one color and two of another, you can obtain a multitone braid as shown in the sequences in Figs. 7, 8, 9, 10, 11 and 12.

Work with two thongs at a time, lacing the first pair from left to right to the end and then interweaving the next pair. Remember the over-one, under-one sequence.

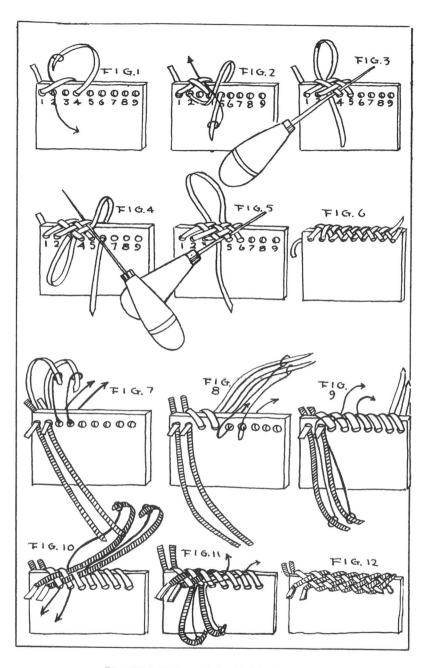

PLATE 120. Round Braid Edge-Lacing.

299

PLATE 121

Eight-String Round Edge-Braiding. The name is confusing. The edge-braid actually is made with one long string, but, when the braid is finished, it looks like an eight-string round braid, with a sequence of over one, under one. braid for securing the lining to the skirting of a saddle and, with wider thongs, is sometimes used on the cantle of the saddle braid for securing the lining to the skirting of a saddle end, with wider thongs, is sometimes used on the cantle of the saddle. Such saddle decorations are not seen nowadays. This is too bad, for a saddle could really be dressed up and beautified with numerous types of braids and fancy knots—and in earlier times they actually were. This is another phase in the lost art of braiding. A book could be written on this subject.

This edge-braid is primarily used to join two pieces together, as well as to cover and decorate the raw edges. In our diagram, for simplicity's sake, we have shown it worked on the edge of one piece of leather.

The rawhide string or leather thong, whichever you prefer, is passed through hole No. 1 from the rear and over the edge through hole No. 5, also from the rear. The arrowline shows the course of the string or thong, passing under its own part on top and then through hole No. 2 from the back. The sequence from then on is clearly illustrated in the diagrams. To finish off the starting point, the original end is worked forward and back, as shown in Fig. 7. To completely finish the braid at this end, the string will have to pass through hole No. 1 at least two more times.

At the bottom of Plate 121, two sequences are shown where two strings, or thongs, of contrasting color are worked simultaneously. The sequence given is the beginning of an under-two, over-two braid, which is explained more fully in the next plate, although of but one string. This edge-braid gives a very pretty effect.

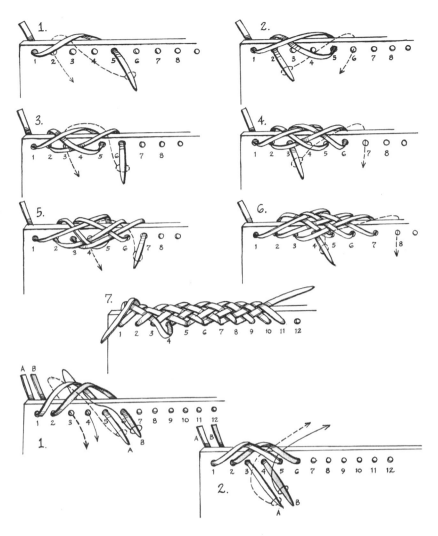

PLATE 121. Eight-String Round Edge-Braiding.

PLATE 122

Eight-String Round Edge-Braiding (Second Method). This edge-braid and similar ones which can be made by this method, are, as far as the author knows, his own invention. Sooner or later in braiding, as in many other arts and crafts, the "original" turns out to be something someone else thought of years ago. Such may happen in this case, as the working out of this braid seems to come as a natural sequence to the one shown in Plate 121.

This is a braid which can be made with an over-two, under-two sequence, and, by leaving a greater number of holes vacant on the first pass, can be made into a braid of over three, under three, and so on. In other words, it can be made to simulate an eight-string round braid of over two, under two, or a twelve-string round braid of over three, under three, and so on. Many combinations can be worked out.

It is a decorative edge-braid and when finished looks, as one fellow remarked, "as if it just growed there."

The first and second moves, shown in Figs. 1 and 2, are similar to the start of the braid in Plate 121. But it will be noticed in Fig. 3 that the thong or string, after passing to the front through hole No. 6, then goes under two. In Fig. 4 it also passes under two in Fig. 5, it passes under two and then over one in the rear before coming to the front through hole No. 4. In Fig. 6, the string passes over one, under two and comes out through hole No. 8. It passes to the back, then (Fig. 7) under two, over one and forward through hole No. 5.

The continued sequence is, in front, always over one, under two; in the rear, under two, over one. By back-braiding at the start, you can finish off this section.

Should you care for a simulated twelve-string round braid, skip six holes at the start and the final sequence will be, at the front, over two, under three, and at the back, under three and over two.

Worked on a saddle, this makes a beautiful—and practical— decoration.

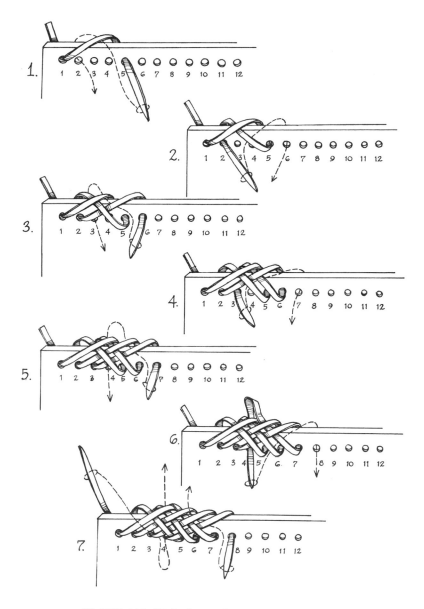

PLATE 122. Eight-String Round Edge-Braiding.

303

PLATE 123

Use of Spanish Edge-Lacing in Attaching Pockets and Flaps. First, cut out the pocket patch marked A in Fig. 1. Around the three edges to be laced on, punch holes about 1/8 inch from the edge and about 3/16 of an inch apart. Lay the pocket patch on the part to which it will be fastened and insert a fid or other pointed instrument into each hole, making a corresponding impression on the leather foundation, marked B.

Punch out these holes at the impressions on B. About ¼ inch from this row of holes, punch the same number of holes in the leather B, each opposite a hole in the inner row. At the curves of the pockets these holes will be spaced wider apart than those on the inner circle—but there should be an equal number of holes on both inner and outer circles.

With a little cement around the edge of the under part, affix the pocket flap, being careful that the holes in the flap are directly over those on the leather beneath. Turn back the flap at the upper right-hand corner and pass the thong (3/32-inch commercial lacing is best) through the first inner hole in the leather B and back up through the outer hole (Fig. 1). Lay the flap corner back with a little more cement on it and on the end of the lacing so that the latter is held fast, and pass the needle through the hole in flap A and down through the corresponding hole in the leather B (the same through which the lacing was first inserted) and up through the second outer hole in B (Fig. 2).

Bring the working end (shown with needle attached) down through the loop formed by the lacing, keeping it inclined to the right (Fig. 3). Draw it snug. Pass the needle down through the second inner hole and up through the outer third hole (Fig. 4). Next, bring it down through the loop formed between the second set of holes (Fig. 5). Pass it down through the inner hole, No. 3, and up through the outer hole, No. 4, and again down through the loop formed. It will be seen by now that this is the same as the Spanish edge-lacing of one loop (Plate 115).

Staggered Slits. To make the thong lie snug on the edge, slant and stagger the slits as shown on the pistol holster in Fig. 7.

Miscellaneous Edge-Lacings. Fig. 8 shows a one-thong spiral or whip-lace; Fig. 9, double one-thong spiral; Fig. 10, double two-thong spiral; Fig. 11, two-thong plain spiral; Fig. 12, one-thong alternate spiral; Fig. 13, two-thong alternate spiral; Fig. 14, one-thong novelty spiral; Fig. 15, a Venetian spiral. The latter is made with very wide, thin lacing.

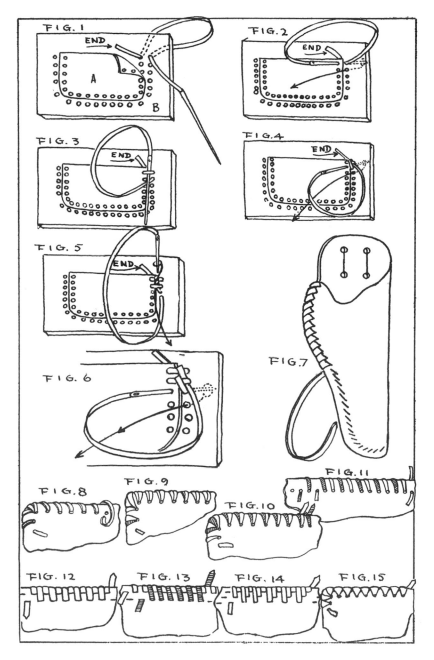

PLATE 123. Applications of Edge-Lacing.

PLATE 124

Gaucho Edge-Braiding of One String. This sturdy but decorative edge-braiding first came to my attention in an article in *El Caballo*, the Argentine horse magazine, written by my friend, Don Luis Alberto Flores. Don Luis presented it, however, in a braid of five strings (Plate 125) and in this account I have sought to simplify it by making it with one string.

In Fig. 1 the rawhide string passes from the front to the rear through hole No. 1, then over the top and through hole No. 2. In this same figure the working end of the string passes from the rear to the front through hole No. 1 (indicated by the arrowline).

In Fig. 2 the working end passes over its own part and through hole No. 2 to the front (shown by the arrowline). Once more it goes through hole No. 1 from the front to the rear, over the top part and through hole No. 3 (arrowline shown in Fig. 3).

In Fig. 4 the working end passes from back to front through hole No. 2 and in Fig. 5 it passes over its own part and through hole No. 3 from the rear to the front and continues through hole No. 2 to the back. These moves are indicated by arrowlines. The sequence is continued for the desired length. Figure 6 shows how this interesting edge-braid looks from the front and the back.

In Fig. 7 the string is middled and both ends are used as illustrated in the remaining figures. Front and back are shown in Fig. 11.

Some of the many designs and braids that can be employed to make belts are shown in the author's collection of belts.

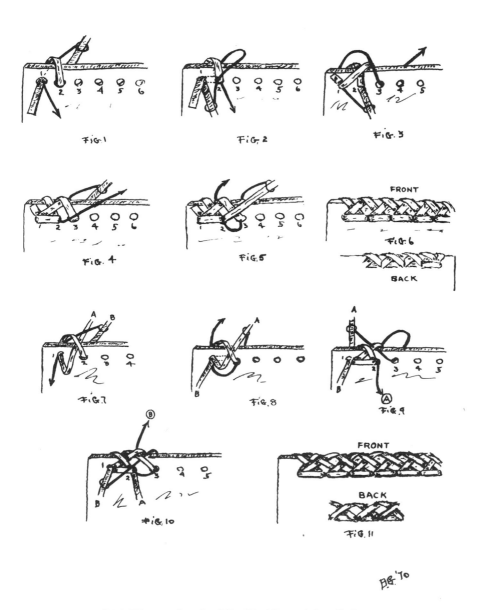

PLATE 124. Gaucho Edge-Braiding of One String.

PLATE 125

Gaucho Edge-Braiding of Three Strings. In this edge-braiding three strings are introduced into hole No. 1 as shown in Fig. 1. String C is laid across the top or edge as illustrated in Fig. 2. Then string A is brought over string C and down through hole No. 2 to the rear. String B is passed under string C and over the edge.

In Fig. 3 string A goes back through hole No. 1 and then passes over its own part and under string B. String C is shown by the arrowline in Fig. 4 how it passes through hole No. 2 then back through hole No. 1. In Fig. 5 its further course is indicated where it passes forward over string B, then through hole No. 3, back through hole No. 2 and over its own part and under string A. The continuation of this braid, using string B, is shown in Fig. 6.

The finished braid is shown in Fig. 7.

In Fig. 8 is the start of a five-string braid, the type used by Don Luis Alberto Flores in his article in *El Caballo*. This becomes a double braid when completed as illustrated in Figs. 12 and 13. As said before, this is a very durable braid and once worked on is difficult to work loose.

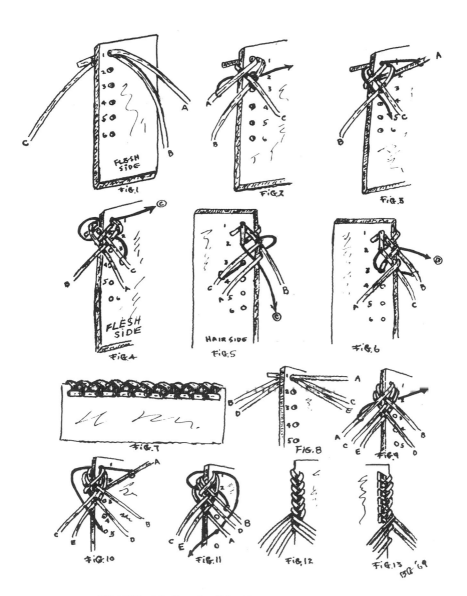

PLATE 125. Gaucho Edge-Braiding of Three Strings.

309

Leathercraft is an excellent hobby. The amateur can begin with simple braids and projects and as skills develop move on to more complex and difficult work.

The objects to make or cover with leather are limitless. Combinations of braiding, lacing, edging and appliqué work in the wide variety of leathers and materials available offer a challenge to any braider.

Mr. Tony Genco of Rochester, New York, a skilled leathercraftsman, has devoted more than twenty years to his hobby. As a participant in the International Assembly of Leathercraftsmen, he has captured many salon ribbons in competitions.

Three fine examples of Mr. Genco's craftsmanship. In his right hand he is holding a *Craftsman's* magazine binder with an original eleven-strand raised circle appliqué braid framing a carving by R.J. Hartmann. In his left hand is a personal scrapbook. This requires 2,900 precision hand-punched nib punchings to execute the half-hitched lace design and used 82 yards (three colors) of 1/8" Duncan hand cut lacing. The personal notebook on the table used an eleven-strand raised appliqué circle to frame Al Stholman's cougar head carving.

310

Buckle and Ring Coverings

PLATE 126

Spanish Type Buckle Covering of One Loop. This is similar to the Spanish edge-lacing of one loop and, once started, is worked in the same fashion (Plate 115).

In the standing end of the thong or lacing cut a small slit and widen it with the fid. Hold the buckle in the left hand with the front toward you. Place the lacing as shown in Fig. 1. Pass the working end, or pointed end, of the lacing through the slit as indicated by the arrowline in Fig. 1 and draw the loop tight. If the tongue of the buckle is free to slide back and forth on the heel of the buckle, be sure it is held in the center.

Pass the lacing beneath the metal part of the buckle from the front, leaving a bight as shown in Fig. 2. The arrowline in Fig. 2 indicates the path of the lacing in the next step. It enters from the front.

Pull out the slack as shown in Fig. 3, but leave a small bight or loop at the pulling point. The lacing again passes beneath the metal part of the buckle and to the rear.

Bring the lacing to the front over the metal part of the buckle. Under the bight which was left, place the fid (Fig. 4) and insert the point of the lacing through this part. Tighten as shown in Fig. 5. Next, pass the lacing beneath the metal part from the front as shown in Fig. 6. Bring it forward over the buckle and through the bight as indicated by the fid in Fig. 7.

Continue thus around the metal part of the buckle. The sequence is always the same: The lacing passes from the front to the rear beneath the metal and then goes through the resulting loop, also passing from front to rear.

Be careful to keep the braid on the outer edge of the buckle. Work it rather tightly so that it holds, but keep the tension consistent.

After working around the buckle and the braid is on the left-hand side of the buckle tongue, draw tight and cement the end to the leather itself. The start and finish of the braid will be hidden when the buckle is attached to the belt.

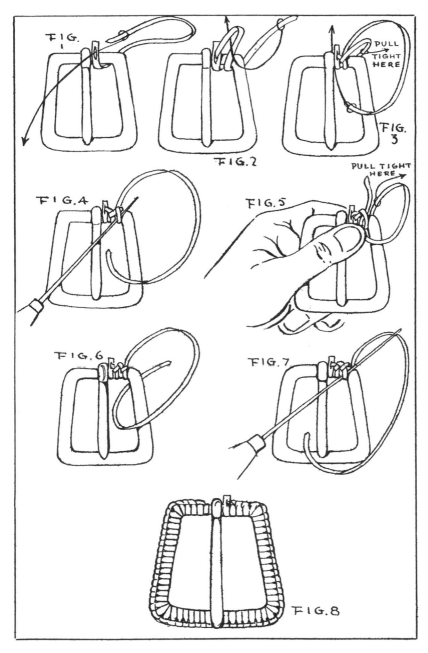

PLATE 126. Spanish Type Buckle Covering of One Loop.

PLATE 127

Spanish Type Buckle Covering of Two Loops. This is similar to the Spanish edge-lacing of two loops (Plate 117) but is worked backwards.

Slit the standing end of the leather thong or lacing and place this end on the left side of the buckle as shown in Fig. 1. Pass the point of the lacing through the slit and bring it to the front. Tighten and pass the lacing beneath the metal part of the buckle and between the original loop and the tongue; that is, to the right of the original loop and left of the tongue (Fig. 2).

Bring the lacing to the front, over the buckle and over the original loop as shown in Fig. 3. Tighten and push the lacing against the tongue of the buckle, being sure the tongue is in the center.

Again, pass the lacing under the metal part as shown in Fig. 3. Insert the fid between this last loop and the original loop and under two loops of the lacing. This step is clearly illustrated in Fig. 3. The lacing follows the course of the fid; again, bring the lacing to the front and under the metal part (Fig. 4).

The fid makes an opening under the two loops as shown in Fig. 5. Be sure that the working end of the lacing always comes out in the rear to the right of its own loop. This is shown in Fig. 6.

Follow this sequence around the metal part of the buckle until the right-hand side is reached. Each time bring the lacing over to the front and under the metal part and then again to the front and under two loops.

This braid must be fairly snug on the metal so that it will not slip. Don't worry about the corners. The underneath loops may overlap slightly but the braid on top will be even.

By thus working this braid backwards it can be kept tight at all times. However, it can be worked as in the edge-lacing of two loops; that is, from left to right.

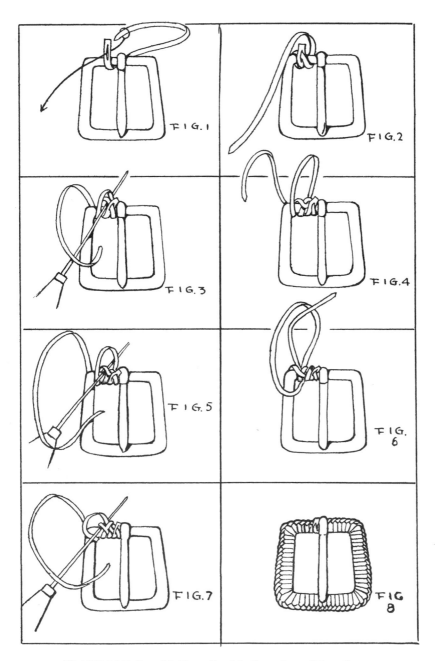

PLATE 127. Spanish Type Buckle Covering of Two Loops.

PLATE 128

Spanish Type Buckle Covering of Three Loops. This is similar to the Spanish edge-lacing of three loops, except that it is worked backwards.

Hold the buckle with the front toward you and place the thong as shown in Fig. 1. If the tongue or pin of the buckle is movable, be sure that it is in the center before the braiding is started.

Pass the working end through the buckle, inclining it toward the tongue and to the right of the standing part as in Fig. 2.

Pass it through a second time, also inclining it to the right of both loops now around the metal heel of the buckle, as indicated by the arrowline in Fig. 2 and shown in Fig. 3.

Bring it down and forward and pass it through the buckle the third time, now inclining it toward the left, as indicated in Fig. 3 and shown in Fig. 4.

It is sometimes difficult to get started, as the loops must not be too tight. At this stage compare your beginning with Fig. 4 to be sure all the loops are in the right place.

The next step has been illustrated in three different ways. First, in Fig. 4, it is shown by the arrowline. Next, in Fig. 5, it has been shown by inserting the fid in the portion through which the thong passes. In Fig. 6, the thong has passed through this place, under three other thongs and emerged on the top.

The thong does not, in this instance, pass around the metal part of the buckle. It comes down in front, inclines to the right and passes beneath the three thongs.

In the next step, which is the beginning of the second stage of the braid, bring the thong down to the front, pass it through the buckle and around the metal part, indicated by the arrowline in Fig. 6 and shown in Fig. 7.

Again the fid is inserted beneath two thongs and under the loop, which makes three thongs (Fig. 7).

Pass the working part of the thong back to the front, over the metal part of the buckle, then down toward the right and through the course followed by the fid, under the three thongs, and, as before, over the metal part.

Continue this until the lacing is completely around the buckle and on the side of the tongue opposite to the starting point. This braid will make a thing of beauty of an ordinary buckle.

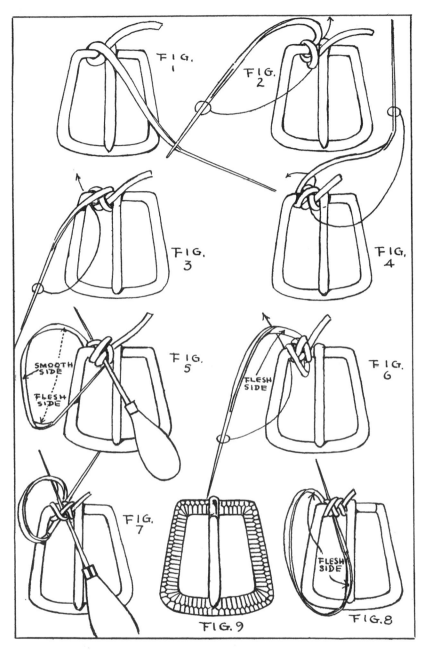

PLATE 128. Spanish Type Buckle Covering of Three Loops.

PLATE 129

Two-Tone Spanish Type Buckle Covering. This two-tone buckle covering goes well with a belt braided from two different colored thongs or strings.

Start your braid as shown in Fig. 1 where the standing end of each thong is slit and the working end passed through to the front. Thong A is passed around under the bottom of thong B and thong B is hitched through the loop of thong A (arrowline, Fig. 2). Thong B is then passed beneath from front to back as shown by the arrowline in Fig. 3.

Next, work thong A, passing it from the front to the back under the two parts of thong B and then down and under as shown by the arrowline. Work one thong and then the other until the buckle is covered. The ends can be tied off as shown in the previous Spanish-type buckle coverings.

Four-Thong Round-Braid Buckle Covering. This braid is worked as the regular four-thong round braid, starting for convenience on the left of the tongue of the buckle as shown in Fig. 6. After braiding completely around the buckle it is finished off on the right of the tongue as shown in Figs. 9 and 10.

Eight-String Round Buckle Covering. Four thongs or strings are middled and the braid started on the left of the buckle tongue as illustrated in Fig. 11. The drawing shows the work from the top. When completed on the right of the tongue, it can be tied off. This is a very popular type of buckle covering in the Argentine.

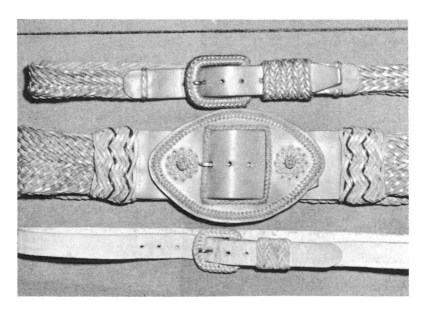

Fancy braided rawhide and leather belts designed and made by the author.

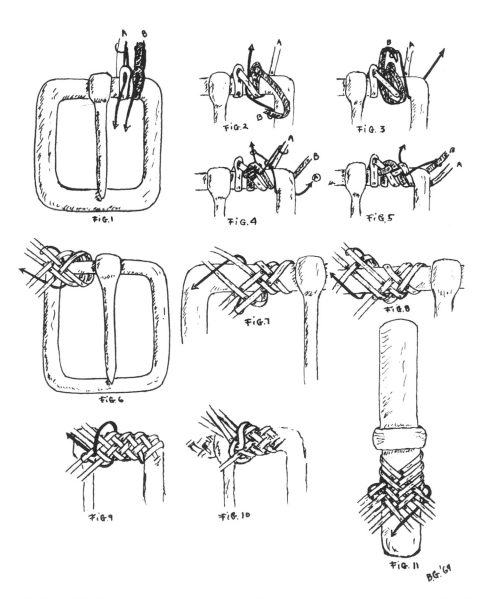

FIG. 1

FIG. 2

FIG. 3

FIG. 4

FIG. 5

FIG. 6

FIG. 7

FIG. 8

FIG. 9

FIG. 10

FIG. 11

B.G. '69

PLATE 129. Two-Tone Spanish Type Buckle Covering; Four-Thong Round-Braid Buckle Covering; Eight-String Round Buckle Covering.

319

PLATE 130

Half-Hitch Ring Covering. This simple covering, adaptable to rings as well as buckles, is made by simply employing a series of half hitches as shown in Figs. 1, 2, and 3. The finished braid is shown in Fig. 3 with a side and a top view. I first saw it on a belt buckle sent to me from Australia, and later effectively employed it in covering harness rings.

Cockscomb Ring Covering. Starting as in the previous braid (Fig. 1) shown again in Fig. 4, after a hitch one way, the next step is to make a hitch in the opposite direction (Fig. 5). Be certain that the flesh side of the string or thong is always against the metal so the finished side is out.

The completed braid is shown in Fig. 6, both from the side and from the top.

Additional braided ring coverings will be found under How to Make a Braided Cincha, in the Twist Braid section.

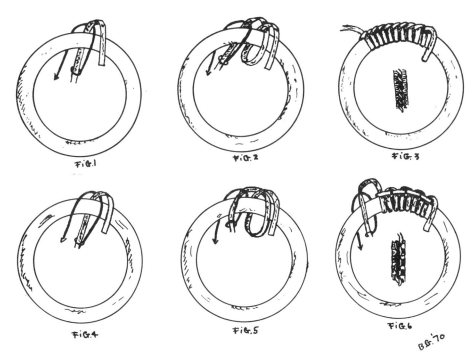

PLATE 130. Half-Hitch Ring Covering; Cockscomb Ring Covering.

320

Other Braided Coverings

PLATE 131

T-Knot for Covering Leather Holding a Ring. One way to cover the leather holding a ring, as well as reinforcing this juncture, is with a plain five-part four-bight Turk's-head. It can be followed around and doubled as well as interwoven, as all such Turk's-heads, and is highly decorative.

Start as in Fig. 1, carrying the working end of the thong around beneath the ring and back over the right-hand side. The arrowline in Fig. 1 shows the next move, which is completed in Fig. 2. Also in this figure the arrowline indicates the next pass.

Continue as in Figs. 3, 4, and 5. The completed knot is shown in Fig. 6.

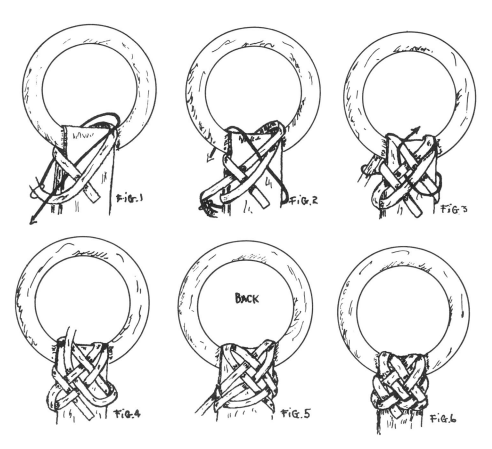

PLATE 131. T-Knot for Covering Leather Holding a Ring.

How to Cover Square and Rectangular Objects. By using the same five-part four-bight Turk's-head, a square or rectangular object may be covered with braidwork (Fig. 7). Be certain that both ends are covered with the four bights of this Turk's-head as shown in the section marked "Top" in this figure. Then follow around, paralleling the previous weave until the entire object has been covered.

Should this object be longer as in Fig. 9, a nine-part four-bight Turk's-head is used. The method of making this Turk's-head will be found under the section on Turk's-heads.

Bricks can be covered for doorstops, or smaller square or rectangular objects can be covered for paperweights.

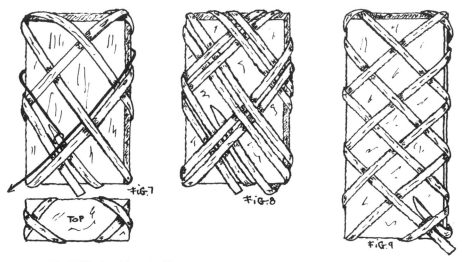

PLATE 131 (Cont.). How to Cover Square and Rectangular Objects.

How to Cover a Pair of Stirrups with the Conquistador Braid. Photo No. 1: This is one of a pair of Visilia-type stirrups. When bought from Fred Mueller of Denver they were galvanized. Here the galvanized coverings have been removed. But this is not necessary.

Photo No. 2: The bolt with its sleeve was removed. A piece of saddle leather 25" x 3½" was cut and soaked thoroughly in soapy water. The leather was then molded around the inside of the stirrup. Holes were punched and the leather was molded over the top and the bolt and sleeve of the stirrup replaced. The bottom was tied down as shown and the leather allowed to dry. When dry, mark the inside of the leather around the stirrup and cut off so the leather comes flush with the outside of the stirrup.

Photo No. 3: Here a rectangular thread of the same leather has been laced over the bottom of the stirrup, holes punched and the conquistador braid started. As the braid is carried back and forth, appropriate holes are punched in the covering. The string enters these

322

holes from below and then back through or beneath itself (shown by the fid).

Photo No. 4: This illustrates the braid as it progresses.

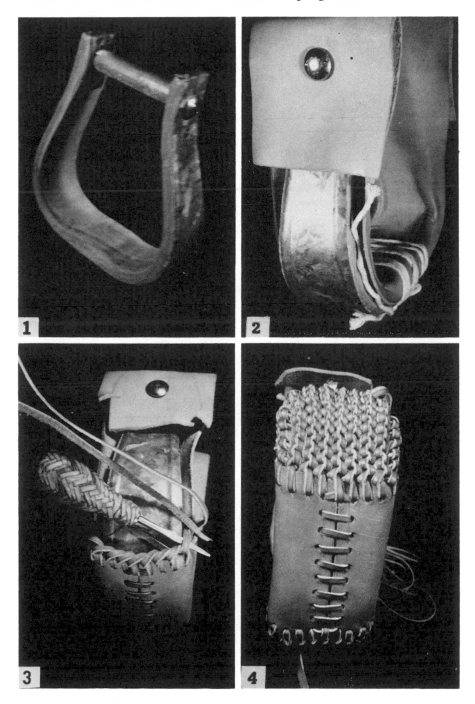

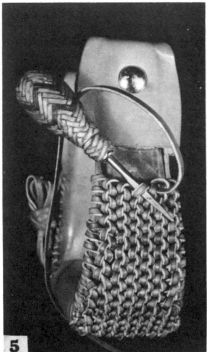

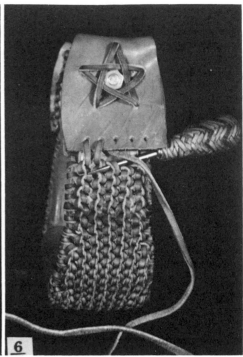

Photo No. 5: At this point, stop the conquistador braid, remove the bolt and sleeve, lift the leather and punch five holes for the lone star appliqué. When this is completed, replace the bolt and sleeve.

Photo No. 6: The conquistador braid is continued and the string passes through the flap as well as the braid and holds both together.

Photo No. 7: The top part or flap is fastened with the stairstep appliqué as shown. Both inside and outside of this flap were cut so they could be joined together thus.

Photo No. 8: This shows the finished braid.

Photo No. 9: This is the covered stirrup with a spurred boot in it. At the top the stirrup leather has a silver dollar inserted and ringed with the stairstep applique.

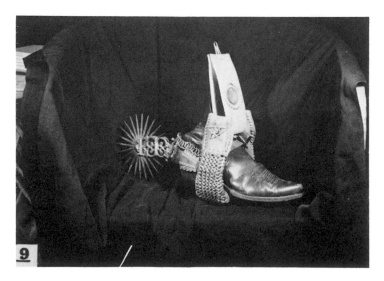

Handle Coverings

PLATE 132

Slit-Leather Handle Covering of One Thong. Cut a piece of leather the length of the handle to be covered. The supposed handle is shown in Fig. 2 and the corresponding piece of leather in Fig. 1. Then wrap the leather around the handle and cut off so that the ends exactly meet.

Now slit the leather so that it is divided into five sections, A, B, C, D, and E (Fig. 1). The leather may be slit into more or less than five sections if desired so long as the total is an uneven number; for example: three or into more or less than five sections if so desired so long as the total is an uneven number; for example: three or seven sections.

The thong (Fig. 3) should be the same width as the width of each section.

Lash the leather around the top of the core as shown in Fig. 4. Insert the end of the thong under the right-hand edge of the leather with some cement on both sides so that it will hold to both the leather and the handle. It is better to thin this part so it will not bulge through the leather.

Bring the thong to the left over the first section, which is E, Fig. 4; then under the next, which is section D (Fig. 5); over the next (not shown in the diagram, but which is section C); under B, over A and under E (Fig. 6). Continue this alternative weave of over one, under one.

Keep working the thong up snug but also keep the leather pulled down. Go around and around until the thong will pass through the last slit without pinching the leather. Conceal the working end inside the leather covering and lash down the bottom.

This gives a vertical pattern and is very effective with contrasting leather and thong (Fig. 7).

To obtain a spiral pattern, cut the leather covering as explained above. This example shows six slits, dividing the leather into seven sections (Fig. 8). The thong should be one-half the width of each section. Start as before but go over two sections (Fig. 9), then under two sections, and then over two (Fig. 10).

The bottom and top of this covering may be concealed with Turk's-heads or woven knots, as explained later in the book under Turk's-heads and Spanish knots, beginning with Plate 143.

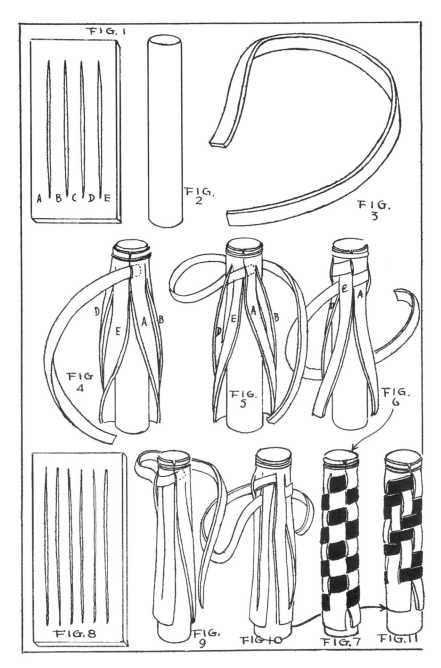

PLATE 132. Slit-Leather Covering of One Thong.

PLATE 133

Spanish Hitchings. For the sake of clarity in the illustration a minimum of thongs has been used and larger spaces left between them than is actually necessary in the working of this braid.

Space the thongs around the circumference of the handle so that a space is left between each one equal to the width of the thong; that is, if 1/8-inch thongs are used, leave a space between them of 1/8 inch.

Take a longer thong, which is designated as thong X in Fig. 1. Slit one end and fasten it around the top, thus binding on the other thongs as shown in Fig. 1.

Pass the thong X around the core in a counterclockwise direction. Bring thong No. 2 over thong X and then under to the left of its own part, as shown in Fig. 2. Thong No. 3 is brought over and then under and to its left. Repeat this operation with thongs 4 and 1.

On each turn of the longer thong, tighten up the braid by pulling the other thongs, and keep the work snug. As in all braiding, a consistent pull must be used to keep the braid even.

Continuation of the work is shown in Fig. 3 and in Fig. 4 is a clearer key to the braiding process. When the handle is completely covered, lash down the working ends of the thongs. Both top and bottom will be covered with Turk's-heads or Spanish knots, detailed later. The finished braid is shown in Fig. 5.

Zig-Zag Braid. This braid is worked in the opposite way from the above braid but on the same principle. First, wrap the longer thong around the handle from top to bottom in a spiral fashion. It should not be too tight and it is well to saddle-soap the thong thoroughly before winding it around the core.

Work down with one thong at a time as shown in Fig. 6. The pattern can be varied by working the hitch either to the right or to the left. Use different colored thongs if desired.

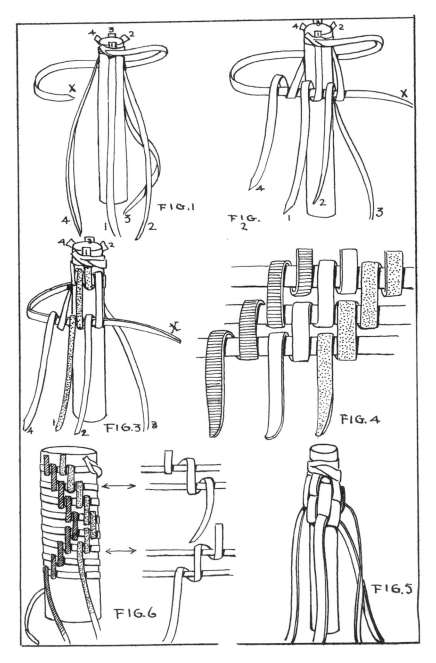

PLATE 133. Spanish Hitching and Zig-Zag Braid.

329

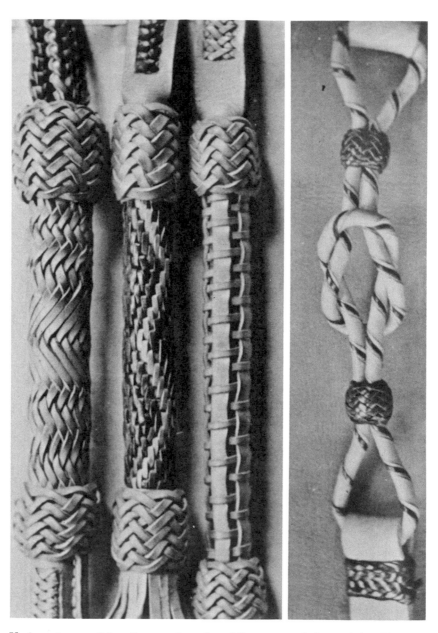

Various types of handle coverings for riding crops. Left to right: Multiple Braid Covering (Pl. 136); half-hitching zig-zag type (Pl. 133); Slit-Leather covering (Pl. 132). Pineapple-type woven knots at each end of handle-braid (Pl. 173). Use of twist braid (Pl. 15) in back part of woman's belt. This is "wormed" with black lacing. Pineapple knots (Pl. 173) and gaucho knot of three passes (Pl. 165) shown.

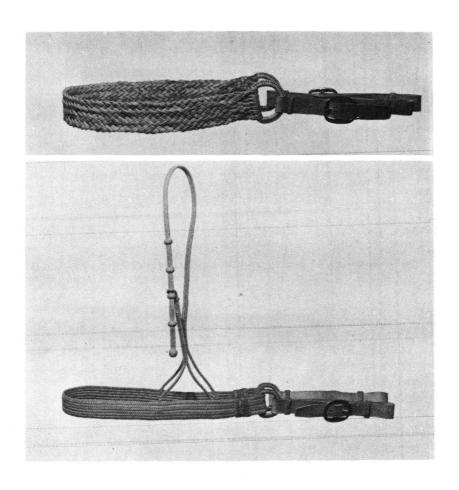

Braided rawhide breast collars made by John Conrad, Bellflower, California.

PLATE 134

Mosaic-Type Braids. This is similar to the slit-leather covering with one thong shown in Plate 132, but it is worked with independent thongs, which will enable one to vary the color of the thongs to form various chromatic patterns.

In the illustrations spaces have been left between the thongs which are lashed to the core. In the actual work, however, these should be close together. Thus, if the circumference is 1-1/8 inches, nine 1/8-inch thongs will be needed. An uneven number is always required.

The longer thong, which is wound around the core, should be the same width as those lashed to the core. Slit it, pass the end through and tighten it over and around the other thongs as in Fig. 1.

Working counterclockwise, pass the long thong under thong 1 and over thong 2; then under and over all the way around. When back to thong 1, pass the long thong over, and at thong 2 pass it under.

A spiral effect may be obtained by passing under two thongs and over two thongs.

Horizontal Braid. This is similar to Spanish hitching except that it is worked horizontally. The thongs, in this case thirteen, are lashed about the core, and the long thong is tightened at the top of the handle. Pass the long thong beneath thongs 4 and 3, bring it back around thong 3 and then under 3 and 2 (Fig. 4).

This is the sequence: Under two, over one, under two, over one. When back to the starting point, it will be noticed that the long thong passes under 4 and 3, over 3 and under 3 and 2. The arrowline indicated the next step.

Figure 6 is an enlargement of the way the braid is worked. In Fig. 7, it is shown how, instead of going under two and over one, you pass over two and under one.

Hitching. This is done entirely with one thong. Pass the thong around the core and over its own end, as in Fig. 8, before the hitching begins. Pass the thong over the part around the core, behind it, and then over its own part. In the illustrations this braid appears loose, but in the actual working it should be kept tight.

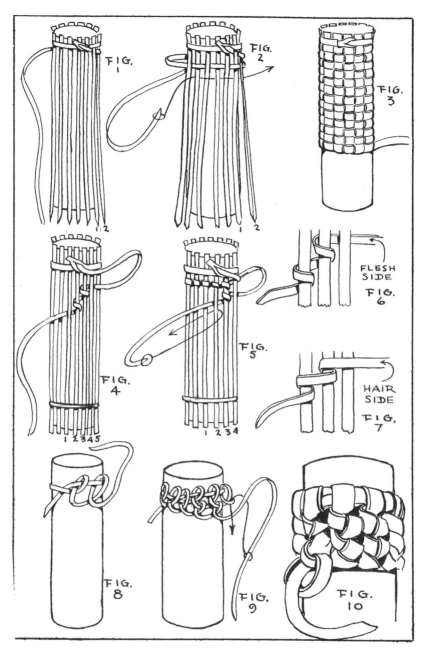

PLATE 134. Mosaic Type — Horizontal Braid — Hitching.

PLATE 135

Four-Thong Twist Braid Covering. This, as well as similar braids shown in Plates 100 and 102, can be used for handle covering. When working with a core, or heart, usually six thongs are employed, but for the purpose of simplifying the technique, four thongs are used in the illustration.

The sum of the width of the thongs should equal the circumference of the handle to be covered. That is, if the handle measures one inch around, each thong should be 1/4 inch.

Lash the thongs, flesh sides out, to the bottom of the handle, as shown in Fig. 1. The first step is the same as in the square braid in Plate 100. Bring thong 1 up inclined to the right (Fig. 2). The smooth or hair side is now uppermost. The arrowline in Fig. 2 indicates the course of thong 2.

Bring thong 2 up under and then over thong 1 (Fig. 3). Bring thong 3 up and over thong 2 in the same fashion, as indicated by the arrowline in Fig. 3.

In the next step, bring thong 4 up and over thong 3 and then pass it through the bight or loop of thong 1. This is indicated by the arrowline in Fig. 4 and shown in Fig. 5. Work the braid down snug, in fact rather tightly, as shown in Fig. 6, which view is straight down on the braid from the top.

Continue now in the same direction, or counterclockwise, and pass each thong over the one to its right: 1 over 2, 2 over 3, and so on. When thong 4 is reached and has been brought over thong 3 it goes down through the bight or loop of thong 1.

However, as shown in Fig. 7, each thong is twisted or given a half turn at its base so the smooth side always is uppermost. Care should be taken that this twist is as close as possible to the base, and as each section is tightened be sure that the smooth side is out. This is the purpose of the twist. In some cases it will be necessary to use your fid in readjusting this twist after tightening.

The colors of the thongs may be varied. When the twists have all been evened up, roll the braid gently under your foot to smooth it out.

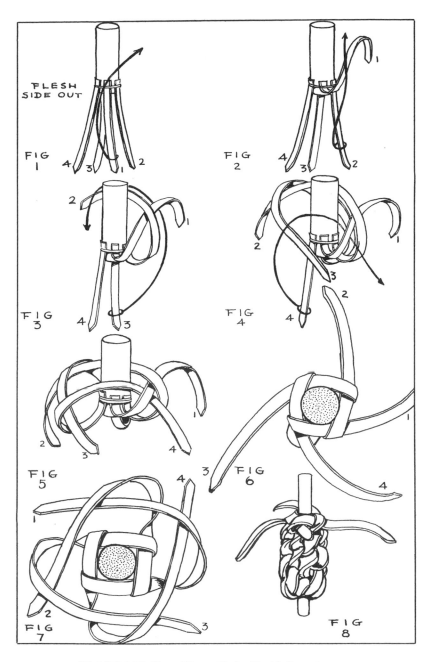

PLATE 135. Four-Thong Twist Braid Covering.

PLATE 136

Six-Thong Multiple Braid. In this type of braid both ends are finished and need not be covered. It is popular in covering a core with varied circumferences as the process of first spiraling the thongs makes it possible to compensate for bulges and depressions.

Six thongs are used. Their total width should be the same as the circumference of the core, although this is not absolutely necessary.

Lash the thongs to the bottom of the core, as shown in Fig. 1, with the flesh sides out. Bring thong 1 up and over the lashing and spiral it around the core as shown in Fig. 2; then thong 2, keeping it snugly along the under side of 1 (Fig. 3).

Continue to spiral the other thongs, smooth side out, until they are all at the top and close together as shown in Fig. 4. Lash them at the top in this position.

A crown knot is formed with the six thongs as shown in Fig. 5. For instance, thong 1 is turned downward, behind 2, smooth side out. Pass thong 6 beneath thong 1; 5 beneath 6; 4 beneath 5; 3 beneath 4; and 2 beneath 3.

Begin the over-and-under sequence, braiding downward at a corresponding angle of the spiral thongs. Pass over one, under one (Fig. 6), or over two, under two (Fig. 7). In fact it can be varied in the over-and-under sequence to suit, being sure that where one thong goes over two and under two, the other five also go over two and under two. In this case the sequence is varied so that it is first under one, over one and then over two, under two (Fig. 7). The bottom is finished off in the over-one, under-one sequence (Fig. 8). Tuck the ends out of sight.

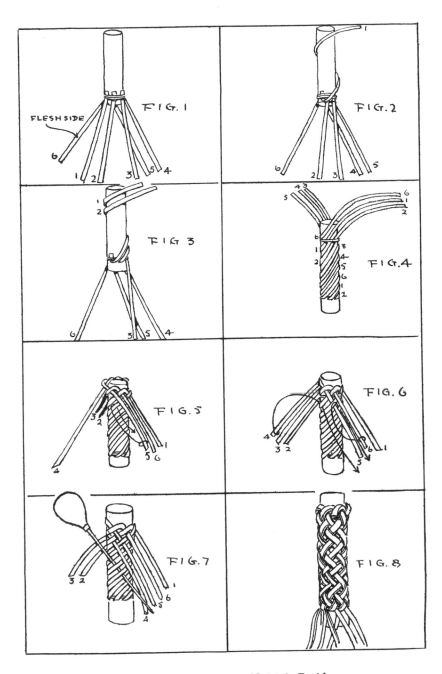

PLATE 136. Six-Thong Multiple Braid.

337

PLATE 137

Multiple-Braid Top and Core Covering. This braid may be used to cover the top of any handle as well as the handle itself. Here is shown the over-one, under-one sequence, but it can be developed into over-two, under-two or other combinations of braids. Start by arranging the thongs in the sequence desired to cover the quirt handle, cane or other similar object.

In Fig. 1 the thongs are laid out in the manner shown. The core to be covered is illustrated just beneath, in Fig. 2. After weaving the thongs in their middle on a flat surface, push them close together and then lay this braided part on the top of the core, which should be slightly rounded at the top (Fig. 3). Secure the thongs just below the braid with cord or thread, as shown in Fig. 4, and arrange them evenly at the top.

In this braid, like any others around a core, the total width of the thongs should be equal to the circumference of the core. In this braid sixteen thongs are used. The measurement around the core is two inches; therefore, each thong is 1/8 inch wide.

Take every other thong (as in Fig. 5, even numbers have been taken) and pass each upward. It is best, as shown in Fig. 6, to tie these together with a string, so that they will be out of the way for the time being. It will be noticed that the thongs carried upward are those which come from beneath other thongs.

The thongs with uneven numbers are spiraled around the core to the full length (Fig. 6). Tie them at the bottom and be sure they are not too tight, but are edge to edge. This may not be possible at the very top, but in any event get them as close together as possible without disarranging the braid.

Take one of the upper thongs, in this case No. 12, and after having made a path for it with the fid (Fig. 7), braid it over the first one to its right, No. 11, and under the next one, which is No. 9. Then take thong 14 (Fig. 8) and braid it in a similar manner, over the first one to its right, which is thong 13, and under the next one, which is thong 11. Continue around, braiding each of the upper thongs over one and under one. Then start back with thong 12 and braid it over one and under one, and so on until the bottom is reached.

Incline these thongs in the upper group at an angle to the right, corresponding to the angle to the left of those which are spiraled around the core. Work the braid up carefully, tightening the thongs until they are snug. Remove the upper binding.

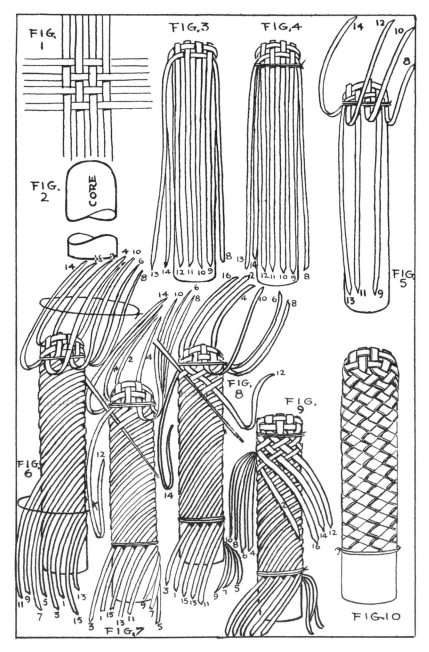

PLATE 137. Multiple-Braid Top and Core Covering.

PLATE 138

How to Make the Corncob Braid. The first time I saw this useful and unique braid in the Argentine I thought it originated there. However, I have found that it also is made in Australia, and later I discovered it on a "talking whip" of the Hungarian *cziko* (cowboy). This elaborately decorated whip was given me by Dorothy Silvus Grant, who took the first American riding group into Hungary.

There are two ways to make this braid. The first, begun in Fig. 1, shows how two thongs or strings are made into a two-string braid and laid around the object to be covered. In Fig. 2, where the ends of the strings are designated by A,B,C, and D, it is shown that after going round the handle or core, string B passes up beneath string D, and then string A passes down over B and under C.

In Fig. 3 string B passes down over A and under D. String C passes upward over D and under A. This last move is to finish the bottom of the braid and from then on all braiding is done with the top strings A and B. The completed braid is shown in Fig. 4. However, the braider can continue indefinitely.

In the Argentine this braid has a rather unpronounceable Indian name of *Corredor Avati Igue*, which translated means much the same as corncob braid.

In the second method starting with Fig. 5, two strings are crossed as shown in the back. These strings are of contrasting colors so the braiding sequence can be more easily followed. Figure 6 shows the front and in Fig. 7 the braiding begins. A crown knot is made and end D is turned up over C and string B passes down over string D and under string D. Figure 8 shows the continuation of this sequence—string B is turned up over string C and string D passes down over B and under C.

The end result is much the same as shown in Fig. 9 as that of the previous braid. However, the last braid is used to cover smaller surfaces than the first.

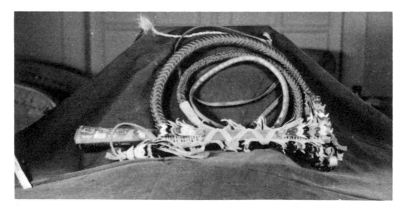

Elaborate Hungarian cowboy "talking whip." Given to author by Dorothy Silvus Grant.

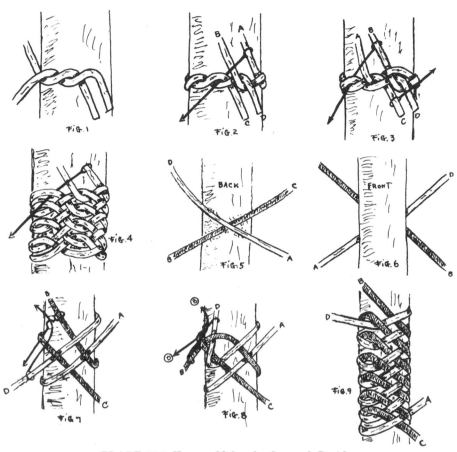

PLATE 138. How to Make the Corncob Braid.

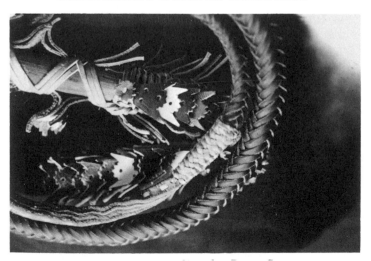

Another view of author's talking whip.

PLATE 139

The Corredor Cordobes. This binding and attractive braid is native to Cordoba, an Argentine province, though it is to be found in the Province of Santa Fe and other sections of the Argentine littoral. It is described in *El Guasquero- Trenzados Criollos,* written by Luis Alberto Flores, who graciously allowed me to detail it. The word *corredor* is freely translated as "running," and is usually applied to braids where one string is utilized.

This braid often takes the place of a woven knot or Turk's-head to cover the ends of other braid on reins, etc.

The start is shown in Fig. 1 where the string first has been wrapped around the object to be covered, passing over the standing end. The working end is passed down under all strings and then up over two and under two. It is worked around in this manner in a clockwise direction and when it comes to the front again, as in Fig. 3, it passes over two and under two as before. Then it starts to pass between the previous loops until it reaches the top when the string is passed under and the end cut off. The finished braid is shown in Fig. 4.

Another way to make a similar braid is shown in Figs. 5 and 6 where both ends of the string become working ends. Instead of working around the braid, make stairsteps up or down.

Fid Work. This type of work is comparable to what is called marline-spike work in sailor's rope work. In the Argentine it has been brought to a high perfection and is termed *trenza de alezna,* weaving or braiding with the fid. An endless number of combinations can be achieved. In Fig. 7 is shown a braid of over-two, under-two sequence. Strings are wound diagonally around the object to be covered and tied at both ends, where small grooves have been made. Then with a separate string start braiding down diagonally as shown with string A. The fid is continuously used, of course, to lift those strings which are passed under. Here we have, as I have said, an over-two, under-two combination. However the first pass can be under one, over one; the second, under two, over two; the third, over three, under three, and so on. After reaching the center of the braid which may be over four, under four, you begin decreasing the strings passed over and under—as, over three, under three; over two, under two, and so on.

See also Plates 136 and 137.

342

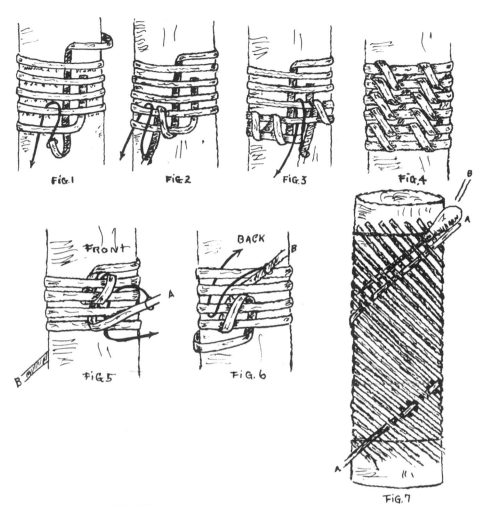

PLATE 139. The Corredor Cordobes; Fid Work.

Beautifully braided knife handle and sheath made for the author
by Martín Gómez, one of the best braiders in Argentina. This
type of braiding is known as "fid work."

343

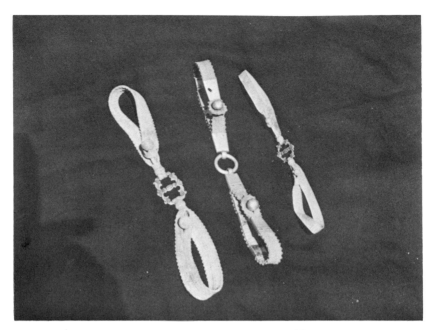

Hobbles in collection of John Walter Maguire.

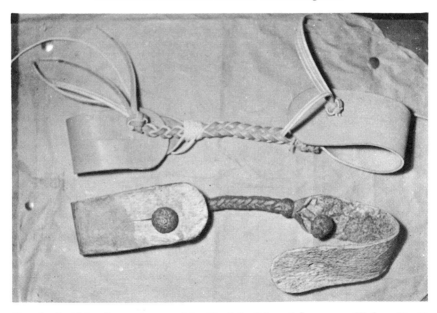

Gaucho hobbles *(upper)* owned by the late Edward Larocque Tinker. Duplicate *(lower)* made by author to illustrate the trick method of making these hobbles.

Hobbles

PLATE 140

How to Make Simple Types of Hobbles. Hobbles come in many styles. They vary from the simplest form, such as is made from a torn gunny sack and piece of rope, to the more elaborately braided article.

Attractive and workable hobbles may be fashioned from ordinary strap leather (or softened rawhide, if you like) of about 1/8 inch in thickness.

The over-all length of the strap is 29 inches and it is 3 inches wide. Taper it from each end for 12 inches, so that the center portion is 2 inches wide (Fig. 1). Round off the ends and punch a hole an inch from each end, in the center of the strap. Make a slit 2-1/2 inches long from each of these holes toward the center, or middle portion, of the strap. These slits serve as holes to accommodate the button.

One method of making the button and securing it to the strap is shown in Fig. 1. This is by a three-hole fastening. Holes are punched as shown, each set of three holes being about 3 inches from the middle of the strap. Thus they would be 6 inches apart.

Thread a 1/4-inch thong through the holes as illustrated and then split the ends. Tie these ends in a terminal Turk's-head knot, as explained in Plate 77, or the end knot shown in Plate 78.

In Fig. 2, another method is demonstrated for making the button and securing it with only one hole punched on each side.

Also, the rolled leather button may be used with three holes, as shown in Figs. 3,4, and 5.

In Fig. 6 a methal ring, 1-1/2 inches inside diameter, is used in the center of the hobble shown. The ends of the strap are folded over the ring, secured with a Spanish ring knot (Plate 161), and the ends are slit and worked into a terminal knot. This terminal knot can be covered with a woven knot, such as the pineapple (Plate 50).

A slit-braid hobble that I worked out, and which has proved a practical one, is illustrated in Fig. 7. It is made of two pieces of leather, each 26 inches long. These are tapered down from 3 inches in width at the button-end to 1-inch width at 12 inches from that end. (The taper is not plainly shown in the drawings.)

The two inside ends are joined together by a slit braid. Strap A is placed over strap B and two slits are made, one in strap A and one in strap B, as shown in Fig. 8. Slit in B should be 12 inches from the button-end of the strap. The one in A should be 13 inches from the button-end.

Strap A is pushed down through B and then B up through A, indicated by arrowlines in Fig. 8. A final slit is made in B, and A is pushed up through this (Fig. 9).

The leather should be damp in working this slit braid.

In Fig. 10, it is seen that both the ends A and B have been slit into four thongs. These thongs are worked into terminal Turk's-heads and then covered with a woven knot (pineapple knot, Plate 50), if desired.

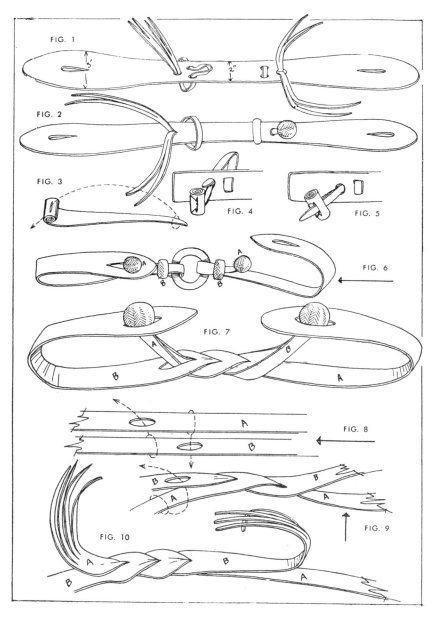

PLATE 140. How to Make Simple Types of Hobbles.

PLATE 141

How to Make a Pair of Braided Gaucho Hobbles. These hobbles are made in the most tricky fashion of any I've ever seen. They were brought back from the Argentine by the late Edward Larocque Tinker, who acquired them while writing his book, *Los Jinetes de las Americas y la Literatura Por Ellos Inspirada* (Horsemen of the Americas and Literature They Inspired). Tinker loaned me the hobbles with the suggestion that I "figure this one out."

At first glance it appears almost impossible that the inside eight-string braid could have been made in the middle section of the hobbles. However, a closer study shows they are fashioned in two parts, ending in buttons A and B (Fig. 1).

First take two pieces of leather (or softened rawhide, as used for the originals) each 26 inches long and 3 inches wide. Mark off 12 inches from one end and taper this down to 2 inches wide, tapering on both edges, of course. The remainder of 14 inches should be 2 inches in width, and this is split into eight 1/4-inch thongs. Then, as in Fig. 2, cut out every other thong, leaving only four thongs. (This also is done for the other piece, marked A in Fig. 5. It will be noticed that you start cutting out the thongs from opposite side on A.)

Take a small round stick, about 3/8 inch in diameter, for use as a mandrel, as shown in Fig. 3.

Begin a four-thong braid (Plate 77) for some 3 inches. As this braid must be interwoven by the thongs on the other piece of leather, make it loose (Fig. 4).

In Fig. 5 you marry or join the other thongs of A. To do this, thong No. 5 passes along the upper side of thong No. 2; No. 6 along the upper side of No. 1. Continue doubling these thongs toward the left, until they come out on the inside of the leather piece marked B (Fig. 6).

In Fig. 6 you begin to interweave. You will note that the remaining, or lower thongs of A, split pairs as shown. The sequence is over two, under two, until thongs are also on the left inside of leather piece B.

Remove the mandrel and tighten your braid. The four thongs on either end are braided for an inch or so in a four-thong round braid (Plate 77) and then tied in a terminal Turk's-head, as indicated by the arrowlines in Fig. 7. For this Turk's-head, see Plate 77, or you might wish to use the one in Plate 78.

Cover both ends of the eight-thong braid with a pineapple knot (Plate 50) and also work a similar knot over the terminal Turk's-heads.

There are other ways of making this inside braid of eight thongs, but I have found the above method the simplest and least confusing. However, if you like, you may first braid the eight thongs on the part B into an eight-thong braid (Plate 47)—that is, before cutting out four thongs as previously described. But the four that would have been cut out should be clearly marked. These are then replaced by four thongs

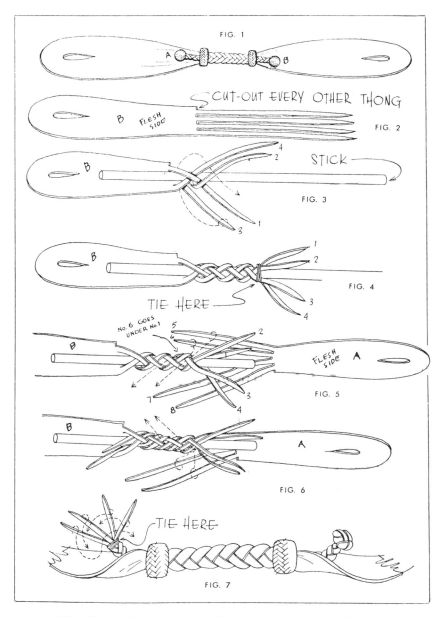

FIG. 1

CUT-OUT EVERY OTHER THONG

B FLESH SIDE

FIG. 2

B STICK

FIG. 3

4
2

B

1
3

B

TIE HERE

1
2
3
4

FIG. 4

NO. 6 GOES UNDER No.1

B

FLESH SIDE A

5
2
7
8
3
4

FIG. 5

B

A

FIG. 6

TIE HERE

FIG. 7

PLATE 141. How to Make a Pair of Braided Gaucho Hobbles.

on the part A. As replacement progresses, draw back the marked thongs and finally, when all thongs on the A end have been interwoven, cut off excess strings on B. This produces the same result as before.

PLATE 142

How to Make a Pair of Braided Hobbles. These are made entirely of braidwork and have the lone star design woven in the buttons.

The first step in making these fancy hobbles is to cover a metal ring, 1½ inch in diameter, with rawhide braiding as described in Plate 52. This covered ring is indicated as A in Fig. 1.

The cuffs, B and C in Fig. 1, are made as follows:

Take eight 1/8-inch rawhide strings, each 56 inches long. Middle them and from this point measure off four inches. Start an eight-string braid (Plate 47) here, working back toward the middle of the strings and beyond until you have six inches of the braid. This will form the loop for your button.

Now bring the strings from each end of the braid together. There will be sixteen of them. Arrange them as shown in Fig. 3. Interweave the strings as shown and then begin your braid by first bringing the highest string on the left (No. 1) around to the rear and forward on the right under two, over two, under two, and over two. Next, string No. 2 on the right passes around to the back and forward under two, over two, under two, and over two.

This 16-string braid is continued for 15 inches. As it is made without a core, it should be pressed flat from the top when finished. It then will appear as a double flat braid and the front part will look like the top drawing and the edges like the lower drawing in Fig. 2.

When the 16-string braid is finished, tie it together at the end. Now, when the loose strings make a terminal knot. This can be done by taking four outside strings and working them into a terminal Turk's-head (Plate 77) around the other twelve. Cover this Turk's-head with the lone star knot (Plate 87).

Two keeper-knots are necessary on each side, one to hold the cuff part of the hobbles to the ring, the other to close the loop around the button. These can be any woven knot you wish—the Spanish ring knot (Plate 61) is a practical one.

Should you care to make your hobbles with the eight-string braid throughout by doubling it, the two braids can be held together by lacing in a long string, as shown in Fig. 4. At the bottom of this drawing is shown the method of starting and at the top is shown some of the finished braid. It will be noticed that the V's on the left of the braid point up, while those on the right point down.

Both this 16-string braid flattened out, and the eight-string ones laced together are good braids to be used on other articles, such as nosebands, browbands, and cheekpieces on headstalls.

At the bottom of Plate 142 in Figs. 5, 6, and 7 is a unique type of hobble used in the Argentine which enables a rider to restrain his horse until he releases the hobbles when in the saddle. These are used when he has no companion to hold the fractious animal. Such hobbles are called *manea desprendedora*, which might be translated as "let-loose hobbles." See also Twist Hobbles under Twist Braids, and Crocodile Ridge Hobbles under Crocodile Ridge Braids.

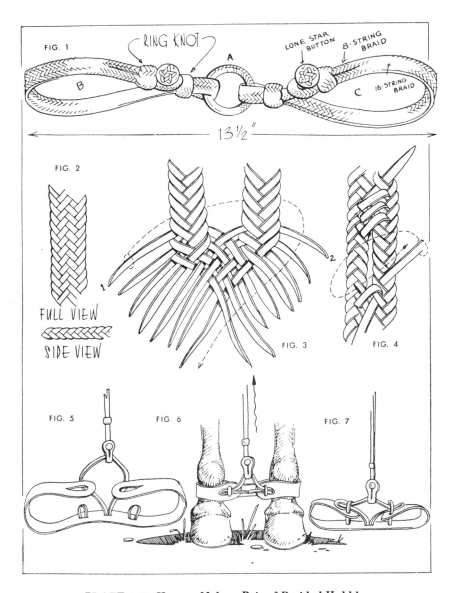

FIG. 1

RING KNOT

LONE STAR BUTTON

8-STRING BRAID

A

B

C

16-STRING BRAID

13½"

FIG. 2

FULL VIEW

SIDE VIEW

FIG. 3

FIG. 4

1

2

FIG. 5

FIG. 6

FIG. 7

PLATE 142. How to Make a Pair of Braided Hobbles.

351

Braided rawhide hobbles made by John Conrad, Bellflower, California.

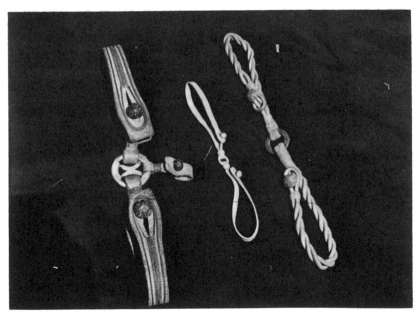

Three hobbles, two braided, in collection of John Walter Maguire.

Turk's-heads

PLATE 143

Braided Paper Turk's-head. The so-called Turk's-head, while serving a practical purpose in leather braiding, should be considered more as the basis or foundation for the beautiful Spanish woven knots.

The Turk's-head has long been one of the most puzzling of knots for the amateur. Observing the finished knot, it seems almost impossible to follow the course of the thong.

Basically the Turk's-head is simple. It is in every respect symmetrical around its circumference, and, like the flat braid, is amphichiral; that is, has the right and left sides alike in figure or pattern and dimensions. It presents the same appearance at any point and in the true Turk's-head the working end of the thong always comes back to the exact starting point, or the same place as the standing end, when the knot is complete.

The Turk's-head might be defined as an endless ring or wreath of any one of the flat braids. To demonstrate the anatomy of a Turk's-head the simplest of the flat braids has been used, the so-called hair braid of three thongs (Plate 28).

Take a strip of writing paper of the size shown in Fig. 1. Cut it into three smaller strips, leaving the section at the top closed, as shown by the dotted lines in Fig. 1.

Now braid these three strips into a three-part hair braid. In doing this, remember the law governing Turk's-heads. No Turk's-head may have the same number of bights, or outer loops (Fig. 2), as it has number of thongs across, or as they are termed, parts. Nor can a Turk's-head have a number of bights and a number of parts which a common divisor.

For example, this Turk's-head is composed of three parts. Therefore, it cannot have three bights, nor six, nine, twelve, nor any number divisible by three. This law applies to all Turk's-heads.

An example with four bights: When the ends are pasted to the uncut portion of the paper as shown in Fig. 4, this immediate part forms one bight. The other three are plainly shown. After pasting down the ends, cut the closed portion, and the Turk's-head reveals itself as an endless wreath of three parts and four bights (Fig. 5).

To demonstrate, place this paper Turk's-head over something round and follow around with a thong until the working end comes back to the standing end. Tear off the paper Turk's-head and the leather one remains (Figs. 6 and 7).

Also, three thongs may be braided and tied together as shown in Figs. 8, 9 and 10, which will result in a Turk's-head of three parts and five bights. Similar experimentation is possible with other flat braids.

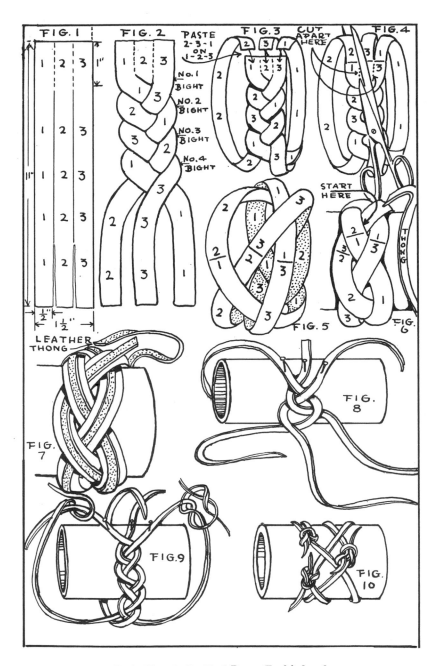

PLATE 143. Braided Paper Turk's-head.

PLATE 144

One-Part One-Bight Turk's-head. This particular Turk's-head is unique in that it is the only exception to the rule that a true Turk's-head cannot contain the same number of bights and parts nor can it contain bights and parts that have a common divisor. In Fig. 1 is shown the method of making the one-part one-bight Turk's-head, which turns out to be simply an overhand knot. But if followed around several times, it makes an attractive small covering knot.

Four-Part Three-Bight Turk's-head. This is made by what I term the "running method," that is, the knot is partially completed at each pass instead of being interwoven on a skeleton knot. It comes, too, under the classification I have designated as "headhunter's type," where the parts are even and exceed the bights by one.

The knot is started as in Fig. 1, but as seen in Fig. 2, the working end is brought around and under the standing part and over the lower bight. Figure 3 shows the sequence in the back where the working end passes over one and under one. Figure 4 illustrates the completion of this and the finished knot is shown in Fig. 5.

Three-Part Two-Bight Turk's-head. This I call the "running gaucho type." Turk's-heads made by this method have an uneven number of parts and an even number of bights, as well as one more part than bight. The start is shown in Fig. 6 and goes *over* the upper bight as well as the lower, as illustrated by the arrowline. The finished knot is shown in Fig. 8.

Five-Part Four-Bight Turk's-head. Continuing as in Figs. 9, 10, 11, and 12 and using the same "running gaucho" style results in a five-part four-bight Turk's-head, as shown in Fig. 13. This is a popular and widely used knot.

Long Three-Part Turk's-head. A long three-part Turk's-head to cover any large circumference can be made as shown in Fig. 14. It can be interwoven into a long Spanish ring knot (or woven ring knot) of one or more passes. It also can be increased to five parts by following the method in Figs. 1 through 7 in Plate 157.

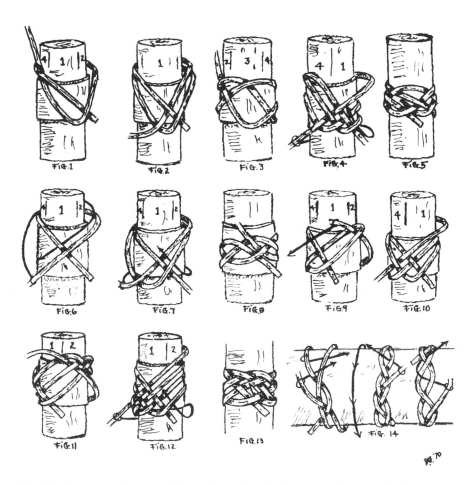

PLATE 144. One-Part One-Bight Turk's-head; Four-Part Three-Bight Turk's-head; Three-Part Two-Bight Turk's-head; Five-Part Four-Bight Turk's-head; Long Three-Part Turk's-head.

357

PLATE 145

Four-Part Three-Bight Turk's-head (Another View). Start this Turk's-head with the mandrel turned so that sections 1 and 4 are toward you, with section 1 uppermost.

Lay the thong on the mandrel so that it is in the area of sections 1 and 4 and the working end is inclined toward the right (Fig. 1).

Pass the thong around the mandrel, inclining it to the left as shown in Fig. 2. The arrowline indicates the next move in which the thong is passed beneath two of its parts in the sections 1 and 4. Keep the loop of the thong extended to the right at the juncture of sections 1 and 4, although the working end, after passing under the second of its parts, is inclined to the left.

In Fig. 3 it is seen that the thong has passed beneath its two parts, with the loop inclined to the right. The arrowline indicates the beginning of the final steps—the important interlocking steps.

Figure 4 shows this first interlocking step. The thong has passed over one and under one in sections 4 and 1.

In Fig. 5 the mandrel has been turned toward you in a clockwise direction so that the back of the knot is visible. Here is another interlocking path of over-one, under-one sequence.

In Fig. 6 the working end has been brought up alongside the standing end and the Turk's-head is complete. Tighten the knot by working it carefully, beginning at the standing end and continuing around.

Figure 7 is a diagram pattern of the four-part three-bight Turk's-head. Follow previous directions.

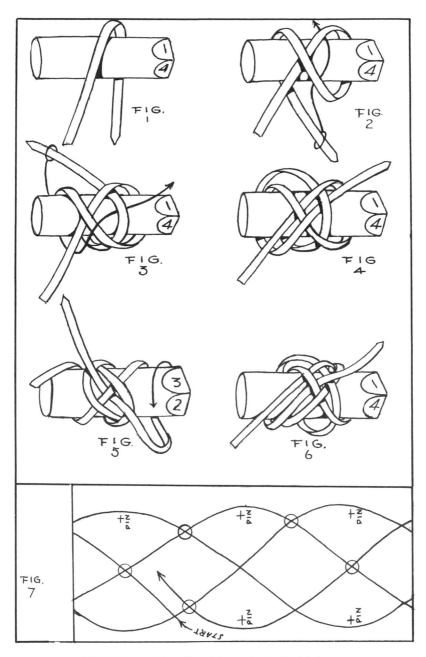

PLATE 145. Four-Part Three-Bight Turk's-head.

359

PLATE 146

Gaucho Knot of One Pass. The Gaucho Knot of One Pass is in reality a nine-part eight-bight Turk's-head. In this instance it is braided instead of tied in the usual way.

Use a mandrel with a leather collar as shown in Fig. 1. If this knot (or the other gaucho knots to follow) is used as a neckerchief slide, turn the leather collar so the smooth part is on the innter side, and work the knot over the flesh side. When the knot is finished, slip the knot and collar off the mandrel and the smooth side of the collar will slide over the neckerchief.

The mandrel is numbered at the top so as to indicate when it has been turned (clockwise, in this instance). Start by laying the thong around the mandrel (and collar) as shown in Fig. 1. Pass the thong again to the rear and over the loop there bringing it to the front, where it passes under one and over one (Fig. 2).

Now proceed as follows:

Rear: Under one, over one (Fig. 3). Front: Over one, under one, over one (Figs. 4 and 5). Rear: Over one, under one, over one (Fig. 6).

Front: Under one, over one, under one, over one (shown by fid in Fig. 7). Rear: Under one, over one, under one, over one (shown by fid in Fig. 8).

Front: Over one, under one, over one, under one, over one (shown by fid in Fig. 9). Rear: Over one, under one, over one, under one, over one (shown by fid in Fig. 10).

Front: Under one, over one, under one, over one, under one, over one (shown by fid in Fig. 11). Rear: Under one, over one, under one, over one, under one, over one (shown by fid in Fig. 12).

Front: Over one, under one, over one, under one, over one, under one, over one (indicated by fid in Fig. 13). Rear: (The work is now moving around so the rear and front are practically one.) Over one, under one, over one, under one, over one, under one, over one (Fig. 14).

Front: Under one, over one, under one, over one, under one, over one, under one, over one (Fig. 15).

In the next move the working end comes up alongside the standing part and the knot is completed (Fig. 17). It should be understood, however, that the working end met the standing end several times before and at any of these points there would have been a complete knot.

In Fig. 18 is a diagram pattern for making this knot.

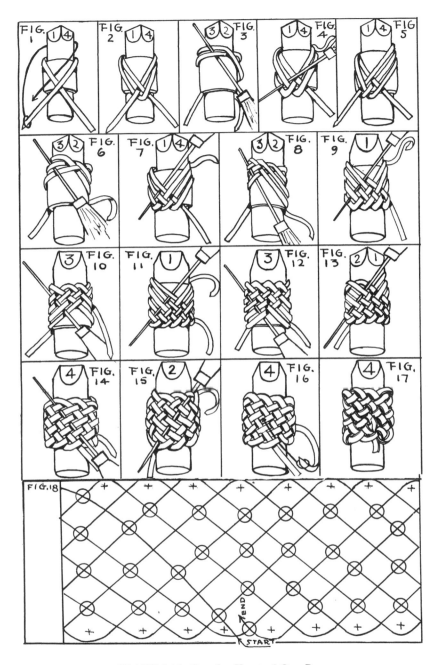

PLATE 146. Gaucho Knot of One Pass.

PLATE 147

Three-Part Five-Bight Turk's-head. This is the regular free-hand method of tying the three-part five-bight Turk's-head, the same Turk's-head worked out in Plate 143 by braiding three thongs and then tying the ends together.

In Fig. 1 the thong has been passed over the mandrel with the standing end, A, at the left and the working end, B, inclined to the right. The working end, B, makes another complete circuit (Fig. 2) and when it comes back to the front as in Fig. 3 it passes under the standing end.

Now take the bight of the standing part as shown by the arrowline in Fig. 4 and pull it beneath the bight to its left. Pass the working end, B, under and through this bight as indicated by the arrowline in Fig. 5 and shown in Fig. 6. Turning the mandrel slightly to show the rear, pull the bight of the standing end under the bight to its right. The working end passes upward through this bight (Fig. 7) and around the mandrel to come up alongside the standing end (Fig. 8). The knot is complete.

In Fig. 9 is shown a diagram pattern for making this Turk's-head. Place a piece of heavy wrapping paper beneath the page, and using a carbon, trace over the pattern. Be sure to trace all the circles shown on the pattern and the X marks shown in the bights.

At the top of the pattern, where indicated, cut the paper off flush. Then roll up the paper from the bottom end, having left it sufficiently long beyond the pattern at this end, until a cylinder is formed and the ends of the wavy lines on the pattern exactly meet.

Place a rubber band around the cylinder on the left side of the pattern, and then stick pins through the ten places in the bights marked with an X. Be sure all the lines at the ends come together.

With the standing end of the leather thong placed beneath the rubber band, start laying the thong around the cylinder, following the line from the point marked "Start," and around the pins at the points marked X. The working end always passed *over* a thong except where there is a circle, in which cases it passes *under*.

When the point designated as *end* is reached, the knot is complete. Withdraw the pins, slip off the loose Turk's-head and adjust it over the lace where it is to be used. Then tighten it up by going completely over the knot from start to finish.

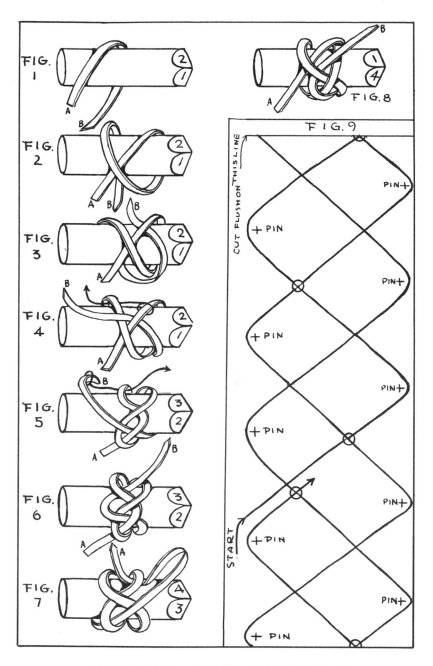

PLATE 147. Three-Part Five-Bight Turk's-head.

363

PLATE 148

Five-Part Four-Bight Turk's-head (Another View). Hold the mandrel (Fig. 1) so that the sections marked 1 and 4 are visible, with the figure 1 uppermost. Lay the standing part of the thong so that it covers these two sections and is well inclined to the right.

Pass the working end of the thong around the mandrel and back over its own part as in Fig. 1, after which it circles the mandrel again, inclined this time to the left. Bring it forward, beneath the standing end, with the working end in the area of section 1 (Fig. 2). The arrowline in Fig. 2 indicates the next pass which is under the loop in section 1.

Draw the thong to the extreme left and under the mandrel bringing it up alongside and to the right of the standing part (Fig. 3). The arrowline in Fig. 3 indicates how it follows parallel to the standing part under the thong in section 4.

The next pass is shown in Fig. 4 where the thong, still parallel to the standing part, has passed under one in section 4, over one at the bottom of section 1, is inclined to the right and then passed over the standing part at the top of section 1. The arrowline indicates its path under the next loop in back.

In Fig. 5 the mandrel is turned clockwise to illustrate section 2, with section 1 at the bottom. This shows how the thong passes under the loop indicated by the arrowline in Fig. 4.

Now turn the mandrel back to its original position with sections 1 and 4 in view (Fig. 6). Observe that there is a path around the knot, in which one section of the thong goes over two, and another under two. The idea is to pass the end of the thong in such a manner that the complete knot will be in a sequence of over one, under one throughout, in other words, *lock* these sections.

The path is clearly shown by the arrowline in Fig. 6. Pass the end over that part in section 4 and under that part in section 1 and the thongs will be locked so far as this part of the knot is concerned.

In Fig. 7 the end has been passed over one, under one, and over one and at the top there is a loop which is passed under two other parts, shown by the arrowline. In Fig. 8 the mandrel is turned in a counterclockwise direction so that sections 4 and 3 are in view, showing the bottom of the knot. Pass over one and under one, as shown by the arrowline. The last and final move is indicated by the arrowline in Fig. 9, when the working end is placed up alongside the standing end. The completed knot is shown in Fig. 10. A diagram pattern for this knot will be found on Plate 149.

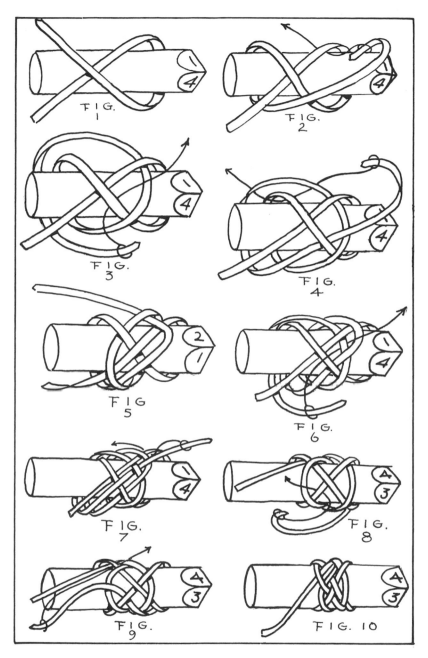

PLATE 148. Five-Part Four-Bight Turk's-head.

365

PLATE 149

Labyrinth Method of Making a Five-Part Four-Bight Turk's-head.
The theory behind this method is, that the more ways you learn to tie a
Turk's-head the better. When completed by this procedure, it may
readily be observed that each ring interlocks in an under-one, over-one
sequence.

It takes a comparatively long thong in relation to the final knot
obtained, to tie the Turk's-head by this method so be sure to keep the
kinks out of the thong and see that the hair side is always uppermost.

Start by laying the working end of the thong on a flat surface and
making a loop in it as shown in Fig. 1. The next loop is indicated in this
figure by the arrowline.

In Fig. 2 this second loop has been made and the arrowline indicates
the third step. The letter X indicates in each case the center of the knot
and where the mandrel will be if the knot is tied by the previous
method in Plate 148.

In Fig. 3 the third step has been executed and the arrowline shows
the final phase of tying this intricate knot, which truly presents the
aspect of a labyrinth. Attention should be called here to the *path*
spoken of in the text for Plate 148. It is more clearly shown here just
how, by passing the thong along it, the interlocking process of the knot
is completed.

In Fig. 4 the working end has been brought up alongside the standing
end and the knot is complete. A mandrel is inserted at the point
marked X and the flat knot is carefully worked down to cylindrical
shape by tightening along the arrows shown on the thong itself.

A diagram pattern for making this knot is given in Fig. 5. Follow the
previous directions for making this knot by the foolproof pattern
method.

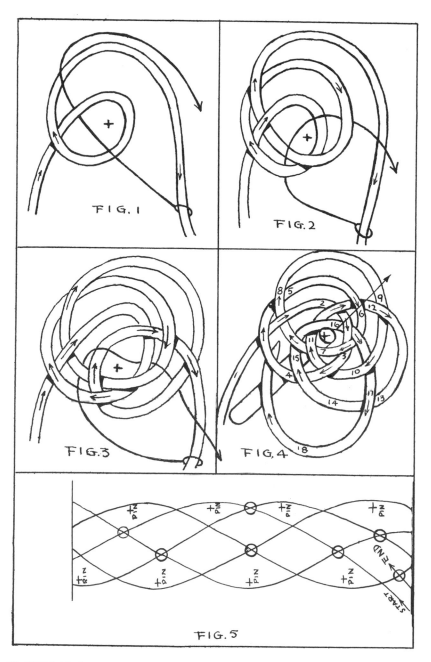

FIG. 1

FIG. 2

FIG. 3

FIG. 4

FIG. 5

PLATE 149. Labyrinth Method of Making a Five-Part Four-Bight Turk's-head.

367

PLATE 150

Sliding Knot or Five-Part Two-Bight Turk's-head. This is a relatively simple but very important Turk's-head. It is the key to some of the more intricate Spanish knots. In itself it is a valuable knot because it can be made over small diameters, thanks to its two bights, and yet is wide because of its five parts. Cowboys double and triple the knot to increase its width.

Begin with the mandrel turned so that sections 1 and 4 face you. Lay the standing part of the knot over the mandrel, covering these two sections (Fig. 1), the working end of the thong inclined to the right.

Turn the thong twice around the mandrel as in Fig. 2, spiraling it towards the left.

Pass the thong underneath the mandrel and to the front and then to the right and over the two spirals as indicated by the arrowline in Fig. 2, and then pass it under the loop at the top of section 1.

Figure 3 shows this step completed and indicates the next step by the arrowline. Bring the thong down in the rear and up to the front between the two spiraled thongs. Here, by going over one and under one, the interlocking pass is accomplished.

The previously indicated step is illustrated in Fig. 4 and the arrowline indicates the final step. Bring the thong to the extreme left, over one of its parts on the left and back up to the front alongside the standing part.

This completes the knot, unless it is desired to double it—in which case, continue as in Fig. 5. Start along the right side of the standing part and follow it with the thong, passing under when it passes under and over when it passes over. In other words, where there was originally one thong, there will now be two. To triple, pass in the same way once more, following the two parallel thongs.

Enlarging Turk's-heads by doubling is a common practice, and in rope work, it actually beautifies the knot. But in leather work it is quite unsatisfactory, because the flat thongs overlap at the curves, giving the work an unfinished and uncouth appearance. When one becomes completely familiar with the Turk's-head knot in all its phases, he will realize that there are Turk's-heads, as well as Spanish knots, that can cover any surface, without the slightest necessity for doubling or tripling.

A diagram pattern for the sliding knot is given in Fig. 7.

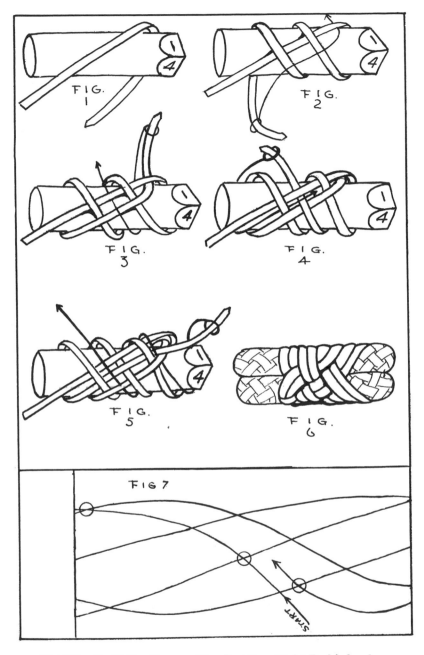

PLATE 150. Sliding Knot or Five-Part Two-Bight Turk's-head.

369

PLATE 151

Five-Part Three-Bight Turk's-head. This Turk's-head will assume an almost spherical form when tied and is, therefore, valuable as the covering for the handle end of canes, quirts and such. While it adapts itself to the circumference of the core, it also can be closed over the top by virtue of its three bights.

Hold the mandrel so that sections 1 and 4 are toward you, with section 1 uppermost. Lay the working end of the thong so that it is within the area of sections 4 and 1 and inclined to the right, as shown in Fig. 1.

In the next step, bring it underneath toward the left and pass it completely around the mandrel again, the part in front inclined to the right, and the part in the back to the left, as shown in Fig. 2. It now passes over three of its own parts, the two in sections 4 and 1 and the other in the rear, without passing under any. Incline the thong far to the *left* or *top* side of the standing end as shown in Fig. 3. Pass it upward and over two of its own parts, to the left of the standing part and under the standing part at the top of the mandrel. This is indicated by the arrowline in Fig. 3.

Figure 4 shows the mandrel turned so that sections 4 and 3 are in view, illustrating the finished operation, and then the mandrel is turned back so that sections 1 and 4 face you, revealing the course of the working end of the thong. A path lies open along the arrowline in Fig. 5, which, when followed by the thong, will interlock the parts as the over-one, under-one, over-one sequence is executed (Fig. 5).

With the mandrel again turned to sections 2 and 1, the end of this interlocking path will be seen. Pass the thong under one of its parts as in Fig. 6, then bring it around underneath, over one thong and alongside and to the right of the standing end (Fig. 6). The finished knot is shown in Fig. 7.

This knot can be followed around again to double it, and still again to triple it, as shown. For more details on this type of woven knot, see Lazy-Man and Pampas Button Knots (Plates 179—181). Be as careful as possible to keep the thongs from overlapping in doubling and tripling.

A diagram pattern is shown in Fig. 9.

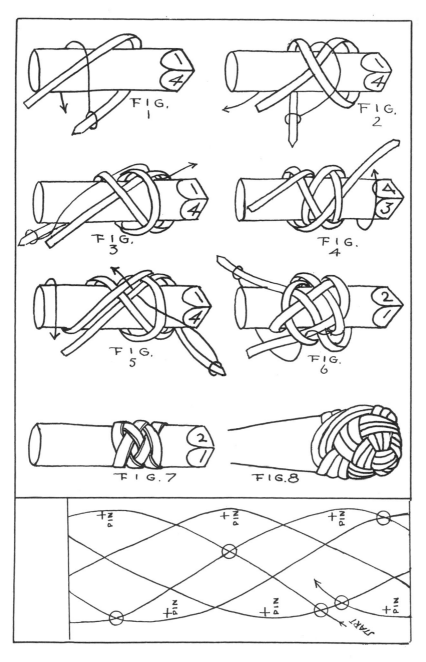

PLATE 151. Five-Part Three-Bight Turk's-head.

371

PLATE 152

Six-Part Five-Bight Turk's-head Raised from a Four-Part Three-Bight Turk's-head. The four-part, three-bight Turk's-head shown in Plate 145 is the foundation upon which may be woven the larger knots of even parts. It can be raised to the six-part, five-bight Turk's-head and the six-part, five-bight can be raised to the eight-part, seven-bight Turk's-head and so on.

The key is given in this plate. Fig. 1 shows the four-part, three-bight Turk's-head tied according to the previous instructions. The numerals on the thong indicate in progressive order the course of the working end from the start to the finish.

First, place the working end of the thong alongside and to the right of the standing part (Fig. 1), allowing it to follow the right of the standing part to the top of the mandrel as indicated by the arrowline in Fig. 1.

Now turn the mandrel as indicated by the curved arrowline in Fig. 1, so that sections 3 and 2 are toward you, as shown in Fig. 2. The thong marked with the sequence number 2 is the standing part, and the working end, marked with a 6, passes *beneath* it and follows to its left, as indicated by the arrowline in Fig. 2. Leave a small bight in the working end where it passes under the standing part.

Turn the mandrel back to the front so sections 1 and 4 are in view (Fig. 3). The arrowline indicates the interlocking path in which the procedure is over one thong and under one.

Turning the mandrel again, so that sections 2 and 1 are toward you (Fig. 4), continue along this interlocking path passing over one and under one. This latter pass, indicated by the arrowline in Fig. 4, shows the path of the working end beneath the bight which is left in Fig. 2, where the working end passed under the standing part.

Continue to turn the mandrel so that sections 3 and 2 are in view and the interlocking path is indicated by the arrowline in Fig. 5. Pass over one, under one, over one and under one, each time locking the other parts of the thongs so their sequence also is over one, under one.

Turn the mandrel back to show sections 1 and 4 and bring the working end alongside and to the right of the standing end (Fig. 6). The completed knot is shown in Fig. 7. A diagram pattern is provided in Fig. 8. To raise the six-part to the eight-part, follow exactly the same procedure.

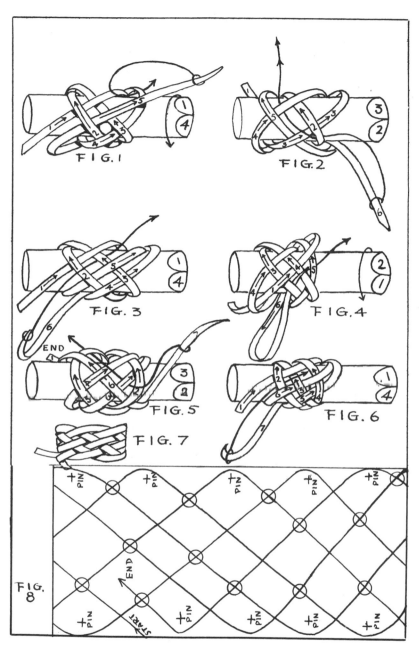

PLATE 152. Six-Part Five-Bight Turk's-head Raised from a Four-Part Three-Bight Turk's-head.

PLATE 153

Seven-Part Six-Bight Turk's-head Raised from a Five-Part Four-Bight Turk's-head. Begin with the five-part, four-bight Turk's-head shown in Plate 148. Notice in Fig. 1 that the end of the standing part is numbered 1 and the working end is numbered 6. These are the progressive numbers denoting each move in making the original knot. They will be continued as the knot progresses.

The working end is alongside and to the right of the standing part (Fig. 1). The working end follows the course of the standing part, passing along to the right until the top of the knot is reached, as indicated in the arrowline in Fig. 1.

In Fig. 2 the mandrel has been turned so that the rear is in view. This section of the standing part is numbered 2 and the working end passes over it (but under the same thong it passes under) and goes down to its left side. Figure 2 indicates this pass and in Fig. 3 the next step is shown.

The working end is now back alongside the end of the standing part (Fig. 4). This time do not follow the path of the standing part, but where it goes *under* pass the working end *over*, and where it goes *over* pass the working end *under*. The first step is indicated in the arrowline in Fig. 4. This shows the interlocking path which can easily be followed completely around the knot.

Turning the mandrel again, so that the rear shows, the arrowline in Fig. 5 continues to follow this interlocking path, that is, under one, over one, under one, over one, under one and over one at the extreme left.

In Fig. 6, the working end is back at the start and this time the knot is finished when the working end is brought alongside the standing part as indicated by the arrowline.

Tighten the knot by drawing on the thong from the start, and, following the sequence in which it was made, pull up the slack until the point shown in Fig. 6 is again reached. It may be necessary to go around several times to get it completely tight. Insert a little cement where the standing part and working part touch beneath the other portions of the thong; cut the ends off flush and tuck in.

To increase the seven-part to the nine-part, follow the same procedure that was used to increase the five-part to the seven-part. This Turk's-head can be made as large as desired; each time it is raised increases it by two bights and two parts.

To make the seven-part, six-bight Turk's-head, follow the diagram pattern in Fig. 7.

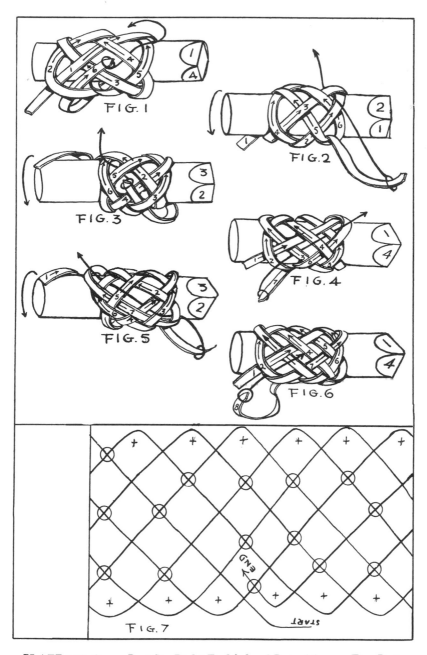

FIG. 1

FIG. 2

FIG. 3

FIG. 4

FIG. 5

FIG. 6

FIG. 7

PLATE 153. Seven-Part Six-Bight Turk's-head Raised from a Five-Part Four-Bight Turk's-head.

375

PLATE 154

Two-Bight Turk's-head of Any Length. By the following method you can make a Turk's-head any length you wish. The number of times the thong is wrapped about the mandrel in the beginning is the determining factor. When the thong is brought back toward the starting point, the number of times it touches the thong first wrapped around will determine the number of sections of the knot. It it touches twice, it will be a two-section knot; if three times, a three-section knot, etc.

Pass the thong around the mandrel three times toward the right (Fig. 1). The small numbers on the thong itself indicate its progress.

The arrowline in Fig. 1 shows the second pass, which is already completed in Fig. 2. Now go around for the third time, in the direction indicated by the arrowline in Fig. 2 and shown in Fig. 3. Up to this point the working end of the thong always passes over each of its parts.

Next, pass the working end beneath the outer part of the thong marked with the numeral 3 (Fig. 3). This is the beginning of the interlocking path. Close study will reveal this path spiraled around the mandrel, where the thong passes over two, the next under two and the next over two.

To *lock* these thongs, pass over the thong which lies over two, and under the thong which is under two, as shown in Fig. 4. Continue in Fig. 5, following the same pattern: over one, under one, over one, under one.

Having reached the extreme left-hand side (Fig. 6), pass over the thong there, then under one and finally over one. The working end now comes alongside the standing end (Fig. 7) and the knot is completed (Fig. 8).

This knot is sometimes doubled and not infrequently tripled. To do this, start following the standing part around and around, keeping on the same side of it all the time and passing *over* where it passes *over* and *under* where it passes *under*. This doubled knot is shown in Fig. 9. To triple, go around and around again in the same fashion.

A diagram pattern is given in Fig. 10 for making the single knot.

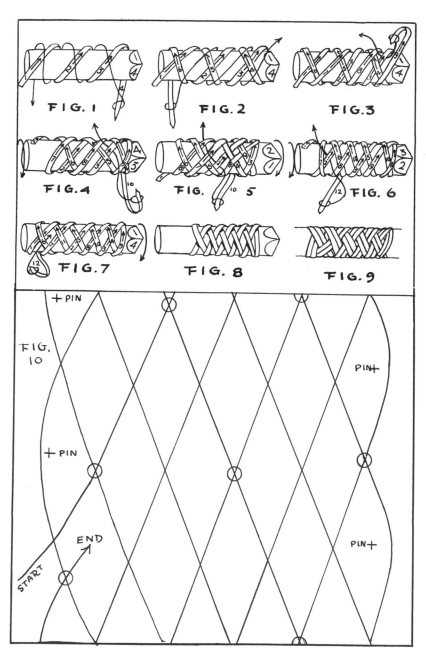

PLATE 154. Two-Bight Turk's-head of Any Length.

377

PLATE 155

Long Three-Bight Turk's-head. This knot is similar to the one in Plate 154, except that it has three instead of two bights. With three bights it can be used around a core of larger circumference. Remember, the greater the number of bights, the larger in diameter the knot will be; this is the reason why Turk's-heads are made with varied numbers of bights.

Wrap the thong around the mandrel twice and then bring it back over its own loop at the right and toward the left under the standing part as shown in Fig. 1.

Take another turn over the standing part and around the mandrel and bring the thong up alongside the standing part to the right side. It is passed to the right and goes under its own part in the center of the mandrel (Fig. 2).

Continue toward the right with the working end, pass over the outer loop and then back to the front and over this same loop again and also over the next thong as indicated by the arrowline in Fig. 3.

Now pass the working end beneath the next two thongs, indicated by the arrowline in Fig. 4 and shown in Fig. 5.

In Fig. 6 the working end passes over the standing part and the extreme outer left-hand loop, indicated by the arrowline in Fig. 7, and is brought to the front, this time to the *left*, or top, of the standing part. It goes over two thongs and under two thongs, indicated by the arrowline in Fig. 7. In Fig. 8 it passes over the next two thongs, and under the outer loop to the right, as indicated by the arrowline.

Now the interlocking path can be seen, where the working end will first pass under the outer loop, over the next thong, under the next, over the next and under the next, going toward the left, of course. This path is indicated by the arrowline in Fig. 9. Continue locking the thongs, over one, under one, over one and under the outer loop at the left (Fig. 10). Bring the working end back, over one, and under the thong alongisde the standing end and the knot is finished.

A diagram pattern is given in Fig. 12.

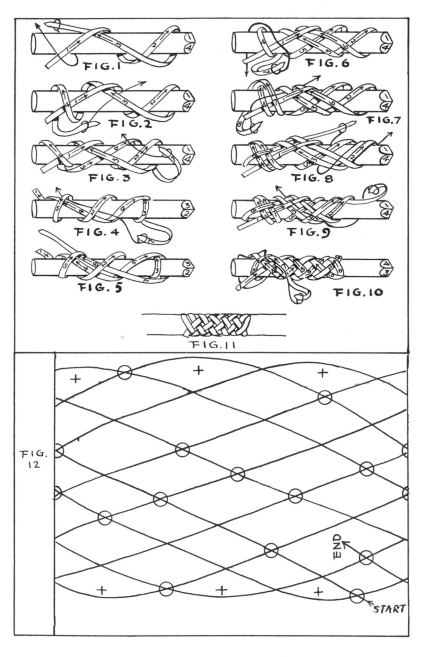

FIG.1

FIG.2

FIG.3

FIG.4

FIG.5

FIG.6

FIG.7

FIG.8

FIG.9

FIG.10

FIG.11

FIG. 12

END

START

PLATE 155. Long Three-Bight Turk's-head.

379

PLATE 156

Two-Part Three-Bight Turk's-head. This is the first of what I have named the Dayville Series. I was introduced to this type of braid years ago by Ed Rickman, who then lived in a little western town named Dayville. In these knots the number of bights exceeds the number of parts. With patience and by using pins or nails on a mandrel, as many bights as you wish can be made. The braid is of the running type and can be made in the same manner as shown in Figs. 1, 2, 3, and 4, and the subsequent knots in this plate.

Figure 1 shows the start of the two-part three-bight knot. The working end passes around back and comes up to the top before crossing the standing part (Fig. 2). For an uneven number of bights, pass under at the bottom.

For an even number of bights and an odd number of parts, start as in Fig. 5 where the working end passes over both the bottom and top bights. Figure 7 shows a three-part four-bight Turk's-head.

A four-part five-bight Turk's-head is started in Fig. 8. Here again we get an uneven number of bights and an odd number of parts by passing below the lower bight and over the top.

A knot with an even number of bights and an odd number of parts (in this case, six bights and five parts) is started in Fig. 11. Here it will be noticed that the working end passes over the lower bight and upper bight. The finished knot is shown in Fig. 14.

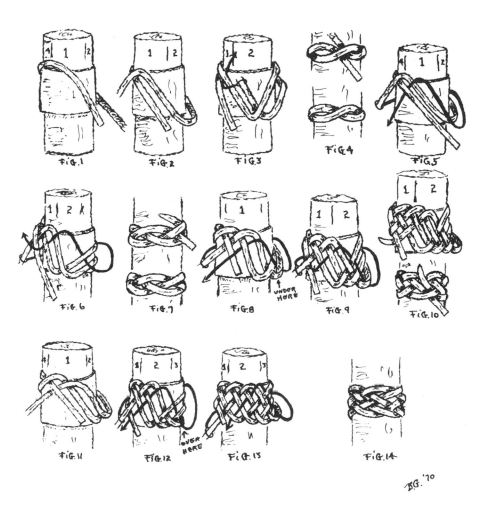

PLATE 156. Two-Part Three-Bight Turk's-head.

PLATE 157

Five-Part Nine-Bight Turk's-head Raised from a Three-Part Five-Bight Turk's-head. This system of raising the three-part Turk's-head to one of larger size is valuable, especially when increasing the elongated Turk's-head shown in Plate 144.

Figure 1 shows the beginning of this process. The working end has been shaded so its progress might more easily be followed. Work first on the right side of the standing part and when passing down, work on the opposite side. Once around and the interlocking path will easily be seen and the sequence is then under one, over one, under one, over one.

Seven-Part Four-Bight Turk's-head. The string or thong first is wrapped around the mandrel as shown in Fig. 8, including the arrowline. In Fig. 9 this pass is completed. In Fig. 10 going up, the sequence is under one, over one, and under one (the top bight). In Fig. 11 passing down, the sequence is under one, over two, under one and then over the standing part. Going up (Fig. 12), the sequence is under one, over two, under one, and then over one (the top bight not shown in the drawing). Going down (Fig. 13), the working end passes under the top bight, then over one, under one, over one, under one, and over the lower bight. The working end is then brought up alongside the standing end and the knot is complete (Fig. 14).

Eight-Part Three-Bight Turk's-head. This Turk's-head is started as shown in Fig. 15. The arrowline shows the next step where the working end is brought around, and up under its own part and then over the top bight. In Fig. 16 this step is completed and the arrowline indicates the path of the working end—down, over two and under two. The working end is now brought aroudn and, as the arrowline indicates in Fig. 17, passes over the standing end and then up, under two, over two, and under one at the top. In Fig. 18 the interlocking path downward is shown where the sequence is over the top bight, then under one, over one, under one, over one, under one, and over the lower bight. The working end is passed around up alongside the standing end, the knot adjusted, and the result is shown in Fig. 20.

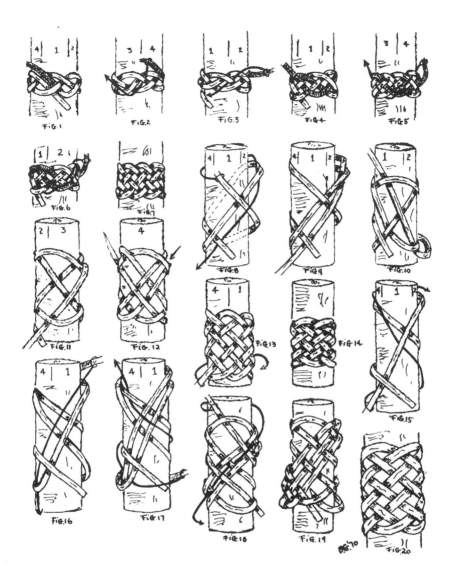

PLATE 157. Five-Part Nine-Bight Turk's-head Raised from a Three-Part Five-Bight Turk's-head; Seven-Part Four-Bight Turk's-head; Eight-Part Three-Bight Turk's-head.

383

PLATE 158

Nine-Part Four-Bight Turk's-head. The first step in making this Turk's-head is indicated in Fig. 1 where the string or thong is wrapped around the mandrel as shown. The arrowline indicates how the working end is passed up, over two (the second being the top bight) and then down, under one, over one, under one, then over one, the bottom bight. In Fig. 2 the working end follows the path of the arrowline which is up, under one, over one, under one, and over one (the top bight) and down, over one, under one, over two, under one, and over one, the bottom bight. The next pass upward is shown in Fig. 3 where the working end goes over one, under one, over two, under one, over one, the top bight. In the next figure (No. 4), the interlocking path downward is shown and the working end goes under one, over one, under one, over one, under one, over one, under one, and over one, the bottom bight. The working end is passed around up alongside the standing end. The adjusted knot is shown in Fig. 5. This is the Turk's-head indicated in Plate 131 for covering rectangular objects.

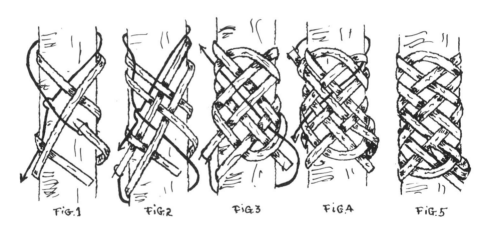

PLATE 158. Nine-Part Four-Bight Turk's-head.

Braided Knots

Braided Knot with Turk's-head Foundation. The simplest form of braiding is the flat braid, or the so-called hair braid of three thongs. This is working each outer thong alternately over the one nearest it toward the center.

Such a working procedure is the basis of flat braiding. Work your outer thongs in rotation—that is, each time bringing the highest thong on each side toward the center. If it passes over one thong and under one thong on one side, the thong on the other side also passes over one and under one.

But the hair braid is not as simple as that. It may be made to form the toughest of all knots, the Turk's-head, which is nothing more than a flat braid made into a wreath or ring by means of a single thong.

The Turk's-head is a practical knot and an old sailor's favorite. But the braider should think of it as a foundation upon which to fashion the woven knot, or the braided knot. While it is customary for present-day braiders to double or triple the leather or rawhide Turk's-head by following around to make it larger or longer, this is a sailor's trick and is not too practicable in leather or rawhide work. Why? Because leather thongs or rawhide strings will invariably overlap on the scallops; the round rope will not do this. The Turk's-head then is best used without being doubled or tripled, and only as a foundation knot, or at times by itself.

I must repeat, there is a rule to be observed in making Turk's-heads as well as braided knots. A relationship exists between the bights, or scallops, and the number of thongs directly across the Turk's-head. By the number of thongs across—which we call "parts"—is meant that if you cut straight across the Turk's-head at right angles you would sever three thongs in the hair braid. So this is called a three-part Turk's-head.

The relationship between bights and parts is this: The number of *bights* and the number of *parts* cannot have a common divsor. A three-part Turk's-head cannot have three bights, six bights, nine bights, or any number divisible by three. It can have two bights, four bights, five bights, seven bights, eight bights, or any number which cannot be divided by three.

If you try to tie a Turk's-head with bights and parts which have a common divisor, the ends will come together or meet before the knot is complete. Turk's-heads are perfect in every respect and are the delight of mathematicians.

Always observe then the rule that no one number can be divided into both the number of parts and the number of bights of your Turk's-head.

The simple three-part flat braid and three-part Turk's-head do not constitute anything elaborate in braiding, but to know how to make them is important as a beginning. They illustrate how you can take any flat braid—one of four thongs, five thongs (Figs. 1 and 2, Plate 159), six thongs, or any number up to infinity—and make from it a Turk's-head.

386

Take a look at Fig. 1, Plate 159. Here is a five-thong braid which has been braided down until there are four bights on each side (including, of course, the bight which will be formed when the ends are tied together). To make this into a Turk's-head you tie the lower part of thong 3 to the upper part of thong 1; the lower part of thong 1 to the upper part of thong 2; lower 4 to upper 3; lower 5 to upper 4, and lower 2 to upper 5. Follow around and you will have a Turk's-head, of four bights and five parts.

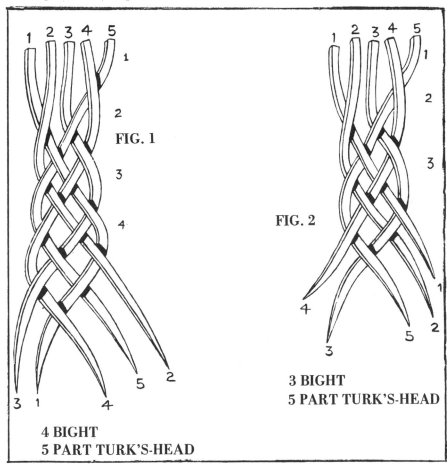

FIG. 1

FIG. 2

4 BIGHT
5 PART TURK'S-HEAD

3 BIGHT
5 PART TURK'S-HEAD

PLATE 159. Braided Knot with Turk's-head Foundation.

In Fig. 2, Plate 159, is a three-bight, five-part Turk's-head. Lower 4 is tied to upper 1; lower 3 to upper 2; lower 5 to upper 3; lower 2 to upper 4, and lower 1 to upper 5.

There is another way to braid five thongs and make them into a Turk's-head. This is shown in Figs. 1, 2 and 3 in Plate 160.

387

Take five thongs and first pass the one on the extreme left (thong 1) to the right and over two and to the center. Then take the thong on the extreme right, thong 5, and pass it to the left over two and to the center. Thong 2 on the left is next brought to the right over two. This is shown in Fig. 1.

In Fig. 2 we see thong 4 on the right has been passed to the center over two thongs. Then you work thong 3 toward the center and over two. Then thong 1 to the left, and so on.

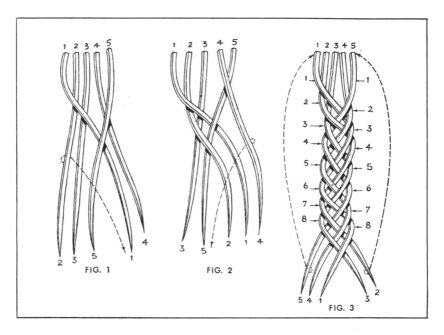

PLATE 160. Braided Knot with Turk's-head Foundation (Continued).

In Fig. 3 you will see the anatomy of the woven knot, which is commonly called the Spanish ring knot. We have braided down until there are eight bights or loops on each side (including the one which will be formed when the ends are joined). Now if you take the lower end of thong 5 and tie it to the upper end of thong 1; the lower end of thong 4 to the upper end of thong 2; the lower end of thong 1 to the upper end of thong 3; the lower end of thong 3 to the upper end of thong 4, and the lower end of thong 2 to the upper end of thong 5—then you will have the Spanish ring knot.

By starting at any point and passing your finger along over the joined thongs, you will finally come back to the beginning. If you thus follow around with a long thong, then untie the original braid and pull it out, you will have the knot of one thong.

Always remember the rule of such knots—you cannot have a number of bights and a number of parts (counting the thongs across) which will have a common divisor.

You can make a Spanish ring knot as long as you please, in fact I use them sometimes for wrist loops on quirts and riding crops. As you experiment, you will become increasingly interested in braiding and do your part in keeping alive this old-time cowboy handicraft.

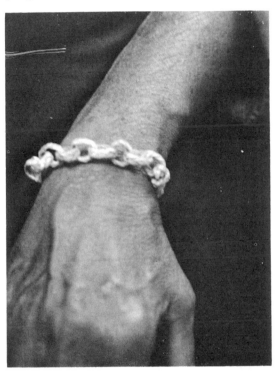

Link bracelet made with Spanish Ring Knots over an ordinary lead pencil. When the first is made another is woven into it. The fastening (not shown) consists of a longer ring knot with a keeper which is woven in one end—in the other end a four-string round braid is made onto the link and then worked into any of the holding knots. Used here are 1/16 of an inch drumhead rawhide strings.

PLATE 161

The Spanish Ring Knot. In the previous lesson we have seen how to make the Spanish ring knot by braiding down five thongs and then joining the ends. This should have given a pretty good idea of the knot.

However, this knot usually is made in a different fashion, in a free-hand way. Only one thong is employed and the completed knot is made with this, first tying a Turk's-head and then interweaving.

We will start with a three-part, five-bight Turk's-head, which is the foundation knot. The mandrel or rounded stick on which it is made has been divided into four areas, so you can tell at a glance when the mandrel has been turned. When you twist the mandrel toward you, the numbers run from 1 to 4.

The leather thong or rawhide string is laid across the mandrel as shown in Fig. 1, Plate 161. The working end is marked A. It is passed around again over the standing part (Fig. 2); then brought forward and passed beneath the standing part (Fig. 3).

Pay particular attention to Fig. 4 where the standing part is pulled from beneath that part of the thong to its left. The working end A now passes beneath this, as in Figs. 5 and 6. In Fig. 7 we see the standing part, which was on the left, pulled again beneath the thong to its right (in a way similar to the procedure in Fig. 4) and the working end is again passed beneath it. Bring the working end of your thong around and to the front and when it passes up alongside the standing part, the Turk's-head is complete (Fig. 8).

We begin the woven knot in Fig. 9. First withdraw your working end from along the right side of the standing end and pass it over and along to the left side of the standing end (Fig. 9).

In Fig. 10 it passes over the standing part and then down along to its right side, having gone under the same part of the thong on the edge as did the standing part. In Fig. 11 it again passes over the standing part, and up along to the left side of the standing part, having gone under the same part of the thong on the edge that the standing part did.

Now we begin the braid or weave. In Fig. 12, the fid shows the path the working end follows, passing beneath two thongs and up, splitting a pair of parallel thongs. On the other side, the working end passes under two thongs and up, splitting two parallel thongs (Fig. 13).

In Fig. 14 it passes under two and splits two from the other side. It is now brought up alongside the standing end, to its left, after passing under three thongs (Fig. 15). The completed knot is shown in Fig. 16.

Here we have shown a Spanish ring knot of over-two, under-two sequence. It can be increased to an over-three, under-three sequence—or a greater one if desired—by passing the working end around, following the standing part as you did from Figs. 9 to 11 inclusive, and then passing around again, splitting the parallel pairs.

This knot will never shake loose or go adrift.

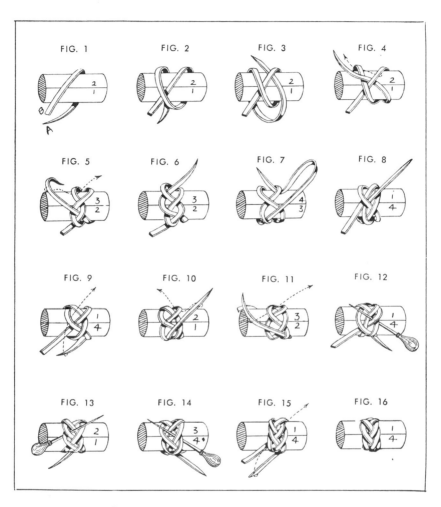

PLATE 161. The Spanish Ring Knot.

391

PLATE 162

Spanish Ring Knot of Three Passes. Start with the woven ring knot of two passes shown in Plate 161. This knot is shown on the mandrel in Fig. 1. The standing end is designated as A and the working end as B.

With the working end, B, follow the path of the standing part. A. The arrowline in Fig. 1 illustrates how the working end is brought up alongside and to the left of the standing end.

In Fig. 2 the mandrel has been turned to show the back. Pass the working end, B, up alongside the left of the standing end and then over it, and at the same time under the two thongs as shown and to the right side of the standing end.

Again pass the working end, B, which is now to the right of the standing part, A, over the latter and follow it to the left side, indicated by the fid. In Fig. 3 the mandrel has been turned to illustrate this operation.

This completes one circuit of the knot, starting with the working end alongside the left of the standing part, then passing over it to its right side, then again over it to its left side, each time following the course the standing part takes, going under and over the same thongs as does the standing part.

In Fig. 4, where the working end and standing part are parallel, the fid has passed between them, separating them, thus providing a course for the working end, B.

The sequence from now on for the working end will be over three thongs and under three thongs, each time separating two parallel thongs.

Pass the fid beneath three thongs and split the parallel thongs, this time from the left-hand side, making an opening through which to pass the working end, B, as shown in Fig. 5.

Follow the same procedure on the right side, passing the fid beneath three thongs and splitting the parallel ones, as shown in Fig. 6. The working end, B, goes through this aperture.

In Fig. 7 the final move is shown. Bring the working end, B, up alongside the standing end, A, and under the same three thongs and the knot is complete.

This knot can be made over a leather collar or even over another Turk's-head, such as the ordinary three-part, five-bight knot shown in Plate 147. This gives it a pleasing raised effect.

A diagram pattern to make the knot is given in Fig. 9.

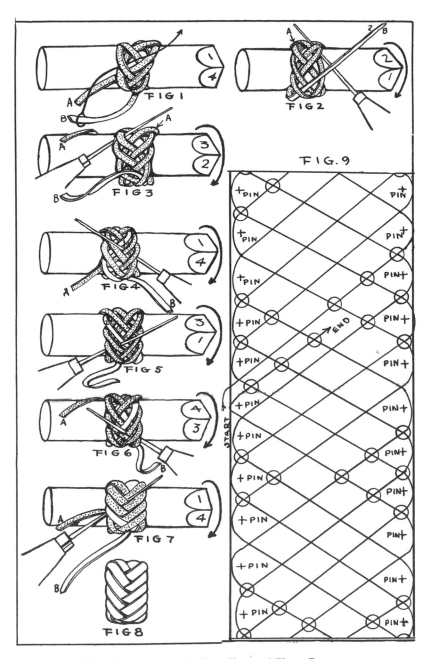

PLATE 162. Spanish Ring Knot of Three Passes.

PLATE 163

Ring Knot of Four Passes. This attractive knot must be used on a collar which will keep its outer edges or bights even.

Wrap the thong around the mandrel (with leather collar) four times, passing over the thongs in both front and rear. Then bring it around a fifth time as in Fig. 1 and pass the working end beneath the first thong, which is the standing part. Pass it over the last four.

In Fig. 2 the mandrel has been turned to show the rear. Pass the working end under one thong and over four.

Back to the front again in Fig. 3, pass the working end under two thongs and over four.

In the rear (Fig. 4), make the same pass under two and over four.

Returning to the front (Fig. 5), now pass under three thongs and over four.

The knot is closing and front and rear are almost one in Fig. 6. Bring the working end up under three thongs and over four.

Bring the working end to the front and pass it under four thongs (Fig. 7). It is alongside the standing part in the next move (Fig. 8). The knot is completed (Fig. 9).

This knot can be made by wrapping the thongs around five times in the beginning and then the sixth time before the weaving is started. In such case, always pass over the last five thongs in both front and rear. It can be made also with an over-six, under-six or an even greater sequence, but it soon gets out of hand.

As cautioned in the beginning, when used on a quirt, whip, hackamore, cane or as a neckerchief slide knot, always work it over a collar so that the edges will not draw inward beneath the knot when it is tightened.

Figure 10 provides a diagram pattern for this knot.

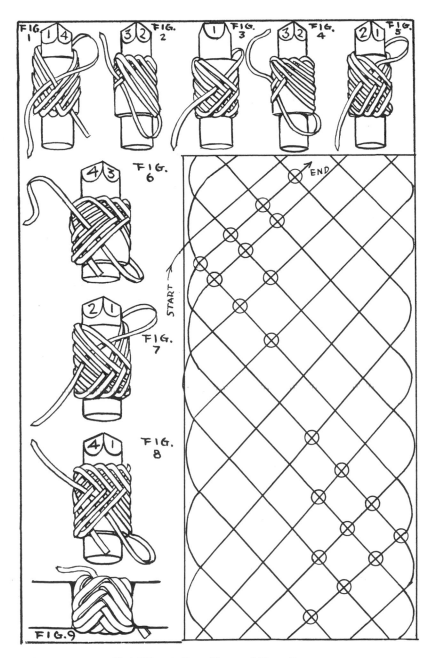

PLATE 163. Ring Knot of Four Passes.

PLATE 164

Gaucho Knot of Two Passes. Made over the same type of leather collar as shown on the mandrel—a collar which can be slipped off with the knot—this knot provides an excellent neckerchief slide. If the knot is to be so used, the hair or smooth side of the leather collar should be *next* to the mandrel.

Begin as in Fig. 1 with the mandrel upright, and pass the thong around as shown. Then make another circuit, passing over the standing part, A, at all points (Fig. 2). Continue around again, going over both thongs in the rear, as shown in Fig. 3.

Start the braid by passing beneath the standing part, A, and over the next two thongs (Fig. 4). Do the same in the rear (Fig. 5).

Now proceed as follows:

Front: Under two and over two (Fig. 6). Rear: Under two and over two (Fig. 7). Front: Over one, under two, over two (Fig. 8). Rear: Over one, under two, over two (Fig. 9). Front: Over two, under two, over two (Fig. 10). Rear: Over two, under two, over two (Fig. 11).

Front: Under one, over two, under two, and over two (Fig. 12). Rear: Under one, over two, under two, and over two (Fig. 13).

Front: Under two, over two, under two and over two (Fig. 14).

In Fig. 15 the working end, B, comes up alongside the standing end, A, and Fig. 16 shows the finished knot.

A larger knot can be made with the same sequence of over two, under two, by continuing around from Fig. 15, passing under two, over two, under two and over two, then to the front, over one, under two, over two, under two and over two, and the same in the rear. This is the sequence followed in Fig. 9 except that there are now a larger number of thongs. To continue, follow the sequence in Fig. 10, which in this case would be over two, under two, over two, under two and over two. Keep on as in Figs. 11, 12, 13, 14 and 15 until the larger knot is finished.

A diagram pattern (Fig. 17) shows how to make the first knot.

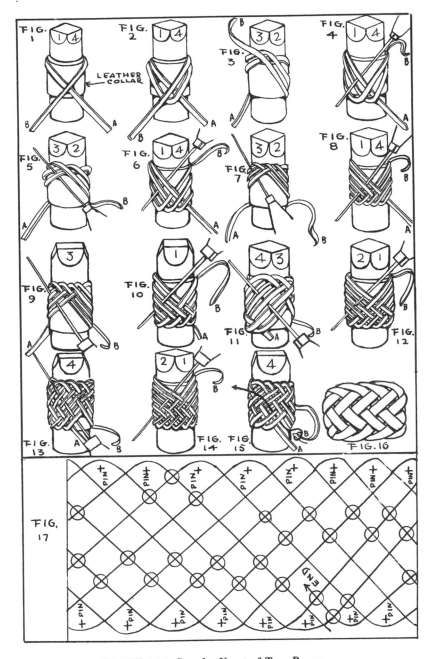

PLATE 164. Gaucho Knot of Two Passes.

PLATE 165

Gaucho Knot of Three Passes. Two plates are necessary to illustrate adequately the manner of making this beautiful knot. So, upon completing the work demonstrated to this plate (165), continue with Plate 165-A. Use an extra long thong and work carefully.

This knot is worked on a leather collar as were the two previous ones. As in the other cases, the collar can be turned so the smooth side is innermost, and the knot used as a neckerchief slide. The knot may also be used as a slide knot on lanyards, bridle reins, etc., not only to hold them together, but to adjust them to shorter or longer lengths and for decorative purposes.

Begin as in Fig. 1 by wrapping the thong around the mandrel (and collar) three times, always passing over each part of the thong.

In Fig. 2 make another turn, passing over the three thongs in the front and the rear as before (Fig. 2 shows the back of the knot). We shall designate that part where the working end passes downward as the "front," and the opposite side of the mandrel where the working end passes upward as the "rear."

Here, then, is the sequence:

Front: Pass the working end under the first thong, which is the standing part, and (following the course of the fid as shown) the sequence will be, under one, over three (Fig. 3).

Rear: Under one, over three (Fig. 4).

Front: Under two, over three (Fig. 5).

Rear: Under two, over three. (Follow the course of the fid in Fig. 6).

Front: Under three, over three (Fig. 7). (This first move after passing under three completes a small knot, as the working end now meets the standing end. But continue to make the knot larger.)

Rear: Under three, over three. (Follow the course of the fid in Fig. 8.)

Front: Over one, under three, over three (Fig. 9).

Rear: Over one, under three, over three. (Follow the fid in Fig. 10.)

Continue this sequence on the next plate.

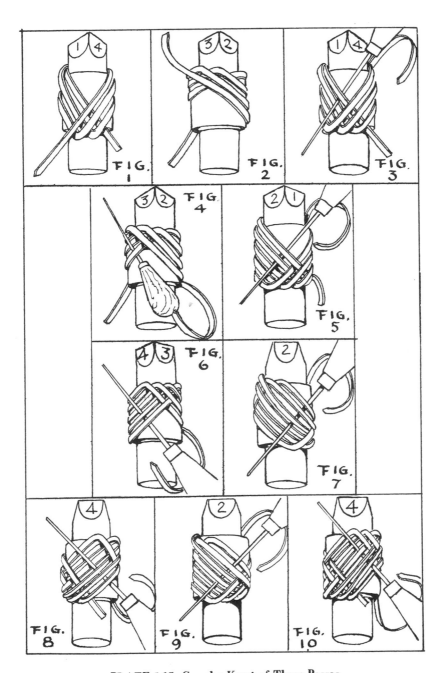

PLATE 165. Gaucho Knot of Three Passes.

PLATE 165-A

Gaucho Knot of Three Passes (Cont.). To continue from the previous plate, pass the working end of the thong along the course taken by the fid in Fig. 11. This sequence is over two, under three and over three.

Rear: Over two, under three, over three (illustrated by the fid in Fig. 12).

By now it may be seen that the working end always makes the same pass in the rear as in the front. However, we shall continue to detail each move. Back to the sequence:

Front: Over three, under three, over three (Fig. 13).

Rear: Over three, under three, over three (Fig. 14).

Front: Under one, over three, under three, over three. (Follow the path of the fid in Fig. 15.)

Rear: Under one, over three, under three, over three (fid in Fig. 16).

Front: Under two, over three, under three, over three (shown by fid in Fig. 17).

Rear: Under two, over three, under three, over three. (Illustrated by the course of the fid in Fig. 18. The knot is closing up now.)

Front: Under three, over three, under three, over three (fid in Fig. 19).

Rear-front: Bring the working end around and under three, which places it alongside the standing end and completes the knot (Fig. 20). The finished knot is shown in Fig. 21.

This knot can be enlarged still further by continuing around. When the front is reached, again pass over one, under three,

This knot can be enlarged still further by continuing around. When the front is reached, again pass over one, under three, over three, and the same applies in the rear. When the point is reached where the pass is over three, under three, over three, under three, over three, start with under one, over three, under three, over three, under three and over three. Continue until an under-three, over-three, under-three, and over-three sequence is reached. When the working end comes alongside the standing end, the knot is completed.

A diagram pattern for making this interesting knot is shown in Fig. 22.

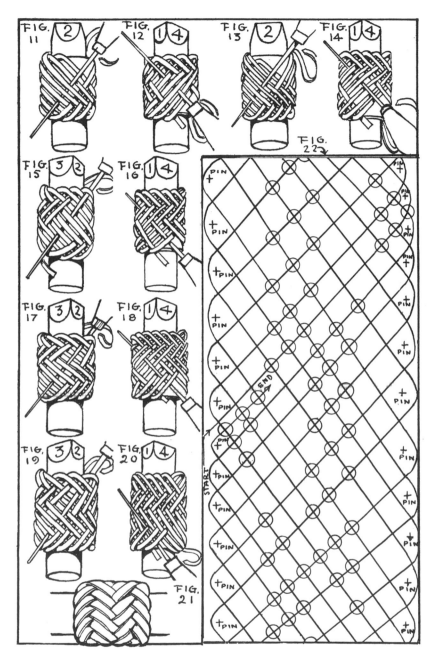

PLATE 165-A. Gaucho Knot of Three Passes (Continued).

401

PLATE 166

Gaucho Knot Worked on a Turk's-head. First make a five-part four-bight Turk's-head. Continue as in Fig. 1, where the working end of the thong or string is brought up alongisde the left side of the standing part.

In passing down, the working end goes beneath the first bight to its left (Fig. 2) and over one, under two, over two. The sequence upwards is under one, over one, under two, over two (Fig. 3).

Fig. 4: Down, under one, over two, under two, over two.

Fig. 5: Up, under one, over two, under two, over two.

Fig. 6: Down, under two, over two, under two, over two.

In Fig. 7 the knot is shown completed with an over-two, under-two sequence and the working end is brought up alongside the standing end. The arrowline indicates the first pass to make this knot with an over-three, under-three sequence. In going down, it will pass under two, over two, under three and over three, and so on. The finished knot of over-three, under-three sequence is shown in Fig. 8.

Figure 9 illustrates how this method can be used to increase a flat braid.

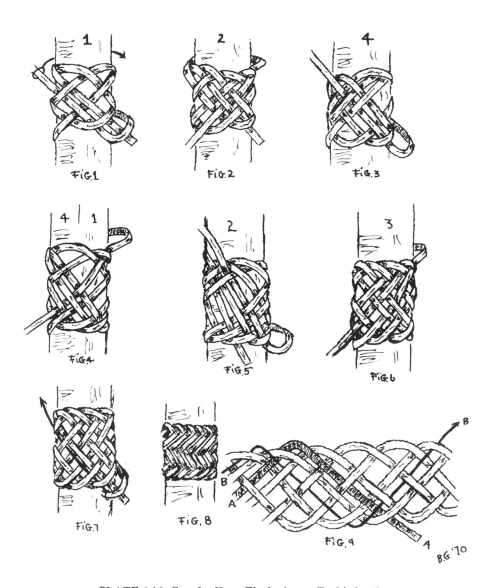

PLATE 166. Gaucho Knot Worked on a Turk's-head.

403

PLATE 167

Double Gaucho Knot of Two Passes. In the two-bight knot of any length (Plate 154) the number of crossings the thong made on its second pass indicated the number of sections of the knot. If it crossed twice, it formed a two-section knot; if three times, a three-section knot, and so on.

The same rule also holds in this knot. It is a two-section or double knot having an over-two, under-two sequence, the same as the one-section gaucho knot of two passes (Plate 164). It can be made in three sections, or four sections, etc., by crossing, on the second move, three thongs, four thongs, or as many as desired.

It will be necessary to demonstrate this knot in two plates, so the work will continue on Plate 167-A.

Start as in Fig. 1, by wrapping the thong around one and one-half times and bringing it back, passing the working end over its own part twice. Do this once more, as indicated in Figs. 2 and 3, never passing *under*, but always *over* each thong. Go around once more, inclining to the right as in Fig. 4, and then pass under one thong and over two as in Fig. 5. This is the beginning of the braid.

In the section of the knot on the left illustrated in Fig. 6, pass again under one and over two. In working to the right, repeat this in the left-hand section, under one, over two (Fig. 7), and again in the right-hand section, under one, over two (Fig. 8).

Now proceed as follows:

Under two, over two (Fig. 9). Under two, over two (Fig. 10). Under two, over two (Fig. 11).

In Fig. 11, after passing under two (as indicated by the fid), a completed knot is shown, as the working end here meets the standing end. This makes a finished small knot, but can be enlarged in the following manner. Continue as in Fig. 12, under two, over two.

Now pass over one, under two, over two (Fig. 13). Over one, under two, over two (Fig. 14). Over one, under two, over two (Fig. 15).

For instructions on completing this knot, turn to Plate 167-A.

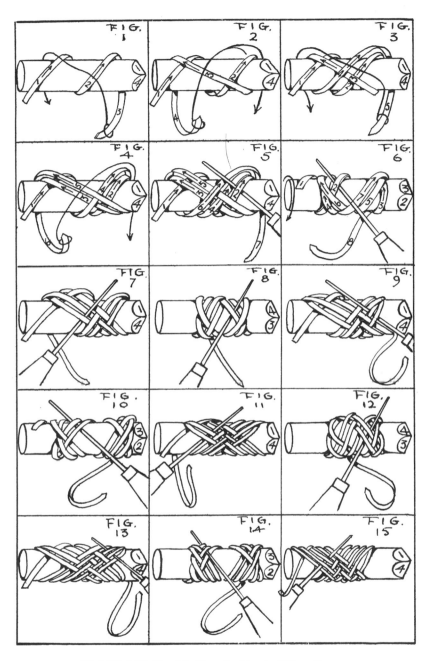

PLATE 167. Double Gaucho Knot of Two Passes.

405

PLATE 167-A

Double Gaucho Knot of Two Passes (Cont.). Take the double gaucho knot of two passes in Fig. 16 and proceed by passing over one thong, under two thongs and over two. Then pass over two, under two and over two (Fig. 17).

Next, in the left-hand section, pass over two, under two and over two, indicated by the path of the fid in Fig. 18. (It will be noted here in combining the sequences of Figs. 17 and 18 that in the middle of the knot the working end actually passes over four thongs. This may look wrong but it will adjust itself in the over-two, under-two sequence as the work proceeds.)

Continue as follows:

Back toward the right, over two, under two, over two (Fig. 19).

Over two, under two, over two (Fig. 20).

Toward the left, under one, over two, under two, over two (Fig. 21).

Under one, over two, under two, over two (Fig. 22).

Toward the right, under one, over two, under two, over two (Fig. 23).

Under one, over two, under two, over two (Fig. 24).

Toward the left, under two, over two, under two, over two (Fig. 25).

Under two, over two, under two, and over two (Fig. 26).

In Fig. 27, after passing under two thongs, the work comes back to the starting point and the working end is alongside the standing end, so the knot is complete. However, as with the other gaucho knots made by this braiding process, it may be continued around again and again, each time terminating at the point where working end and standing end meet. This will result in a knot with a greater number of bights, which will fit over a larger circumference and still close up when tightened. The finished knot is shown in Fig. 28.

Figure 29 provides a diagram pattern for this knot.

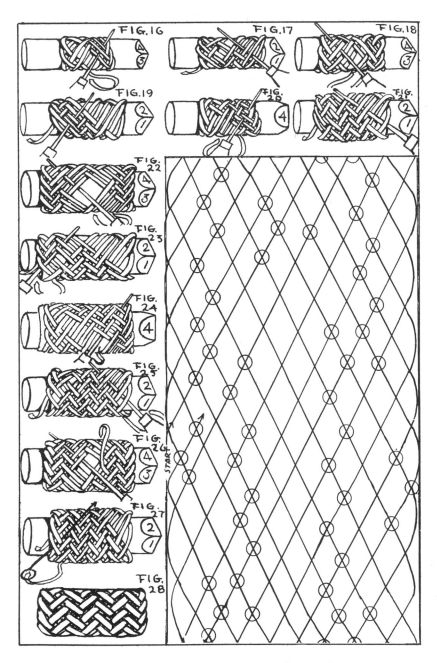

PLATE 167-A. Double Gaucho Knot of Two Passes (Continued).

407

PLATE 168

Double Gaucho Knot of Three Passes. To make the double gaucho knot of three passes, wrap the thong around the mandrel two and one-half times. Then continue until at the right there are four thongs alongside each other, all of which have been passed over the top in going around. The sequence now is this:

To left (Fig. 1): Under one, over three in the right-hand section; under one, over three in the left-hand section.

To right: Under one, over three in the left-hand section; under one, over three in the right-hand section.

To left: Under two, over three, and again under two, over three.

To right: Under two, over three, and under two and over three.

To left: Under three, over three; under three, over three. (The next move where the working end meets the standing end, completes a small knot. But we shall continue to make a larger knot.)

To right: Under three, over three; under three, over three.

To left: Over one, under three, over three; over one, under three and over three.

To right: Over one, under three, over three; over one, under three, over three.

To left: Over two, under three, over three; over two, under three, over three.

To right: Over two, under three, over three; over two, under three, over three.

To left: Over three, under three, over three; over three, under three, over three.

To right: Over three, under three, over three; over three, under three, over three.

To left: Under one, over three, under three, over three; under one, over three, under three, over three.

To right: Under one, over three, under three, over three; under one, over three, under three, over three.

To left: Under two, over three, under three, over three; under two, over three, under three, over three.

To right: Under two, over three, under three, over three; under two, over three, under three, over three. Then pass to the left under three, over three, under three, over three; under three, over three, under three, over three.

The next move is under three, with the working end alongside the standing end, and the knot is finished (Fig. 2).

In using this pattern it is best to work it with 3/32 inch commercial lacing and a thonging or lacing needle. Be very careful the ends of the pattern lines are true and coincide.

A diagram pattern is given in Fig. 3.

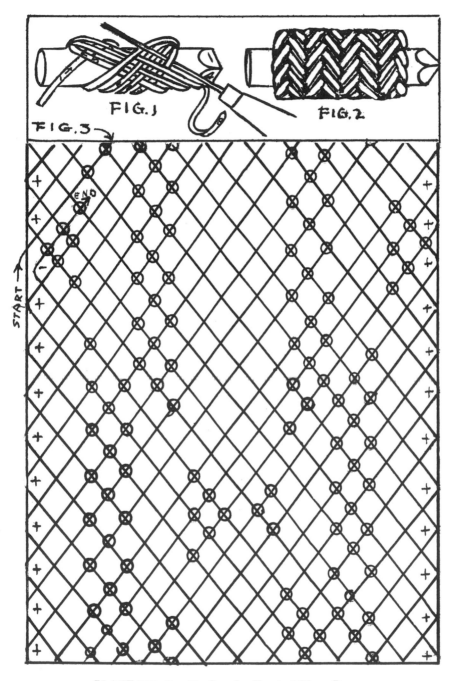

PLATE 168. Double Gaucho Knot of Three Passes.

PLATE 169

Headhunter's Knot of Two Passes. The man who first introduced the headhunter's knot to civilization never told how it was made. As the story goes, a chieftain of a savage tribe had explained to him how to braid the knot and then warned him that he would suffer dire consequences if he gave away the secret. However, as I have worked it out myself, I am violating no confidence and fear no savage vengeance.

Start as in Fig. 1 by wrapping the thong around the mandrel (with leather collar). When the working end reaches the rear (the mandrel has been turned in Fig. 2 to show this), it passes *beneath* the thong there. This is the secret of the knot.

Proceed as follows:

Front: Over two (Fig. 3).

Rear: Under two (Fig. 4). (From now on always pass *over* the last two in front and *under* the last two in the rear.)

Front: Under one, over two (Fig. 5).

Rear: Over one, under two (Fig. 6).

Front: Under two, over two (Fig. 7).

Rear: Over two, under two (Fig. 8).

Front: Over one, under two, over two (Fig. 9).

Rear: Under one, over two, under two (Fig. 10).

Front: Over two, under two, over two (Fig. 11).

In Fig. 12 the working end comes up under two thongs and alongside the standing end which, by our mathematical law, completes the knot. The finished knot is shown in Fig. 13.

If a larger knot is desired, keep passing around, varying the sequence at the top and bottom each time so that when working from the top down, the working end always comes out over the last two thongs, and when working up in the rear, the business end of the thong passes *under* the last two. When the working end comes up alongside the standing end, the knot is finished. This is true, we repeat, of all the knots of this fascinating series.

A diagram pattern for this knot is provided in Fig. 14.

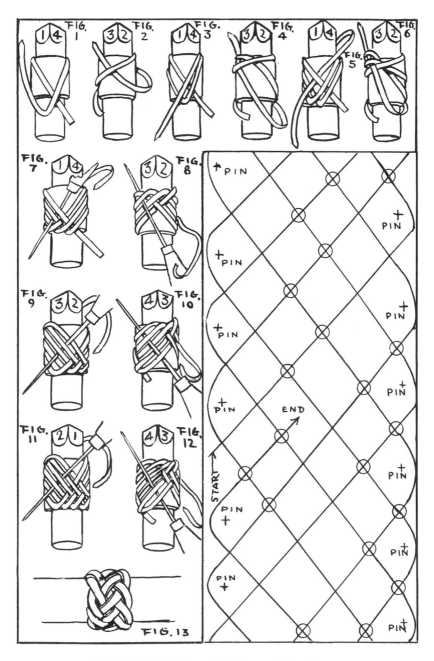

PLATE 169. Headhunter's Knot of Two Passes.

411

PLATE 170

Headhunter's Knot of Three Passes. As a headhunter's knot of over-three, under-three sequence, this may evoke a triple curse from the chief of the cannibal tribe for revealing the secret. But here goes:

Figure 1 illustrates the same rule that was given in the beginning of the headhunter's knot of two passes (Plate 169); that is, the working end passes on top of all the thongs in the front and *beneath* all the thongs in the rear. The rear is not shown in Fig. 1 but all the thongs there go under each other.

Start by passing under one thong and over three (Fig. 1). Then to the rear (the mandrel has been turned to show) in Fig. 2 and pass over one and *under* three. The sequence from now on is:

Front: Under two, over three.

Rear: Over two, under three.

Front: Under three, over three.

Rear: Over three, under three.

Front: Over one, under three, over three.

Rear: Under one, over three, under three.

Front: Over two, under three, over three.

Rear: Under two, over three, under three.

Front: Over three, under three, over three.

Rear: Under three. The working end is now alongside the standing end and the knot is finished.

The completed knot is shown in Fig. 3.

If desirable to enlarge the knot, continue from this point with an under-three, over-three, under-three sequence and when the front is again reached, pass under one, over three, under three, over three. The rear this time will be over one, under three, over three, under three.

Keep going in this manner, being sure that in the front the working end passes *over* the last three thongs and in the rear it passes *under* the last three thongs.

The savage tribes of the Philippines use split bamboo and weave this knot into finger rings. They also use it to adorn their spears and other warlike implements.

A diagram pattern for the over-three, under-three headhunter's knot is given in Fig. 4.

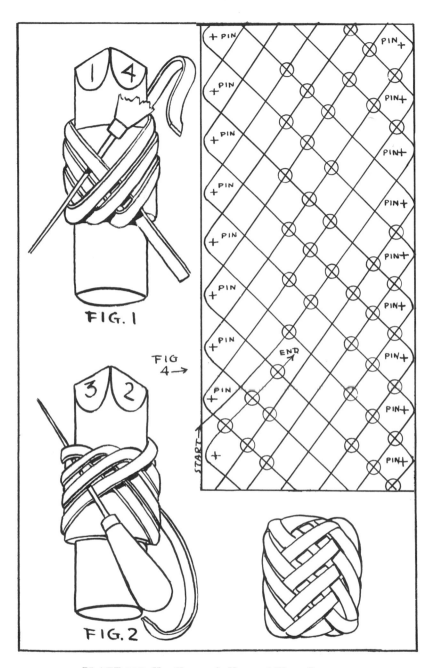

FIG. 1

FIG 4 →

FIG. 2

PLATE 170. Headhunter's Knot of Three Passes.

413

PLATE 171

Herringbone Knot. This is a very dressy and decorative knot for the top of a quirt handle. It can be woven on any of the Turk's-heads having uneven parts, such as the five-part, seven-part, nine-part, etc. This particular knot will be made with the five-part, four-bight Turk's-head as the skeleton knot. While the five-part four-bight Turk's-head can be tied as shown in Plate 148, we will be consistent and weave it.

Wrap the thong around the mandrel (with collar) in the manner shown in Fig. 1. On the second turn pass it under the standing part (Fig. 1), and in the rear pass it under one and over one (Fig. 2).

Continue as follows:

Front: Over one, under one, over one (Fig. 3).

Rear: Over one, under one, over one (Fig. 4).

Front: Under one, over one, under one, over one (Fig. 5). This brings it back to the start, with the working part meeting the standing part (Fig. 6).

Now, instead of tucking it under one thong alongside and to the right of the standing part, tuck it under the standing part and under that thong which is looped over the standing part and up alongside the *left* of the standing part (Fig. 7), so that it follows the standing part upward, passing over one thong and under one thong (Fig. 7).

Pass the working end to the other side of the standing part beneath it and also beneath the thong on top of the standing part (Fig. 8).

With the working end follow the standing part down on its other side, passing under the same thong the standing part does (Fig. 9).

At the bottom of the knot in Fig. 10, the working end has returned to the point where it first passed along to the left of the standing part. Now pass it over the standing part and under its own part, as well as under the two adjacent thongs at the point where they cross each other. In other words, the sequence is over one, under three.

Pass the working end upwards, following to the left of the thong on its right, until it reaches the top, where it goes over one thong and under three, as indicated by the arrowline in Fig. 11. The braiding sequence is continued on Plate 171-A.

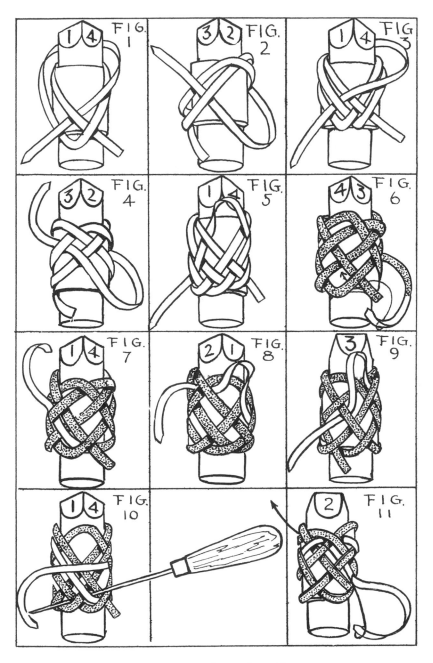

PLATE 171. Herringbone Knot.

PLATE 171-A

Herringbone Knot (Cont.). The last step in Plate 171 reached the top of the knot and the next pass will *split* two of the parallel thongs. Bring the working end down over one, under one, over two and under three, drawing it out at the bottom to the left as shown in Fig. 12.

Going up, the working end passes over one, under one, over two and under three, emerging at the top and left (Fig. 13).

Passing downward, the working end goes over one, under two, over two and under three, emerging at the bottom left (Fig. 14). (Note: Watch the numbers at the top of the mandrel which show when it has been turned.)

Going up, the working end passes over one, under two, over two and under three, emerging at the top left (Fig. 15).

Fig. 16: Going down, the working end passes over two, under two, over two and under one (Fig. 16).

Figure 17 shows the finish of the knot. Pass under two more thongs, including the standing part, and the knot is complete. This last pass could have been included in the previous one and the working end could have been brought under all three thongs at once. However, for the sake of clarity in instructions, it is here done the longer way.

Both the shaded thongs and the white thongs in the completed knot (Fig. 18) represent a five-part, four-bight Turk's-head. In other words, this complete knot is simply the result of weaving or interweaving these two Turk's-heads together.

The same type of knot can be made with a seven-part, six-bight Turk's-head, which would be the result of interweaving two seven-part Turk's-heads together. Also it can be made from the nine-part, eight-bight Turk's-head and so on.

It might be of interest here to say that Turk's-heads and woven knots have engaged the attention of many profound mathematicians and a ponderous literature has been written on them. They follow rules as inviolate as those of the planets, and the winding and intricate, even labyrinthine, twistings can be calculated to a nicety.

A diagram pattern for this knot is given in Fig. 19.

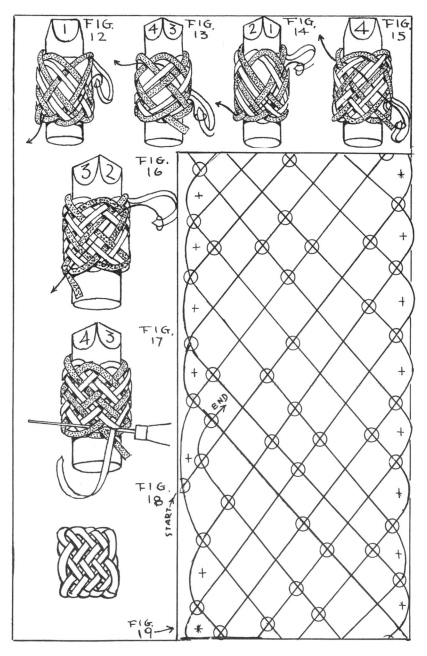

PLATE 171-A. Herringbone Knot (Continued).

417

PLATE 172

The Bruce Knot. This knot is a small type of herringbone woven on a three-part five-bight Turk's-head. Start as in the Spanish ring knot, Plate 161, up to and including Fig. 8. The working end of the string or thong is passed up along the right side of the standing part (Fig. 1).

In Fig. 2 the working end passes along parallel with the standing part, but in Fig. 3 it goes beneath the crossed strings (Fig. 4). It continues to follow the original string but in Fig. 5 it splits a pair downward and then in Fig. 6 splits another pair.

In Fig. 7 the sequence is under one, over two, and under three. The same sequence in Fig. 8 and then the string is brought up alongside the point where the weave started. The finished knot is shown in Fig. 9.

The Catharine Knot. This herringbone knot is similar to the preceding one, except it is woven on a three-part, four-bight Turk's-head. Also, unlike the above knot which is woven at the top, this one is woven at both top and bottom.

Start the foundation knot or Turk's-head as in Fig. 10. It is completed in Fig. 11 and in Fig. 12 the working end is brought up to the right of the standing part. The working end does not cross the standing part but follows around above it to the second crossed strings then passes down over one, under one, over two (one the standing part) as shown in Fig. 13.

Fig. 14: Up, over one, under one, over two.

Fig. 15: Down, over one, under one, over two.

Fig. 16: Up, over one, under two, over two.

Fig. 17: Down, over two, under two, over two.

Fig. 18: Up, over two, under two, over two.

Fig. 19: Down, under one (not shown in drawing), over two, under two, over two.

Fig. 20: Up, under one, over two, under two.

The interweaving string can be a contrasting color and both knots can be made on larger Turk's-head. I believe both types of knots to be original.

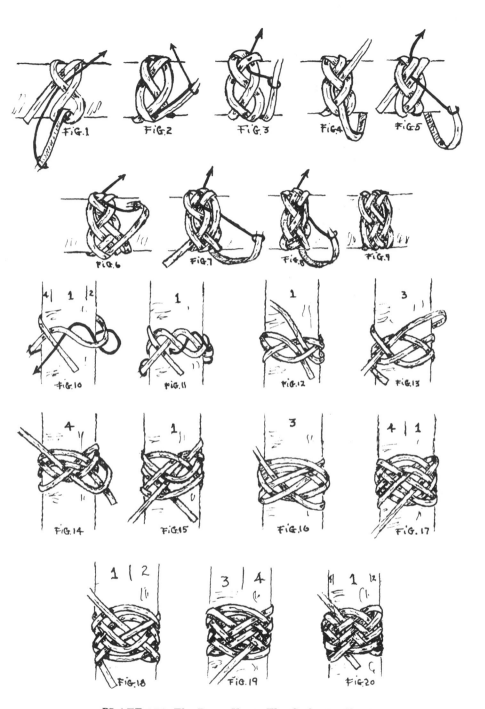

PLATE 172. The Bruce Knot; The Catharine Knot.

419

PLATE 173

Pineapple or Gaucho Button Knot. Where the herringbone knot (Plate 171) was an interweave of two Turk's-heads of the same number of parts and bights, the pineapple knot is an interweave of two Turk's-heads of the same number of bights but different number of parts.

In this case, the basic or skeleton knot is a seven-part, six-bight Turk's-head and the one interwoven is a Turk's-head of five parts and six bights. This knot is usually made over a rounded core and can be used on the heads of canes and quirts. It has, because of its double row of staggered bights at each end, the faculty of closing completely over a round surface.

If tightened around a small spherical core, it makes a beautiful button. The interweaving thong can be of a different tone or color, which gives a very unusual pattern.

The knot can be made any size or length; however, it should be made on a skeleton knot of uneven parts, such as the five-part, seven-part, nine-part, etc. A longer one can be made by interweaving the double or triple section basket-weave Turk's-head.

In Fig. 1 is shown the start of the basic, or skeleton knot. It illustrates a Turk's-head of five parts and four bights which will be raised to one of seven parts and six bights. Tie the five-part, four-bight Turk's-head as shown in Plate 144. Beginning at the front of the knot (Fig. 1), pass the working end, along parallel to the standing end, on its right, under one, over one, under one, over one.

At the top, working down (Fig. 2) pass over one, under one, over one, under one and over one (the bottom loop). The working end passing down in this last step was to the *left* of the standing part.

In Fig. 3, pass upward, again to the right of the standing end, over one, under one, over one, under one, over one and under one (top loop.) Follow the interlocking path downward, over one, under one, over one, under one, over one (Fig. 4).

This portion of the knot is shaded in Fig. 5. Begin with the unshaded part of the working end in Fig. 5, again follow alongside upward to the right of the standing end, under one, over one, under one, over one, and then pass toward the left under the two thongs which cross each other.

Fig. 6: Down, over one, under one, over one, and under two (where the two thongs cross). Fig. 7: Work up, over one, under one, over one and under *three* where the working end divides two parallel thongs. Fig. 8: Work down, over one, under one, over one and under three, splitting a pair.

Fig. 9: (Not shown clearly in the drawing) work up, over one, under one, over one, and under three (splitting a pair).

The sequence is continued on Plate 173-A.

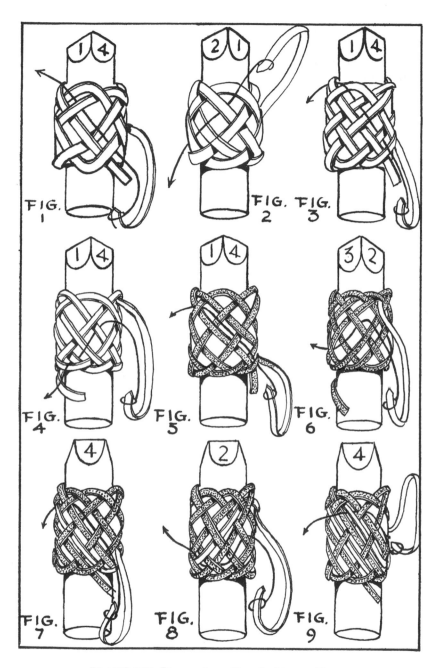

PLATE 173. Pineapple or Gaucho Button Knot.

421

PLATE 173-A

Pineapple or Gaucho Button Knot (Cont.). The sequence of the pineapple knot is continued; pass down (Fig. 10) over two (splitting a pair), under one, over one, and under three, splitting another pair.

Fig. 11: Pass up, over two (dividing a pair), under one, over one and under three. The last move splits a pair of parallel thongs.

Fig. 12: Pass down, over two (splitting a pair), under two (splitting a pair), over one and under three. The last move divides another pair.

Fig. 13: Proceed upward, over two (dividing a pair), under two (dividing another pair), over one, under three (splitting a third pair).

Fig. 14: Over two (dividing a pair), under two (dividing another pair), over two (splitting a third pair) and then under three (dividing a fourth pair).

Fig. 15: Pass up, over two (dividing a pair), under two (dividing a second pair), over two (dividing a third pair), and under three (splitting a fourth pair).

Fig. 16: Pass down, over two (splitting a pair), under two (splitting a second pair), over two (splitting a third pair), and then under three, bringing the working end alongside its own original part. The finished knot is shown in Fig. 17.

A diagram pattern is provided in Fig. 18.

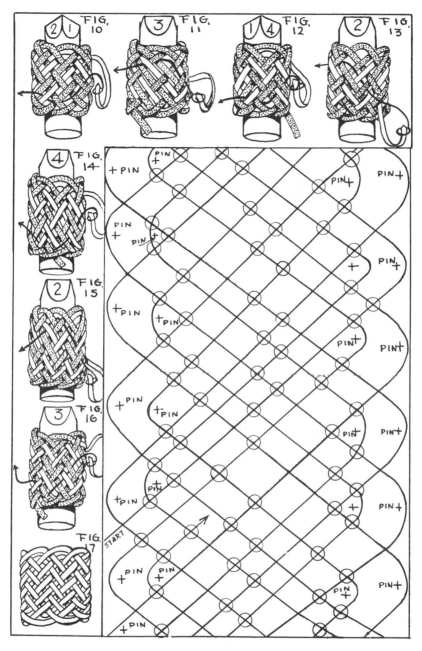

PLATE 173-A. Pineapple or Gaucho Button Knot (Continued).

PLATE 174

The Flores Button Knot. This beautiful little button knot was shown to me in November, 1966, in Buenos Aires by my amigo, Don Luis Alberto Flores. It illustrates a unique way to make a herringbone weave on a five-part, six-bight Turk's-head —or *armadura*, as they say in the Argentine.

First, the Turk's-head is constructed as shown in Figs. 1-5. In Fig. 5, note that the working end comes up alongside the right of the standing end. The weaving begins in Fig. 6 where the working end passes to the left (arrowline) under two inside crosses.

Fig. 7: Down, over one, under four (two crosses).

Fig. 8: Up, over one, under five.

Fig. 9: Down, over one, under five.

Fig. 10: Up, over one, under six. (Split pair, one of which is the standing part.)

Fig. 11: Down, over one, under six.

Fig. 12: Up, over one, under six.

Fig. 13: Down, over two, under six.

Fig. 14: Up, over two, under six.

Fig. 15: Down, over two, under seven (split two sets of pairs).

Fig. 16: Up, over two, under seven.

Fig. 17: Down, over two, under seven and up alongside the first string to the right of the standing part.

There are some Turk's-heads where you find it impossible to weave a herringbone or pineapple braid. This is one of them, when the usual method is used. When the bights are unequal, say five or seven, and exceed the parts, the working end is brought up to the left of the standing end, crossed under two crosses at the top, and one cross at the bottom.

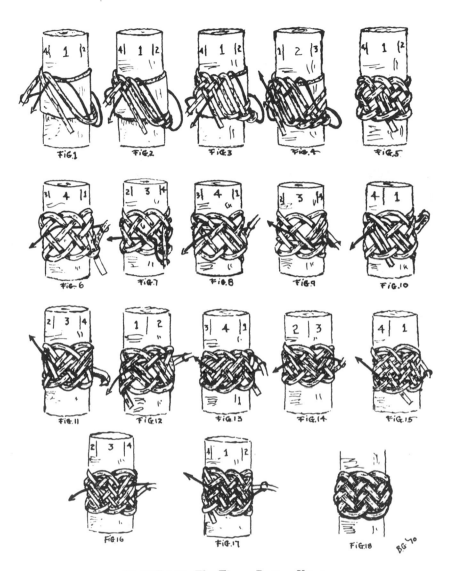

PLATE 174. The Flores Button Knot.

425

PLATE 175

The Small Fan Knot or Botón Oriental. The Botón Oriental comes in various lengths. Named in the Argentine, this knot resembles a Chinese fan. In this small version, where the edges are of a sequence of over two, under two, and the center over three under three, start as in the gaucho knot of two passes, Plate 164. Beginning at Fig. 8, Plate 164, instead of passing down over one, under two, over two, the sequence is as shown in Fig. 1 of this plate—under three, over two.

Fig. 2: Up, under three, over two.

Fig. 3: Down, over one, under three, over two.

Fig. 4: Up, over one, under three, over two.

Fig. 5: Down, over two, under three, over two.

Fig. 6: Up, over two, under three, over two.

Fig. 7: Down, over three, under three, over two.

Fig. 8: Up, over three, under three, over two.

Fig. 9: Down, under one, over three, under three, over two.

Fig. 10: Up, under one, over three, under three, over two.

Fig. 11: Down, under two, over three, under three, over two.

The working end is now brought around and under two alongside the standing part. Figure 12 shows the knot completed.

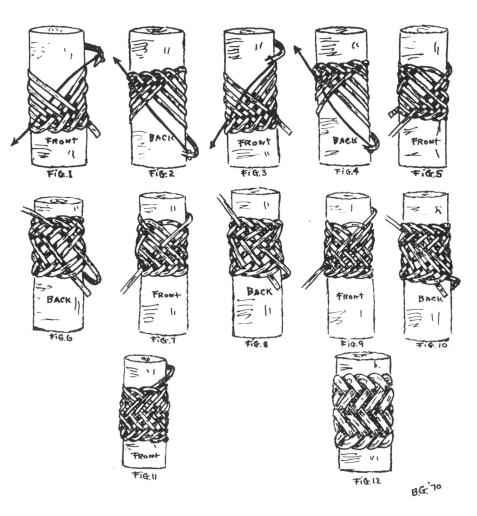

PLATE 175. The Small Fan Knot or Botón Oriental.

427

PLATE 176

The Ginfer Knot. This knot has an over-three, under-three sequence on the ends and over-one, under-one sequence in the center. This center part can be interwoven in various patterns, as will be shown in the section of Braid on Braid.

Start the knot as in Fig. 1 by passing the working end completely around over everything. Do this three times, passing over everything, and then in Fig. 2 pass the working end beneath the standing part as shown, and over three.

Fig. 3: Up, under one, over three.

Fig. 4: Down, over one, under one, over three.

Fig. 5: Up, over one, under one, over three.

Fig. 6: Down, under one, over one, under one, over three.

Fig. 7: Up, under one, over one, under one, over three.

Fig. 8: Down, under two, over one, under one, over three.

Fig. 9: Up, under two, over one, under one, over three.

Fig. 10: Down, under three, over one, under one, over three.

Figure 11 shows complete knot.

John Walter Maguire, affectionately called Don Juan Maguire, in his private museum in Buenos Aires. He is holding a pair of silver reins of exquisite pampas workmanship.

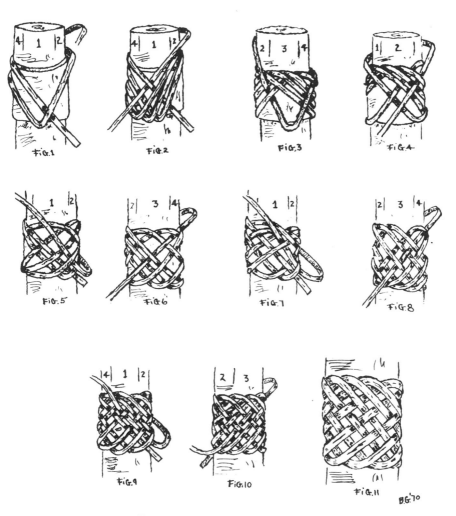

PLATE 176. The Ginfer Knot.

429

PLATE 177

Three-Section Fan Knot or Botón Oriental. Mario A. Lopez Osornio, who made a scholarly study of Argentine Braiding for *La Cómision Nacional de Cultura* of that country and wrote three important books on rawhide braiding, said of this knot: "Few times have I seen a botón so difficult to make."

The edges are of a sequence of over two, under two, and the center or "fan" section is over six, under six.

The knot is started as in Fig. 1 where the string or thong is wrapped around the mandrel as shown. It will be noticed that it goes over all parts except on the way down it passes beneath the standing part at the point marked X. The arrowline shows the progress upward—over one, under one, over one.

Fig. 2: Down (follow the arrowline), over two, under two, over two.

Fig. 3: Up (arrowline), over two, under two, over two.

Fig. 4: Down, under one, over two, under four (one of these the standing part), over two.

Fig. 5: Up (arrowline), under one, over two, under four, over two.

Fig. 6: Down, under two, over two, under six, over two.

Fig. 7: Up, under two, over two, under six (the arrowline does not show the other two this string passes under), over two.

Fig. 8: Down, over one, under two, over three, under four, over one, under two, over two.

Fig. 9: Up, over one, under two, over three, under four, over one, under two, over two.

Fig. 10: Down, over two, under two, over four, under four, over two, under two, over two.

Fig. 11: Up, over two, under two, over four, under four, over two, under two, over two.

Fig. 12: Down, under one, over two, under two, over five, under five, over two, under two, over two.

Fig. 13: Up, under one, over two, under two, over five, under five, over two, under two, over two.

Fig. 14: Down, under two, over two, under two, over six, under six, over two, under two, over two.

The working end is now brought around two, alongside the standing end. The finished knot is shown in Fig. 15.

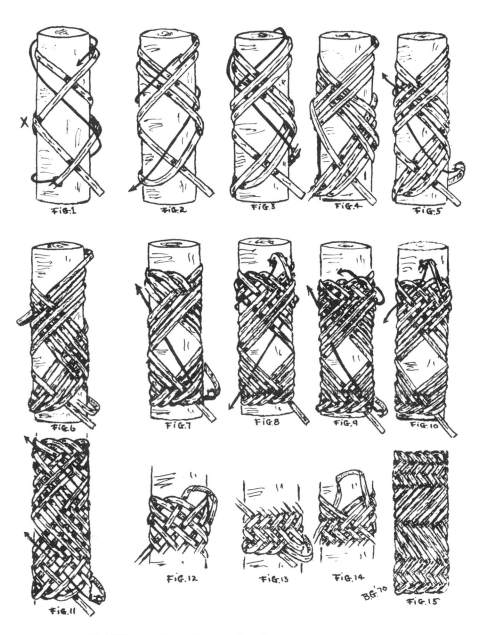

PLATE 177. Three-Section Fan Knot or Botón Oriental.

431

PLATE 178

The Perfect Pineapple Knot. This perfect pineapple knot is made without interweaving a Turk's-head skeleton knot as is the regular pineapple knot. It is made in one continuous sequence. Thus, it is the perfect knot as the working end of the thong comes up alongside the standing end when it is complete.

I see in my notes that I began struggling with this knot back in 1954. Recently Señor Luis Alberto Flores, an enthusiastic braider, wrote and said he had not found explained how to make a perfect pineapple knot, or, as he termed it, *pasador pluma sin armadura*, in any of my books on braiding. He said he had worked out this knot. We exchanged ideas and while the end results proved the same, the method of making the knot was relatively different. Señor Flores had never found anyone who could make the knot. Neither had I.

In Fig. 1 you wrap your thong twice around the mandrel as illustrated. On the second wrap the thong does not cross in the back. Continuing upward in Fig. 2, pass beneath the double thong. Down in Fig. 3, pass over one, under one (but not the lower thong), and incline upward. This is the secret of making this knot, as it has double bights or scallops at top and bottom.

Fig. 4 up (forming an outside bight), over one, under one. Fig. 5, down (outside bight), under two, over two. Fig. 6, up (inside bight), over two, under two. Fig. 7, down (inside bight), under one, over two, under one. Fig. 8, up (outside bight), under one, over two, under one. Fig. 9 (outside bight), over two, under two, over two.

At this point, if you bring your thong around and up alongside the standing part and tighten the knot, you have a 5-bight, 7-part pineapple as shown in Fig. 11. If you wish to make a longer and larger knot as shown in Fig. 12, continue after Fig. 9:

Up (inside bight), under two, over two, under two. Down (inside bight), over one, under two, over two, under one. Up (outside bight), over one, under two, over two, under one. Down (outside bight), under two, over two, under two, over two. Up (inside bight), over two, under two, over two, under two. Down (inside bight), under one, over two, under two, over two, under one. Up (outside bight), under one, over two, under two, over two, under one. Down (outside bight), over two, under two, over two, under two, over two. Then up, under one alongside the standing part.

This knot can be used for many purposes to dress up horse gear, quirt handles, etc. You will not find it simple to make, but rewarding, once you get the hang of it.

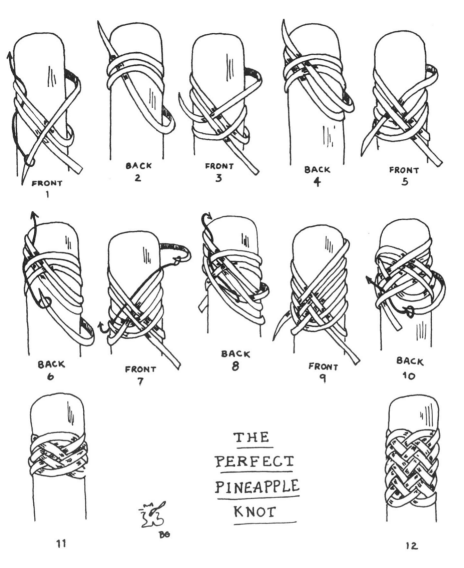

FRONT 1
BACK 2
FRONT 3
BACK 4
FRONT 5
BACK 6
FRONT 7
BACK 8
FRONT 9
BACK 10

11

THE
PERFECT
PINEAPPLE
KNOT

12

PLATE 178. The Perfect Pineapple Knot.

433

Lazy-Man

and

Pampas Button Knots

PLATE 179

The Lazy-Man Button. This type of button knot is very popular and is frequently found on braided cowboy horse gear. In terming it the Lazy-Man Button, I do not mean to infer that it is just a knot or button that a lazy man would make, instead of the more complicated braided ones; but that it is one that can quickly and easily be made because of its simplicity.

This is a very practical knot and its origin is nautical—it is found extensively in sailors' ropework. In seaman's language it is made by "following the lead," or "following around" a Turk's-head or skeleton knot—that is, paralleling the first-laid strand with an identical over-and-under sequence. Once can follow around as many times as desired to increase the knot.

Three different button knots are shown on Plate 179. In each case the Turk's-head or foundation knot first is made and then increased by following around.

The first one (Figs. 1-5) has a foundation a three-bight, five-part Turk's-head. A bight is the scallop at top and bottom and a part is a thong on the sides or body. This knot is started in Fig. 1 where the lead passes up and around the mandrel and in back and down in front over the standing part; then around once more over everything. In the third phase the lead—or working end—passes around to the back and in front where it goes beneath the standing part, then up over two and under one (follow the arrowline).

In Fig. 2 the lead is brought down over one, under one, over one, under one, and around to the front (follow arrowline). This completes the Turk's-head. In Fig. 3 the process of doubling by following around begins. The working end-lead-passes up and alongside the standing part and continues to follow it, never crossing it, until the knot looks as in Fig. 4. Figure 5 shows the knot after three more similar passes have been made. Figure 6 shows the top of the knot and how it closes completely.

A four-bight, five-part Turk's-head is started in Fig. 7. First the working end passes up and then around back and to the front and then down over the standing part. In the next pass it goes beneath the standing part and over the lower bight. Figure 8 illustrates how it passes up under one and over one in the back.

434

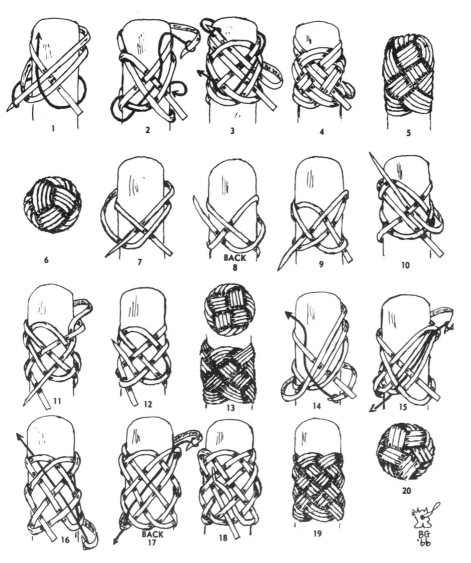

PLATE 179. The Lazy-Man Button.

435

Fig. 9 (down): over one (standing part), under one, over one. Fig. 10 (up): over one, under one, over one. Fig. 11 (down): under one, over one, under one, over one. Fig. 12 (up): under one, alongside the right of the standing part. Follow around as in the previous knot. Figure 13 shows the top and side of this button knot after it has been followed around three times.

In Fig. 14 is illustrated the start of a five-bight, seven-part Turk's-head. Referring back to the first Turk's-head (Fig. 1), it will be noticed that the working end or lead has been wrapped around twice. In this knot it is given one more turn, or wrapped around three times. (I have designated the two knots as "wrap-around knots," and with practice they can be made quickly on the hand instead of on a mandrel.)

In Fig. 14, in passing up, go over *three* and under one.

Fig. 15 (down): over two, under one (standing part), over one, under one. Fig. 16 (up): over two, under one, over one, under one. Fig. 17 (back) (down): over one, under one, over one, under one, over one, under one.

In Fig. 18 bring the working end up alongside the right of the standing part and begin following around as before. In this instance the knot is tripled. If a larger knot is desired, follow around again. Figure 19 shows the side of the finished button and Fig. 20 the top.

Any type of Turk's-head can thus be followed around to make the Lazy-Man Button. These buttons are used on tops of quirts, as side buttons on bosals, and for many other purposes.

PLATE 180

The Colima Lazy-Man Button. I found this button knot on a quirt given to me in Colima, Mexico. Tearing it apart, I learned that it was woven on a five-part, four-bight Turk's-head.

Start as in Fig. 1 where the working end of the string is passed upward to the right of the standing part. As shown, the working end parallels the standing part to the very top. In Fig. 2 the arrowline shows the course of the working end in the back of the knot. It passes under two, over one, under one, and over two, one of which is the end of the standing part. In Fig. 3 the working end passes upward under two, over one, under one, and over two.

The sequence after Fig. 3 (not shown in the drawings) is: Down: Under two, over one, under two, and over two. Up: Under two, over one, under two, and over two. Down: Under two, over two, under two, and over two. Up: Under two, over two, under two, and over two. Down: Under three, over two, under two, and over two. Up: Under three alongside the standing part (Fig. 4).

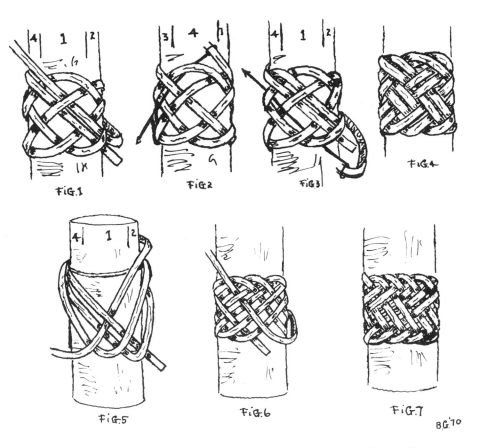

FIG.1 FIG.2 FIG.3 FIG.4 FIG.5 FIG.6 FIG.7 B.G.70

PLATE 180. The Colima Lazy-Man Button; The Small Pampas Button Knot.

The Small Pampas Button Knot. As I am partial to what I term the "running" method of making woven knots, or building them up as you braid, I devised this knot. In deference to the Pampas Button which follows, I call it The Small Pampas Button Knot.

Start as in Fig. 5 where the string passes around and over everything twice and on the third time goes under one, over two, as shown. The sequence then (not shown in the drawings) is: Up: Under one, over two. Down: Under two, over two. Up: Under two, over two. Down: Under three, over two. Up: Under three, over two. Down: Under four, over two.

Here the sequence radically changes. In Fig. 6 the working end passes over three, under one, and over two. Down: Over three, under two, over two. Up: Over three, under two, over two. Down: Under one, over two, under three, over two. Up: Under one, over two, under three, over two. Down: Under two, over one, under four, over two. The working end then passes up under two alongside the standing end (Fig. 7).

437

PLATE 181

The Pampas Button. This decorative button knot is a sophisticated version of the Lazy-Man Button. In the Pampas Button the follow-around is only in the center of the knot and the ends are woven. This knot is much in vogue in the gaucho regions of the Argentine Pampas, hence the name.

Take a long string or thong and start working it around the mandrel as in Fig. 1. Beginning at the lower right-hand side, wind the string to the left upward in a clockwise spiral and then downward crossing the original string three times (Fig. 1). The arrowline in Fig. 1 shows the path of the string in the next move. It goes upward over one, under one, over one. Then downward over all strings to the position shown in Fig. 2.

The mandrel is divided into four sections, each section numbered from 1 to 4 in a counterclockwise direction. The No. 1 section is the front, No. 3 is the rear, No. 4 the left side and No. 2 the right side. The sequences shown here can thus be more easily followed.

In Fig. 2 the arrowline shows the progress of the string which is upward over two, under two, over two. Also in Fig. 2 is shown a second arrowline for the down braid which is under one, over five, under one, over two. This is shown completed in Fig. 3.

Up: (Fig. 3) The arrowline shows a part of the next move, which is completed in Fig. 4 after the knot has been tightened and adjusted. The entire sequence is upward under one, over two, under four, over two. The arrowline in Fig. 4 indicates the downward move which is under two, over six (in the rear), under two, over two (completed in Fig. 5).

Up: (Fig. 6) Under two, over six (in the rear), under two, over two.

Down: (Fig. 7) Over one, under two, over two, under four, over two, under two, over two.

Up: (Fig. 8) Over one, under two, over six (in the rear), under one (in the rear), over one, under two, over two.

Down: (Fig. 9) Over two, under two, over two, under four (in the rear), over four, under two, over two.

Up: (Fig. 10) Over two, under two, over six (partly in the rear), under two, over two, under two, over two.

Down: (Fig. 11) Under one, over two, under two, over two, under four, over three, under one, over two, under two, over two.

Up: (Fig. 12) Under one, over two, under two, over six, under four, over two, under two, over two.

Down: (Fig. 13) Under two, over two, under two, over two, under four, over four, under two, over two, under two, over two.

Up: Under two alongside the standing part. The finished knot is shown in Fig. 14.

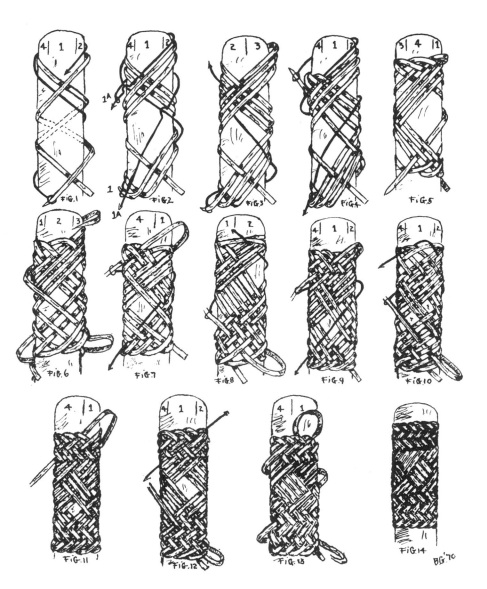

PLATE 181. The Pampas Button.

439

The Braiding Detective

PLATE 182

Duplicating Strange Braids and Creating New Ones. The braided knot, or even the Turk's-head is a mathematical marvel. It goes round and round and comes out perfect—the working end of a braided knot returns to its point of origin.

It is interesting to analyze, more absorbing to create, and definitely a challenge. Distinct variations are limitless and all of them are adjusted to a mathematical scale of easy deduction.

Dr. Almanzor Marrero y Galíndez, in the prologue of his book, *Cromohipologiá*, said this of his Argentine father: "During his last years almost each day he made an original *criollo* button, which he first posed as a problem, resolving it mathematically, and later executing the formula he had worked with success. Some of these buttons were of such complexity that he had to use several strings in the same knot, whose total length reached several meters."

Alas, his mathematical techniques in planning his buttons have been lost to posterity. Many serious scientists and mathematicians have given profound thought to the Turk's-head and as an independent result of the studies of Clifford W. Ashley of New England, and George H. Taber of Pittsburgh, the "Law of the Common Divisor" was discovered.

Ashley, for instance, setting a limit of knots of twenty-four parts and twenty-four bights, found there were, in all, 576 combinations—240 had a common divisor and could not be tied as Turk's-heads, while 336 had no common divisor and could be tied. I have pointed this out before, but wish to stress it. If one number can be divided into both parts and bights, the knot is impossible to tie.

If you wish to duplicate a braided knot, count the number of bights, the number of parts, and the over-and-under sequence. If this does not give you a key to how the knot is made, then start with a small string or thong of different color at the standing end of the knot and parallel or follow around this standing end, noting each move on paper as the new string crosses itself, viz., "Up: Over one, under one, over one," etc.

Luis Flores, of Buenos Aires, has a different method. He takes an unfamiliar braided knot and as he unbraids it, using the working end of the knot, he notes the sequence backwards. But when he is done, if he has made a mistake in his counting, he has no knot.

440

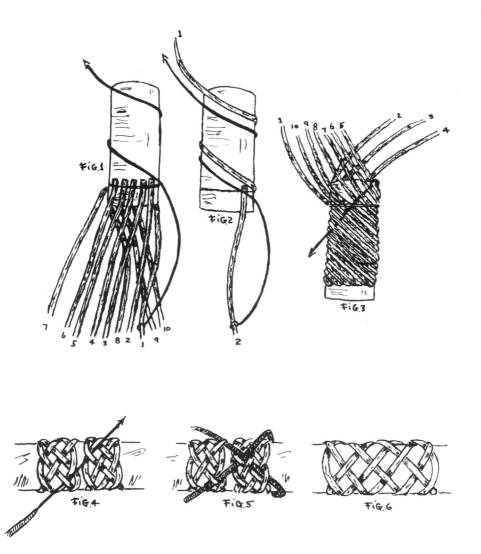

PLATE 182. Duplicating Strange Braids and Creating New Ones.

441

For many years I have used what I call a "Braiding Detective," see Figs. 1 through 3. Cut a broom handle about five inches long and about half an inch from the bottom cut a groove all the way around. Take ten strings (this number is arbitrary) three times as long as the piece of broom handle and fasten them on with string or wire, the strings pointing downward (Fig. 1). Then, string by string, wind them upward (Fig. 2). If you are going to use them all, wind the ten and then temporarily tie them (Fig. 3).

These strings are now woven down in any sequence you wish—under two, over three, etc. If ten strings are used, be certain the parts and bights do not have a common divisor. When the knot is complete, start following around with a long string and when the working end meets the standing end, pull out the strings of the "Detective" and slip off the knot.

In duplicating a strange knot, use the same number of strings as there are bights in the knot. If eight bights, use eight strings; if the knot starts with an under-two sequence, you do the same. Follow carefully the sequence to the end and then remove the "Detective" strings and slip off your knot.

Another method I have used in creating new knots is to make independent knots of the same number of bights, using the running method explained in braided knots. Arrange the knots side by side on the mandrel (Fig. 4) in such a fashion that the emerging string on one bight is *over* and the string on the other goes *under*. Then follow around with a long string and finally pull out the original knots. In this case I have used two knots of five parts and four bights. The result is a knot of nine parts and four bights (Fig. 6).

By this means you can create long knots of varying sequences. The one rule is that all original knots must have the same number of bights.

442

Braided Appliqués

PLATE 183

Stairstep Appliqué of One Thong. Like edge-lacing, appliqué handicraft is both practical and beautiful. It is useful in joining pieces of leather and at the same time is pleasing to the eye. With the proper use of thong appliqué no thread or metal brads will ever be necessary. And it is needless to say that there is a harmonious relationship between a leather thong and the leather it joins and whose beauty it complements.

One of the simplest forms of appliqué is the stairstep type. It can be used not only in joining leather pieces at the edges, but also as a means of decoration in itself by following a pattern, such as initials or some particular design.

Space the holes the width of the thong. Enter the thong from the back through hole 1 (Fig. 1). Then pass it through hole 2 from the front (Fig. 1) and up and back through hole 1 from the rear (Fig. 2). Always be sure it consistently emerges either to the right or left of the portion of the thong already in the hole or slit. In this case it is always on the right.

Now bring the working end of the thong down from hole 1 to hole 3 and pass it through from the front to the back (Fig. 3). Pass it up from the back through hole 2, to the right of both thongs at that point (Fig. 4).

Next, pass the thong down through hole 4 from the front (Fig. 5) and up through hole 3 (Fig. 6). Keep it to the right. Then down through hole 5 (Fig. 7), and so on in the same order until the finish.

In Fig. 9 is shown a diagram of how the braid looks from the rear. There are several variations of this attractive braid, which will be detailed later.

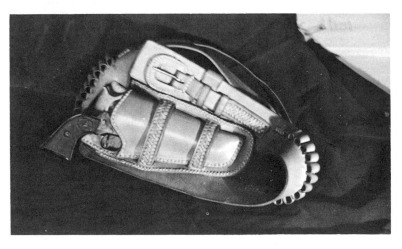

Holster and belt for Colt .45 single action decorated with appliqué work in rawhide. The belt and holster proper are of heavy saddle skirting leather.

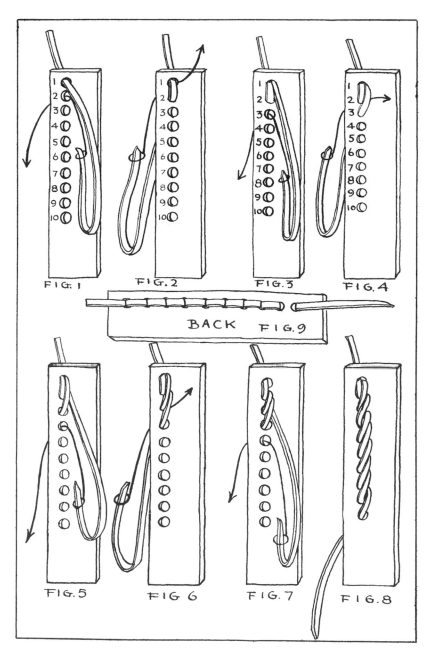

PLATE 183. Stairstep Appliqué of One Thong.

445

PLATE 184

Stairstep Appliqué with Similar Braid on Both Ends. This is a one-string braid as in Plate 183, but the back and front have the same type braid. It is particularly valuable in sewing together two pieces of leather or rawhide where you wish both sides to be dressy and showy.

In Fig. 1 ten holes have been punched and the string enters No. 1 hole from beneath and then passes down through hole No. 4. The arrowline indicates the next pass where the string is brought back and emerges to the right of its own part through hole No. 2 (Fig. 2). Also in Fig. 2 the arrowline shows how it is passed back and out hole No. 3 and then down (to the right) through hole No. 6.

In Fig. 3 this move is complete and the arrowline indicates that the string emerges to the front from hole No. 4 and down through hole No. 7. The front of this braid is shown in Fig. 4. The back, with the same stairstep applique, is shown in Fig. 5. Note the back is one hole shorter. There is no need to worry about the back as you proceed; this sequence takes care of itself.

Four-Part Appliqué Same on Both Sides, Made with One String. Ten holes are punched on both edges, with an extra hole punched between the No. 1 holes as shown in Fig. 6. Ten are merely used for convenience; any number can be made. Start with the string at the bottom where it passes to the front in the lower center hole (Fig. 6). The string is continued upward as shown in this figure. After the string goes through the upper center hole, start the interweaving indicated by the arrowlines (Fig. 7). This interweaving is continued downward by the same method, taking care to interweave in the back as you proceed. The braid on the back will be shorter by one hole, but of the same type.

Five-Part Appliqué Same on Both Sides, Made with Two Strings. This braid is started by introducing two strings in the two lower center holes (Fig. 8). In the back, string A passes to the front through hole No. 9 and string B to the front through hole No. 10 (Fig. 9). Keep working both strings, front and back, as indicated in the drawings. This is a consistent braid, front and back. More elaborate appliqués can be made by using three, four, five, or more strings.

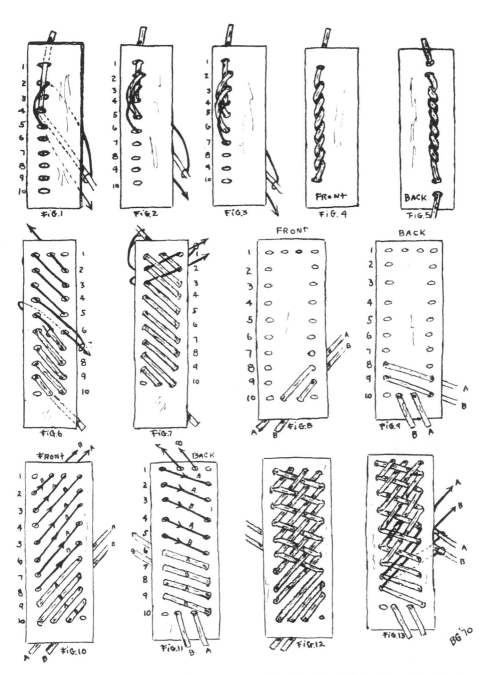

PLATE 184. Stairstep Appliqué with Similar Braid on Both Ends; Four-Part Appliqué Same on Both Sides, Made with One String; Five-Part Appliqué Same on Both Sides, Made with Two Strings.

447

PLATE 185

Two-Thong Four-Part Appliqué. As this is built upon the stairstep appliqué (Plate 183), first make the stairstep braid. Then, with a second thong, this one of a different color if desired, pass through the first hole at the top from the rear to the front as shown in Fig. 1. The original thong of the stairstep appliqué is white and the second thong is shown as shaded in the drawing.

Pass the shaded, or working thong over the white thong between holes 1 and 2, under the white thong to its right, then over the next and down through hole 3, from the front to the rear, as indicated by the arrowline in Fig. 1.

Now bring the working thong back up through hole 2 from the rear to the front and on the left side, indicated by the arrowline in Fig. 2.

Next pass the working thong over one thong, under one and over one, then through hole 4, illustrated in Fig. 3. Bring it back again from the rear to the front through hole 3, to the left, as indicated by the arrowline in Fig. 4.

The next step is the same as the preceding ones. Pass the working thong over one, under one, and over one, always inclined to the right, and then down through hole 5 (Fig. 5).

In the rear view (Fig. 6) it can be seen that the thongs overlap, as the shaded or working thong is brought through a hole on one side and up through a hole on the other side.

The finished work is shown in Fig. 7. This gives a pleasing, two-toned effect, but it can also be worked effectively with thongs of the same color. The braid simulates, after a fashion, the four-thong flat braid.

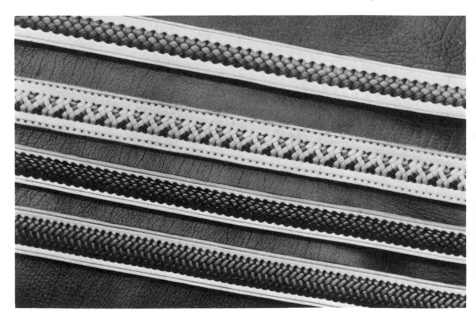

Appliqué braidwork applied to belts made by Tony Genco.

This type of thonging is very popular among leather braiders in Switzerland. It can be made with thongs of different widths; usually the original stairstep appliqué foundation is made of the wider thongs. It is an effective trimming on belts and other articles, although it must not be forgotten that it has the utilitarian value, as does all appliqué braiding, of joining together two or more pieces of leather.

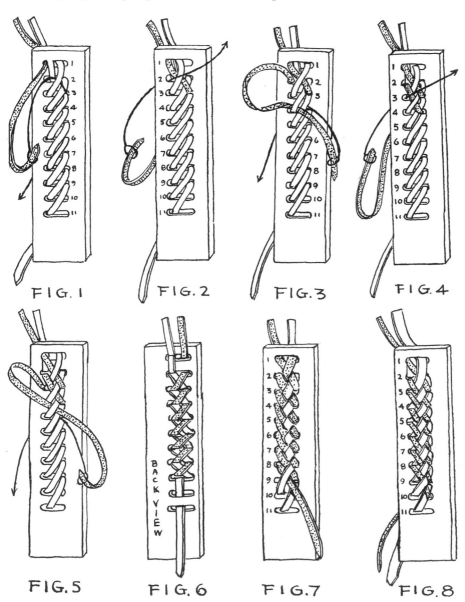

FIG. 1 FIG. 2 FIG. 3 FIG. 4

FIG. 5 FIG. 6 FIG. 7 FIG. 8

PLATE 185. Two-Thong Four-Part Appliqué.

449

PLATE 186

Stairstep Appliqué of Two Thongs. This is similar to the stairstep appliqué of one thong (Plate 183) except that a closer braid is obtained by the use of two thongs.

It is used for joining pieces of leather and at the same time for decoration. For a pleasing effect, use a thong of contrasting color. Different leathers, such as goatskin thonging lace on cowhide or calfskin, are quite effective.

To begin, insert the thong designated as B in the top hole from rear to front. Next, pass the one designated as A through the second hole from the rear to the front and under B (Fig. 1). In this drawing the arrowline indicates the course of thong B. Pass it through the second hole from front to rear and to the left of thong A.

Now bring thong B forward through the third hole and inclined to the right, indicated by the arrowline in Fig. 2. Pass thong A down through the third hole over thong B and to its left in the hole. Follow the arrowline in Fig. 3.

In Fig. 4 the next move is indicated. Bring thong A from back to front through the fourth hole and inclined to the right. Pass thong B down over thong A and through the fourth hole from front to back and to the left of thong A at that point (Fig. 5).

When the two thongs are in the position shown in Fig. 6, tighten by pulling on both at the same time. Bring thong B back up through the fifth hole and incline it to the right.

Pass thong A down through the fifth hole over thong B and to its left in the hole (Fig. 7). The finished braid is shown in Fig. 8.

A back view of this braid is illustrated in Fig. 9 and resembles in every way the single thong braid.

Make the holes with a punch or with a small thonging chisel. The symmetry of the braid depends on the care used in spacing the holes evenly. When using slits made by a thonging chisel, always enlarge them with the fid before inserting the thonging end. Braid made with slits is much neater than when made with holes.

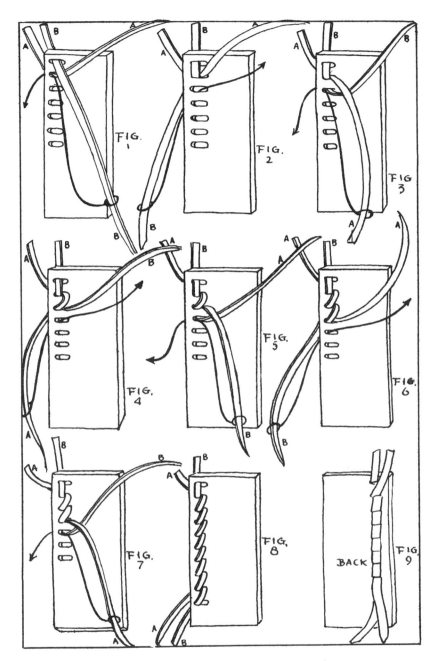

PLATE 186. Stairstep Appliqué of Two Thongs.

PLATE 187

Chain Appliqué of One Thong. Pass the thong through the top hole from the rear to the front and down through the third hole as shown in Fig. 1. The arrowline in this drawing indicates its path which is up through the second hole from the rear to the front and to the *right* of the standing part.

Next pass it down through hole 4 from the front to the rear.

Pass the working end up through hole 3, this time to the *left* of the standing part, as shown by the arrowline in Fig. 2. Then bring it down through the fifth hole from the front to the rear.

Now bring it up through hole 4, this time to the *right* of the standing part, as indicated by the arrowline in Fig. 3, and down through the sixth hole from the front to the rear. Continue thus, first passing back to one side of the standing part and next to the other side.

Split-Thong Appliqué. This provides a double security in joining two pieces of leather and also gives a pleasing effect. First pass the thong through hole 1 from the rear to the front and down through hole 3 (Fig. 5). Now, in that part of the loop which is directly over hole 2, cut a small vertical slit in the thong with a thonging chisel or the point of a knife. Enlarge it from the rear with the fid and pass the working end through the hole in the leather and through the slit in the thong, as indicated by the arrowline in Fig. 5.

In Fig. 6 the working end is shown through the holes in both leather and thong. Bring it down through hole 4. In that section of the loop of the thong directly over hole 3 stab another vertical slit, being careful not to cut the thong beneath. Pass the working end through hole 3 and through the slit in the thong as indicated by the arrowline in Fig. 7. Continue for the desired length.

Split-Thong Appliqué of Two Thongs. This is the same as the preceding appliqué except that two thongs are used and thus there is no necessity of slitting them. Work the thongs as a unit as shown in Figs. 9, 10, 11 and 12. One thong of one color and one of another may be used and by overlapping them each time in the rear, a pleasing, two-toned effect is achieved.

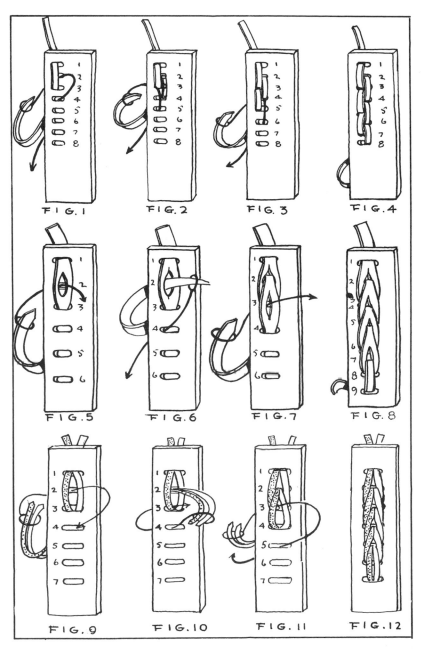

PLATE 187. Top: Chain Appliqué of One Thong. Center: Split-Thong Appliqué. Bottom: Split-Thong Appliqué of Two Thongs.

PLATE 188

Hair-Braid Appliqué of Two Thongs. Begin this appliqué by passing two thongs of equal width through the top hole from the rear to the front (Fig. 1). The left-hand thong (unshaded) is designated as A, and the right-hand one (shaded) as B.

Pass thong A down through hole 4 and thong B down through hole 3.

The arrowlines in Fig. 1 show the next pass of the two thongs. Bring thong B through the second hole from the top and to the extreme right of the other two thongs. Pass thong A back through the third hole from the top and to the extreme right of the other two.

In bringing both thongs from rear to front always have them emerge to the extreme right. This will incline the finished braid toward the left and if the holes are not too far from the edge of the leather or pieces of leather being joined, the braid will lie on the very edge, giving an attractive edge-lacing effect.

Pass thong B to the left over one thong, under one and down through hole 5, as indicated by the arrowline in Fig. 2. Now pass thong A over the first thong to the left, under thong B and down through hole 6. This is indicated by the arrowline in Fig. 3.

Bring thong B up from rear to front through the hole 4 and to the right, as indicated in Fig. 4 by the arrowline. Pass thong A up from rear to front through hole 5, as indicated by the arrowline in Fig. 4.

In the next step, shown in Fig. 5, pass thong B over one thong (its own part) under the white thong (A) and down through hole 7. Thong A follows the corresponding path, passing over its own part, under thong B and down through hole 8, as shown in Fig. 6.

Continue this as far as desired. By tracing a design or initials on a piece of leather it can be followed with this appliquéd braid. The finished braid, shown loosely woven so the operation can better be observed, is shown in Fig. 7. The back of the braid is illustrated in Fig. 8.

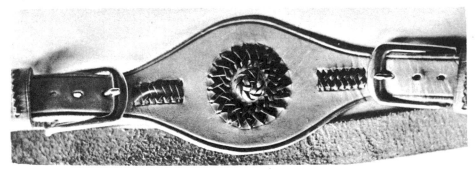

Woman's belt (front) showing "S" type applique of one thong (Pl. 189) braided in circular fashion—also as decoration near buckles. Round button knot (Pl. 111) in center of appliquéd circle.

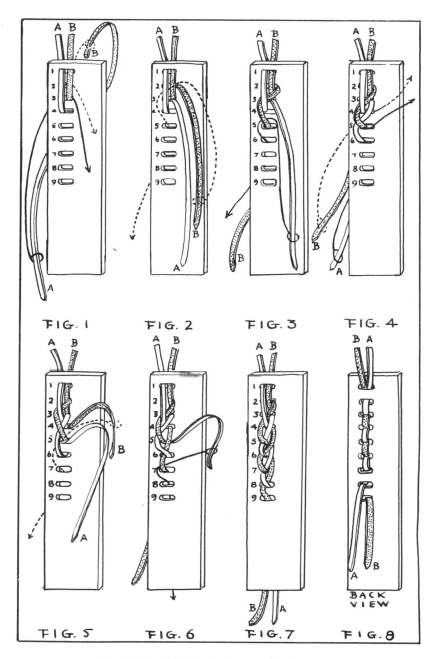

PLATE 188. Hair-Braid Appliqué of Two Thongs.

PLATE 189

"S" Type Appliqué of One Thong. The width of the thong will determine the distance of the holes from each other and the distance between the two vertical rows of holes. If an 1/8-inch thong is used and the braid is to be closed up, space the holes 3/16 of an inch from each other and the vertical rows ½ inch apart.

This appliqué, like other appliqué braids, is not only used to join two pieces of leather, but for decoration.

Pass the working end of the thong through the top hole at the right from the rear to the front and then down and across through the second hole on the left, shown in Fig. 1.

Next, bring the thong up through the top hole on the left from the rear to the front and down to the right over its own part and through hole 3 on the right-hand side. Pass it back to the front through hole 2 on the right, as indicated by the arrowline in Fig. 2.

Incline the thong to the left over its own part and down through hole 3 on the left. Then pass it back to the front through hole 2 on the left, as indicated by the arrowline in Fig. 3.

Incline the thong to the right, over its own part and down through hole 4 on the right-hand side. Then pass it back and up through hole 3 on the same side, as indicated by the arrowline in Fig. 4.

Incline the thong to the left, over its own part, down through hole 4 on the left-hand side and up through hole 3 on the same side, as illustrated in Fig. 5.

Incline the thong to the right, over its own part, down through hole 5 on the right-hand side and up through hole 4 on the same side, as illustrated in Fig. 6.

Continue thus until the braid has reached the desired length. The finished braid is shown in Fig. 7, with the back view in Fig. 8. This latter figure illustrates how the ends are secured.

In Fig. 9 this applique is used to fasten the part of a belt that holds the buckle. The braid can be continued down the middle of the belt, the shaded portion to the left showing a *bed* or depressed part in the leather. To make this *bed*, the leather should be dampened, then cut along the sides of the bed to about one-third of its thickness and depressed with ordinary background stamping tools. The braid will then lie flat on the surface. The bed is not necessary, however, and the braid can be emphasized by working it over a narrow strip of leather laid between the rows of holes.

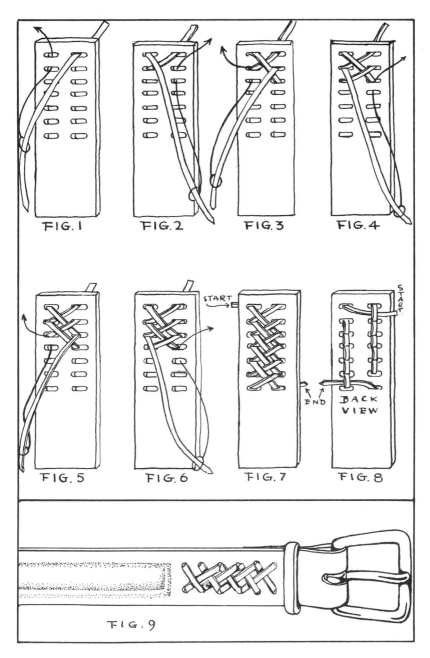

PLATE 189. "S" Type Appliqué of One Thong.

457

PLATE 190

Appliqué of Three Thongs. This beautiful appliqué of three thongs gives the effect of a five-part flat braid. The color of the thongs may be varied. It is, of course, used to fasten together parts of leather as well as for decoration. Space the rows of vertical holes about five times the width of the thong.

Thongs are designated from left to right as A, B and C. Pass thong A from the rear to front through the upper left-hand hole and down through the third right-hand hole (Fig. 1). Pass thong B through the middle upper hole from rear to front and down to the left, over thong A and through hole 3 on the left (Fig. 1); thong C through the upper right-hand hole from rear to front, under thong A and down through hole 4 on the left-hand side (Fig. 1).

Now, bring thong A (on the right) up through the second hole on the right (b) from rear to front, incline down the left, over its own part and through hole 5 on the left-hand side, as indicated by the arrowline in Fig. 1.

Bring thong B (on the left) up through hole 2 on that side, incline down to the right and over its own part, under thong C, over thong A and down through the fourth hole (d) on the right-hand side (indicated by the arrowline in Fig. 2). Next, bring thong C up through hole 3 on the left, incline down to the right, over its own part, under thong A and down through the fifth hole (e) as indicated by the arrowline in Fig. 3.

Bring thong A up through hole 4 on the left, incline down to the right and over its own part and through hole (f), the sixth hole on the right (Fig. 4).

The three thongs are now on the right-hand side (Fig. 5). Pass thong B up through the third hole (c) on the right, incline down towards the left, pass it over its own part, under thong C, over thong A and down through hole 6 on the left. Bring thong C up through hole (d), the fourth one on the right, incline down toward the left, over its own part, under thong A and down through hole 7 on the left. Pass thong A up through the fifth hole on the right (e), incline down to the left, over its own part and down through the left-hand hole, 8. These moves are all indicated by arrowlines in Fig. 5.

Figure 6 shows the finished braid, and Fig. 7 shows the back of the braid and the method of securing the ends.

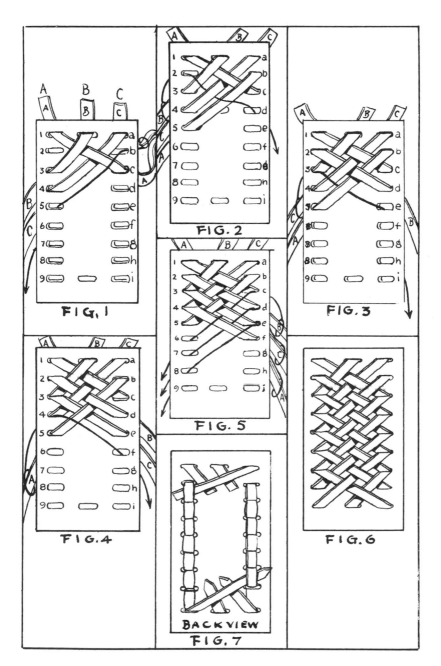

PLATE 190. Appliqué of Three Thongs.

459

PLATE 191

Appliqué of Five Thongs. Braiding with five thongs in the following manner gives the effect of a seven-part herringbone flat braid.

Space three holes across the top between the upper holes of the two vertical rows (Fig. 1). The thongs are designated from left to right as A, B, C, D and E. Pass thong A through the upper left-hand hole from rear to front and down through the fourth (d) right-hand hole; thong B through the second horizontal hole from the left and down to the right through the third hole (c) on the right-hand side; thong C through the third horizontal hole from the left, over thongs B and A and down through the left-hand hole, 3: thong D through the fourth horizontal hole, incline down to the left, under thong B, over thong A and down through the left-hand hole, 4; thong E through the upper right-hand hole, incline down to the left under thongs B and A and down through the fifth left-hand hole (all shown in Fig. 1).

Next, bring thong C up through hole 2 on the left, incline down to the right, over its own part, under thong D and E and down through the fifth hole (e) on the right, designated by the arrowline in Fig. 1.

Bring thong D up through hole 3 on the left, incline down to the right, over its own part, under thong E and down through the sixth hole (f), on the right-hand side (Fig. 2). Pass thong E up through hole 4 on the left, incline down to the right, over its own part, and down through the seventh hole (g) on the right (Fig. 3).

All thongs are now on the right-hand side (Fig. 4). Start with the top one, thong B, and bring it up through the second hole on the right (b), over its own part, under two thongs, over two thongs, and down through hole 6 on the left, indicated by the arrowline in Fig. 4.

Pass thong A up through the third hole on the right (c), down over its own part, under two thongs, over one and down through hole 7 (Fig. 5). Bring thong C up through the fourth hole on the right (d), down over its own part, under two thongs and down through hole 8 on the left (Fig. 6). Pass thong D up through the fifth hole on the right (e), down over its own part, under one and through hole 9 on the left (Fig. 7). Pass thong E up through the sixth hole on the right (f), down over its own part and through hole 10 on the left (Fig. 8).

Now work the thongs back to the right in the same manner; each goes up through the hole above, then down over its own part, under the next two and so on. The finished braid is shown in Fig. 9.

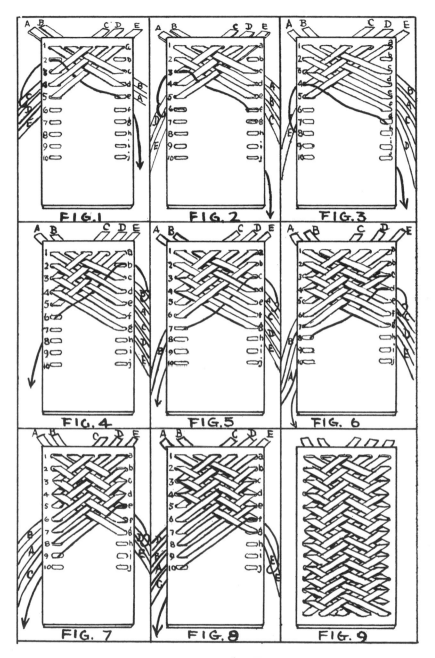

PLATE 191. Appliqué of Five Thongs.

461

PLATE 192

Five-Thong Circular Appliqué. This is the same as the five-thong appliqué in Plate 191. It gives the equivalent of a seven-part braid and when made in this circular fashion, usually is raised by placing a small strip of leather beneath, over which it is braided.

As the outer circle of holes will be spaced wider apart than those of the inner circle, be careful in laying out the circles to see that the outer holes are not too far apart and those in the inner circle too close together. There must be the same number of holes in the outer as in the inner circle.

The circles in Fig. 1 are divided into sixteen parts. Punch the holes on the inside of the outer circle and on the outer rim of the inner circle (Fig. 1). The width between the two rows of holes, the space between the holes themselves, and the width of the thongs, will all determine how close the braid is to be.

Pass thong A through hole 1 in the outer circle (all outer circle holes are numbered) from underneath and down through hole (e) in the inner circle (Fig. 2). (All inner circle holes are designated by letters.) Pass thong B through hole 2 and down through hole (f); thong C through hole 3 and down through (g); thong D up through hole (b), over A, under B and C and down through hole 5; thong E up through hole (e), over A, and B, under C and through hole 6.

Pass thong A back through hole (d), then under its own part, and over B and C, and down through hole 7 (arrowline in Fig. 2). Bring thong B back through (e), under its own part, over C and down through hole 8 (Fig. 3). Pass C back through (f), under its own part and down through hole 9. The working ends of all five thongs are now on the outer circle.

Start with D and pass it back through hole 4, under its own part, over E and A, under B and C, and down through hole (h). Follow the same sequence with the other thongs; pass each back through the hole to its rear, under its own part and then over and under, so that each

A book jacket, for Bruce Grant's *Leather Braiding* made by Tony Genco. A nine-strand filigree circle of braidwork executed on gold leather.

thong from hole to hole in the finished braid will have a sequence of under one, over two, under two and over one.

To close the braid (Fig. 4), pass D under three, over one and into hole 4; C under one, over one, under one, over one and into hole 3; B under one, over three, into hole 2; A under one, over two, under two, over one and into hole (d), and E under one, over two, under two, over one into hole (c).

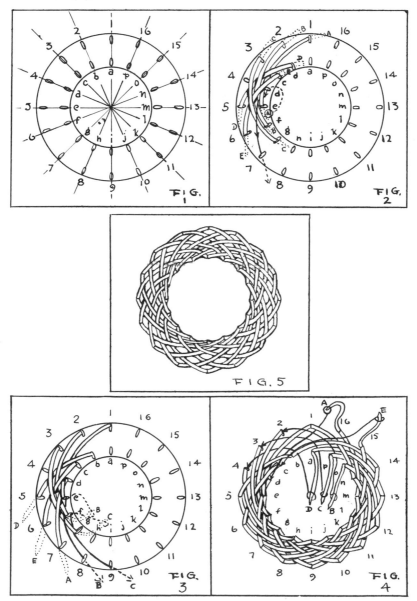

PLATE 192. Five-Thong Circular Appliqué.

463

PLATE 193

The Zig-Zag Appliqué. The Zig-Zag Appliqué makes an attractive decoration when worked on a belt, but it can be used also as a border for carved leatherwork as well as for other purposes that imagination and ingenuity might inspire.

For purposes of illustrating this appliqué I have chosen a belt, one inch wide. The first step is to set the buckle as shown in Fig. 1. Skive the short end of the belt as it is to be brought back and cemented to the underside. The buckle is held in place with a three-hole fastening—the top hole is that punched for the base of the buckle tongue (Figs. 2-6). Before cementing down the underpart, make the belt loop or loops—if you prefer more than one. As this loop is appliquéd before it is put into place, work the zig-zag appliqué on it in the same fashion as explained in Figs. 11-15 for the belt proper.

The fastener for the loop is shown in Figs. 8 and 9. When the ends of the thong are drawn tight, bringing together the ends of the loop, the loop is placed between the folded leather below the buckle. The loop should be just large enough to accommodate the thickness of the belt end that is fastened by the buckle.

In Fig. 10 I have shown the appliqué on the belt just below the belt loop. However, this actually is the end of the appliqué and it should be started from the other end of the belt, as will be explained. For the time being, cement the folded and skived part to the underside of the belt.

Try the belt on for size, determining the position of hole (x) in Fig. 11. Later you can punch two or three holes on either side of this hole to take care of an increase or decrease in girth.

Set the wing dividers or compass at ¼ inch and score a line for the full length of both sides of the belt leather. This is the guide for the thong holes.

Set off the thong holes along this line ½ inch apart, but start the first hole (y) opposite hole (x) in Fig. 11 and work both ways. When all holes have been marked off on this side, begin on the other side, making sure that these holes are exactly in the center of the space between the opposite holes (Fig. 11). The first hole of this series is (z).

Start the appliqué as shown in Fig. 11 with one long thong. Each end will be worked alternately. In Fig. 12, looking at the back, fold over end A and insert end B in the same hole as shown and again through the hole on the other side. In Fig. 13 end B is folded back and end A passes through the same hole and on through the hole on the other side. Figures 14 and 15 show the sequences from the front. This appliqué is carried on back to the belt loop and further secures the cemented fold-over as shown in Fig. 10. To secure the working ends, tuck them beneath the braid at the back and cut off the excess.

In this appliqué on the belt proper and the belt loop I have used an 1/8-inch dark brown goatskin lacing.

If you wish a double zig-zag appliqué, work it as in Figs. 16 and 17, using different color lacing. Three rows can be made on a 1¼-inch belt.

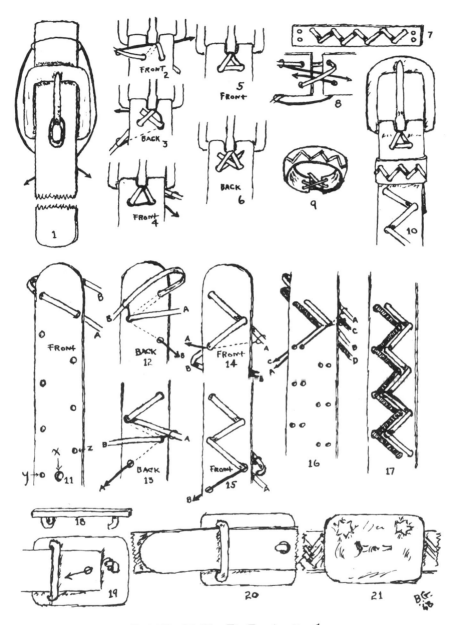

PLATE 193. The Zig-Zag Appliqué.

On a wider belt, more rows can be appliquéd.

However, in the case of two or more rows, it is difficult to locate the holes for the buckle tongue. When more than one row is used I prefer a buckle known as the "hook and bar," or trophy-type buckle (Figs.

465

18-21). With such the appliqué can be worked just under the edge of the buckle on each side.

Usually this buckle is mounted by folding the stationary end of the belt around the bar and then securing it. However, this usually causes a bulge in the front and the working end of the belt comes out on top of the belt. I skive the stationary end on the hair side, punch a hole in it to accommodate the hook, pass it through the bar and over the hook (Figs. 19 and 20). A little cement between the skived leather and the underside of the buckle will usually hold it in place. The working end of the belt goes over the hook and through the bar, beneath the standing part.

In such case I use one hole for the fastening, exactly measured. The working end is thus hidden beneath the other section and the buckle looks like it "jus' growed on the belt."

If the belt is to be taken up, punch a new hole in the standing end, cut off the section with the original hole, and re-skive. If it is to be enlarged, punch a new hole in the working end and then splice out the appliqué so it disappears under the edge of the buckle.

The best way is to watch your diet!

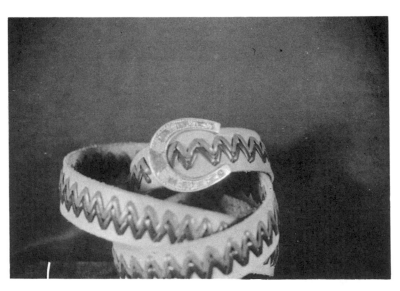

Belt decorated by the author with a Zig-Zag applique.

Three-inch-wide belt decorated in the center with appliqué similar to that of Plate 191 and with a four-thong round edge braid on the edges (Pl. 119).

Executive's briefcase. The case is black leather, medallion type circle appliqué braidwork over silver leather; cut medallion underlay. This example of Mr. Genco's work demonstrates how braidwork, lacing and design complement any project.

PLATE 194

Making and Decorating a Belt Buckle. This type of appliquéd buckle makes a decorative woman's belt. It also can be used on the cheekpieces of a headstall. Select the metal buckle to suit your needs, place it on the strap or belt and then sew it down to a round piece of leather (Fig. 1). Cut a second round piece the same size as the first and then cut out the center so the metal part of the buckle is covered (Fig. 2). Punch holes around the edge for the braid. Punch through both pieces of leather to make holes 1-8 and 12-17. In the section where the billet of the belt passes, punch holes only in the top piece (9-11 and 18-20). Now pass the braid through both pieces of leather (holes 1-8), just through the top piece (holes 9-11), back through the two pieces (holes 12-17) and just through the top for holes 18-20. Figures 3-7 inclusive show the hair-braid appliqué that is illustrated in Plate 188.

If using thongs or strings of a contrasting color, be sure there is an even number of holes. Otherwise, when the braid is finished, the string of one color will join that of the other.

The completed braid is shown in Fig. 7. In Fig. 8 four strings are used with an over-and-under sequence of two. In Fig. 9 three strings are used with an over-and-under sequence of one, giving a simulated four-string braid.

An ordinary belt buckle covered with leather and the edges held together with circular appliqué.

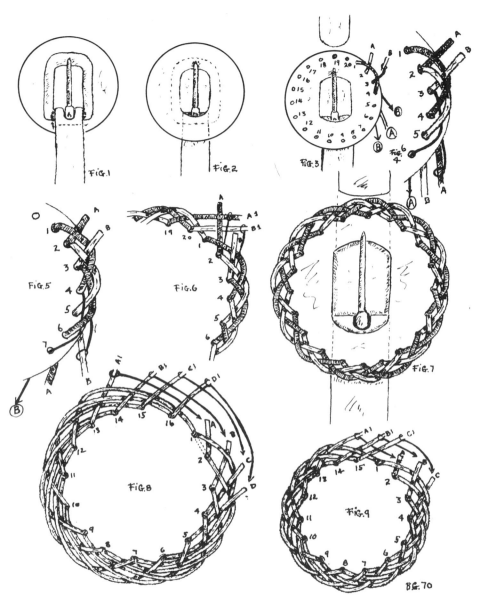

PLATE 194. Making and Decorating a Belt Buckle.

469

PLATE 195

Star Appliqué of One Thong. With a pair of calipers make five equidistant marks on a circle. Then punch five holes and number these in a clockwise direction, 1 to 5. The thong or string enters hole 1 from beneath, passes down through hole 3, then back upwards through hole 2 and over its own part (Fig. 1). The arrowline in this figure shows the progress of the string which goes down through hole 4, up through hole 3 and over its own part and down through hole 5.

The arrowline in Fig. 2 shows the string passing back through hole 4, over its own part, and down through hole 1. Then it passes up through hole 5 over its own part, then under a string and down through hole 2.

At this point (Fig. 3) the single-string star is complete. But it can be doubled by using the same string or one of a contrasting color, and punching five more holes inside each preceding hole toward the center. The arrowline in Fig. 3 shows the string emerging from hole 1 (inside hole), under one string, over one string, and down through inside hole 3. It is then brought back up through inside hole 2.

The procedure in working these inside strings is the same as previously shown in the one-string star. The result is illustrated in Fig. 5. Figure 6 shows the back of the braid. With very narrow strings other holes can be punched toward the center to make a three, four, five, etc., star. By utilizing this method, three-pointed, four-pointed, six-pointed or more stars can be made.

Chevron and Diamond Appliqués. These appliqués make attractive decorations for belts, reins, etc. In Fig. 7, string A passes from underneath through the center hole, down through the second hole on the right, across beneath to the center hole and down to the left through the third hole, and so forth. B goes up through the top center hole, down through the second hole on the left, across beneath and up through the second center hole and down through the right center hole, etc. The method of making the diamond appliqué is shown by arrowlines.

The Mosaic Appliqué. This appliqué, starting with string A, stairsteps upward, and upon reaching the top two holes, begins to stairstep downward. B also goes up, and when reaching the top, either another string goes down on the right of A or it crosses beneath to the other side. For C, reseat. Multicolored strings make this an attractive appliqué for a belt. If you have the patience, punch holes in leather so the ends meet and then continue the appliqué to close around a bottle or other object. Figure 9 gives an idea of how this appliqué looks.

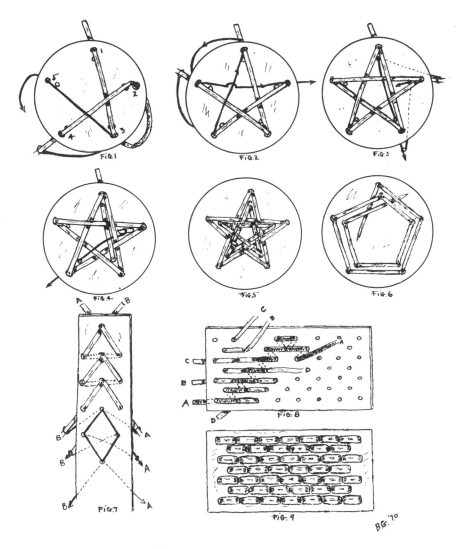

PLATE 195. Star Appliqué of One Thong; Chevron and Diamond Appliqués; The Mosaic Appliqué.

PLATE 196

Saddle Decoration—Appliqué Braids. Fortunately, there are many horsemen who still consider leather carving and braidwork the richest and most agreeable form of decoration for all types of horse gear. That this form of decoration can be applied to saddles is to be seen in many old-time saddlers' catalogues, where fancy braidwork is emphasized. Unfortunately, braiding on saddles has been supplanted today by ornate and heavy metal ornaments. Only fancy carving has survived and braiding, as a saddle decoration, has become a lost art.

There are many types of braid which may be applied to saddle decoration. In an endeavor to revive this interesting and beautiful type of ornamentation, several original braids have been created by the author, and methods of utilizing standard braids have been worked out.

In Fig. 9 of Plate 196 is shown the sketch of a saddle decorated in this fashion. This saddle was made by Lee M. Rice and decorated by the author. The carving is supplemented by different types of braidwork. The seat, back jockey, skirt and fender are decorated with an appliqué of five strings. The swell, seat, back jockey, skirt and fender carry circles of hair-braid applique, and in the center of each circle is an appliquéd Lone Star knot. Edge-braiding is on the cantle, swell, rigging, skirt, back jockey and fender. Around the horn and on the stirrups is a hair-braid appliqué.

The method of making the appliqué of five strings is shown in Figs. 1-4, inclusive. The five strings are inserted in holes or slits, as shown in Fig. 1. Each end on the left side is then brought up through the hole above it and then passed down, as shown in Fig. 2, to the holes on the right. The five ends on the right are brought up, each through the hole above, and then down through the holes on the left (Fig. 3). The completed braid is shown in Fig. 4, where the corner ends are interwoven to finish these sections.

The circle of hair-braid appliqué is shown in Figs. 5-8, inclusive. This braid is worked with two strings. If strings of a different color are used, the number of holes must be even, otherwise it doesn't matter. String B passes down through the first hole to the fourth and then back up through the hole above it, on the inside of the circle. String A passes through the second hole, down through the fifth and up through the hole above it, also emerging on the inside of the circle (Fig. 5). In Fig. 6 is the key to the sequence to be followed. String B passes over its own part to the left under string A and down through the sixth hole. String A goes over its own part under string B and down through the seventh hole and so on.

Many other types of appliqué braid which can be used in such decoration are described in this book. White rawhide strings or latigo thongs may be used.

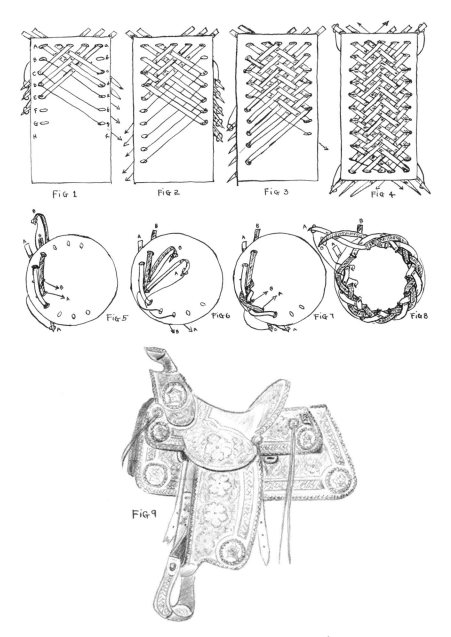

FIG 1   FIG 2   FIG 3   FIG 4

FIG 5   FIG 6   FIG 7   FIG 8

FIG 9

PLATE 196. Saddle Decoration — Appliqué Braids.

PLATE 197

Lone Star Knot Appliqué. To make the Lone Star knot appliqué, first make the foundation or skeleton knot, as shown in Plate 87 up to and including Fig. 10. Do not start interweaving as shown in Fig. 10 of that plate, but begin the interweave as shown in Fig. 1, Plate 197.

Before this, however, the foundation knot is flattened out. The top of the knot becomes the center and the bottom of the knot becomes the edges. Lay this flattened knot in the center of your hair-braid appliqué circle. Then punch five holes, as shown in Fig. 1, Plate 197. These holes are numbered 1 to 5.

Begin the weave by passing the darker colored string, designated as B, up through hole No. 1. The string then follows the course shown by the arrowline in Fig. 1: under one, passing also under, or at the tip of, string A, over one, under one, over one, under two, over one, under one, over one, under one, and then down through hole No. 1, passing over its own part in going through this hole.

In Fig. 2, the first step of the weave is completed. String B now follows the course of the arrowline: down through hole No. 1, as previously stated, up through hole No. 2, under one, over one, under one, over one, under three, splitting a pair, over one, under one, over one, under two, splitting a pair.

Figure 3 shows this second phase of the braid completed. String B now follows the course of the arrowline: down through hole No. 2, up through hole No. 3, under one, over one, under one, splitting a pair, over two, under three, splitting a pair, over one, under one, over two, under two.

In Fig. 4, the third phase of the braid is completed. The string now follows the arrowline: down through hole No. 3, up through hole No. 4, under one, over one, under two, over two, under three, over one, under two, over two, under two.

The fourth phase of the braid is completed in Fig. 5. String B follows the course of the arrowline: down through hole No. 4, up through hole No. 5, under one, over two, under two, over two, under three, over two, under two, over two, under two. It passes down through hole No. 5.

Holster and belt for .38 caliber revolver. Belt is a double braid of 48 thongs. The belt buckle and holster are decorated with appliqué work.

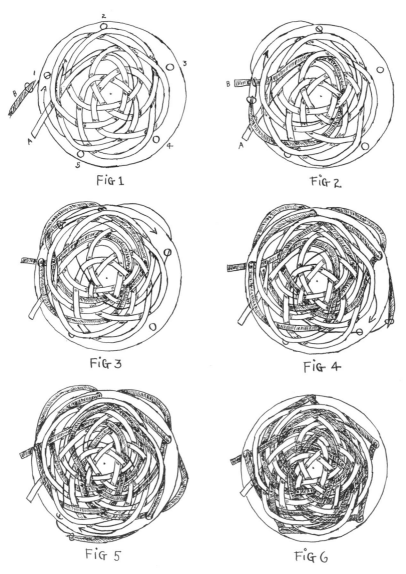

Fig 1

Fig 2

Fig 3

Fig 4

Fig 5

Fig 6

PLATE 197. Lone Star Knot Appliqué.

The finished braid is shown in Fig. 6. The interweaving, whereby string B has passed through five holes, has secured the entire knot to the saddle leather.

Conchas for the tie strings may be fashioned from a circle of leather with edge-braiding, or may be made from a flattened Lone Star knot (Plate 87) with a smaller piece of round leather laid on top.

The Star Knot Appliqué shown in Plate 195 can also be used for this.

475

Leather picture frame decorated with appliqué braid and round buttons and held together by "S" type appliqué (Pl. 189).

Braid on Braid

PLATE 198

Mosaic Type Braid on a Three-Part, Five-Bight Turk's-head. This ring knot can be made not only on the Turk's-head shown here, but on larger Turk's-heads with an over-one, under-one sequence. It results in a very attractive and unique braided knot.

Start as shown in Fig. 1 where the working end comes up alongside the standing end on the left side and over the first crossed strings and back under one of them as illustrated by the arrowline. This step is shown completed in Fig. 2. Turn the mandrel toward you, in the next step carry the working end over the two crossed strings on the right (arrowline, Fig. 3) then under one and over the crossed strings on the left (arrowline, Fig. 4). Continue this sequence until the working end emerges at the start of the braid. Carefully trim off the end. When the working end is a contrasting color, it is very effective.

Joining Two Turk's-heads with the "S" Braid. The two Turk's-heads are placed side by side on the mandrel, and the "S" Braid, explained under Appliques, is used to unite them (Fig. 6). Figure 7 shows this braid on punched leather or rawhide. Again a contrasting string can be used.

Braid on the Aztec Button Knot. The Aztec Button Knot is explained in Plate 75. As the strings cross in a one-one sequence in the center, the Stairstep Appliqué, illustrated in Plate 183, is used for the top or appliqued braid (Figs. 8 and 9). A string in a contrasting color makes this a beautiful knot.

Five-Part Appliqué on a Nine-Part, Eight-Bight Knot. Each edge of this foundation knot (Fig. 10) is of an over-two, under-two sequence, with an over-one, under-one sequence in the center. It is this center section that is to be appliquéd. This basic knot is of the Ginfer-type knot. Figure 11 shows a graphic illustration of the appliqué, which is made with three strings or thongs. Figure 12 shows the same, only worked on a nine-part flat braid. Figure 13 illustrates how this knot looks when finished on the button-type foundation. Each of the three strings used will join up with another and the ends trimmed. A truly beautiful knot.

Mosaic Type Appliqué on an Eight-String Flat Braid. This is a very fine example of how an applique can be made on any type of braid of over-one, under-one sequence. Figure 14 shows this appliqué worked on a piece of leather which has been punched. In Fig. 15 the same appliqué is made on a flat braid, the holes being the interstices in the braid.

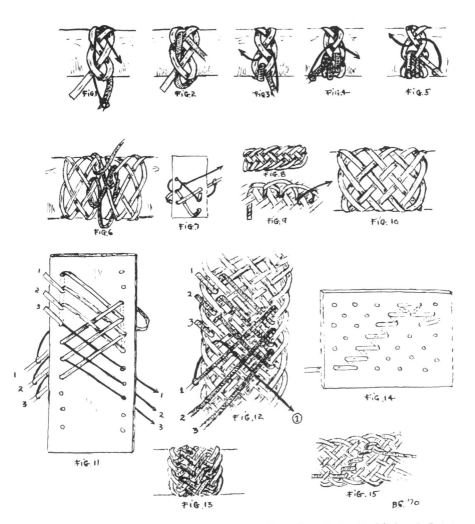

PLATE 198. Mosaic Type Braid on a Three-Part, Five-Bight Turk's-head; Joining Two Turk's-heads with the "S" Braid; Braid on the Aztec Button Knot; Five-Part Appliqué on a Nine-Part, Eight-Bight Knot; Mosaic Type Appliqué on an Eight-String Flat Braid.

479

PLATE 199

Appliqué on Ginfer Knot. This appliqué on a Ginfer knot with over-three, under-three edges and over-one, under-one sequence in the center. In Fig. 1 is shown the area to be interwoven. The working end is first brought up along the left side of the standing part and then over two crossed strings and under one. For contrast this working end can be of a different color.

Figures 2 and 3 illustrate the working of the interwoven string. In Fig. 4 the working string passes under one, over three and under one. Continuing, Fig. 5 illustrates the path of the working string. In Fig. 6 the sequence is over three, under two, over three, and under two. In Fig. 7 the same sequence is followed, and in Fig. 8, with the same sequence, the working end comes up alongside its beginning. The finished knot is shown in Fig. 9.

If this knot is mashed flat it looks like the drawing in Fig. 10. But the hole in the center is much smaller. Say it originally was worked on a mandrel of 7/8 inch diameter, when flattened the hole in the center will be about ½ inch. The flattened knot has several practical uses. It can be employed to decorate reins, or in conjunction with a button knot with the closed end pushed through the hole, it can be used as an interesting drawer pull.

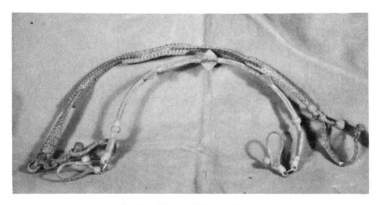

Butterfly braid key chain.

The Butterfly Knot. This knot, which actually is made with the conquistador braid, can be worked on a simple four-string round braid. After the first pass, shown by arrowlines in Fig. 1, taper the knot by failing to pass beneath one element of its own part at the end of each pass. Figure 13 shows the butterfly knot (or *Mariposa* as designated in the Argentine) used on a necklace. It also is employed to decorate key chains, bridle reins, etc.

Appliqué on a Crocodile Ridge Braid. After making the crocodile ridge braid with ridges on both sides and an over-one, under-one sequence in the center, interweave the center strings with a string of

480

contrasting color, using the "S" Braid, as shown in Fig. 14. This combination makes an attractive belt. The billet end should be started by the Australian method employed on all flat braids. Eight strings are used here.

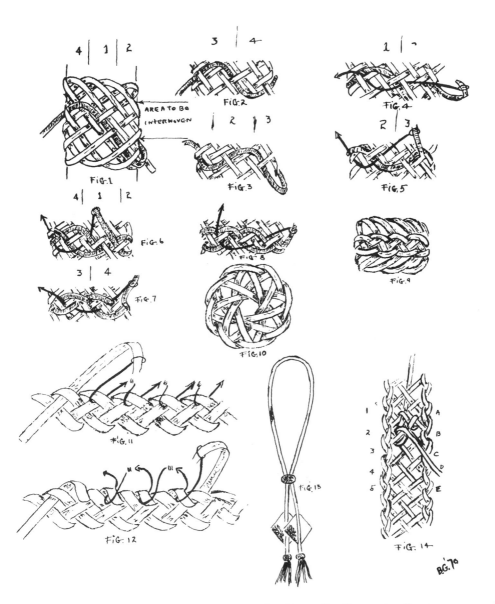

PLATE 199. Appliqué on Ginfer Knot; the Butterfly Knot; Appliqué on a Crocodile Ridge Braid.

Top: Picture taken in private museum of Gaucho Handcraft at Estancia El Cinco in the Province of Buenos Aires. (Left to right) Don Luis Alberto Flores, author and writer for the horse magazine *El Caballo;* the author; and Don Osvaldo Monti, owner of the estancia. *Bottom:* Another view of Mr. Monti's museum.

Additional Projects and Examples

PLATE 200

How to Make "Quick-Draw" Galluses. The old-time cowboy—and the cavalryman, too—had a hankering for galluses or suspenders instead of a belt to hold up his pants. He disliked putting his gun belt on over his pants' belt. Before elastic suspenders, and even afterward, the cowboy wore galluses as shown in the illustration. The loops of the shoulder straps slid back and forth freely, allowing easy play in them as if they were elastic.

These old-time galluses are simple to make. Cut two straps, each 42 inches long and ¾ inch wide, from a medium weight calfskin. (You can vary any given measurements to suit yourself.) At one end slit both straps in hald for 11 inches. At the other ends make slits for the buckles and holes for the buckle tongues (Fig. 1).

Next, make what I term the "sliders," for lack of a better name. These are illustrated in Fig. 2 and two of them are needed. Cut ¼-inch thongs 21 inches long with slits at each end. Dampen the leather and twist these thongs into a tight twist braid, the flesh side in, of course. In twisting there is some shrinkage and when finished the sliders will be about 16 inches long. Or, if preferred, leather can be sewed around a small core as shown in Fig. 2.

Attach the two buckles as illustrated in the assembled drawing (Fig. 5) and in Fig. 1. The buckles are attached with a three-hole thong fastening as shown in Fig. 3. Next make loops for the back (Fig. 4). But before fastening them on either side by sewing or with the three-hole thong method, be sure to interlace the slits in the back as shown in the assembled drawing in Fig. 5.

Back view of "Quick-Draw" Galluses. (See other picture on page 486.)

Two more small loops are needed as shown (A in Fig. 5). Thread the "sliders" through the loops as shown, adjust the buckles to suit, and the galluses are all ready to button on.

If a more elaborate type is desired, the shoulder straps can be made of many of the different kinds of flat braids.

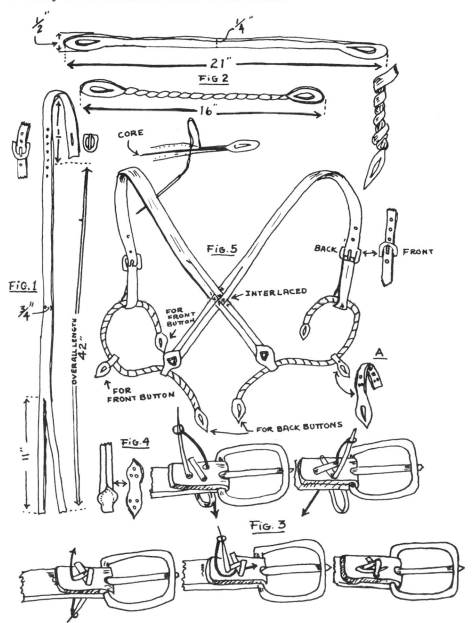

PLATE 200. How to Make "Quick-Draw" Galluses.

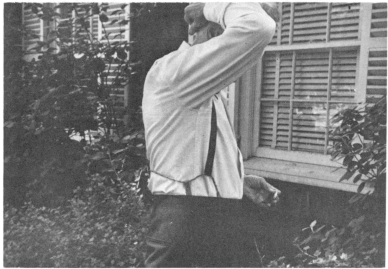

Top: Side view of "Quick-Draw" Galluses showing how they articulate. *Bottom:* Another side view showing how they easily adjust to any movements.

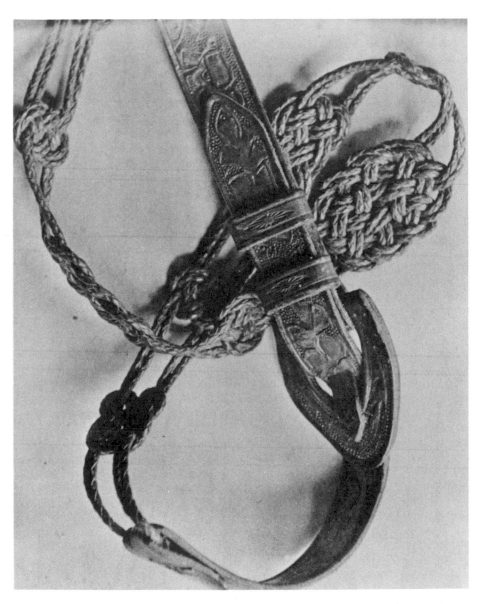

Belt made from a four-thong round braid (without core, 50 feet after braided, Pl. 37) and then tied in Chinese knots.

PLATE 201

How to Make a Rawhide-Covered Suitcase. The feature of this suitcase is the braided mitered corners.

First make a box of ¼-inch plywood, measuring 23¾ by 13 by 5¾ inches. This plywood box is all of one piece. After it is completed, measure one inch from the part that will be the top and draw a line around the entire box. Then, following this line, saw the box into two pieces, one to be the top and the other the bottom.

These pieces are next covered with thin calfskin rawhide (Fig. 1), allowing a couple of inches so the rawhide can be turned in on E, the wooden, part. The rawhide is designated F in the drawings.

I use no cement to hold the rawhide to the foundation. The rawhide should be dampened just enough to make it workable. The best dampening agent is three parts water and one part glycerin. It is applied to the rawhide with a sponge.

A design or initials can be worked on the rawhide before it is placed on the top or bottom. Different types of appliques are used.

Now for the corners (see Figs. 1-4). First cut the rawhide at each edge as shown in Fig. 1, A to B. The section marked C is brought up beneath that marked D and D is brought down so its edge is parallel to the edge of the box.

Stretch the rawhide over the top and bottom parts of the box—but do not stretch it too tight. It will shrink a trifle. Tack the turned-in edges to the inside of the box.

Taking the top part which is approximately 1¼ inch in width (with the added rawhide cover) mark off ¼ inch at the top and about 1/8 inch at the bottom. At ¼-inch intervals make slits in the rawhide. Make six perpendicular slits, each measuring ¾ inch (Fig. 3). An extra ¼-inch slit is made at each end.

The method of braiding is indicated by arrowlines in Fig. 3—an over-one, under-one sequence. The finished braid, with all ends tucked under, is shown in Fig. 4.

Locks and hinges can be bought at most hobby shops and some hardware stores. The handle is placed midway of the width of the suitcase. The one shown is made by taking a strip of rawhide and after threading it through two D-rings (covered or not covered, as you wish) an additional arrow strip is placed between and the ends sewed together underneath. The edges are closed with edge-braiding. The D-rings are held in place by cutting slots through the rawhide covering and the wood and passing a long strip of rawhide through the slots (at each slit a loop is made for the D-ring). The ends of this strip are tacked down inside.

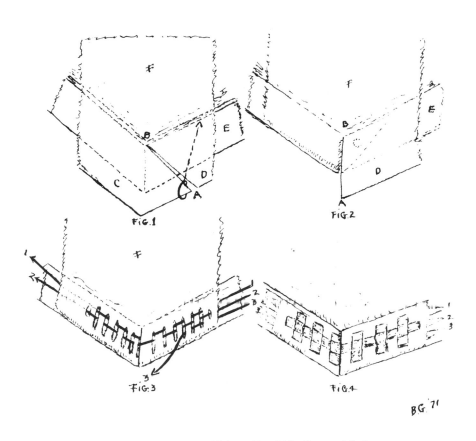

FIG.1
FIG.2
FIG.3
FIG.4

B.G. 71

PLATE 201. How to Make a Rawhide-Covered Suitcase.

489

Closeup of braided mitered corner.

The author's initials are worked in the stairstep appliqué of one string;
the circle employs the hair-braid appliqué of two strings. The design or
initials are worked on the rawhide before it is put on the case.

Top: Front view of the finished rawhide-covered suitcase. *Bottom:* View showing lock, handle and the mitered corners.

PLATE 202

Making a Woven Rawhide Chair Seat. On one of my trips to Mexico I saw an interesting woven rush chair seat. I took a closeup photo of it and later duplicated the woven seat with rawhide strings. I used a sturdy old Elbert Hubbard Roycraft chair with worn-out seat. It proved a most interesting and rewarding task.

Figure 1 in Plate 202 and Photo A show the beginning of this braid or weave. I used ¼-inch-wide rawhide strings, cutting them from head to tail down the center to avoid the belly section which narrows and stretches when wet.

One end of the string is first tacked securely under on the left side bar of the frame (Fig. 1). It is then brought up and over the left side and then across to the right side where it is passed under the side piece and over its own part. It is next passed under the side piece and worked toward the left, passing under the loop as indicated by the arrowline in Fig. 1. At the left side it passes over the side piece and then makes a loop over both strings as illustrated in Fig. 2. It is again carried to the right over the side piece where the same procedure is continued as in the case of the first pair of strings.

As it is difficult to work with a tamale or very long string, I prefer to use strings of seven or eight feet in length, splicing in a new string when necessary. This split-braid splice is illustrated in Figs. 3 and 4. Make a slit about ¼—1 inch from the end of the old string and the same from the new string. If necessary, cut off the end of the old string before making the slit so the splice will be underneath the side piece.

I use dampened newspapers in which to keep the strings properly dampened and tempered. You can keep these dampened strings overnight in an icebox if you do not finish the braiding in one session.

Photo E shows the design of the Mexican rush chair seat. However, a plain basket weave of over one, under one can be used, or an over-two, under-two sequence, as shown in Fig. 5, can be employed.

It might first be well to try out your braiding over an ordinary frame and by using paper with small squares drawn in, make up your own sequence, or design. There are many possible designs and one can even work initials in the center part of the braid, if desired.

When working these dampened rawhide strings, do not pull too tight for the strings will contract when dry and could pull the chair frame apart.

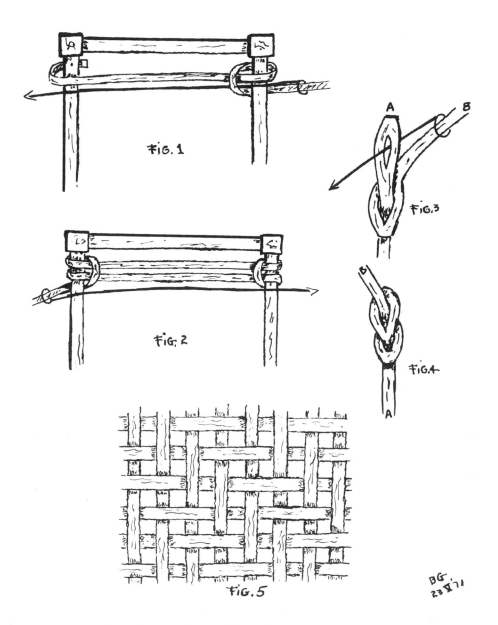

FIG. 1

FIG. 2

FIG. 3

FIG. 4

FIG. 5

PLATE 202. Making a Woven Rawhide Chair Seat.

493

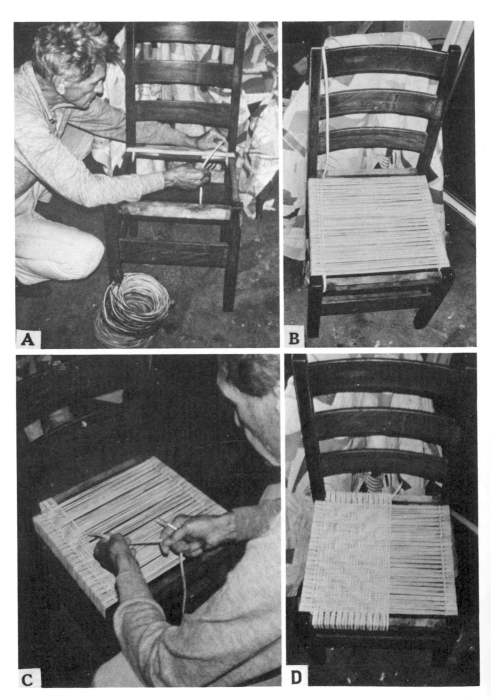

A: The start of the braid, working crosswise on their seat. (Illustrated in Figs. 1 and 2 in the plate.) *B:* The cross strings completed; begin the weave or braid from front to back and vice versa. *C:* Continuing the weave. *D:* The braid or weave half finished.

E: The completed braid. (This can also be made in over-one, under-one or over-two, under-two sequence, or of a design of the braider's choice.)

Covering Boleadoras. Boleadoras, used in the Argentine to catch ostriches as well as cattle and horses, are often covered with elaborate braidwork.

These boleadoras, usually smooth rocks about two inches in diameter and two and a quarter in length, are first covered with rawhide so that a loop is formed at the top. This is illustrated in Photo No. 1 by the bola on the right, It is covered much like the locket shown in Plate 9, Figs. 4-7.

A thinner piece of rawhide cut round and then into strips almost to the center is placed damp on the bola. The bottom, or center, is incised in an *uneven* series of slits and a string of contrasting colored rawhide is braided through these slits in an over one, under one sequence. Be sure the slits are uneven.

On the upper part cut out every other string and braid the others,

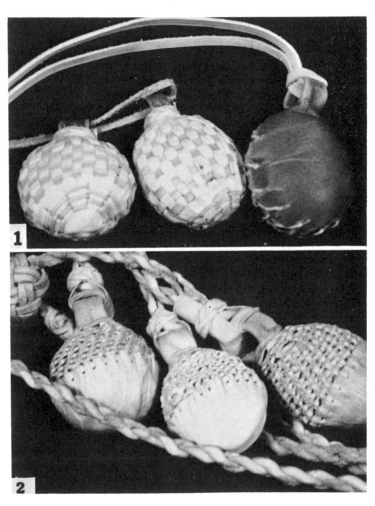

which also are of an uneven number, in an over-one, under-one sequence, with a long string of a different color. Tie at the top and cover the ends with a Spanish ring knot.

Photo 2 shows the same set of boleadoras. After covering the stone, a piece of dampened rawhide is worked over the bottom and holes punched in the edge. Spanish hitching is used to cover the middle and top portions. Usually the type of rope used is a two or three string twist braid.

Photo No. 3 shows boleadoras covered with braided knots. These, of two bolas, also are shown in Photo No. 4 on top of a case for the silver spurs, and encircling the spurs. The handle of this case is of interest. It is fashioned from a single strip of rawhide, folded with covered D-rings at each end. It is held together with two braids—the center portion being covered with the stair-step applique of one string and using the same holes to work edge braiding on each side. The two D-rings are held to the case by a long strip of rawhide which passes through each ring and through two slots in case itself.

497

COVERING A LAMP BASE

Covering a Lamp Base With Rawhide. 1. Select a base. 2. Fit the base with light fixture kit. 3. Cut rawhide to cover the base. Use a revolving punch to make holes down both sides where the rawhide will be joined. Remember to put one prong in the last hole cut to insure even spacing throughout. Draw the rawhide around the base and, using a thong, join the edges with edge-lacing or appliqué. 4. The finished lamp.

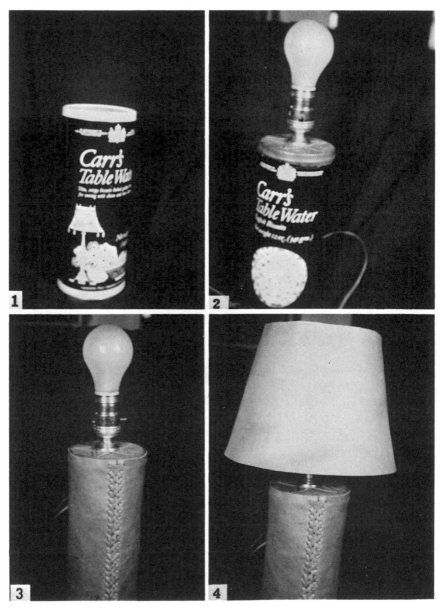

AN EXERCISE IN BRAIDING

Multiple Ring Button. *Top:* The large braided ring is made like one shown in Plates 23, 24 & 25, How to Make a Braided Cincha. The smaller rings in the center are shown in Plate 68, How to Make a Multiple Ring Button. The middle section is cemented on the outer ring.

Center: Photo showing how light comes through the middle section. The outer ring is of red latigo and the middle section of white rawhide.

Bottom: This ornamental combination is illustrated as a medallion.

Woman's pocketbook showing use of stairstep applique of two thongs (Pl. 186) as
edge-braiding as well as holding parts together.

Drum-head type woman's pocketbook showing carved work set off by 7-thong circular appliqué braid (similar to that of Pl. 192) and with Spanish edge-braiding of three loops (Pl. 118). Braid work is in black and pocketbook natural calf.

The author made this braided halter shown on a bell mare.

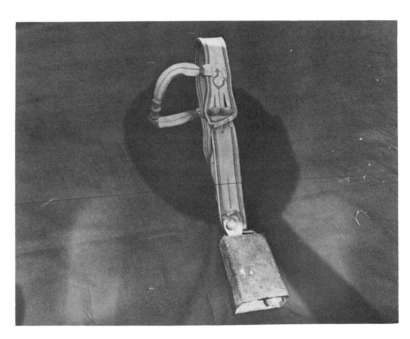

A collar of softened rawhide with bell. It is for the *madrina* or bell mare of a string of horses. The collar was made by a master braider, Tomás Anascolta, and is in the collection of John Walter Maguire, Buenos Aires, Argentina.

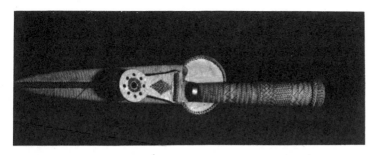

Martín Gómez covered this knife handle with fid work and made the sheath for the author.

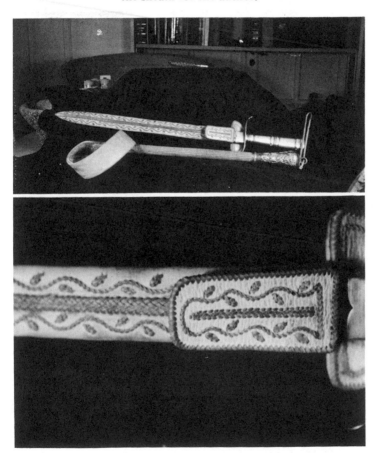

Top: Knife in decorated sheath and an Argentine *rebenque* covered with intricate fid work. *Bottom:* Closeup of decorated sheath. This is the type of sheath used by the South American gaucho to carry a facon (a large heavy belt knife).

503

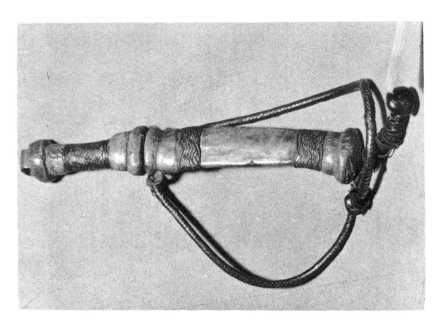

An ancient Arabian knife and sheath owned by Wright Howes, Chicago, Illinois. Note the braided knots on sheath and knife handle. Rawhide and leather braiding originated in Arabia, and was carried into Spain.

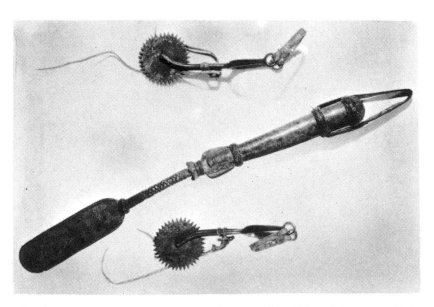

An Argentine *rebenque*, or *heavy quirt*, owned by Edward Larocque Tinker. Note braided knot on handle end of quirt, similar to that of the Arabian knife.

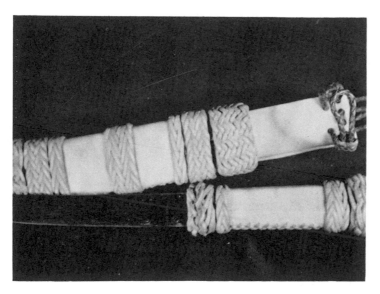

Comanche scalping knife with rawhide covered handle and sheath. Braiding can be considered a universal language. Note braided knots are used on both the Comanche knife and the Arabian knife.

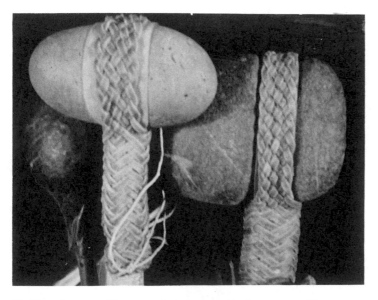

Braidwork generally served some practical purpose. Shown are three types of stone weapons that employed rawhide. *Left to right:* a rawhide covered rock "head breaker," used by the Plains Indians; Apache tomahawk; grooved stone axe.

Covering a Bottle. Leather craftsmen strive to develop the art of leather work. Projects such as these two shown on this page, by Tony Genco will keep the art flourishing. Half gallon bottle completely covered with one piece sunburst-type cut leather brought up from bottle bottom. One piece lacing woven around bottle up to its neck in over-two, under sequence (on right).

Intricate Designed Bottle Covering. To proceed from the basics to complex and original designs is a challenge of braidwork. Bottle covered with half-hitch design. The design repeats three times around in three colored lacings. To excute the design 1,000 plus precision punched nib punchings were made in the leather. Bottom piece molded and joined to the cylinder design area with a false braid, a weave. Top of the cylinder piece is finished with a two-color edge lacing. A pineapple two-two sequence is used for covering beyond the cork area (on left).

Rawhide bottles or containers. In Mexico they are used as to-
bacco pouches. The stopper for each bottle is the metal part of a
shotgun shell.

A CURIOSITY IN BRAIDING

A curiosity in braiding. This is an eight-string round braid worked into a ring like a Turk's-head, and done with one long string, according to the maker, Ernie Ladouceur. He wrote at the time: "All I can remember was that I took a piece of copper wire and bent it in a circle. The wire was about 1/8 inch in diameter. I started working over this wire and when the braid started to get too tight I just pulled out the wire and continued from there. I haven't the slightest idea how I did it."

However, this braid can be made with *two* strings, wrapping them in the same direction, but so as to cross each other, and interweaving them. The braid is of two cycles, which would make it theoretically impossible with one string revolving in one cycle. But Ernie apparently did the impossible, which should confound all mathematicians.

This braid is certainly a challenge to the braider. It is suggested that the work first be done over a rope grommet or a metal ring. Spiral one string or thong around the grommet in a clockwise direction. Then, going in the same direction, spiral the second string around in a counterclockwise direction so that it crosses the first string on the outside and inside of the grommet. Then wrap the first string around, passing over everything. Finally, work with the second string, over one, under one, interlocking all sections. This gives a four-string round Turk's-head.

This can be built into an eight-string by doubling and then splitting pairs, and after that it can be made into a sixteen-string round Turk's-head, and so on *ad infinitum*. If you can make this of rawhide you can do away with metal rings on your horse gear.

This is more fully illustrated in Plates 23, 24 & 25.

The upper, closed pair were made by the author. The lower, open pair were made by Rudy Mudra, Sheridan, Wyoming. Both are made of heavy latigo, but can be fashioned from softened rawhide. First take a strip of latigo or rawhide 56 inches long and 2¾ inches wide. Wet thoroughly and then fold in the flesh side on both edges. On one end fashion a rolled leather button similar to the one in Fig. 3, Plate 140. Five and one-half inches from the button fold the leather again for 8

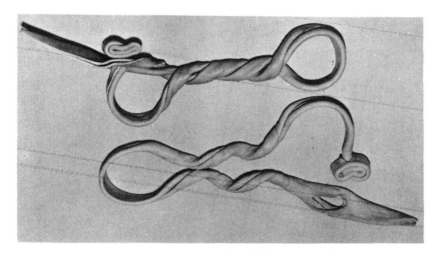

inches, leave 9 inches doubled after that and then fold again for 8 inches. Twist your two 1/8-inch folds together and lash with string until dry. Make a slit in the end opposite from the button. Button the hobbles and allow them to dry in the shape shown in the upper photograph. Those shown were dried around two soup cans, but they can be dried around anything approximately 3 inches in diameter. When dry, remove the string around the twisted parts. These hobbles will then retain their shape.

The section on hobbles contains directions for making Simple Types of Hobbles (Plate 140), Braided Gaucho Hobbles (Plate 141), and Braided Hobbles, (Plate 142). Photographs of various hobbles are also shown.

Margarita del Castillo (shown here) and Gloria del Castillo are two of the fanciest riders in Mexico City and lead all the parades for notables. Their father, who died recently, was Romeo del Castillo, secretary of the Asociasión del

The author is shown as a young man wearing the hat, buckskin jacket and holding the braided quirt—all bought with many other articles from Herbert Cody Blake, a nephew of Buffalo Bill. Blake duplicated Buffalo Bill's outfit and played the role in his own Wild West Show.

GLOSSARY

Alforja *(al-for'hah)*—Wide leather or canvas bag in which a horseman carries his personal effects on a pack animal.

Aparejo *(ah-par-ay'ho)*—Packsaddle.

Appliqué—A form of braiding which is worked directly upon the surface of the leather.

Awl—A pointed instrument or tool for piercing small holes in leather. Used when stitching with waxed thread.

Back—The middle of the hide or skin directly over the backbone. This section supplies the best thongs.

Back Braid—A braid in which the thongs are first braided loosely in an over-one, under-one sequence, then crowned and woven back upon themselves.

Basil—A cheap form of sheepskin.

Basket Weave—Usually where the interwoven thongs are of an over-one, under-one sequence.

Belly—The sides of a skin or hide. A very thin thong can be cut from this section. However, it must be dampened and stretched before the thong is cut.

Bevel—To cut or shape to a bevel angle; to slope the edge or surface of a piece of leather.

Bight—A loop in a thong, as that part of the thong between the working end and standing end, formed by bringing the working end of the thong around, near to, or across its own part. Particularly the "scallops" on the upper and lower edges of a Turk's-head or woven knot.

Bit—The metal part of a bridle which goes in the "bit hole" of a horse's mouth and to which the reins and headstall are attached.

Bit-Chains—Chains for fastening the reins to the bit. Usually fitted because of the tendency of some horses to bite the reins. They add weight when certain types of bits (such as the Mexican bit) are used.

Blanket Stitch—A form of lock stitch. Sometimes called buttonhole stitch in edge-braiding.

Boots—Protective coverings of rawhide or leather in eyes of hondas, reins, and bit-cheek loops on headstalls to prevent wear on the braid. Also called *wear-leathers*.

Bosal *(boh-zal)*—Noseband of the hackamore, usually made of braided rawhide. Bosals are made from pencil size to 1¼-inch diameter.

Braid—The interlacing or weaving of one thong with itself or several thongs with each other.

513

Breast Collar—Harness which passes around the horse's breast and is attached to the saddle. Standard length is 32 inches. Some breast collars have a neckpiece and side straps both of which are adjustable. When used with a saddle it is more properly termed *martingale*.

Breeching—A wide strap which passes around a horse's rump.

Bridle—Head harness consisting of headstall, bit, and reins.

Bucking Strap—A strap placed tightly around a horse's belly to make him buck.

Buckskin—A soft, pliable leather of deerskin, formerly tanned by the American Indians by treating them with brains of the animals and smoking the skins. Today a chrome process is used and the term applies to both deer and elk skins.

Buck-Strap—A leather loop attached to the saddle horn to provide a "hand-holt" when riding a bucking horse.

Bull-Rigging—A broad strap or rope around an animal's body and to which are attached "hand-holts" for wild-steer riding in rodeos.

Bullwhip—A whip with a lash from 15 to 25 feet in length, with a short lead-weighted handle.

Buscadero Belt—A broad belt from which two guns can be hung, one on each side.

Button—Woven leather or rawhide knot on quirts, bridle reins, headstalls, and other gear. Interwoven thongs forming a knot, or a strip of leather rolled into a small cylinder.

Cabestro *(cah-bes'tro)*—Horsehair tie-rope.

Calfskin—Leather made from the skins of calves. The best and most attractive thongs are cut from calfskin.

Cantinas—Saddle pockets which slip over the saddle horn.

Cantle—Up-curved back of a saddle.

Catch-Rope—Working rope or lariat.

Catgut—A tough cord obtained from the intestines of sheep. Used for violin strings, tennis rackets, surgical sutures, and for Turk's-head decorations on canes and whips. Also for ferrules on the latter.

Chamois—A very soft leather made from sheepskin.

Chaps—Leather leggings with wide flaps for the protection of a horseman's legs. From the Mexican **chaparejos**.

Cinch—A wide strap which goes around a horse's belly to hold the saddle on his back. Called *cincha* in some areas.

Coachwhipping—A braid made around a core in which several thongs are worked as one unit.

Concha—Silver or metal ornament used on belts, bits, headstalls, and saddles. Saddle conchas are usually termed "string conchas" and come in sets of eight.

Core—A hard or pliable center of a whip, quirt or crop, usually of twisted rawhide or leather, but sometimes of rattan or French willow. Also a rope center of a braid.

Corona—A fancy saddle pad.

Crown Knot—A knot at the end of a braid where the working ends are laid over each other so that they interlock and are pointing back toward the braid.

Cuff—Leather gauntlet for guarding the wrists and protecting the shirt sleeves.

Curb Strap—Strap which is attached to the bit and passes behind the horse's chin.

Danglers—Pear-shaped ornaments of metal which dangle from spurs.

Draw Gauge—A hand tool for cutting thongs or leather straps.

Drover's Whip—A swivel-handled and shot-loaded whip having a lash from 8 to 12 feet long.

Duffel Bag—A roll containing blankets and personal effects.

Ear-Head—A simple headstall without noseband, browband, or throatlatch, and with a loop or loops for one or both of the horse's ears.

Edge-Lacing—A type of edge-braiding in which the braid covers the edge of the leather. While a decoration, it also serves to fasten two or more pieces of leather together.

False Braid—Braid where leather thongs are pulled alternately through slits in their own parts. Usually is termed slit-braiding and simulates actual braiding.

Fiador—A safety device or throatlatch used on the hackamore. Sometimes called *Theodore*.

Fiador Knot—An intricate knot used on the fiador.

Fid—Sometimes called belt awl in leather work. A long tapering metal tool with a blunt point used for making an opening between thongs in braiding, as well as enlarging slits through which thongs are passed.

Flat Braid—Braid in which thongs are worked alternately from each side.

Flesh Side—The inner or rough side of the leather as opposed to the smooth or hair side.

Frill—A tassel on a quirt or other gear.

Girth—Same as *cinch*.

Grain—The smooth natural exterior surface of leather from which the hair has been removed. Same as hair side or smooth side.

Guilloche—A pattern made by interlacing curved lines in which braiding is simulated; sometimes carved or stamped on leather.

Hackamore—Type of western headstall or bridle without a bit. It consists of headstall, bosal, mecate, and fiador. Commonly used in breaking horses and teaching them to neck-rein.

Hair Braid—The simple, three-thong flat braid.

Headstall—Part of a bridle or hackamore that fits over the horse's head. It consists of cheekpieces, crownpiece, noseband, browband, and throatlatch.

Herringbone—A pattern usually of a V-shape formed by thongs when braided in over-two, under-two sequence or over-three, under-three sequence.

Hide—A pelt from one of the larger animals; cattlehide, cowhide, horsehide, etc.

Hide Rope—Rope made from strips of leather cut from green hides and braided. Formerly used by seamen in rigging.

Hobbles—Cuffs or loops joined together and fastened around an animal's forelegs.

Holster—Leather sheath for a pistol or revolver.

Honda—Eye on the working end of a lariat, or reata, through which the rope passes to form a loop or noose.

Horn—Pommel or knob on the front of a saddle.

Horsehair Rope—A rope of braided horsehair. Best quality is the "clipped" rope made from a horse's mane. When used on a hackamore, it is called a *mecate*, or "McCarty."

Horse Jewelry—Various types of metal ornaments used on headstalls, breast collars, and saddles.

Huaraches—Mexican sandal-like shoes with tops of braided thongs.

Incising—Another name for leather carving. A method of slightly cutting around the ornament with a knife before sinking the background.

Inlay—To set braidwork in a leather surface to form a design. The two surfaces are usually level.

Interlaced—Where laces or thongs cross alternately over and under each other.

Jingle-Bobs—Another term for *danglers*.

Kink—Twist in a thong.

Lace—A small, narrow thong. Usually commercially made and beveled; used mainly for edge-braiding or edge-lacing.

Lacing Needle—Flat needle split at one end to receive the thong or lacing.

Lariat—A throw-rope or catch-rope. Usually made of fiber.

Lasso—A modern term for lariat. However, the word is more properly used as a verb—to lasso.

Latigo—A form of thong of alum-tanned leather; often mistermed rawhide.

Levis—Blue denim overalls, named for the maker, Levi Strauss.

Lock—Thonging in which each turn secures itself.

Lie—The "settling down" of a thong in the right position, usually obtained by tapping it lightly with a mallet.

Maguey *(mah-ghay'e)*—Four-strand rope, handmade by Mexicans from the fibers of the aloe plant.

Mandrel—A cylindrical or conical core used in making Turk's-heads or woven knots.

Marlinspike—A metal pin tapering to a point used in separating thongs in braiding. Synonymous with fid.

Martingale—A breast collar used with a saddle.

Mecate—A twisted horsehair rope used on the hackamore for reins and lead-rope. Sometimes called "McCarty."

Natural—A term applied to unstained or undyed leather.

Neckerchief—Bandanna or handkerchief worn around a man's neck, knot to the rear.

Neckrope—A rope that encircles a horse's neck and through which the lariat passes to keep the horse head-on to a calf or steer after it has been roped.

Parfleche—Rawhide.

Paring—Thinning down the edge of the leather with a knife.

Piggin' Strings—Strings used to tie an animal's feet after he has been roped and thrown.

Pile—The under or flesh side of leather. Also called the velvet side.

Pinking—Cutting the border of leather in an ornamental pattern of small scallops with indented edges.

Plait (Plat)—The continued interlacing of several thongs to form a braided strap. In some sections "plait" means a round braid and "braid" is used for flat braid.

Poncho—Blanket or oiled cloth with a hole in the middle for the horseman's head,

Prong—Tool for punching several slots at equal spacings.

Pulling—A skin is more elastic from side to side than from neck to tail.

Punch—A tool with a sharpened cylinder or tube which acts upon a soft metal base for punching holes in leather. There are also independent punches known as drive punches. The revolving punch has as many as six different size tubes.

Quirt—A short, loaded whip.

Rawhide—An untanned hide.

Reata—A rope 40 to 85 feet in length made from braided rawhide. The 3/8-inch diameter reata is called "light"; 7/16-inch, "medium"; ½-inch, "heavy"; and the 9/16-inch, "extra heavy." Often misspelled "riata."

Reins—Leather or rawhide lines attached to the bit. By these the rider guides and manages his horse. There are two types of reins, *open* and *closed.*

Rigging—Latigo, cinch, and rigging rings, or gear securing a saddle on a horse's back.

Romal—A long flexible quirt or whip attached to closed reins. It measures about 3 feet with its 1-foot "popper," or lash. Sometimes misspelled "ramal."

Rope—A common term for a lariat. The two general types of ropes are the hard-twist, made from vegetable fiber, and the reata, of braided rawhide.

Roping-Reins—Closed reins used in roping. The standard length is 6 feet.

Rosette—A leather tie ornament used both as a decoration and as a fastening on saddles and headstalls.

Round Braid—A braid in which alternate thongs are brought around to the rear instead of straight across as in flat braiding.

Run—The passage of a thong from one hole to another on the front of the leather, without going over the edge to the back.

Saddle—A leather seat with a high horn and cantle, fastened to a horse's back to accommodate the rider. With its rigging, it consists of a tree, horn, seat, cantle, back jockey, skirt, swell, gullet, front jockey, fender (rosadero), stirrup-leathers, stirrups, cinch rings, latigo, conchas and tie-strings.

Saddle Blanket—A blanket or padding between saddle.and horse's back.

Saddle Leather—A vegetable-tanned cowhide leather, tan or natural colored.

Saddle Pockets—Leather bags joined together and hung across the saddle behind the cantle.

Saddle Soap—A special soap used to cleanse and soften leather.

Saddle Stamp—A metal stamp used to impress various designs on leather.

Scabbard—Open-mouthed leather sheath for a rifle or carbine.

Skin—The pelt of the smaller animals, such as calf, goat, sheep, etc.

Skirt Ornaments—Silver ornaments for decorating saddle-skirts.

Skiving—Splitting a skin horizontally into several thicknesses. Beveling an edge by paring.

Slicker—A raincoat made of oiled canvas. Sometimes called a "fish."

Slot—A long, narrow aperture as distinct from a round punched hole.

Spanish Knot—A woven cylindrical knot of one thong worked with a Turk's-head as a skeleton or base.

Spanish Lacing—Edge-braiding or edge-lacing.

Spur-Chains—Small chains attached to spurs and passing under the wearer's instep. Two or three chains are used.

Spurs—Metal implements attached to the heels of a rider's boots. They usually have a wheel or rowel with blunt-end points and may be hand-forged, plain, silver-inlaid, or silver-mounted, with straight or curved shanks, of 1/8- , ¼- , or ½-inch metal.

Spur-Straps—Leather straps securing spurs to rider's boots. Usually carved or stamped, some are decorated with silver conchas. Some cowboys wear the buckles inside; others wear them outside.

Square Braid—Braid usually made by the overlapping or crowning of several thongs.

Stake-Rope—A picket-rope, or rope for tying up a horse.

Standing End—The inactive or secured part of a thong as opposed to the active or working part.

String—A tie-leather used on saddles. Also a term for a rawhide thong.

Surcingle—Girth or strap passing around the body of an animal.

Taps—Leather covering or shields over the front of stirrups. The word is from the Mexican *tapaderos*.

Thong—A narrow strip cut from a hide or skin. Sometimes beveled on the flesh side.

Thonging Chisel—A small chisel with one or more tines or prongs to cut slits for thonging.

Thong Wheel—A tool cutting a continuous line of slots for thonging when rolled under pressure.

Tie-Down Bosal—A pencil bosal with a loop or ring in place of the heel-knot on other bosals.

Tie-Strings—Leather thongs or rawhide strings that pass through leather rosettes or metal conchas on saddles. Used to tie on blankets and other articles, as well as to hold parts of the saddle together.

Trick Braid—An inside braid made with three or more thongs cut in a strap in such a manner that the ends are joined.

Tube Punch—Same as revolving punch.

Turk's-head—A braided wreath or ring in which the braid is similar to that of flat braids but is continuous and made with one thong. A Turk's-head cannot have the same number of thongs across its breadth as bights. The law is that bights and parts must not have a common divisor or the working end will come back to the standing end before the knot is complete.

Twist Braid—Braid made with leather turned or twisted upon itself.

War Bridle—Halter used in leading unruly horses; usually a lariat-noose placed in the horse's mouth and over his head.

Wear-Leather—Another term for boot; used to protect braid in the eyes of hondas and reins.

Working End—The end of a thong used in making a braid as distinguished from standing end.

RAWHIDE AND LEATHER BRAIDERS' BIBLIOGRAPHY

Ashley, Clifford, *The Ashley Book of Knots*, Garden City, N.Y., 1945. Ropework and braiding that can be applied to leather and rawhide.

Berruti, Augusto Diego León, *El Trenzador Sudamericano*, Buenos Aires, 1921. Gaucho rawhide braiding.

Catalogues (Old). Hamley & Company, Victor Marden, Visalia Stock Saddle Company, Walsh-Richardson Company. Pictures of old-time rawhide braidwork.

Coker, Jim, *How to Skin, Make Rawhide, Tan, and Braid*, Kernville, Calif., no date. A mimeographed pamphlet by an old-time braider.

Country Hides and Skins, U.S. Department of Agriculture, Farmers' Bulletin No. 1055, Washington, D.C., revised edition, 1942. Instructions on how to skin an animal.

Dobie, J. Frank, *The Longhorns*, Boston, 1941. Romantic aspects of rawhide, pp. 221-241.

Flores, Luis Alberto, *El Guasquero-Trenzados Criollos*, Buenos Aires, 1960. Argentine rawhide braiding.

Grant, Bruce, *The Cowboy Encyclopedia*, Chicago, 1951. Alphabetically arranged text. Rawhide and horse gear.

Grant, Bruce, *Leather Braiding*, Cambridge, Md., 1950. Leather and rawhide braiding sequences.

Grant, Bruce, *How to Make Cowboy Horse Gear*, Cambridge, Md., 1956. Practical rawhide and leather braiding. Contains a section on *How to Make a Western Saddle*, by Lee M. Rice.

Graumont, Raoul, and Hensel, John, *Encyclopedia of Knots and Fancy Rope Work*, Cambridge, Md., 1958. Much practical knowledge of ropework and braiding which can be used in leather and rawhide braiding.

Griswold, Lester, *Handicraft*, Colorado Springs, Colo., 1951. How to make rawhide and rawhide handicraft, as well as leather braiding.

Handbook of American Indians North of Mexico, edited by Frederick Webb Hodge, Bureau of American Ethnology, Bulletin 30, 2 vols., Washington, D.C., 1907-1910. Skin and skin dressing, Vol. 2, pp. 592-504.

Indians of the Southeastern United States, John R. Swanton, Smithsonian Institution, Bulletin 137, Washington, D.C., 1946. Indian methods of making rawhide, pp. 442-448.

Jaeger, Ellsworth, *Wildwood Wisdom*, New York, 1945. Indian uses of rawhide, pp. 26-27.

Lopez Osornio, Mario A., *Trenzas Gauchas*, Buenos Aires, 1943. Argentine methods of rawhide braiding.

Mason, Bernard S., *Woodcraft*, New York, 1939. Indian method of making rawhide and uses, pp. 394-422.

521

Raine, W. MacLeod, and Barnes, Will C., *Cattle*, Garden City, N.Y., 1930. How cowboys utilize rawhide, pp. 309-313.

Rincon Gallardo, D. Carlos, *El Charro Mexicano*, Mexico City, 1939. Mexican rawhide horse gear.

Saubidet, Tito, *Vocabulario y Refranero Criollo*, Buenos Aires, 1945. Alphabetically arranged text. Gaucho horse gear and the making and uses of rawhide.

Williams, R.M., *The Bushman's Handcrafts*, Prospect, South Australia, 1966. Australian methods of leather and rawhide braiding. Also Australian tanning methods.

Sometimes a braider will be confronted with measurements in the metric system:

1 millimeter equals 0.03937 inches
1 centimeter equals 0.3937 inches ·
1 decimeter equals 3.937 inches
1 meter equals 39.37 inches or 3.28 feet

1 inch equals 25.4 millimeters
1 inch equals 2.54 centimeters
1 foot equals 0.3048 meters
1 yard equals 0.9144 meters

To convert inches to centimeters, multiply by 10 and divide by 4.
To convert feet into meters, multiply by 61 and divide by 200.
To convert yards into meters, multiply by 9 and divide by 10.
To find feet in a given number of meters, multiply by 200 and divide by 61.

Old-time crude measurements are to be found in many Latin American countries, especially Argentina:

Brazada—length of the arms extended.
Cuarta—breadth of the hand at the palm.
Dedo—finger breadth.
Jeme—distance from the end of the thumb to the end of the forefinger, both extended.

SOURCES OF RAWHIDE AND LEATHER SUPPLIES

C. Ralph Dillon
    1930 Pine Grove Drive, Mount Shasta, Ca. 96067
Robert J. Golka Co.
    400 Warren Avenue, Brockton, Ma. 02401
MacPherson Brothers
    730 Polk Street, San Francisco, Ca. 94109
    200 S. Los Angeles Street, Los Angeles, Ca. 90053
David Morgan
    P.O. Box 70190, Seattle, Wa. 98107
    (Kangaroo hides & lace)
Oregon Leather Co.
    110 N.W. 2nd, Portland, Or. 97209
    810 Gonger Street, Eugene, Or. 97402
Salz Leathers, Inc.
    1040 River Street, Santa Cruz, Ca. 95060
Sax Arts & Crafts
    P.O. Box 2002, Milwaukee, Wi. 53201
    P.O. Box 2511, Allentown, Pa. 18001
Texas Leather Co.
    P.O. Box 123, Yoakum, Tx. 77995
    (Lace, latigo, strap, skirting, chap leather, rawhide, garment, & woolskins)
Tandy Leather Co.
    P.O. Box 2903, Ft. Worth, Tx. 76107
R.M. Williams Pty., Ltd.
    5 Percy Street, Prospect, South Australia 5082

526

527